Alchemy of the Word

SUNY Series in
Western Esoteric Traditions

David Applebaum, Editor

Alchemy of the Word

Cabala of the Renaissance

Philip Beitchman

STATE UNIVERSITY OF NEW YORK PRESS

The author acknowledges with thanks the right to quote from HISTORY OF MAGIC
AND EXPERIMENTAL SCIENCE, by Lynn Thorndike. Copyright © 1923–58, by
Columbia University Press. Reprinted by permission of the publisher.

Anne Conway, *The Conway Letters*, edited by Marjorie Hope Nicolson. Copyright ©
1930 by Yale University Press and Oxford University Press. Revised edition, edited
by Sara Hutton, Oxford University Press, 1992. Reprinted by permission of Oxford
University Press.

Production by Ruth Fisher
Marketing by Anne M. Valentine

Published by
State University of New York Press, Albany

© 1998 State University of New York

For information, address the State University of New York Press,
State University Plaza, Albany, NY 12246

Library of Congress Cataloging-in-Publication Data

Beitchman, Philip, 1939–
    Alchemy of the word : cabala of the Renaissance / Philip
Beitchman.
        p. cm. — (SUNY series in Western esoteric traditions)
    Includes bibliographical references and index.
    ISBN 0-7914-3737-X (hc : alk. paper). — ISBN 0-7914-3738-8 (pbk.
: alk. paper)
    1. Cabala and Christianity. 2. Renaissance. I. Title.
II. Series.
BM526.B45 1998
296.1'6'094—dc21
                                                   97-37506
                                                   CIP
                                                   r97

10 9 8 7 6 5 4 3 2 1

Ad Sophiam
Per Shekinam

Contents

Preface   ix

1   In the Beginning   1

    Scholem and Benjamin   7

    The Zohar   9

    The Two Sources of Morality and Religion   15

    Losing the Reader   23

    Exile and the Bride of Sabbath   30

    Lilith and the Shekinah   38

    Cabala and the Medieval Manichees   47

    People of the Book   52

    Cabala as Rhizome   55

    The One and the Two Many   60

2   The Secret of Agrippa   65

    Pico's Conclusions   67

    Reuchlin's Art   71

    Cabala between Freud and Jung   78

    Agrippa's Open Secret   79

    Agrippa and His Shadow   88

    The Two Laws   95

    Cabala as Fad   100

    Cabala as Beginning   104

    The Paradox of Secrecy   108

3   Bibliographica Kabbalistica   115

    Topics in Cabala   117
    The Dissemination of Cabala   169
    Cabala as Motif   187

4   The Kiss of the Spouse, Cabala in England (1497–1700)   209

    Cabala, Shakespeare, and The School of Night   210
    The Cabalas of the Age of Elizabeth   215
    (H)Enoch Clapham Redivivus—Ancient Theology
        and the Protestant Preacher   219
    The Other John Davies   232
    Inebriation as Ascent   236
    The Occult Sir Thomas Browne   245
    Cabala in the Baroque Renaissance   258

Notes   293

Bibliography   321

Index   341

Preface

This is a study of the impact and implications, immediate and long range, of the Cabala of the Renaissance. Although Cabala is a creation of the Late Middle Ages (or even earlier), it is not until the end of the fifteenth century, or after the expulsion of the Jews from Spain, that it began to become widely known in Europe. The Cabala I will be discussing here, therefore, will be *of* the Renaissance and a Renaissance creation. Accordingly when, as in the first chapter, "In the Beginning," I treat Cabala through its essential text, The Zohar, which was composed in the late thirteenth century in Spain and was even attributed, pseudepigraphically (with a fictional or legendary author), to someone who lived more than a thousand years before that, I will be focusing especially on themes, ideas, and styles that were later to fascinate the *Renaissance*. Two elements, for example, in the Cabala in general and The Zohar in particular that anticipate while helping to formulate Renaissance concerns are its flexibility in matters of morality and its concentration on the qualities of language.

One of the "missions" of this Cabala of the Renaissance was to help the "truths" of religion survive the challenges of a dawning secular and material age. Accordingly Cabala was a metaphorical/interpretive, often bold and original reading and rendition of scripture, custom, and tradition, one that allowed people more room in adjusting to what was happening to them, while contributing to their sense that nothing essential was being lost or forgotten. Overall, this goal has been either achieved or abandoned by 1700, when with the desperate extravagance of Sabbatian apocalypticism on the Jewish side, and the failure of the English to complete their Biblically inspired social revolution on the Christian side, mystics and politics go their separate ways.

Cabala runs in three distinct but interrelated currents through the Renaissance. First of all the Jewish stream, which rises in Northern Spain and Southern France in the twelfth and thirteenth centuries, then expands over Europe in the sixteenth century, while being "radicalized" through the "holy community" in Safed, in the Middle East. Cabala's course, through the purifying, exalting, and "Paradise Now" culture of Safed, had been profoundly changed, and in a messianic direction. Effectively, the Sabbatian catastrophe late in the seventeenth century was a long-range consequence of the efforts of the earlier Safed mystics to "live their Cabala." Modern Hasidism, which starts in the eighteenth century, represents the abandonment of the cosmic, world-repairing direction of the revolutionary Lurianic-Safed-Sabbatian Cabala in favor of a more practical and private ecstasy for the believers. Parallel to this important devolution into Hasidism, Jewish Cabala turns into the trickle of sects, cults, a "cranky" delta (or West Bank!) terrain it still inhabits today.

Secondly, a Christian Cabala, though one existed earlier in Spain, contemporaneous and competitive with the Jewish one, first becomes a factor in European culture with Pico della Mirandula's discovery of The Zohar, brought over to Italy by Jewish refugees from Spain. Pico said, before every sacred council that would hear him, that he thought that nothing so well *proves* the divinity of Christ and the truth of the New Testament as Cabala. This conjecture of Pico's, although early on condemned as heretical because of its Neoplatonic demotion of Reason (Acquinian-Aristotelian theology), nevertheless nourished a Christian Cabala for centuries. Thirdly, a demiurgic Neopagan Cabala, one that is God-Angel-and-Demon conjuring and connects with a more-or-less ancient Hermeticism, is spawned in Italy just about the same time as Pico's Christian one. This bold movement, which cuts through millenia of monotheism, refusing its limits, modesty, and restrictions, back to its Pagan provenance, has its heroes and its martyrs. Notable in it, at its very start in the early sixteenth century, was Ludovico Lazzarelli, whose *Crater of Hermes*, which takes the prerogative of creation from the gods and gives it to humans, was a text that was widely read and influential, but dangerous to acknowledge. Some of the martyrs of this Neopagan Cabala were Giordano Bruno (burned, 1600, for refusing to retract his theory of infinite worlds) and Lucilio Vanini (burned, 1619, for flat atheism). Neopagan Cabala in the seventeenth century merges into Rosicrucianism, with demiurgic figures like Robert Fludd and Thomas Vaughan, but by the end of the nineteenth century was on congenial terms with Theosophy.

The Zohar will be my overall guide and standard, which is a little like picking out your biggest problem as your solution. Whatever paths the separate Cabalas take, The Zohar has remained always a determining factor. This book, however, has been interpreted and even translated in many different ways, while, as we'll see a little later, people have been arguing for centuries over even what constitutes it, as well as, very passionately, *who* wrote it and *why*. Although The Zohar will impinge over everything I will say here, through the labyrinths of the discrete Cabalas, I will be following particular guides. For the Jewish Cabala, ineluctably it will be Gershom Scholem; for the Christian, Joseph Blau and François Secret; for the Neopagan, A. E. Waite and Frances Yates.

I've perused, additionally, some collections, catalogues, or surveys of Renaissance texts, mainly so I could acquire a sense—sometimes hard to attain with the "guides," who mostly treat the major figures—of how deep into the culture cabalistic themes, styles, and practices had penetrated. For English-language material or books published in England from 1475 to 1640, I've availed myself of a facsimile collection at the Library of the University of Pennsylvania, based on Pollard and Redgrave's *Short Title Catalogue*. For the Continental material I have depended very much on the last five volumes of Lynn Thorndike's *History of Magic and Experimental Science*, as well as on the still very useful book Scholem published in 1927, *Bibliographica Kabbalistica*.

Two late-nineteenth-century surveys I have found it frequently germane to consult and cite from are Wilhelm Windelband's *History of Philosophy* (Vol. II); and Henrich Graetz's *History of the Jews*.

Cabala, of whatever character, served in the sixteenth and seventeenth centuries to create and maintain that sense of awe and wonder Goethe's Faust has called "the best part of man" and

Rudolf Otto has named so well for us as "the numinous." Although Cabala has a certain literary presence in the Renaissance, for instance in Spenser, Shakespeare, Thomas Browne, Milton, and the Cambridge Platonist "Poetry of Meditation," it is not confined or limited to these texts but can be located in many other places. We find it for instance in astrology, with John Dee, who tells us "that we should raise cabalistic eyes to the sky."[1] It is enormously significant in medicine, where as a mystic theurgy, it combines with Paracelsan Alchemy, coexisting with and lending its authority, sanction, and dignity to the myriad divinatory systems that were always vulnerable, otherwise, to the accusation of triviality. Its impact is noticeable in Renaissance Neoplatonism, as well as in a kind of marginal Theology (of liberation?) that connects with (a certain "lunatic fringe" of) the English Civil War. Cabala, however relevant allusion to it often seemed, was more of a *style* than something that commits one to one side or another of a political issue. Cabala was very much of a *leitmotif*, in the sermons Lancelot Andrewes, a conservative "King's man," gave annually, on Guy Fawkes Day, commemorating the "miracle" that spared England the (Papish) catastrophe of The Gunpowder Plot. Finally Cabala was above all the sign, solace, and science of Conversion, whether of becoming more profoundly what you were (Jewish, in the case of the Safed mystics) or something else (Christian, or even Atheist), a means whereby one could either dignify and hallow one's choices or confirm and accept one's fate.

Far otherwise today, Cabala can be found *only* in literature—an exile, devolution, or sublimation that commences at about the time of the Sabbatian fiasco. *Cabalistic* today are not the slogan/mantra-chanting, land-oriented sects of the West Bank or self-help circles in Queens that use The Zohar, even "on line," as a health and fortune-finding divinatory device. For Cabala, nothing if not syncretic, can never become merely a cult. *Our* cabalists are rather *writers*, such as, among others, Franz Kafka, Bruno Schultz, Anaïs Nin, and Isabelle Eberhardt.[2] This would be, one has to add, more to the glory of their texts than that of Cabala, for the realm of the *aesthetic* might be a place where the the numinous can survive and endure, but never *prevail*. In this sense, although today religion is no longer the near-universal leveling and unifying passage it once was (though its powers to divide seem intact), there *is* no replacement for it. The aesthetic, however wonderful it seems cannot be that place of wonder into which Cabala was wont to transform the world. This is, by way, for instance, of Kierkegaard's telling critique, because the aesthetic can never be the place of equality, justice, or real compassion. What Pierre Bourdieu recently has called the "cultural capital" of the aesthetically endowed, depends more or less directly or subtly on real economic capital. Aesthetics likes the lucky, the healthy (one must be sound enough at least to articulate or chose one's malady), the young (beautiful), and only such suffering as is susceptible to being transformed into spectacle, whatever has been sufficiently overcome to be able to be translated into discourse: the Muses help those who show they don't need help. Proust's Françoise weeps when she hears a sad story, not when sad people turn up at her door. Cabala in literature can only remind us that there is such a thing as the numinous, never, however, put us in its presence.

I would like to add a word of explanation about the *partial* way I will be handling certain figures in relation to Cabala. The fact is that most of the "mystic heroes" of Cabala did many other things that to them, as well as a reader of today, could seem more interesting or important. Occupation with a matter as intrinsically wavering and labile as Cabala, which, even more than other occult heterodoxy in the Renaissance, privileges spontaneity, secrecy, and disguise, could be unsteady and unsteadying work! Additionally the changing moods and needs of Popes and rulers could impinge upon one's direction or determination, that likely had to be changed, or seem so, sincerely or not to meet a new imperative or answer to the latest Bull or Index. Pico, Ficino, Agrippa, Suavius (Paracelsan acolyte), Campanella, and others all wrote more or less strict and credible denials or refutations of the occult principles, including Cabala, which they had once endorsed, or even thought would *save the world*.

Agreed, for a figure as multidimensional as the polymath Renaissance genius, scientist, bibliophile, engineer, alchemist, cabalist, mathematician, and maybe diplomat-spy, John Dee, it might be a little simplistic and distorting to reduce him to the role of Magus. The authors of two recent monographs on the subject don't deny so much a place of Magic in Dee, but say it has been overemphasized. Nicholas Clulee, for example, complains that the mystical reading of Dee (by Yates, French, and Calder)[3] was based too exclusively on the latter's *Hieroglyphic Monad* of 1564. William Sherman, allowing that The Thrice-Great Hermes was part of Dee's library, insists that he occupied only a corner of it. For Sherman, *another* Hermes, that of (naval) engineering, writing, and communication, as projected in the series of texts by that name of the contemporary French philosopher of science, Michel Serres, would be more germane to Dee.

All the same, there wasn't so much respect for Dee as a "modern man, ahead of his time" before Frances Yates and her students had rescued him from a reputation of charlatan-obscuratonist that lasted for centuries. In a book published in 1941, for instance, Lynn Thorndike, the kind of conscientious, "other directed" reader that can be depended upon to express a consensus, will allow, grudgingly, that Dee will sometimes stumble on a truth, in this case a Copernican one, but deserves, because of his vitiating (character) flaws, no real respect: "In any case Dee, with his mystical inclination towards every form of the occult, would hardly bring the Copernican party into good repute by his accession to its ranks. And he believed in so many things that were wrong, that we could not give him personally any high credit, even if in this one instance he believed in something that happened to be right."[4]

Yates's "Magus" Dee was a much-needed and long-overdue reversal of the sort of snide, tempocentric, and patronizing complacency with which figures who seemed to follow very different ways than those that were supposed to have led to our promised land of Science and Technology were traditionally discounted. Yates's ideas about the importance of Hermeticism, Alchemy, and Cabala in Dee, and correspondingly for his age, constituted a rewriting of history that was tonic and exciting for our idealistic-mystical, radical, and psychedelic 1960s and 1970s. Now in our hard-headed, economic 1990s we want a more practical Dee. Dee, Pico, Agrippa, and other mercurial cabalists-and-much-else, were always, anyway, what one wanted them to be.

In the Beginning

Before the conclusive findings Gershom Scholem published about fifty years ago, resumed in his magisterial *Major Trends in Jewish Mysticism*[1]—that Moses de Leon, a Spanish Jew and cabalist writing in thirteenth-century Spain was, in fact, the sole author of most of what we now know as The Zohar— provenance of this strange and influential text had been argued back and forth for centuries. Although, here and there a serious academic will still disagree with Scholem,[2] there seems to be a general acceptance of his research. Adding to the cogency of the idea of de Leon as author is also the fact that Scholem evidently came to his decision reluctantly and grudgingly, having commenced early in the 1920s by trying to prove rather the *antiquity* of The Zohar—that it was, indeed, as de Leon claimed it to be, entirely the work of the famous, quasi-legendary Rabbi Simon ben Yohai, a refugee of the Diaspora that followed the destruction of the second temple, and a mystic, scholar, and cabalist who was supposed to have lived, worshiped, and worked with a small band of faithful acolytes, in certain remote mountain retreats and caves in or near "the holy land" in the second century A.D. Scholem's early efforts were in fact a reaction to a certain nineteenth-century positivist and historicist tendency, an extension of eighteenth-century rationalist enlightenment, to deflate, deemphasize, and discredit The Zohar, in particular, and Cabala and Jewish mysticism in general.

The extraordinary cabalist career of the notorious Sabbatai Zevi, seventeenth-century apostate and "false messiah," the scandal caused by the iconoclastic sexual and religious practices of eighteenth-century Jewish sects that continued to believe in Sabbatai's apocalyptic message, "beyond good and evil,"[3] and also the general temper of our nascent scientific, practical, and empirical world, to which Judaism, as other religions, were trying to adapt, had made many thinkers, of the mainstream at least, distrustful and suspicious of anything as subjective, incalculable, and immeasurable as a mystical experience. By establishing, for instance, that Moses de Leon wrote The Zohar, Heinrich Graetz, foremost nineteenth-century historian of Judaism, meant to subvert its authority, in claiming that, far from being divinely inspired, it was rather a sham and a forgery, or "book of lies," as he called it. Ironically, Scholem found himself confirming Graetz's suspicions about de Leon, while differing from Graetz dramatically over the significance of The Zohar. For Scholem, Cabala, as conveyed most significantly in The Zohar, represented rather an authentic cultural, literary, and religious movement, one with immense, sometimes even awesome influence and consequences. The Cabala of the Renaissance,[4] as Scholem conceived it and so brilliantly communicated to his generation, was nothing less than a major gnostic revival, which was nourished and inspired both by a syncretic neoplatonism and an idealistic utopianism. Heresies, heterodoxies, imaginations, alternatives which had been forced out of official religions of the western world a millennium ago and had led a subterranean, "denied" existence, surface in the Renaissance, for Scholem, in Cabala. The hegemony of this fundamental thesis of Scholem's has been challenged, certainly in orthodox circles but also by a contemporary French school of Cabala translators and scholars, very important among whom is Charles Mopsik, who directs a series devoted to Jewish mystical texts, published by Verdier. Mopsik's ecstatic-practical bias is evident even in the title of his recent magisterial survey of theurgy in Cabala, *The Great Texts of Cabala: Rites Creating God*.[5] The French "ecstatics" are, in their turn, very respectful students of Moshe Idel, who for the English-speaking audience would be notable for his reservations about Scholem's Cabala. In *Kabbalah: New Per-*

spectives, Idel gets even a little personal over it , where he calls Scholem a "theoretical mystic," even going so far as to state, relying on personal and biographical information, that Scholem, who thought of himself as "rather a failure qua mystic, yet one who longed for mystical experience," was the culmination of a tradition that overemphasized the speculative-philosophical current in Cabala, paying insufficient attention to more "ecstatic"-meditative elements, for instance of Eastern European Ashkenazi-Hasidic, and also of Sufi provenance.[6] A major intention of Idel's book, announced early, was, indeed, to right that imbalance.[7]

That Scholem's Gnostic-Sabbatian Cabala has aroused such passionate opposition may, on the other hand, indicate its power and cogency: like Freud's unconscious, Scholem's Cabala forces us to acknowledge hidden parts of our psyche and nature, while placing in question all moral complacencies. Just as Freud obliges us to admit this other dimension—the ceaseless amoral drives of the blind Id—into our psyches, so Scholem obliges us to admit an "other side"—that of the violator, criminal, and even counterfeiter—into our devotions.[8] The fact that The Zohar was written in the thirteenth rather than the second century, according to Scholem, therefore merely confirms *the* major text of Cabala in its *Renaissance* avatar. Pseudepigraphy, or the attribution of the work of a contemporary to a more ancient and hallowed source, is actually no sign necessarily of imposture but rather a familiar hallmark of mystical writings. It was finally important, for Scholem, that we conceive of The Zohar as a Renaissance creation not for the mere satisfaction of scientific curiosity, but so as to be able, by situating it in its context and by seeing it as the major statement of an evolving movement of Cabala, to understand its relevance, impact, and influence, both in its own time and for centuries subsequently.

The problem as to who exactly wrote it has not been the only point in contention for the almost seven hundred years The Zohar has been in existence. There has been debate also about whether there were one or more authors, which complicated the question of whether it was of ancient or thirteenth-century provenance. In addition there has been considerable speculation, because of a variety of manuscript and published versions, as to what exactly should comprise it. While another kind of integrity, that of the authenticity, intentions, and sincerity of its author(s), transcribers, translators, promoters, "believers," and followers has also been frequently attacked, defended, and certainly wondered about, since this would, by affecting drastically its aura of sacredness, modify its reception and influence.

Manuscript versions of the main body of what was going to be known as The Zohar were apparently in circulation in Spain by 1290. Even close to the time of its first appearance the circumstances of its creation and/or discovery were a matter for speculation and curiosity. A traveling cabalist of the period, and some kind of fugitive from the Moslem conquest of Acre, Isaac ben Samuel of Acre, has left an account of a trip he made to visit de Leon's widow in the "author's" house, which she still occupied in Avila, in Spain, in 1305. Isaac ben Samuel had mentioned that Moses de Leon, whom he said he had met previously in Vallodolid, had sworn to him that the Aramaic original was in his house in Avila, yet, when he asked to see it, in Scholem's words, "both the widow of the deceased and his daughter had denied the existence of such an original."[9] This is the kind of "evidence" that was eagerly seized upon later by Graetz in his attempt to assign The Zohar exclusively to de Leon. Another kind of proof or nonproof of the book's "authenticity" has also been that of comparison of other cabalistic-mystic texts by de Leon, written in Hebrew, with the language, expressions, and formulations of The Zohar's Aramaic. So, in 1856, Rabbi David Luria published findings, based on this comparative method, according to which de Leon could not have been the author. Yet, obviously in the field of Zohar studies, how one interprets evidence has a lot to do with the allegiance of the critic, for just a few years earlier, an important German-Jewish scholar, Aaron (Adolph) Jellinek, had used the same approach to come to the opposite conclusion. Jellinek equally agreed with Graetz that Isaac of Acre's testimony was reliable, pointing to de Leon as the author, but, apparently anticipating Scholem, did not feel that The Zohar was thereby discredited.[10]

The controversy that surrounds Cabala from the time it first came to be known to a wider (non-Jewish, or Christians whose goals were other than *only* converting Jews)[11] audience was only an extension of one that was already thriving. Although Cabala might have seemed, for Pico, Reuchlin, Agrippa, and its acolytes in the fifteenth and sixteenth century, to begin with the zoharic texts, actually, they represent more of a culmination, fruition, and climax than any real beginning. Cabala had been an important and original if somewhat exotic and esoteric element in Jewish religious life for at least two hundred years before The Zohar started to circulate. Then, as more recently, Cabala was passionately espoused and opposed. In the slightly over two centuries between the first appearance of The Zohar and the expulsion of the Jews from Spain the book was known, if not widely so, in its country of origin, but had not yet achieved its later international fame, authority, and notoriety, all surely subsequent to the Spanish exodus. Significantly it was Spanish Jews, who had taken up residence in Italy, who initiated Pico, who was to become the major source and fountainhead of a pan-European Christian Cabala, into the mysteries of The Zohar and other cabalistic texts.

Accepting the claim of de Leon that he was only the book's transcriber and editor, from an "original" in Aramaic that no one has ever seen, had been customarily those who believe in its "divinity" and treat it accordingly. On the other hand, Scholem, who as a scholar is interested rather in the phenomenology of the appeal to divine inspiration than in proving a work to be dictated by angels to Simon ben Yohai (a Pascalian wager in any case, the risks of which science can in no way reduce), argues against the book's antiquity on linguistic, philosophical, and textual grounds. De Leon's Aramaic, for Scholem, is rather that of a clever literary convention, an affectation, device, or mask, in the sense of a Late Medieval version (anticipating Renaissance "games with the reader"), of a language in use in second-century Palestine, but no longer current, than convincingly organic. However, between the extremes of conceiving of The Zohar as a fixed holy word or as a secular and modifiable commercial and marketable production, meant to exploit a certain public, there have been nuances too. Leaving aside the question of its ultimate authority, so modern in its antimetaphysical resonances, the book has been a cultural resource, its stories, styles, and ideas borrowed, alluded to, and adapted for literary, philosophical, mystical, and "magical" purposes. It has been the perfect example of a text that can mean many different things to different people. For many Jews, on the one hand, it had represented, especially during the Renaissance, an intensification and culmination of their faith; but since the fifteenth century at least, and probably even earlier, the work has been seminal also for a Christian Cabala, so much so that it was often spared the bonfires lit by an Inquisition that consumed other Hebrew-language books. A whole gamut of shades and degrees of involvement and connection of author to text are implied in one aspect or another of the debate over its authenticity and authority, and composition, the latter both in the sense of *who* composed it and *when* and what exactly it is supposed to have been *composed* of.

Even after accepting de Leon as the originator of the main body of the work, there are other vast sections, the *Raya Mehemna* and the *Tikkune Zohar*, comprising about 40 percent of (what usually circulates as) the whole that everyone, including Scholem, seems to accept are by other, probably later but more radical, experimental, and urgently mystical and/or apocalyptically minded acolytes; and sections from these texts are typically interpolated into subsequent editions and translations of de Leon's text, introducing a permanent element of structural paradox, contradiction, and polysemy, and also keeping editors (who tend to note where they think the style of the text and character of the ideas and language changes markedly) and readers perpetually on the alert. We should add, to these imponderables, issues relating to provenance, acceptability, meaning, and interpretation. How, for example, are we being asked to read and understand The Zohar, given that texts, especially as enigmatic as this one and aspiring as it does to significance, come either explicitly and implicitly with a *mode d'emploi*? Joyce's *Finnegans Wake* never tires of telling us, for instance, on so many different registers how it wants to be read and understood. However, for The Zohar, are we to read it symbolically, literally, anagogically, or teleologically? Or are we to adopt the philosophically sophisticated hermeneutics of its readings of scripture to The Zohar itself, seeing its characters and narrators often as so many abstractions and ideas? Are we to *see through* this Zohar and other classics of Cabala as they have taught us to *see through* Scripture? Some such element of obliged figuration must be operating here, since there are zoharic flights (into Heavenly mansions, for instance, described in absurdly exact detail) that would defy a literal reading, even more characteristically than for the Bible, which, in comparison, is certainly more down to earth. Yet The Zohar, like the Bible, often likes to be homey, practical, and concrete, so we can't get too settled in any hermeneutic system or attitude. What all this must amount to is the notion that The Zohar—apex, confluence, masterpiece, and incarnation of Cabala—is also a consummately Renaissance problematization of writer, reader, and work, which anticipates, prepares, and probably helped to create contemporary critical attitudes and ambivalencies as well as modern textual strategies and deconstructions.

Scholem and Benjamin

It is surely more than a coincidence that our twentieth-century revival or recovery of The Zohar was developed by Scholem, at least in its early phases, at a time when he was in close contact and communication with Walter Benjamin. Cabala was one of their frequent subjects of conversation, at a time (World War I) when their knowledge of and interest in these matters was apparently beginning. Scholem relates, in his memoir of the period, *Walter Benjamin, the Story of a Friendship*, that the very first time the subject of Cabala ever came up between them was connected to their interest in a work by the Christian Cabalist and German-Romantic thinker Franz Josef Molitor: "Between 1827 and 1857, Molitor published anonymously, as an introduction to a projected presentation of the Kabbalah, four volumes under the memorable title *Philosophie der Geschichte oder Über die tradition* [Philosophy of history or on tradition] . . . That period [1916–17] marked the beginning of his [Benjamin's] interest in Franz von Baader and in Franz Joseph Molitor, who was a pupil of Schelling and Baader and the only serious German language philosopher to study the Kaballah, having devoted 45 years to it . . . These [on Molotor] were our first conversations on the Kaballah."[12] This discovery of Cabala was connected with their mutual fascination with mysticism; and the recourse to mystical texts, generally, for both Scholem and Benjamin, must have symbolized their opposition to the war mentality, which they bitterly opposed, and to the prevailing drift of contemporary society toward a reductive materialism and commercialism. Significantly, Martin Buber, Jewish existential philosopher and enthusiastic about Hasidism, with whom Scholem and Benjamin were as disillusioned as they were with the "patriotic" German socialists and who already had an important following, was both anti-Cabala, which he regarded as an individualistic distortion of communitarian Judaism, and also, swept along in the fanatical current of the time, *pro*-war.[13]

These two writers were also, according to David Biale, in *Gershom Scholem, Kaballah and Counter-History*, attracted to the specifically word-oriented quality of Cabala, in contrast to other mystical approaches (for instance, Eastern, or even Buber's I-thou relation, with its Zen connotations) that are built in and around the wordless, or various modes and styles of *silence*. Biale explains that, whatever their later differences, implied by Benjamin's and Scholem's intellectual style at this time was a notion that "Language itself is of divine origin . . . [and that] the experience of revelation is linguistic. Since language is equivocally both human and divine, a basis exists for using language to communicate an experience of the divine."[14] One of Benjamin's innovations, precisely language centered, was an ability to illuminate texts with contemporary and relevant philosophical-critical insights, meant to bring out their political challenges, social implications, and ideological ambiguities. Equally the freshness of Scholem's approach and its fecundity lay, as a matter of fact, in the particularly literary attitude he was able to take, for example, toward The Zohar, which tended previously to be handled more emotionally and subjectively, or as a matter of either reverence or repulsion; and the most compelling evidence in his crucially important attribution of the book to de Leon was indeed of a literary-critical nature, grounded in a close linguistic, stylistic, and textual analysis.

Benjamin and Scholem could converge also, to a certain degree on this revival of the mystical text, endemically idealistic, because of their common passion, and that of their intellectual generation, for *utopia*, in art, thought, and practice, although, of course, they were later to diverge radically in their attitudes on how their ideals could be realized. Benjamin's path was to take him eventually in a Marxist and secular social-aesthetic and political direction, in a process, nevertheless, modeled on ideals, styles, and practices of the German Romantics (among them the Christian Cabalist Molitor) and French Symbolists, whereby much of the energy, absoluteness, and "aura" of the sacred word is displaced onto a literary one. For Benjamin came to conceive that only *this* world, transformed through a revolutionary praxis, personal and social, could become that other, better one; whereas for Scholem, the two domains, a quotidian one ruled by politics and economy and a rarer one where we can aspire to higher things, would need to stay separated, except perhaps for momentary joinings. These connections might be facilitated, for example, by certain sublime moments of insight and knowledge occurring in some protected and demarcated area, as of Sabbath-evening or mystical text; and no one has done more than Scholem, as in his intriguing studies of the mystical heresy of Sabbatai Zevi, to make us aware of the awesome implications and world-shattering and world-creating consequence of the careers of those who have attempted to lay claim to *more* of this "ecstasy" and for *more* people. So Scholem's path led him toward an exploration of possibilities for human elevation into extraordinary, visionary, and numinous levels and experiences through research into the arcana of Jewish mysticism, these flights guaranteed from a territory, secured by a pact or compromise, a Zionist one, with the real, that is not *only* mental or spiritual, and certainly is not always fair. On the other hand, however much, sometimes, he wanted to, Benjamin could never stray too far from a neoenlightenment universalism that Scholem came to think of as a hopeless cause, or one, at least in its Marxist avatar, that would reduce humanity to a narrowly economic dimension. Try as he would and did, Scholem could never bring Benjamin to Jerusalem, perhaps because for the latter it meant leaving too many and too much behind.

The Zohar

The Zohar is mainly a massive commentary on the Five Books of Moses, also known as the Torah, or Pentateuch. Like other important Jewish commentaries, which (we now know) predate it, on the Bible, like the Talmud, Mishnah, and Gemora, it expounds the quandaries, problems, seeming conundrums, and general relevance of scripture for comportment; but The Zohar purports to be, in addition to its quality as commentary on some of the most provocative and intriguing portions of scripture, also an introduction to "the mysteries of the Bible," invisible as it were to the untrained eye and ear. For it, the Bible would be a labyrinthine mystery and secret to explore, one to conceal while revealing, reveal while concealing.

Including various strata, some manifestly not de Leon's responsibility but which it would be inconceivable still not to regard as an essential and integral portion of the work, The Zohar will amount to from about three thousand to five thousand printed pages, depending on the version and translation. Until the the late nineteenth century it existed mainly in its Hebrew-Aramaic "original" version, first printed in the Mantua and Cremona edition of 1558–1560, with an important introduction by Isaac de Lattes, and in Latin translations, anthologies, and selections of passages, more or less representative and comprehensive. In our own century there have been translations of The Zohar into French, by Jean de Pauly [1910][15] and Charles Mopsik [1981–96].[16] S. L. G. Mathers (of Rosicrucian fame) published an English translation (from the Latin of Knorr Von Rosenroth's 1677 anthology, *Kaballa Denudata*) of some of the most important and "curious" portions of The Zohar in 1887, which was the only place to go to read The Zohar in English until the five-volume English translation, by Maurice Simon and Harry Sperling, from the "original" Hebrew-Aramaic appeared in 1933. This is, in spite of its quaint editorial position on The Zohar's antiquity, still the definitive version. Translations as well as editions of The Zohar would seem to be, however comprehensive and well intentioned, structurally incomplete, inevitably for a text like this, probably impossible to establish definitively, or whose very indefiniteness is part of its charm. In our century there have been a number of anthologies, in English, of parts of The Zohar: for instance Mather's anthology, *The Kaballah Unveiled*, which last appeared under that title in 1926, some of which resurfaced in Dagobert Runes's selection, *The Wisdom of the Kaballah*, in 1967; a slender, but widely known book of passages chosen by Scholem, *Zohar, the Book of Splendour* [1949]; and, most magisterially, Isaiah Tishby's impressive edition, from a translation into Modern Hebrew of selected passages, *The Wisdom of The Zohar*, arranged thematically and commented on extensively, which has appeared in English in 1989.

Although other very important, though much more summary cabalistic works were known before the appearance of de Leon's Zohar—the most renowned and important of which were the Sefer

Yetzirah, or Book of Formation, which may date back to the fourth or fifth century A.D. and the enigmatic Sefer Bahir, or Book of Brightness, thought to be the oldest cabalist work, whose roots go back into gnostic antiquity—no other cabalistic text had ever approached the comprehensiveness, ambition, amplitude, and sheer encyclopedic exhaustiveness of The Zohar, which, especially since the Spanish Diaspora, has truly made the Cabala its own. So compact has this identity of Cabala been with The Zohar that, starting at least in the fifteenth century, all cabalistic writings tend to be, are just about obliged to be, zoharic, that is commentaries on and interpretations of this Book of Splendour, to the point that it would not be straining a comparison to say that what Marx's *Capital* has been to Communism The Zohar has been to Cabala.

Thinking about the Cabala in general and The Zohar in particular for a theory-drenched modern is certainly an intellectually dizzying enterprise, full of traps, aporias, paradoxes, and outright contradictions. One cannot read for long in and about Cabala, for instance, without noticing that this is a tradition in which an *oral* component pretends to be all important, one made necessary and ineluctable because the *written* word of God, comprised first and foremost of the Torah, together with its canonical commentaries and accretions, Talmud, Mishna, and Gemora, is insufficient, or rather inexistent without it. However, whether this Torah is an oral tradition or a written text, or both simultaneously, concurrently, and undecidably, The Zohar is never more ecstatically hyperbolic than when telling us that the world was created for the purpose of Torah, and indeed *by* Torah, not, as might seem reasonable to suppose, the other way around: "When God . . . created the world, He did so for no other purpose than that Israel should one day come and receive the Torah. It was by means of the Torah that the world is established" [*Zohar IV*, 177].[17] Yet what exactly we mean by Torah, by this text by which and for which the world was created, cannot always be so clear; for Torah is not identical with the literal letters and words that comprise it, even if they are Hebrew and ostensibly more proximal to the divine than that of another language. Nor on the other hand can Torah be separated from its literal, written manifestation or avatars.

When especially The Zohar likes to comment and interpret is where the letter of Torah seems puzzling, enigmatic, or contradictory.

Certain explanations and motivations very urgently demanded by ethics, morality, and common sense are just not present, or not amply enough, presumably, for Cabala's sophisticated Renaissance audience, in the literal "letter of the law." The Zohar, accordingly, is concerned with finding a higher logic behind that rather blunt partial ethnocide Moses seems to have carried out on his own people subsequent to the first, disappointing descent from Mount Sinai and the breaking of the tablets of the law. The breaking of the tablets was ineluctable in any case, The Zohar will explain, since there was as yet no oral law, indispensable, exactly because of human frailty, to receive, explain, and contain any written one; Moses receives this *cabal* or oral word on the *second* ascent, along with a new edition of the written one, in response to the *fall* involved in the episode of the worship of the Golden Calf. Moses' zoharic Jehovah, like Milton's later Puritan one, likes to give humans every chance to be perfect, before visiting them with the well-deserved consequences of their not being so. Even for the killing of the masses who had turned to idol worship or crass materialism and luxury, we are not to think of it, according to The Zohar, as really internecine slaughter: what essentially seems to have been eliminated, as the rationalizing zoharic commentary explains the matter, were impure pagan elements that had followed Israel into freedom, motivated rather more by license than religion, but whose pleasure-loving proclivities had now become an obstacle, preventing those faithful others from observing the Sabbath strictly: "and R. Isaac next began a discourse on the text: *And Moses assembled all the congregation of the children of Israel etc.* 'The object', he said, 'of this assembling was to give them anew the law of the Sabbath. For the previous promulgation of the Sabbath before the Israelites made the golden calf was not observed by the mixed multitude [ostensibly recent converts, plus Jews of longer standing]. When they heard the words . . . they said in protest: Are we to be excluded from this? . . . Then, after the guilty ones were put to death, Moses assembled the children of Israel separately and gave them the Sabbath anew" [*Zohar IV*, 187].

On another, more abstract level, The Zohar likes to explain such enigmas as why the wicked prosper on this earth, which is because "the side of impurity, the other side, has rule only in this world and none at all in the one to come" [*Zohar* II, 190]; or why the good are so often unrewarded and/or die young. This later question is considered such a troubling one that it is answered very early in our text, during the prologue or overture to the main body of the work, where we are told to love God "even if he deprive thee of life . . . it was for this reason that the light of creation which first emerged was afterwards withdrawn [meaning the abandonment of the earth to the powers of evil] . . . in order that there might be perfect [disinterested] love" [*Zohar I*, 50]. This gnostic argument is thematic indeed in the zoharic conception of life on earth, with its proto-Nietzschean reversals and transvaluations, as in a later passage when we are assured flatly that "when suffering befalls a righteous man it is on account of the love God bears to him" [*Zohar II*, 190].

The Zohar is equally illuminating and consoling in its ways of justifying and explaining the existence of unenlightened strata, according to which we require our opposites, since "each class can win credit for itself though the medium of the other, that is, the righteous through the wicked, the wise through the stupid, the rich through the poor" [*Zohar II*, 288]. Even more ingenuity is required on the very sensitive question of why it is that the virtuous need to be malign. Naturally the potential for confusion and abuse in this area is maximal; and certainly in this matter of the incorporation of evil into the lives of the ostensibly just were sown the seeds of later "adventures on the other side," including the catastrophic cabalistic messianic movement of the seventeenth century.

At the same time such nuanced handling of matters of morality became part of the later appeal of Cabala. This was an aspect, of gnostic-dualist inspiration, which was already well established by the time of The Zohar. A particular province that Cabala had staked out for itself was that of Theodicy, or justification—that is, to confront and account for the existence of evil. In the gnostically tinged Bahir, or Book of Brightness, for example, so very important in the late Medieval stirrings of Cabala in Provence and Northern Spain, it is even suggested that evil is a *middah*, or aspect or quality of God: "And what is this [principle of the seduction to evil]? It is Satan. This teaches us that God has a *middah* which is named 'Evil'."[18] Although it treats gnostic ideas so seriously, Cabala does not surrender to the pessimism or apocalyptic desperation that has often accompanied them. In stressing an idea of incorporating evil into the divine, Cabala was thereby trying to eschew recognizing in it an independent principle, thereby being forced to assign this world to the rule of Satan, as in the troubling and dangerous contemporaneous revival of Dualism-Manicheanism, in its Cathar and Albigensian forms in twelfth- and thirteenth-century France.

On the other hand, by bringing evil in so close to the heavenly, Cabala runs a different risk, that of a process of contamination of the very principle or possibility of the good, at the end of which moral judgment of any sort would be a frank absurdity because the divine on which such a thing could be based had been irremediably compromised. However, even at its inception Cabala was distinguished by a willingness to take such risks, for stakes that seem to have been nothing less than a more honest and intimate understanding and toleration for the ambiguities of existence. In the thought, for instance, of Isaac the Blind, a major figure in early Cabala, whose influence radiated from Provence to Northern Spain early in the thirteenth century, there is a special tendency to find a place for evil, which is allocated a position in the hierarchy of the *sefiroth*, or forms, before even any worldly manifestation or materialization. The position of evil was, according to Isaac, an honorable and legitimate one until an episode of rebellion and an effort at usurpation against other powers in the cosmic scheme of things. Nevertheless, we still cannot demarcate evil definitively from "the holy," but must keep it in mind and view, paying it all due respects, for its "fall" is only a temporary one. In a messianic era, and perhaps as one of its harbingers, Satan will be reinstated, an essential element in the repair of the Throne of God, which had been damaged, presumably, during the War in Heaven, and incomplete ever since.[19]

Isaac seems to have gone so far in his "faith in evil" as to become an advocate of the doctrine of apocatastasis, or theory of the "ultimate restoration of Satan." It should be added too that, since, in Judaism, authority tended to be fragmented rather than centralized, such speculations like these on the place and destiny of evil could never become a matter of dogma or doctrine but remained discretionary and open. It is not surprising, therefore, that later in the Renaissance we find Christian writers turning to Cabala and also to gnostic sources, with which it is connected, for nuances and explanations in this matter of evil when they found their own traditions insufficiently comprehensive.

Generally it seems that this problem of evil, which was already an important and characteristic element in early Cabala, becomes a matter of extensive and obsessive concern in The Zohar, where, for example, an opportunity is never missed to elucidate the very ambiguous issue of the "use of evil to overcome evil." The Zohar concludes its discussion of one of the most obvious and notorious Biblical examples of this situation, Jacob's cheating Esau out of his birthright, by claiming flatly: "It was in this way that Jacob dealt with Esau, who was on the other side, so as to outwit him by craft, as was necessary in order to keep the upper hand of him from the beginning to the end, as befitted" [*Zohar II*, 114–15]. This use of "the weapons of the enemy" is thereby not only prescribed but also commanded and *enjoined*. It is not peculiar, therefore, according to The Zohar, that Job was punished, because his vice was that of an excessive and self-conscious purity, a sort of complacency or pride, besetting sin of the good, or those who like to think of themselves as such:

> And when Job made sacrifices, he did not give Satan any part whatsoever . . . had he done so, the Accuser would not have been able to prevail against him. Hence in the end he only took what was his due. As to the question which might be asked, why then did God allow Job to suffer thus, the answer would be that had he given Satan his due, the "unholy side" would have separated itself from the holy, and so allowed the latter to ascend undisturbed into the highest spheres; but since he did not do so, the Holy One let justice be executed on him. Mark this! As Job kept evil separate from good and failed to fuse them, he was judged accordingly: first he experienced good, then what was evil, then again good. For man should be cognizant of both good and evil, and turn evil itself into good. This is a deep tenet of faith. [*Zohar III*, 109]

The Two Sources of Morality and Religion

Certainly a founding narrative for Cabala would be the story of Moses' return to Mount Sinai, there to receive, along with another edition of the Decalogue, literally "in his ear" (another meaning of Cabala, from which we get the modern *cabal*, denoting something that tends to be whispered, conspired, and secret rather than written and open), an oral *supplement* that would make the revised written rendition tolerable. The episode of the worship of the Golden Calf having revealed that humanity is unready to confront the challenge of the naked written word, just *there*, demanding attention and devotion—not until a Day of Judgment perhaps, or other messianic event, we need, in the meantime (and Cabala is an ideology for this *mean*-time, or time of exile), the constant help, consolation, warmth, and life of this spoken wisdom. Cabala's function is at once a guiding, sheltering, and challenging one, from which the idea and reminder of a *voice* is never very far away, like a parent, the sound of whose very words connotes care for the child, encouraging, calming, and reassuring, gently correcting and explaining when there's been misbehavior or when upsetting or contradictory things happen.

The association of oral and written, already implied by Torah, with Cabala becomes a formal rule and, in fact, its very reason for being. Dating from that time of primordial revelation of human insufficiency and dependency, symbolized by the need for a second Mosaic ascent, according to Cabala, the written and the oral have coexisted: "Since the only aim and object of the Holy One in sending man into this world is that he may know and understand that *YHVH* is *Elohim*. This is the sum of the whole mystery of the Faith, of the whole Torah, of all that is above and below, of the written and Oral torah, all together forming one unity. The essence of the mystery of Faith is to know that this is a complete Name. This knowledge that *YHVH* is one with *Elohim* is indeed the synthesis of the whole Torah, both of the Written and the Oral, the former being symbolic of YHVH and the latter of *Elohim*" [*Zohar IV*, 58].

As with the confirmation of a cosmic and "righteous" place for evil, this dialogue, symbiosis, and dialectic between a written and oral Torah, which so pervades The Zohar, was already amply adumbrated earlier in the Cabala of Isaac the Blind, according to whom no written Torah is even conceivable without an oral one. As paraphrased by Scholem, from an important fragment left by Isaac, "we find a conception according to which there simply is no Written

Torah within reach of the ordinary mortal. Everything we call by that name has already passed through the mediation of the Oral Torah . . . The Torah scroll itself symbolizes that. The ink and the parchment form a unity. But the element rendered visible by the ink is the blackness, the 'obscure mirror' of the Oral Torah; the true secret of the Written Torah, which embraces everything, is contained in the signs, still not visible, of the white parchment."[20]

Just as in this striking image (that may recall Mallarmé, who made us very much aware of the whiteness of the page) of the materiality of the writing, perceptible only because of the emptiness it shows against, so the word and the letter come together for Cabala. The written and the spoken here are intertwined inseparably, analogous, if not identical to other borders, margins, and divisions across which traffic continues to flow—such as Heaven and Earth, Human and Angel, Evil and Good, Man and Woman, Jew and Muslim, Living and Dead, Wise and Foolish—leaving it to the imagination of contemporaries to supply the current polarities between which there is still, hopefully, some flow.

Strategically, then, the very notion of Cabala, that of a written law, is a way of dealing with a present that is likely to be making very different demands and posing other problems than the past, without sacrificing the orientation and anchoring provided by the "sacred" written word. An oral line can change with the times, and, as in The Zohar, where opinions frequently differ on issues and difficulties are often resolved in conversation, an opinion expressed verbally is intrinsically less permanent. From the point of view of the oral, the *spirit*, which has to do, as conveyed etymologically by "inspiration," with breath and breathing, would be what matters. With the spoken word a mutability or drift is immediately there, not only in the process of production and amplification but in the aspect of reception and dissemination; and this quality of contingency returns us necessarily to the spirit or intention behind the word, as supported by the gestural or body language that accompanies it. In respect to the written word, and especially when its author would be the divine, the *spirit*, of course, still is all-important—in Torah the spirit *is* the letter, inseparably, unalterably, unchangeably. Nevertheless writing involves intrinsically the illusion or suggestion of permanence, whether product of a divine authority or of a demonic impertinence. What, for instance, expresses the unmodifiability of the decalogue with which Moses descended is their status as inscribed, therefore staying elements in an otherwise passing world. If commentary has found an oral component to be implicit in Torah, on the other hand, in Cabala, and preeminently in The Zohar, the written text is its own commentary, since it is replete with signals of its essential oral accompaniment. "Cabala," anyway (and *cabal*), means something conspired, that is whispered and received in each other's ear.

A written Zohar thereby absorbs much of the fluidity, flexibility, and possibility for confusion, fragmentation, and correction that would belong to a spoken one, thereby altering, by making more contingent, also the way we read and understand Torah. This impermanence in The Zohar is intensified further because it is a text, which, even though it claims divine provenance and inspiration, has never, unlike Torah, assumed a final, set, and authoritative form. The very notion of what exactly comprises it is fluid, since for every scholar, editor, translator, certainly every era, it seems to be something else, not to mention even *what* it means!

Traditionally (Cabala means "tradition" also, in the sense of something absorbed, "drunk with one's mother's milk," as we say, or told to us by our elders), Cabala thinks of itself as the vehicle of a body of lore, therefore, that was given to Moses directly from God, in the form of an *other* revelation he received (Cabala also means "reception") at the same time when he was given the literal written one in its material embodiment of the ten commandments. Cabala then is the Renaissance Latinization of the Hebrew word *cabal*, making of it a singular noun of the feminine gender, appropriately also, since another attribute of Cabala is to supply a softer feminine presence, known as the *Shekinah* (which in precabalistic Judaism meant simply "divine immanence),"[21] to complement the severity of the male God or *Jehovah*. This, of course, involves a modification of a traditional image—which turns out to be somewhat of a misconception—of Judaism as a sexist religion. Recently, Raphael Patai, for instance, has done much to correct the distorted impression that Judaism was (is) so exclusively patriarchal. Interestingly, the ancient worship of the feminine, was not, however, as Patai points out (relying on Philo), really an expression of the principle of mercy but one of severity and rigor.[22] The "softer," more consoling Shekinah was a later creation, inspired perhaps by Christian worship of Mary. The feminine in the Jewish divine has come a long way since Leo Baeck insisted, seventy years ago, that such a notion was inconceivable: "Its language [Hebrew], plastic though it is, contains no word for 'goddess,' for the concept behind that word is alien to it."[23] The word *cabal* means ineluctably, then, in Hebrew that which is not, cannot be written down, the oral as opposed to written, but which the very substantial, though confusing (in the sense of who to ascribe them to) texts, the most illustrious of which is The Zohar, continue to *represent*. The very concept of an oral tradition that is written is a paradox in itself, which commentators, beginning at least as early as the Renaissance, have wondered about. Interesting also is the fact that The Zohar, now somewhat marginal in Jewish religious practice, or maybe relegated to cult status, was widely considered a sacred text for three or four hundred years, that is, treasured and revered as divinely inspired, along with the Torah and its canonical commentaries. This changed when Enlightenment rationalism and then nineteenth-century Jewish positivist scholarship attacked the mystical currents, especially Cabala, that were held responsible for messianic "excesses" of the previous centuries. The best known of these were the seventeenth-century apocalyptic movement of Sabbatai Zevi and Joseph Frank's eighteenth-century Sabbatian cult—both masters of what Scholem calls a "heretical Cabala," the first notable for eschatological deviation (principally claiming to be the messiah), culminating in conversion to Islam; the second for conversion to Catholicism, cooperating in the infamous "blood libel" (whereby Jews were accused of murdering Christian children, so as to drink their blood at Passover), and for polygamous-incestuous sexual orgies and rites.

This paradox of an oral tradition-in-writing as embodied in The Zohar was certainly evident, especially to the opponents of Cabala, even during the centuries of its greatest prestige, approximately between 1500 and 1700. Yet the damage of the contradiction may have been contained and attenuated by The Zohar's peculiarly fragmented and "dialogic" style. It is the burden of *this* particular written text, so obsessed with voice and voicing, to demonstrate so vividly and constantly, and to embody the existence and importance of an oral tradition, not only in its content, but also in its typically conversational way of proceeding. What happens when people are allowed to talk, as Bakhtin has called to our attention in his studies of the "festive" style of Rabelais and Dostoevsky, is a threat to all central power and control. So, here, in The Zohar, where each has their say, authority—even the most commanding one, that of the legendary Rabbi Simon ben Yohai, to whom the original is attributed by de Leon, finder of the manuscript, whom many haven't believed anyway—is always provisional, temporary, distributed, questionable, and frequently questioned.

A problem of accreditation, for instance, arises at one point when it is mentioned that the books, presumably Indian or Zarathustrian of "the children of the East" are identical in many respects to the teachings of The Zohar.[24] A similarity might be the presence of *gilgul*, or something like a doctrine of reincarnation, referred to at times in The Zohar, and growing in importance in the later Cabala but inexistent in Torah, as in mainstream Judaism. An essential aspect, additionally, of the theodicy of Sankara Vedanta, well established by the time of the inception of Cabala in the thirteenth century, was a separation of Brahman into upper and lower categories, of which only the lower was knowable. On a different register, this dichotomy was the basis of the pioneering explorations of Rudolf Otto into correspondences between the mystical systems of East and West. In *Mysticism East and West*, Otto compares Eckhart and Sankara, stressing however, for the former, a dichotomy between Godhead and God, that would parallel the cabalistic distinction between Ain Soph and the Sephiroth. Sankara (c. 788–820/50 A.D.) insisted that only the "upper" Brahman was real, all below being merely illusion; but the thirteenth-century Vedantic reformer, Ramanuja, insisted on "reality" for the lower realm as well, so in a sense, as for the cabalists with which he was contemporary, in the theurgic possibilities of the lower to influence the higher. The debate between Ramanuja and Sankara is the classic one between immanence and transcendance, respectively. In cabalistic terms this would surely mean the opposition between the intimate revelation of the *Sephiroth*, always here and now, and the distant secrecy of the *Ain Soph*, forever somewhere else. This maybe explains why some intellectually very exigent Christians were attracted to Cabala like bees to honey: that god-man, Jesus, would be the incarnation of a miracle that has long eluded philosophers, that of an *immanent* transcendance and a *transcendant* immanence.[25]

Raphael Patai's research into the connections between Cabala and Indian religion[26] might make us wonder, also, whether the very strange, mystical stress The Zohar places on sex, certainly one of its main "roads to the absolute," is linked to the Tantra of the East. Worship of the Goddess, although episodic, was still a factor, if a controversial one, in Jewish religious practice in ancient Israel. Judaism, apparently was quite porous to such "pagan" devotions, so attractive as to be sometimes irresistible, as were intrinsic to the religion of surrounding tribes. This went along with the presence in the Temple, which Patai documents that lasted, more or less discreetly, for centuries of sexually suggestive statuary, both of goddesses and very sensual Cherubim. Sometimes the mere sight of such idols unleashed sexual orgies, which behavior was a factor evidently in their eventual exclusion from the sanctuaries about the time of Christ, and also in the segregation of the sexes, still practiced in orthodox Judaism. Patai wonders whether the Jews might have derived this suggestive (and apparently arousing) sculpture, directly or indirectly, from Alexander's armies' exposure to "prototypes of that type of Indian temple sculpture which we know from such late examples as the Konorak façade, showing divine pairs in various positions of ecstatic embrace."[27] Sabbatian sexuality might then represent not so much a departure as a revival.

However accurate such ideas are, that The Zohar entertains, as to its congruence with the "Books of the East," it decides, nevertheless, that tempting though such conjectures might be, these Eastern texts are to be rejected as dangerous and heretical since they lack the guarantee of the divine authority of Cabala! Strange, if symptomatic too, is the fact that The Zohar, different in so many ways from traditional Judaism—for instance, in its insistence on ecstatic (although monogamous) sexuality, its "Paradise Now" mentality—is so sensitive about demarcating itself from other teachings, however compatible, which it is inclined to regard as heresies.

In spite of an occasional "anxiety of influence" that inspires, seemingly in this case, its insistence that a similar Eastern spirit is *different*, there is, more typically, a profound sense in The Zohar of the partial nature of all knowledge, no matter how reliable its provenance. Even Angels know no more than they are told, and tell you no more than you need to know.[28] In Cabala, generally, there is a perpetual sense and awareness both of the possibilities and the limitations of human perception and cognition; and, seemingly, the closer to extraordinary knowledge the subject comes the more caution is to be exercised, since the probability of delusion and its corresponding cost would be similarly maximized. The Zohar, for example, which tends to be attracted to and even, maybe, to attempt to induce nonordinary states of mind, is nevertheless cautious about them: "What a man is shown in a dream corresponds to his own character, and his soul ascends just so far as to obtain for him information suitable to his grade" [*Zohar II*, 238].

Dreams, indeed, in The Zohar, are a privileged form of access to other and (hopefully) higher worlds, or "revelation" as it is commonly called, as befits a visionary text; and, as a matter of fact, dreams, for instance those of Joseph and Nebuchadnezzar, are a frequent recourse in Scripture also, where it seems that they were more to be relied upon. In Cabala, on the other hand, the dream is considered to be merely one of a set or series of states, others of which are those of vision and prophecy, and, indeed the lowest in this ladder—and, from this point of view, to be mistrusted as always containing elements of falsehood and error. For it is thematic also in The Zohar that evil, tempting spirits delight in visiting us in our sleep, for instance, with perverse sexual fantasies—anything other than the Sabbath "heavenly" sexual intercourse with the Shekinah one's wife has become, being considered to be of Satanic provenance. Edmund Spenser seems to utilize a thoroughly zoharic and cabalistic motif in the dream of the Redcrosse Knight, in *Fairy Queen*, Book I, Canto I, st. 45–48, when Archimago, whose evil character was based on the demonic reputation of the sixteenth-century cabalist, Agrippa, sends a replica of the knight's ladylove into his chambers to disturb, arouse, corrupt, and "weaken" the knight in his sleep. James Nohrnberg, in *The Analogy of the Faerie Queene*, quotes from The Zohar in analyzing this episode: "When a man dreams in his sleep, female spirits often come and disport with him."[29]

Elsewhere, The Zohar, breaking down prophetic epistemology into six grades of divine revelation, is quite specific, through a striking imagery of light and darkness, on the relativity of all this exalted knowledge. The light (of understanding), at best, is fitful, indirect, and unreliable, and at the topmost grade, where the stakes are highest the obscurity is densest, which is why this grade is

called "burden": "In regard to the word 'burden', it should be noted
that there were six grades in the divine revelation to prophets:
'appearance' (*mahzeh*), 'vision' (*hazon*), 'revelation' (*hezyon*), 'aspect'
(*hazuth*), 'word', and burden'. The first five are all like unto the
vision of one who beholds a reflection of light from behind a wall,
and some of them are as the vision of one who sees the light of the
sun through a lantern. But 'burden' signifies that the light came
with great difficulty, and was barely revealed. Here it was even a
'burden of silence' (*dumah*), for which no words could be found"
[*Zohar III*, 374].

Losing the Reader

Often very singular also is the way in which The Zohar is to be
taken or understood as it is read: quite limpid, even straightforward sections of lecture and conversation yield suddenly to ab-
strusely lyrical and baroquely ornate flights of fancy and rhetoric
on such items as tents or candelabras, with all kinds of heavenly
analogies, concomitants, and implications, as sheer extravagance
takes over, forbidding any kind of calm reading, which would be
defied or downright impossible. No doubt Scholem has something
like this in mind when, in introduction to his Zohar anthology,
where, nevertheless, he seems cautious enough not to include any
of like extravagance, he admits "in a certain number of passages a
passion for the association of ideas which is pushed to the extreme,
degenerating into *a flight from conceptual reality*."[30]

However, Scholem generally, adapting perhaps to positivist
criticism, which might regard such pages as evidence of irrespon-
sible elitist esoterics, tries to minimize the importance of the "exceptional" in The Zohar, whether literary, sexual, or mystic,
understanding, rightfully, from his point of view, that a book like
this is very much what you make of it. This depends on which
aspects of the work, so multifarious, varied, and variable, you decide would be most meaningful or representative. Whether, indeed,
the "flight from conceptual reality" involved above would be so
irrelevant from the point of view of experimental modernism in
literature is not so sure. From such a perspective, such "wild passages" and flights might seem too frequent, extensive, serious, and

developed to be anything less than intrinsic and essential to a Cabala and a Zohar that nevertheless was (and is), understandably, not entirely comfortable with them; inasmuch as The Zohar is aware that it promotes trips that not everyone might want to take, for instance, as Scholem implies also, in demarcating, as if marking for caution, its more outrageous extravagant pages, so that the readers know what they're in for, or to avoid. But thoroughly cabalistic and zoharic is an antinomian style of finding much value in what seemed at first nonsense. Typically some of the wisest words in The Zohar come from people of seemingly low social rank and accomplishment, donkey drivers, boys, ranting hermits, whose discourse it then requires the insight of Simon ben Yohai to "see through," as well as to show the truth behind the mask to his followers.

Let's interrupt briefly one of these flights, the kind that for Scholem's good reasons you won't find in his slim anthology but that you can't miss noticing will take off here and there from any reasonably comprehensive text. The context here is that of what is certainly a mystical commentary on the symbolic meanings of the three metals (as subject, only a launching pad, it turns out) used in the fashioning of a tabernacle to house the Torah that Moses had received, as we break into a conversation between cabalistic Rabbis, participants in a conversation that is supposed to have taken place about 150 years after the destruction of the Second Temple:

> AND THE BRASS OF THE WAVING WAS SEVENTY TALENTS. Said R. Judas: "All this descends here below in the supernal image, containing the mystery of Faith. To the same pattern did Nebuchadnezzar make the image that he erected." R. Jose said: "It was not the image that he made that was after the same pattern, but the image that he saw in his dream, an image made of gold, of silver and brass. Now, iron and clay were not worthy to enter into the work of the Tabernacle, but only those three metals. There is a recondite significance in the triad of metals. There were other materials that formed into tetrads, as the four fabrics consisting of blue, purple, scarlet, and fine linen, or the four rows of stones in the breastplate." R. Judah said: "Some of them formed into threes, some into fours, some into twos, and again others were

kept single. Nevertheless, an Order proper consists of a triad.[31] The world is divided between forty-five varieties of the light, seven of which are assigned to the seven abysses. Each light impinges on its Abyss, where there is a great rolling of stones, and penetrates into and pierces those stones so that water issues from them. The light impinges on the four sides of the Abyss, and then each light becomes entwined with the next and they join together and divide the waters, and all the seven lights overwhelm the seven Abysses, and hover over the darkness of the Abysses so that the light and darkness intermingle. Then the waters rush up and down, and there is a fusion of light and darkness and waters, from which emerge lights in which darkness is not intermingled. The lights then impinge on each other, with the result that they split into seventy-five channels of the Abyss along which waters course. Each channel roars with a sound peculiar to itself, so that there is a quivering of all the Abysses. At the sound of the roaring each Abyss calls to its neighbor, saying: 'Divide thy waters.' Thus Scripture says: 'Deep calleth unto deep at the voice of thy cataracts' (Ps. XLII, 8). Underneath these there are the three hundred and sixty-five veins, some white, some black, some red, all of which intertwine and fuse into one color. These veins are woven into seventeen nets, each of which is a called a net of veins, and descend to the nethermost parts of the Abyss. Underneath these there are two nets of the appearance of iron and another two nets of the appearance of brass. Over above them there are two thrones, one on the right and one on the left. All these nets join into one, and water flows from these channels and enters the nets. As for the two thrones, one is the throne of the black firmament and the other of the variegated firmament. When the nets ascend, they go by way of the throne of the black firmament, and when they descend they go by way of the throne of the variegated firmament. The throne of the black firmament is on the right, and the throne of the variegated firmament is on the left. When the nets ascend by the throne of the black firmament, the throne of the firmament of the left lowers itself, and they descend by it, as the two thrones balance one another. Thus all the nets descend by means of them and enter into the nethermost parts of the Abyss. Then one of the thrones rises above all the Abysses and the other throne lowers itself underneath all the Abysses. Between these two thrones whirl themselves all the Abysses, and all those channels are fixed between these two thrones. There are seventy-five channels, seven of which are higher than the rest, which, however are attached to them, and all of them pass through the wheels of the two thrones on either side. Their waters course upwards and downwards. The downward-coursing waters form caves in the Abysses and cleave them asunder, while the upward-coursing waters enter into the caverns of the stones and continue rising until they fill them, which happens once in seven years. So far the seven varieties of lights with their profound symbolism.

The 'brass of waving,' previously mentioned, represents the so-called 'Brass Mountains,' and the 'sockets of brass' represent the gates through which entrance is made to the King. Now of that brass were made all the ministering vessels of the altar. They are, indeed, ministers to the altar, because when the souls of men come up on the altar it is they that execute the service of the altar, and help it to perform its function, and hence they are named 'vessels of the altar.' " [*Zohar IV*, 277–79, where I've stopped in the middle of a paragraph that goes on for another two pages]

We might grasp, but dimly and only after having been instructed, that such a tale, in the context in which it is recited and written, would have something to do with travels in the hyperreality of the outer space of the Sephiroth or in the four worlds of Cabala. But essentially such a consent would be a mere formality, for anyone who makes even minimal demands of coherence on language would be left wondering not only about understanding such a text but what understanding it would mean. The speaker, the signs, the referent, the intention are all sublimely floating "eight miles high" above merely human comprehension, yet the writing insists on being there, perhaps intransitively, in the sense that Barthes and Sollers meant—or as the "paradox of its own unreadibility," to use the language of Paul de Man. This written excursion into other worlds is presented also as a spoken discourse, which turns into a lecture, implying that there is something there to be learned, cogitated, questioned, and followed. But how follow such a trip as this, and on what guiding thread? The spoken quality, for which conventional quotation marks seem absurdly insufficient for the "he said that he said that he said" quality of the text, exercises a charm, difficulty, and a fascination all its own. Among the impossible questions implied would be whether we are to believe that such things were really said and listened to, not to mention what we are supposed to do about them. Is this a text meant to be appreciated, as literature, or is it illocutionary, in Austin's sense, performing an action, or are the words supposed to have some other magical effect just by our sheer exposure to them?

Some light might be shed on these mysteries by reflection on Cabala's dialogic style. Almost everything, indeed, in The Zohar is introduced as spoken, whether as lectures, arguments, dialogues, or conversations, and words are likely also to come from the unlikeliest sources, beggars, merchants, youths, even women that become vehicles for the divine afflatus. This interpenetration of the verbal and spoken, metaphor and reality of dialogue, lends to the written text an aura of the evanescent, arguable, and temporary, where an "elsewhere" is dangled always beside the written word, awaking in that strange combination of listener, worshiper, and reader a sense that there is always something more to be known, something one isn't quite with.

On the other hand The Zohar certainly does not underestimate or in any way deflate the importance of the scripted, of which Torah is the constant embodiment, past and future. Rather the written and the oral *come together* in the dance that is, temporarily, this life on earth. This symbiosis, dialogue relation between oral and written have certainly been very important in recent critical theory; and one of Derrida's constant themes has been the subtle ways in which a "logocentric" culture's notions of presence, tyrannies of control, and unity rely on the implicit support and authority of the spoken word even in the texts of the most text-conscious writers and thinkers (Nietzsche, Lacan, Heidegger, Lévinas). Not surprising also is the fact that this centuries-old cabalistic dialogue between oral and written is singled out for special comment by that most writerly of contemporaries, Maurice Blanchot, who finds it natural, relevant, and very current, that for Cabala, as for Derrida (for whom the oral would represent an usurpation whose political, social, and ethical consequences we are just beginning to be aware of), the *written* has always already come first.

Harold Bloom has approached Cabala from a similarly literary angle. In his important little book, *Kaballah and Criticism* (1975), he mentions Cabala in connection with Malcolm Lowry and Thomas Pynchon—after also finding analogies in English Romanticism, Structuralism, and the "modern outlook" in literature in general. This "literary modernism" of Cabala was noticed also by Dov Hercenberg, who drew parallels between Cabala and Umberto Eco's idea of the "open work," a seminal concept in the modernist critical vocabulary, invented by Eco to deal with such infinitely suggestive works as *Finnegans Wake*.[32] Openness in Eco's semiotics may have these occult echoes, but Cabala has entered Eco's fiction literally too, with a stunning, even *sublime* and thoroughly cabalistic "Explication of the Dove" that anchors, if anything does, his free-floating recent voyage into the abstruse realms of seventeenth-century metaphysics, *The Island of the Day Before*.[33] Connections have also been made to Cabala in relation to Borges,[34] where it seems tied in rather with his gnostic sensibility, and to Kafka, because of his sense of existence as obscure but ineluctable allegory as well as his appreciation of the specifically cabalistic culture of the Jews from Eastern Europe.[35] In the literature from Eastern Europe, where zoharic moods and texts were apparently still part of the fabric of daily life in the Jewish communities well into the twentieth century, there is sometimes a particularly intense cabalistic presence—for instance, in the fictional world of Isaac Bashevis Singer, where it is almost thematic, though a distanced, exotic, maybe soft-core, ironic, and gently mocking kind of Cabala. A more Sabbatian, engaged, and demonic Cabala seems rather to imbue the mystical narratives of Bruno Schulz,[36] but is openly and proudly proclaimed as such in that wildly speculative and experimental fiction and last testament, *The Hermit of 69th Street*, by the mysterious Jerzy Kosinski, who was obsessed, not so coincidentally, with pseudepigraphy. Somewhat of the spirit and even the letter, although with a more anodyne resolution, of Kosinski's iconoclastic-surreal-modernist Sabbatianism may have passed into Philip Roth's recent novel, *Sabbath's Theatre*, whose hero was named after the great apostate-and-"messiah" himself—"They wrote it in all kind of ways: Shabas, Ahabbus, Shabsai, Sabbatai"—but who ends up identifying with a more orthodox Cabala, answering rather to the name of "Rabbi Israel, the Baal Shem Tov—the Master of God's Good name."[37]

According to Idel, Cabala's provoking fascination with naming, language, and letters makes it compatible with Surrealism. The theurgic iconoclasm of Breton's manifesto-aphorism, "Language was given to man so he may make Surrealist use of it," was anticipated by the language- and rationality-cracking, meditative, Sufi-like methods of de Leon's great contemporary and rival, Abraham Abulafia, who aimed at the "disintegration of social language into meaningless units" for the purpose of the "transformation of human language into divine names."[38]

For Blanchot, as well as for Harold Bloom, Cabala would convey, from a literary point of view, a language-oriented protomodernism, in the ways in which it reflects incessantly on the status of the oral and the written, making of the latter a question that can neither be answered nor dismissed, that indeterminate expression of an "ethic of ambiguity" we've agreed to call *text*.[39] So it is that Blanchot, coincidentally, lingers over that strikingly Mallarméan passage from a fragment of Isaac the Blind that we've cited, that is where the black of the ink and the white of the page incarnate, respectively, a written and oral Torah. Blanchot's reading orients Isaac's brilliant figure, which although it had established the priority of the written had emphasized our inaptitude for it, more toward the writing. Blanchot, therefore, is all the more fascinated over finding in this tradition of the Cabala, so sensitive to the presence of the spoken, and of the having spoken, also the absolute precession of the written, the oral—intriguingly, paradoxically coming from and leading only to the written: "It's quite remarkable that, in a certain tradition of the book (such as has come through to us through the Kabbalists' formulation, even if their intention was to stress the mystical meaning of a literal presence), what we call the 'written Torah' has preceded the 'oral Torah', the latter yielding then to the revised version which then alone constitutes The Book. This involves an enigmatic proposition for thought. Nothing precedes writing. Nevertheless the writing of the first tablets becomes readable only after and by way of the break—after and through the oral decision, which leads to the second writing, that which we know, rich in meaning, capable of commandments, always equal to the law that it transmits."[40]

Exile and the Bride of Sabbath

Moses de Leon claimed to have been working from a manuscript of The Zohar, written in the Aramaic of the period by the great Rabbi Simon ben Yohai, a Jewish mystic and quasi-legendary charismatic religious figure of the second century A.D., who, whether he wrote the book or not, is a major presence in The Zohar as a character and narrator. Depending on whether his claim is correct, and to what degree—or assuming de Leon as the author, there is a difference of about one thousand years on the date of conjectured composition. No original Aramaic manuscript of The Zohar, dating from that period or any other, has ever been discovered; so if the antiquity of the work is assumed you are forced to believe flatly de Leon's assertion. Possibly de Leon was working with some manuscripts of considerable antiquity and did a job of editing, translating, and writing, so that The Zohar that resulted would be of multifarious provenance, even though he would have been the main one responsible for it. This issue of the origins of The Zohar had never been satisfactorily resolved, at least not until Scholem's recent conclusive efforts; generally the scholars who, whatever their convictions, approach the work with a secular bias, tend to attribute it more or less to de Leon. For Scholem The Zohar is eminently a literary masterpiece, with the genius of de Leon, if not quite reflected on every page, obvious enough. Not everyone is as sanguine as Scholem, yet most seem to grant it some kind of literary status, which depending on how you think of things, can either enhance or discredit it. For Idel, for instance, who likes to play down a discursive, theosophical Cabala in favor of a more ecstatic-meditative one The Zohar is still "one of the few Kabbalistic books whose literary quality is sometimes dominant."[41] It's interesting how the Hegelian Owl of Minerva still flies at dusk—in other words, the issue of the literary comes up at a time when Cabala would be, at most, a marginal element in the worship or ritual in any major religion, however manifold the evidence is of it once having been there or however carried away a cult or two becomes. A cabalistic hymn to welcome The Bride of Sabbath is a part of all orthodox Jewish Friday evening prayers. One is not told, of course, that this Bride is, in fact, God's, and also the Shekinah who has a midnight date with members of the congregation. Although this represents a subtle survival of zoharic (sexual) mysticism, one may wonder, for example, just how much of the spirit of The Zohar, which likes to refer to *this world* as belonging to the "other side" there would be in the answered prayers of West Bank "cabalists," for the elimination of one whom they were afraid was going to cost them a piece of it![42]

Cabala certainly was a style that played, teasingly, on the margins of the literary, creating the kinds of texts that would make one wonder whether indeed they were literary, with a "merely" thrown in for its opponents. The Zohar, correspondingly, anticipates modernism in the sense that it provokes and inculcates wonder, imagination, curiosity, and insecurity about its own status as a text. Probably we can agree that Cabala is just as literary as literature is cabalistic, where it would be in the spirit of the subject that we would not quite know what exactly we were agreeing to.

Even Scholem will consider much of what has been known as The Zohar to be accretions, in particular certain very radical-messianic texts (the *Raya Mehemna* and the *Tikkune Zohar*), which were especially important for the Sabbatian eschatological movement that was to earn, by the end of the nineteenth century, a special exile for Cabala even within the greater Jewish diaspora. De Leon's motive in the invention of an ancient author would have been, then, ostensibly, to make the work more fascinating to a contemporary public. "Finding a manuscript," anyway, is one of the most common literary ploys, the most distinguished example of which would be Cervantes' *Don Quixote*, which, we may remember, he only pretends to *translate*, while the ostensible reason for volume two was that there was an unauthorized version in circulation! Other scholars, especially writing before Scholem's definitive "revelations," had cited an already established and abundant Cabala tradition and a plethora of surviving manuscripts relating to it by the time de Leon "received" it, and so were able to accept his guarantee of the work's antiquity. Abelson, writing in the authoritative position of introduction to the five-volume English translation of The Zohar, is sure of the work's age and authenticity, though his main evidence is its variety, which he insists would be impossible for a single person to encompass—so there seems to be a certain subjective element involved in his decision. For those who practice Cabala currently, or pretend to, the merest hint that de Leon is the author smacks, of course, of anathema. Idel is, if anything, understating the case when he remarks that "modern research is notorious in religious circles for its denial of R. Simeon ben Yohai's authorship of The Zohar, a very important issue for Kabbalists"[43]—who are about as interested in listening to evidence that de Leon wrote The Zohar as fundamentalists are in hearing the arguments for the nonexistence of God![44] For one would be thereby trading ben Yohai's divinely inspired Mosaic-type authority against the suspiciously secular and protomodern writerly games of the early Renaissance.

Cabala's uneasy status, its traditional and apparently ongoing identity crisis, swaying as it does currently between the roles of modernist critical strategy and (barely) surviving mystical style, stems also from the very needs it has been historically called forth to fulfill and create. Its literature relates much more directly to diaspora and exile than does the Pentateuch, or Torah, whose commentary it is. For Torah exile is a characteristic and frequent plight or state, but a temporary one, whose length is measured not in millennia but in centuries at most. The *galuth*, or slavery in Egypt, and the wanderings in the desert are long and arduous ordeals but also challenging rituals of passage, adventure, revelation, and discovery; and the end is always in view. Cabala, on the other hand, relates to another exile, a second, endless wandering that can only be stopped at the end of time by such as a messiah. This is an exile that is metaphysically structural, for it is not only of a people, but also one within the Godhead, from itself: "Exile [in sixteenth-century Safed] is no longer a human term, relating to the fate of the Jewish people; it is a mysterious process within the Godhead, which began long before the creation of man or of the people of Israel."[45]

For even those who deny de Leon's composition of The Zohar, insisting on ben Yohai's, don't seem to take Cabala back any farther than late Roman times, or to a time when the "wandering Jew" was to become a permanent entity, and there *is* no earthly end or goal in sight—so that the heavenly one looms as all the more imminent and necessary: at midnight sharp God descends to visit with his faithful in their earthly-heavenly Paradise, whether in Smyrna, Safed, or Gerona (or today in Cincinnati). At midnight, the point in time outside of time when God, attracted by their devotion. likes to visit them, the cabalists rise to study the Torah: "For the world on high requires to be stirred by the impulse of the lower world . . . The real night only begins with the actual stroke of midnight, for at that moment the Holy One . . . enters the Garden of Eden in order to have joyous communion with the righteous. For this reason it behooves the pious man to rise also at that time, for then the Holy One and all the righteous in the Garden listen to his voice" [*Zohar I*, 274 and *III*, 140]. Additionally every Friday night the practicing cabalist is enjoined to have intercourse with his wife, because at that time she has become *Shekinah*, God's female emanation: "Students of the Torah . . . make themselves 'eunuchs' during the six days of the week for the Torah's sake, and on Sabbath nights have their conjugal union, because they apprehend the supernal mystery of the right moment when the Matrona [Shekinah] is united with the King . . . On Sabbath, at midnight, when [after?] the wise consummate their conjugal unions, at the time when they are sleeping peacefully in their beds, and their souls are eager to ascend and behold the glory of the King, the supernal spirits with which they crowned themselves at the sanctification of the Sabbath take those souls and bring them up unto the heights. These souls are there bathed in the spices of Paradise, and behold all that is within their capacity to behold" [*Zohar III*, 274, 389].

This carnal advice is repeated often in The Zohar. Instructions are weirdly specific; for instance, it is recommended that the relations be frontal: "When the lower union was rendered perfect, and Adam and Eve turned face to face, then was the upper union perfected."[46] Intercourse on Friday night is not only indicated but rather *enjoined* and indispensable, a form of welcome to and congress with the Shekinah, who is partial to the beginning Sabbath and who descends to inhabit the body of the man's wife. Sexual experience, about which The Zohar is particularly insistent and emphatic, is also generally a *rite* in Cabala,[47] an aspect that has been remarked by just about every commentator and also makes it exceptional and possibly unique as a Western tradition, perhaps linking it with certain Tantric practices of the East. Although cabalistic sex is monogamous, the power, implications, and effect of intercourse are quite awesome, reaching far beyond the couple concerned to cure an entire cosmos. About this "penetration to the mysteries" there is none of the grudging Pauline "better to marry than to burn" resignation about it, for here it is not a matter of not being damned, but of being saved—for which purpose one must have a wife for the Shekinah to become, and fuck her "royally"! Meanwhile, the purely earthly, the leavened (yeast is a recurrent zoharic symbol of impurity, identified with paganism and the idol-worshiping nations), the everyday is honored in its way, but as something alien, temporary, passing, the province of evil, the serpent, the other, who are deeded this world because they have no other to look forward to, to look up to.

The definitive exile from Spain, pronounced in 1492, though foreshadowed much earlier in the progressive marranization (whereby Jews, given the choice of either conversion or exile, pretended to be Christians outwardly while remaining privately faithful to their own religion) of the community, gave an enormous impetus to the dissemination of Cabala, its spread, influence, and relevance, since it was regarded as a confirmation and a deepening of the first estrangements and eloignings of Biblical and post-Biblical times. Nowhere had the Jews—especially before the twelfth century when the Arabs were more securely in control—been so much at home; yet their welcome turned out to be temporary. What was needed was a philosophy that made a home out of exile. So powerfully salutary did the cabalistic medicine seem to be at the time that it rapidly attracted the attention of some mystically inclined Christian students (most notably Pico della Mirandola) who borrowed from it massively, applying its styles, methods, and madnesses (numerology, letter magic, mystical hermeneutics) to their own problems in accepting a world that was just as ineluctably passing. That which was the mark or stigma of a particular group becomes a distinction of the human condition in general, so idealistic Christians too could feel that their exile, in a world of Machiavellian power politics and ethical relativism, of demonic or amoral technology, had just begun.

Whenever, more recently, we have resorted to the trope, myth, or ideal of exile—emerging, for example, in an oppositional vocabulary of alienation, reification, nomadism, persecution, decentering, and fragmentation—Cabala can loom into view, justifying, explaining, preceding, collecting. This outsider quality, which has always inhabited Cabala, even in those critical times when it approached the dimensions of a mass movement, may account for its especial congruence and affinity with literature, with which it shares qualities of rootlessness, search, and movement, as well as ambiguous and existential attitudes toward authority, tradition, and precedent. What has been left for us moderns, according to Michel de Certeau, of the mystics' incessantly restless motion toward an end or goal in the absolute, once faith in the absolute has disappeared, is simply movement itself as a blind force, compulsion, energy, and need: "Of that self-surpassing spirit, seduced by an impregnable origin or end called God, it seems that what for the most part still remains, in contemporary culture, is the movement of perpetual departure . . . The traveler no longer has foundation or goal. Given over to a nameless desire, he is the drunken boat. Henceforth this desire can no longer speak to someone. It seems to have become infans, voiceless, more solitary and lost than before, or less protected and more radical, ever seeking a body or a poetic locus. It goes on walking, then, tracing itself out in silence, in writing."[48]

However, when this search takes the form of words, *literature* is what we may call it, where change is a matter of language, or getting the words right. This is a task for Sisyphus, since the right word one instant is wrong the next: from a literary as well as cabalistic point of view, *holding on* to the word is what would make it wrong. We should, according to Cabala, not count on the integrity of any word, even a Biblical one, the reading and interpretation of which is far more significant than what was merely said. For instance, anticipating the sophistication and playfulness of current notions of textuality, the maggid (heavenly visitor and advisor) of an important sixteenth-century cabalist, mystic, lawyer, and rabbi, when challenged over the inaccuracy of a quote from the Bible, replied: "Though at times I expound a scriptural verse which does not exist in the form in which I quote it, [this happens] because I quote as it is in your mind. None the less my explanation is true and it is your duty to make it fit the correct reading of the text."[49]

Cabala is, then, a mysticism that is both radical and conservative, or harbors the potential for both positions. It is cautious and elitist in its *withdrawal*, analagous to its guiding idea of *tsimtsum*, or divine retreat from created matter, whose concomitant is a retreat from the possibility of earthly rescue for the community, except for episodes, conspicuously dangerous, when it declares its people free and leads its followers into utopian extravagance and autodestruction. Returning then to its *elect*, it becomes socially conservative. Contemporary Hasidism would be merely the latest of these conservative, or what Scholem calls "neutralizing" turnings in the series of attempts to popularize Cabala,[50] which are caught in a kind of double bind, certainly an example of the paradox and anguish of the discourse de Certeau called "mystics": either the challenge and provocation of the original inspiration is lost in the attempt to spread the message or a Cabala that is faithful to its order-shattering principles tends to be cut off from the society with which it must nevertheless come to some kind of terms.

However, even within the framework of an acceptance of state authority, very radical indeed is Cabala's insistence, amounting to exigence, on an unlimited potential of cosmic realization and knowledge for certain self-selected individuals. One is able, according to Cabala, to aspire almost to divinity, or at least be treated to its sight, taste, and presence. This latter, overreaching, and elevating aspect is doubtless what attracted Pico, for whom the "dignity of man" consisted precisely in his angelic possibilities, in addition to being a quality that Cabala shares with mysticism in general, as remarked, for instance by Henri Bergson, for whom philosophy itself amounts to the human aspiration to go beyond the known, and who, accordingly was interested in the challenge of mysticism as a self-surpassing ideology: "In fact mystics are unanimous in testifying that God needs us, as we need God. Why would he need us, if not to love us? Such would obviously be the philosophical conclusion which would be called forth by mystical experience. Creation would appear to the philosopher like God's enterprise of creating the creators, so as to join to himself those who are worthy of his love."[51]

In Cabala, indeed, this power of worship and the worshiper are very frequently mentioned. God, through his Shekinah, is attracted, through the magnetic energy emanating from the devotions of his faithful, to descend on Sabbath eve. This uncanny dependency of the divine on the human has not escaped notice by Franz Rosenzweig, who was interested especially in the existential quality of the Jewish experience and who talks glowingly in *The Star of Redemption* of the Cabala's God of Love's need for man.[52] In The Zohar, confirming Rosenzweig's intuition, the symbiosis of human and divine is strict indeed, but the balance of power, which teeters surely on the brink of colossal heresy or hybris, seems strangely weighted on the side of the humans. About these cosmically powerful, loved worshipers The Zohar says, astoundingly, "When their works are not according to the Divine Purpose, they actually weaken the power of the Holy One Himself, but when they do His will they, as it were, increase his power and might" [*Zohar III*, 105].

This is, in fact, the most signal way in which Cabala departs from traditional Judaism, in its emphasis on the individual and in its exploration of a path to salvation that only the few, the rare, and the qualified can hope to travel. Among the Jews, already chosen, the cabalists were, presumably, the elect of the elect. For ordinary Judaism, on the other hand, what was to be saved was the people, or nothing; and the individual was significant only so long as he contributed to that—or, as in the case of Moses, he would be redeemed only after he had accomplished the maximum service socially. Israel, therefore, or the community, is the real and ever-recurrent theme of the Pentateuch, as well as of its indispensable commentary, or Talmud, whose purpose it is to inform how the community is to survive and even flourish in the various historical contexts in which it has been placed.

The Zohar also is a commentary on the Bible, but its theme is not as much Israel, or community, but Adam, who is community all to himself: as *Adam Kadmon* he is heavenly man, and as *Adam Belial* demonic man, man being the microcosm, the theater where the two Adams are perpetually in strife. This Adam's marriage with his heavenly bride, the *Shekinah*, through his Eve or earthly spouse, represents the culminating moment, the ecstasy of his existence, a rite to be repeated as often as the Sabbath comes, and seemingly Tantric in its resonance, with the telling difference, however, that the zoharic sexual style involves not the indefinite retention of the sperm and the attainment of a nirvana of permanent arousal, but its release at the moment when the female comes to meet the male in the simultaneous orgasm that is obviously one of Cabala's ideals: "For the seed does not flow save when the Female is present, and their mutual desires are blended into one indissoluble ecstasy" [*Zohar II*, 121]. It is, furthermore the very *desire* of the female that creates the force of the male.[53] Here, apparently, the female (desire) plays the role of the worshiper's devotion in attracting God's visits, so it likewise takes precedence over male desire, which like God's power, strengthens or wanes according to how much it is wanted. A Cabala ratio seems to be that woman is to man as man is to God; yet, in this "world turned upside down" power, paradoxically, remains below.

This Shekinah whom one joins when one joins one's wife, whom one travels with and sleeps with when one travels and sleeps alone is another peculiarly cabalistic notion. This purpose of this feminine divine avatar or emanation is to attenuate the severity, cruelty, and violence of the jealous, possessive, military, and aggressive Old Testament Jehovah. It is certainly through the *Shekinah*, or the feminine, that the cabalist is in relation with the male Godhead. Woman is the same means of exchange in the heavenly, as she has been so often in earthly society. De Certeau, after alluding to Javary's research on the place of the cabalistic Shekinah in Christian apologetics of the Renaissance, stresses this *complimentary* aspect also: "The *Shekinah* implied a spiritual indwelling, a presence, a glory, and, later, a femininity of God—themes that played an important role in the Christian *mystics* [discourse of mysticism] of that era."[54]

For Rosenzweig, equally, the Shekinah was the compassionate god(dess) of exile, worshiped by the "remnant of Israel" and symbolizing God's analogous and sympathetic separation from himself. Cabala, indeed, has long been noticed for the preeminence in it of the feminine. H. C. Agrippa, the model for Edmund Spenser's demonic enchanter Archimago, in *The Fairie Queene*, remarkable also for being one of the first scholars to make the connection between Gnosticism and Cabala,[55] noticed in a provocative little feminist monograph of 1509, *Female Preeminence*, that a zoharic interpretation of the name of Eve would bring her closer to the numerical value of the Tetragrammaton (name of God) than Adam's would bring him, therefore she stood closer to the divine![56]

Lilith and the Shekinah

This power of the feminine, Cabala's unquestionable contribution to Judaism, played its part in the attraction of Cabala for Christianity in the Renaissance. By way of this feminine addition, which insists on remaining sexual, one could worship one's Mary and have her too, though one must assume that on the trip from the bed of the carnally practicing cabalist to the Christian poet or mystic's (or both) cell the Shekinah had quit insisting on intercourse from her lovers, the desire doubtless having been displaced onto proto-Freudian symbols or baroque visions, as in the very fleshly "mariolatry" of Richard Crashaw's devotional poetry, with its oddly suggestive and synesthetic imagery of a carnal contact with the divine mistress-mother that seems too close to incestuous to be very innocent: "Oh Mother turtle dove!/Soft source of love/ That these dry lids might borrow/Something from thy full Seas of sorrow!/Oh in that breast/Of thine (the noblest nest/Both of love's fires and floods) might I recline/This hard, cold, Heart of mine!/The chill lump would relent and prove/Soft subject for the siege of love . . ./Oh let me suck the wine/ So long of this chaste vine/ Till drunk of the dear wounds I be/A lost thing to the world and it to me"[57]

As opposed to this erotic-feminine quality of the dialogue between the earthly and the heavenly, whether in what seems a close to oral sex or maybe infinite polymorphous-perverse preplay mood of Crashaw's adorations, in the intercourse and arousal figures and analogies of The Zohar, the communication between individual and the divine in Torah is always, however, between *men*. This may be noticed in that founding conversation that Moses carries on with Jehovah, even though the subject of this dialogue is the Woman, or feminine entity, constituted by the community of the people of Israel. Likewise, in the very beginning, it was only by way of her husband that Eve was in touch with God. On the other hand, hers is the ear of choice, entry for a *cabal* of the "other side" when Satan has something to say to humanity.

Israel, or the community, symbolically Eve or Woman, is identical also, in Cabala, when she is what she should be, with the Shekinah. Yet, equally, for Cabala, good and evil come together. Israel, as Woman, has the potential of receiving the divine Shekinah but is profoundly attractive to and attracted by the demonic Lilith, who, in any case, is proximal to and ineluctably intertwined with the Shekinah on the *sefirotic* tree, since they both "fell to earth" from its lowest or tenth branch, that of *malkuth* or World. Wherever the Shekinah is Lilith is never very far away, and, for certain purposes, at least, they can be thought as being interchangeable. Because of the intimate, probably gnostically inspired association of sex with evil, Lilith's function is every bit as necessary as that of the Shekinah, for not only does she prepare the woman for love, she also is the breaker that brings forth progeny,[58] that makes possible the perpetuation of Israel. According to Joseph Dan, there is a tradition going back at least to the thirteenth century that makes of the enchanting wisdom of Lilith an apprentice stage (in this "fallen world") on the way to prophetic powers.[59] That Lilith ruled in the plain, therefore, while Moses was on the mountain, was only a foregone conclusion. She needed to rule in order to prepare for and to justify the violent creation and birth of a people, who required to have lapsed, in a "fortunate fall," first into paganism and idol worship. By the time of the second descent the community has been reshaped, ethnically cleansed of recent converts—naturally untrustworthy, according to The Zohar—into a unit that is capable of receiving the revelation.

It is, however, only retroactively, cabalistically, that we are enhancing the feminine role in this cosmic drama, one that is more or less subdued, or at least invisible, in Torah, where the awesome Sinai conversation was between men. Likewise, in Torah, a crucial initiating covenant takes place between Abraham and the Godhead, which concludes with promise made to him to make his seed, or Israel, as numberless as the sands on the beach. In The Zohar, on the other hand, the very Godhead itself has separated into male and female quantities, so that it is rather men who communicate with the divine through women than the other way around. In addition to being *Adam Kadmon's* heavenly mate (link with the divine), the Shekinah is also the real mistress of Jehovah, and Jehovah's greatest joy is the delight with which he beholds his Shekinah. Adam's goal on earth is to partake somewhat of Jehovah's joy by gazing upon her with the selfsame eyes; for the purpose of the cabalist's study and life is to become one with the Godhead in the most intimate sense, through intercourse with the divine mistress, sublimely the wife he's with. Through a Platonic hermeneutics of the macrocosm and the microcosm, social context is restored, then, if only by means of some powerfully invested symbolism: If the cabalist is a microcosm, a theater of the community, then the latter is taken along in the ecstasy of the former. On the other hand, on the level of the macrocosm the earth would be the ideal body of the Godhead, divided into two archetypal anatomies, male and female, Jehovah and Shekinah; and earthly life corresponds, in miniature, to this map of the godhead. This intimacy of the cabalist with the divine is exemplified in the minute physical detail in which these correspondences are worked out in The Zohar; for instance in the *Idra-Rabba,* or *Greater Assembly* section, where Jehovah's penis, his testes, the Shekinah's vagina and breasts are measured and lavishly expounded. Here also the "parts" are counted, explained, and interpreted. The *face* of God is especially important, and in the face the *nose,* which in the two countenances of God, the greater and the lesser, is either elongated or abbreviated—the longer version, or *macroprosipus* belonging to the greater countenance, symbolizing infinite tolerance and patience, the shorter nose, or *microprosipus* standing for the blending of severity and judgment in with mercy, in amounts suitable for worldly use.[60] Habitually, we on earth get to glimpse only the lesser, less pure countenance, and even that can be faced only if we are "good"; a sinner can't even look on the lesser countenance![61]

Here again the confidence and ambition of Cabala seems to be going up against the modest caution of the Jewish as well as other Western religious traditions, exemplified prominently, antecedently in the story of the temptation in Genesis: Adam sinned, by way of Eve, through the desire to become God-like, through pride; but Cabala, on the contrary, makes of this curiosity, this aspiration, a virtue and even a necessity, with its focus not on avoiding knowledge but in being able to tolerate, or experience, in what we might think of as a Nietzschean sense, what one is *able* to know. Of all ideas difficult to incorporate into a practical attitude, or *a fortiori,* into a system of judgment, moral questions, where hypocrisy is arguably ineluctable, must be the most supremely resistant, since we all contain all possibilities within us, which only await the right combination of circumstances to be externalized. No one has been more persuasive or definitive on this matter than Spinoza, who thereby justified his removal of God, which Leibniz thought of as cabalist in inspiration, from all involvement in the material affairs of people. We deserve neither credit nor blame for our deeds, determined in so many ways, simply because: "Those who believe that they speak or keep silence or act in any way from the free decision of their mind, do but dream with their eyes open."[62]

In The Zohar, as later for Spinoza and Nietzsche, questions of good and evil tend to be handled dialectically rather than polarized; the cabalist errs more in trying to forget and abolish evil rather than in attempting to accept, incorporate, and work with it, consistent with a vision of existence that sees life on earth as exile, and evil, therefore, for the present (except for brief moments or hours), as being inescapable. Those passages in the Bible where good resorts to the cunning and manipulations of evil, for instance, Jacob's maneuverings to secure Esau's birthright, are, indeed, the special province of zoharic commentary, expostulation, and rationalization. This factor of accommodation to a resolutely secular world also helps explain the dissemination, fame, and use of the Cabala in the wider Renaissance context of power politics and incipiently "demonic" technology.

Enduring Dualist elements, which connote an equality for good and evil, equipped Cabala for this function of adaptation to the moral ambiguities and nuances of a Renaissance world, one that was becoming increasingly exigent, complex, and confusing. However, although Cabala flirts with Dualism, it does not cross over into its patently polarized terrain, committed as it is to a vision of ultimate integration and realization. This ultimately optimistic mood of cabalistic visionary systems could make them somewhat of a fortress from which one could survey the demonic sides of experience, and with comparative impunity. The Manicheans, following Zoroastrian precedents, posited principles of light and darkness as eternal antipodes involved in a struggle that has no end, to which there is no final resolution, but at best only a series of uneasy truces. For Cabala these two principles would be the Adam *Kadmon* and *Belial*, respectively their heavenly and earthly manifestations; however, their struggle, though arduous, daily, and ineluctable is in no way conceived to be interminable, while the two entities, like the Shekinah and Lilith, partake also in each others' nature. Individuals, perhaps entire communities are considered to be capable, now and/or in the future, of transcending the antinomies, by way of an Hegelian-like *aufhebung*, or overcoming, accomplished by the (self?)-elected soul(s). Meanwhile, momentarily, if in an evanescent, hallucinogenic manner, such anguished but essentially privileged

selected ones may be nourished, fortified, and consoled with their
weekly intimate mingling with the divine in the sex of their wives,
those indispensable Shekinah surrogates.

That Cabala, whatever its antiquity, was also a Renaissance
ideology, should not obscure its connections and correspondences
both with idealizing philosophical motifs as well as mystical heterodoxies that predate it. Like Gnosticism, Cabala is much concerned with maximizing knowledge of God, but for the latter the
wisdom that is attained becomes a sensuous, emotional, and finally—
as has often been remarked and celebrated and, as often, resented
or even denied—*a sexual experience*—rather than remaining only
abstract. It would be disingenuous, however, not to consider that
there has been, understandably, some controversy over this point.
Werblowsky, for example, makes a point of rejecting the idea, which
must have had some currency, that Cabala involves anything like
"erotic and bridal mysticism," insisting instead on a kind of
nonsensual sexuality of what he calls "the first ascetic system to
develop a mystical metaphysic of the sexual act,"[63] referring, for
substantiation of his suggestion that sex in Cabala has been overemphasized, to Scholem's *Major Trends*. The latter, indeed, responded there to what he considered to be certain already traditional
misunderstandings and distortions of cabalistic sexuality, a prime
example of which would be A. E. Waite's "Mystery of Sex,"[64] based
on a mistranslation of a Hebrew phrase as sexual intercourse that
actually meant only communication. Waite's misapprehensions,
however, were widely shared, apparently, for instance, by Denis
Saurat, in his chapter on cabalistic sexuality, "The Sexual Law,"[65]
according to which he reinterpreted mystically some of the classics
of English Literature (Spenser and Milton). Anaïs Nin's very sexual
ideas of Cabala certainly were owing to a combination of Saurat
and the very imaginary de Pauly French translation of The Zohar,
inspiring perhaps her love affair with her father, as well as the
very Tantric life style we may read about in some recently published collections from her journals. *Lilith* is, after all, the original
title of her *House of Incest*![66]

It's curious too, that while Scholem rejects the idea of a "sexual
key" for the Cabala as a whole he notices that sexuality is very
important in The Zohar, guessing at some special characteristic
or obsession of its author, then remarking, with wonder, on the

staggeringly cosmic imagery of sexual intercourse that accompanies the apotheosis or death of Simon ben Yohai. Scholem perhaps is on his guard, ambivalent and hedging on this matter of sexuality because of his caution over what he brands "the eloquent denunciation of so-called obscenities which Graetz and other detractors . . . have permitted themselves."[67] Sensual, kinky or not, the imagery of intercourse does indeed pervade The Zohar and, therefore to some extent at least, Cabala. About the Shekinah, for instance, it is implied, typically, that existence practically hinges on the consummation of her divine pleasure, as The Zohar turns the very psalms into a scene of sexual chase and aftermath: "And when he is aroused by her, how many are they that stand on every side in order to be refreshed and blessed from there, as it is said, 'the young lions roar after their prey, and seek their food from God' (Psalm 104: 21). Then she ascends into the mystery of mysteries ['Into the mystery of intercourse,' Tishby explains in a note], as is fitting, and receives pleasure from her husband, as is proper, when they are alone, as it is said 'there was no one with him,' for it is written 'Take everybody away from me'. And after she has received pleasure from her husband they are all refreshed and nourished, as it is said 'They give drink to every beast of the field; the wild asses quench their thirst' (Psalm 104:11)."[68]

The hedging of both Scholem and Werblowsky over the sexual perhaps may extend to the contiguous area of the feminine in general. The latter admits, for example, that "From a psychological point of view, one of the great feats of the Kabbalistic movement that culminated in The Zohar and similar texts was its discovery of a "female' principle within the Godhead."[69] Yet, although he comments that (cabalistic) "marriage is a state of perfection" that deepens and promotes divine perfection between God and the Shekinah, still he insists that this prestige of the feminine was merely formal and rejects flatly the idea that there was any new relation to women involved in it or any "novel conception of love and spiritual intimacy," especially since the woman was not being promoted as an individual but as a replaceable and expendable symbol of the Shekinah.[70]

The indecision and turnings of authors of the authority (and sympathy) of Werblowsky and Scholem on the subject of the sexual, I think, are evidence that Cabala is also very much what is made of it. Elements that might have at one time seemed symbolic, poetic, and metaphysical can, for example, suddenly leap into the arena of real life. Such was the destiny, of an influential passage in The Zohar, in which God is described lending his Shekinah to humanity, which became the justifying text for wife swapping, ritual copulations, and other licentious practices of the eighteenth-century Frankist Sabbatians. The followers of Joseph Frank, mistranslated, according to Scholem—somewhat it seems like Waite above, although presumably not with the excuse of not knowing Hebrew-Aramaic—a word that meant "service" into "service of love" to justify their promiscuous practices.[71] Similarly, whether or not cabalistic enhancement of the role of woman meant different rapports between the sexes in the Renaissance, by now Cabala, and especially what is taken to be zoharic precedent, is cited as a model and forerunner of profound changes in this area, in the direction of equality. Judith Plaskow, for instance, finds "It is not surprising that, in seeking female images for God, Jewish feminists turned early on to the one developed image Judaism has to offer—the image of the Shekinah as the indwelling presence of God," regretting, nevertheless, that "While the image of the Shekinah was an important constituent of Kabbalism that gained widespread popularity, it was never incorporated into the liturgy as an accepted counterweight to the masculinity of God."[72] Coincidentally one of the ways the controversial "Reimagining 1993" conference, which gathered two thousand women from various Christian denominations, rocked the (Presbyterian) establishment most was in invoking "a female personification of God," or the Old Testament Sophia figure.[73] It is interesting that this Sophia, or Goddess of Wisdom, of Proverbs 8–9, which is serving today to feminize the Godhead has typically been associated with the Shekinah, for instance, by Edmund Spenser, in his "Hymn to Heavenly Beautie," Stanzas 27–37, where the poet's Sapience, necessary feminine mediation between the human and the divine, is at once very obviously the Old Testament Wisdom, or Sophia, but also has been commonly identified with the Shekinah: "Spenser's Sapience also reflects something of the Shekinah of the Talmud, which is both distinct from and identical with God, at once a separate being and a personified attribute, mediating between God's immanence and his otherness."[74] This Wisdom-Sapience-Sophia-Shekinah figure is also one of the more solid ways Spenser has been linked to Cabala, for example by Denis Saurat.[75] It is curious also that Saurat's provocative thesis that Spenser was influenced by Cabala, which had been derided by the academic establishment, nevertheless is considered to shed some light on the poem in the most contemporary authoritative edition. However, Saurat's name is discreetly or unwittingly omitted by the editors from their commentary, which alludes, nevertheless, to many other critics.

Cabalistic emphasis on sexuality, at and for the pleasure of the woman and under her sign, should not suggest that pleasure in itself was the goal in cabalistic sex, as may have been the case for hedonistic-pagan varieties. That much admitted, the fact remains, starkly, that very differently, for example, from the Christian ascetic approach (sublimations like St. Teresa's iconic dream of the arrow notwithstanding), in order to reach out to the divine in Cabala one must pass by way of sex, initiated always by the arousal and desire of the worshiper, who, even as a male, takes the feminine side when it is a matter of congress with the divine; whereas, in The Zohar, even for earthly intercourse, homology, and trigger of divine ecstasies between God and the Shekinah, it is the ardor and arousal of the woman that sets the whole process in motion in the first place. In Cabala that part of God which can be known (only the emanation, and a lower one at that, the *real* beginning, together with the sefiroth closest to it, remaining unknowable) can and must also be possessed carnally, and, in the form of Shekinah, "known" in the Biblical sense. Nevertheless, until the heretical age of Sabbatai and the sects that followed his doctrines into the eighteenth century and beyond, the emphasis in regard to physicality of any kind would have been on *knowing* about things, essentially so they can be surpassed and transcended. This is why it would be a mistake to interpret zoharic recommendations for a sacramental sexual practice as being an invitation to hedonism. Cabala, for which everything becomes *discourse*, stresses rather the metaphysical implications of orgasm than its qualities of physical or emotional release or satisfaction. It was not so much the *woman*, as Werblowsky thought, that was merely a means to an end, but *sex*, itself only the gate to the mysteries. In its transformation of body into mentality or spirit Cabala shares with an ancient Gnosticism, which helped create it, a titanic intellectualist ambition, which was eventually to find an outlet and an awesome efficacy in the Cartesian cogito, to penetrate, no matter how seemingly resistant the material, barrier, or obstacle, into the domain of truth through mind.

Cabala and the Medieval Manichees

Among mystical styles, curiously, Cabala tends to be known for "keeping its head," leaning rather toward theosophy than theurgy.[76] It has been remarked, for instance, with some wonder, that cabalists, experimenting with automatic-writing techniques that Surrealism was to revive in our century, who claim to have taken dictation from supernal authors, or to hear their voices, which, even more remarkably, have been *overheard* by others also, invariably produce a brilliantly reasoned and organized discourse, often relating very relevantly with problems and quandaries of the day, and therefore showing a deep familiarity with more conventional (halakhic) wisdom. Very important, for instance, in the cabalistic canon is a book of revelations that were supposed to have been communicated to Rabbi Joseph Karo by a Maggid, or heavenly visitant from the "world of souls," sometimes called the "answering angel." Karo kept a diary of these events, an abbreviated version of which (about five percent, apparently, of the original), which was published posthumously as the *Maggid Mesharim*, then republished frequently over the centuries. What has amazed many is that Karo, in his "day self" was a sober, responsible, reasonable, and practical person, author as a matter of fact, of important, long classic works of talmudic commentary and interpretation, from which the mystical side of his nature seems to have been missing. The disproportion between the Karo of the Maggid and of his life style and the other works has led some to suppose that another was the author of the former; yet, Werblowsky argues convincingly to the contrary, insisting, anyway, that in sixteenth-century Safed the mystical and the practical could coexist, partly through the mysterious synthesis and balance that Karo and others, like Moses Cordovero, Isaac Luria, and Hayim Vital, were able to achieve in that time and place of cabalistic Eden. The revelations were spoken by the Maggid to Karo, who didn't transcribe them until afterward, so essentially in his diary he transcribed his memories of the Maggid's speeches. "Automatic writings," though respectable and conventional tools of cabalistic revelation, Karo, interestingly, considered less reliable than voiced ones. Karo expressed the phonocentric opinion that his own revelations were more valuable, for instance, than those of a contemporary cabalist rabbi, a Joseph Taytazak, because the latter's "answering angel" communicated only in writing! Finally, according to a contemporary memorialist, a Solomon Shlomel Dresnitz, who presumably ruled out the possibility of ventriloquism, the speeches of Karo's Maggid were overheard by others, although in other rooms.[77]

Feeding into this Cabala, which won't "lose its mind," even on the outer limits of speculation, or in the throes of copulation, was also a Platonizing current, first of all, in the form of the Hellenistic mystical hierarchies and emanations of Philo, Plotinus, and Porphyry. These were seen to be the *sefiroth* or forms of creation that had separated from the unknowable kernel of divine mystery, or *Ain Soph*. Cabala, in its turn, obviously becomes one of the styles that inform and help create, amplify, and justify Renaissance Neoplatonism, by helping the latter, through expanding the margins of what could be acceptable to include more visionary experience. Thereby Neoplatonism was in a better position to eschew the accusations, frequently leveled, of paganism, polytheism, or even frank demonism. A radical, left wing of the neoplatonic current was never very far away and could easily be drifted into by visionary intellectuals who could lose their sense of what was still orthodox. As recounted by D. P. Walker (who depended on the research of Paul Oscar Kristeller), in *Spiritual and Demonic Magic*, that work of titanic pagan theurgy and demiurgy, Ludovico Lazzarelli's *Crater of Hermes*, published in 1505, was not just an eccentricity but the coherent expression of a reawakening tradition that had its master, disciples, and scandals. Later on in the century, we have, very much in Lazzarelli's occult spirit, the project and works of Giordano Bruno, burned at the stake for his pride in them. Before that sad conclusion, Bruno connected, through his proselytizing visit to England, very likely with the "demonic polytheism" of such as Christopher Marlowe, Sir Walter Raleigh, and their circle, as well as being a probable source, by way of John Dee, directly or indirectly, for Cabala in Spenser.[78]

The polymorphous provenance and inspiration, Gnostic, Talmudic, Dualist, Platonic, even Sufi,[79] its daring flights and experiments, as well as the philosophical and intellectual competence, curiosity, and range of Cabala had helped create a syncretic quality that made it a useful if controversial tool in opening up Christianity to new thoughts and practices, or ancient ones that had been expelled from the Church. Cabala was not just "raided" for structures that resemble Christian ones, for instance, its concept of three worlds (spiritual, intellectual, and physical), sefirotic categories that could be seen as representing the trinity; but, significantly, a Christian Cabala was the creation as much of Jewish converts, deeply versed in Hebrew language, texts, and traditions, as of "born," if unusually experimental, Christians (Pico, Reuchlin). Paul Ricci and Pietro di Galantini were two very important Jewish converts turned Christian cabalists. Ricci, who flourished in the early sixteenth-century, was physician to Maximilian I, professor of Greek and Hebrew at the University of Padua, and a prolific and popular writer on Cabala. Ricci's significance was such that more than half of Pistorius's magisterial and widely disseminated anthology of Cabala, of 1587, really the standard source of the period, was composed of works with which Ricci had something to do, either as translator or writer. Galantino was another catalytic figure in Christian Cabala of the early sixteenth century. First published in 1518, his book, *Of Arcane Catholic Truth* , important also for its lengthy excerpts from The Zohar, was in print for over 150 years, going through at least six more editions by 1672. Galantino was one of the mystics who had gathered in the Joachamite and esoteric circle of Eugenio da Viterbo in Italy in the 1520s, apparently also considering himself the latest in a line of "angel popes."[80] On the nonconvert, Christian side, Pico della Mirandola was at once confluence, origin and culmination of many heterodox currents—occult, neoplatonic, and cabalist—of the late fifteenth century. John Reuchlin, of Basel, followed in Pico's footsteps in the matter of Cabala, publishing an influential work, *On the Wonder-Working Word*, in 1494, pursuing and deepening his studies in Cabala well into the sixteenth century. Because his focus on the subject was so intense and single minded (unlike more mercurial and varied figures like Pico and Agrippa), Reuchlin's was *the* most important name in Christian Cabala of the Renaissance.

It is no coincidence that Cabala was conceived and flourished in the South of France and Catalonia, in the twelfth and thirteenth centuries, in proximity to the transplanted (from the East) Albigensian and Cathar mystical heresies. Although no direct relation of influence between Cabala and this tumultuous revival (and genocidal extirpation) of Dualism, with which it is contemporary, has been established, there are certainly lines of congruence between the two movements. The religion of the doomed French Cathar heretics shares with Cabala elements of a world view with roots in ancient Gnosticism and Dualism; additionally, like the controversial Catholic Joachimism of about the same time, Cabala was also millennial and apocalyptic. Nevertheless, efforts to prove direct relation between these movements and Cabala have been inconclusive.[81] It has been opined, for example, that elements of cabalistic eschatology, in particular the theory of world cycles or *shemittoth*, were inspired by the millenialism of Joachim of Fiore, which the Church agonized over, finally declaring it heretical. Joachimism had an enormous impact in the Europe of the twelfth and thirteenth centuries, but had certainly not been forgotten much later on in the Renaissance. Enthusiastic students, translators, and disseminators of a Christian Cabala in early sixteenth-century Italy— for instance, those who gathered in the circle of Eugenio da Viterbo—were also followers of the cosmic apocalypticism, however dubious its orthodoxy, of Joachim.[82]

As for the doomed Albigensian Cathars, the fact that they, apparently, *practiced* a Dualism, which in Cabala was more of a symbolic and metaphorical element, would however separate the two religious movements. For one thing, cabalists, at least until the Sabbatianism of the seventeenth century, probably, in fact, very Albigensian-Manichean in mood, have never been fond of defying either civil authority or religious orthodoxy. Cabalistic sex, until the much later Sabbatian episode and its Frankist aftermaths, though extravagant and significant metaphysically, never drifts into license or promiscuity, since the cabalists, although they agree with Dualism that "this" world belongs to Satan, nevertheless do not see themselves as belonging (only) to it. Very much involved in its theories of creation is Cabala's notion of *withdrawal* (of light), which became increasing important in the Renaissance, especially after the Spanish expulsion, but, already in its comparatively early version, that of The Zohar, this *retreat* is rather a matter of nuance, relation, ebb and flow, and intermingling, rather than any sudden separation or polarization: "At the Creation, God irradiated the world from end to end with the light, but then it was withdrawn, so as to deprive the sinners of the world of its enjoyment, and it is stored away for the righteous, as it stands written, 'Light is sown for the righteous' [Ps. 97:11]; then will the worlds be in harmony and all will be united into one, but until the future world is set up, this light is put away and hidden. This light emerged from the darkness which was hewed out by the strokes of the Most Secret; and likewise, from the light which was hidden away, through some secret path, *there was hewed out the darkness of the lower world in which inheres light.*"[83]

The Albigensians, in contrast, evidently divided this world very clearly from a heavenly one, prophesying a transformation that could only be hastened by the escalation of evil. Cabala, more nuanced, cautious, and patient, or less linear, allowed for more movement in the here and now between the domains, therefore for a greater tolerance for accomodation with authority. The divagations of the Albigensians, being nominally Christian, also were naturally more of a threat to established order. While cabalistic sex, however intense, was monogamous and procreative, the more extremist Albigensian life styles were obviously more threatening. Some of the most serious accusations leveled at them were in fact sexual in nature, either that they practiced a polymorphous and satanic free love, or a life-denying total celibacy. These were, however only apparently contradictory, being the two classically gnostic responses, opposite sides of the same pessimistic coin, to a Manichean ideology that hands this world over to the rule of "the powers of darkness."

Nevertheless the congeniality of the Cabalists with these medieval Manicheans and Christian Dualists, as Steven Runciman demonstrates the Albigensians to have been,[84] was indeed assumed at the time of the Albigensian crusade. Harold Bayley, for example, cites a document according to which one of the crimes the Albigensians were accused of was "harboring and sheltering cabalists."[85] Curiously, this Christian Dualist Heresy, in its Manichean, Bulgar, and Albigensian avatars, was dead by the fifteenth century, at a time when Cabala, with which it had much in common, was about to come into its own. According to Runciman, Christian Dualism was doomed because it was a religion of total hopelessness, so it "died without issue, before the swords of the Turks [Bulgar version] and the fires of the Dominicans [Albigensian]."[86] To this we may add that its idea of an eternal struggle between the principles of good and evil left no room for a vision of a redeeming Shekinah, confluence, rapture, or vision, as Cabala does, however fancifully. Indeed the very promiscuity of the Albigensians, so prominent in the indictment against them, must have had more to do with despair over good's impossibility than a rendezvous or emission with and from any absolute, as was surely the case for Cabala's Tantric Sabbath eves! Cabala was able to live on, possibly, because it had something to live for, in the sense that its Paradise Now could be a palliating sample, evidence or foretaste of one that is both past and to come.

People of the Book

Cabala seems to have been able, at least until the nineteenth century, when it was excoriated by post-Enlightenment Jewish positivism, to survive the disasters its potentially messianic streak could lead it into, because it had the texts, its own Zohar preeminently, and also its rock, The Torah, to fall back on, so it wouldn't be so totally identified or committed with what was going to happen to its followers, to the extent that it would not be able to survive the disappearance (or conversion) of many of them. Judaism is indeed a primordial religion of the Book, the Text, in a way that was more essential than for any other major religion. The reader-losing, extravagant hyperbole, for example, of the passage from The Zohar cited above (24ff.) is *sublimely* symbolic of the ingredients that went into building the tabernacle, meant to receive Torah. When one reflects on how Torahs are considered to be the word of God, and even, cabalistically, as spelling out the letters of his name, with what ceremony they are written, scrolled, clothed, crowned, housed, read, reread, memorized, danced with, buried (as with anything in Hebrew, the "sacred language," when they have deteriorated), one might even go so far as to suggest that Jewish worship of the Torah was another, maybe more advanced, form of idolatry, that of the Book, eventually to be displaced, perhaps, into literature as worship of all "good" books. Cabala, from this point of view, would be both an extension and a corrective to this singular and very strange and enduring obsession of a people with a text. From a Hegelian point of view, however, Judaism's reverence for the text would represent a spiritual materialism, which in turn would mean an advance over paganism, in the way the letter is less substantial than the idol or representation of a being; but, in its turn, Christianity would have carried the process on further toward an ineffable and immaterial end of history. Such is the notion of Judaism, for instance, when it happens to come up in the notebooks of a Hegelianizing Kierkegaard, where, for example, the Jew becomes a metaphor for a declaimed sensuality of fashion: "In a country where Jews are not tolerated, one at times sees a Jew roaming around and hawking; in the same way fashion's sneaking sensuality fears morality's commandment."[87] This is a relegation of Judaism to the lower realm of the senses, specifically to a kind of Limbo between the Hell of Pagan Flesh and the Heaven of Christian Soul. Kierkegaard conceives of Jewish consciousness, even on its more discursive levels, in a thoroughly Hegelian way, as a step past paganism, but an incomplete one, still trammeled by too much clinging matter.[88] Such, indeed, was the philosophical critique, anti-Semitism aside, that anticipated and prepared for Hegel, that Judaism has had to deal with for millennia. Judaism was seen as childish, in the sense of insisting on having that "lollipop" of something to hold onto. Jews are scorned for having, for instance, scanted that too-impalpable afterlife, mention of which is scarce or nonexistent in Torah, which would rather accord its milk and honey to its chosen in this one. Indeed, Judaism has had to create parallel texts, traditions, and commentaries, the latest and most controversial of which was Cabala, in order to ground and deepen its sense of such imponderables as soul and heaven and thereby meet the Christian-platonic challenge in spirituality. Cabala, was, anyway, in its late medieval stirrings, partly a response to a philosophical critique of Judaism, as is clear from that famed defense of the religion, The *Kuzari*, written in the Arabic of the Islamic Aristotelians, by Judah Halevi in the twelfth century, a work that was to play an important and inspiring role in the creation of the Spanish Cabala. Ironically it was the strength of the same cabalistic and spiritualizing defense that made some Jews and many Christians regard cabalism as Christian. Equally, Gershom Scholem's idealizing affinity with Cabala has had something to do with a stubbornly Hegelian streak in his mentality, raised and educated as he was in the intellectual milieu of Berlin, which pointed him early toward his lifelong exploration of limit-defying and self-transcending, and self-testing aspects of the Jewish experience.

In Christianity and Islam the sacred aura of certain writings was also a distillation of the precedent and concurrence of Jewish awe, ritual-cyclic repetition, and worship. The Gospels have never had, could never have had, the sacral place in Christian ceremony that Torah has had in the Jewish. Rather the story they tell, which can be very well rendered other ways, for instance, pictorially, as in medieval stained glass, and an imitation or approximation of it, *is* their message, never the words themselves. The Gospels, indeed, were taken to be the second installment of the words of God, the first of which was Torah, but it took over one thousand years for them to assume, and then only under the influence and pressure of a Hebraizing Protestant Reform, anything like the aura of Torah. Christianity remained a religion of sacrament, act, performance, and sacrifice, for which the central symbol was not a Book, of letters and paper, which is read, recited, repeated, but a Cross, of wood and nails, which is mounted, suffered on, remembered, and relived. The early fathers, indeed, seemed well aware that Christianity could never trust entirely to its texts, as sacred as they were, but needed to confide, and immediately, in the legitimacy and guidance of an oral tradition. Ironically, Cabala, understood as an oral component, which took until the Renaissance to push its way closer to the letter of the Jewish law, and then only for a few centuries, was already, in a way, sublimely Christian from the year one: "The problem [of an oral tradition] haunts Christian thought from its beginnings, as soon as they became aware that the Word of God could not be reduced to his texts, and that, as Ireneus had already insisted (*Against Heresy*, III, iv, 2), the written tradition had to admit the existence of an oral tradition—*sine charta*, without text—therefore never objectively identifiable, but, on the contrary, enigmatic, although also constituting an authority."[89] An Islamic sense of aura of their sacred text is indeed closer to the Jewish, surpassing it even, than to the Christian, for Mohammed's revelations were modeled on those of Moses. Yet even in the Koran Jews are known as "The People of the Book!"[90]

It was surely no coincidence that the sixteenth-century cabalistic community of Safed was within walking distance of the caves that were supposed to have sheltered Simon ben Yohai and his followers, fugitives from Roman persecution, in the second century A.D., and where Rabbi ben Yohai, under the spell of and therefore transmitting faithfully and automatically the words, divinely inspired, of Moses and Abraham, was believed to have *written* (down) The Zohar. These caves, it might go without saying, were the object of frequent and ritualistic peregrination for the Safed faithful, as well as constituting a landing place of choice for visitors from the world of spirits, or *maggadim*! Understandably, at Safed, they did not want to hear that The Zohar was written by de Leon, and in the thirteenth century; but this was not the first example, nor the last, of life copying art. Cabala, whose company, audience, and consolation could be the Book, was a truth that did not depend on large numbers or popularity for its durability; it could always retire to the isolation and protection of its mountain caves with its elect, where according to legend, virtually effective if not empirically true, its texts of exile and millennial aspiration were born anyway.

Cabala as Rhizome

Not the least of the challenges of interpreting Cabala is the development of a critical vocabulary appropriate for it. A discourse-oriented approach such as we have generally been deploying here is, it must be admitted, likely to run up against some determined opposition. It is interesting that in France, where deconstruction was invented, there also has been a defiant resistance to extending its parameters to include religious or sacred writings, as if a fissuring of authority might be acceptable for the literary text but must not be pursued into the inner sanctum of faith. The fragmented modernity, for example—against which Claude Vigée, a contemporary French poet and essayist, whose works are imbued with Cabala, protests—is nothing less than the style of *difference* that deconstruction has disseminated. The debate as Vigée carries it on is hardly temperate: "The great masters of modernity . . . think of all

of human experience as an explosion, the endless division of the
original mental dust. Because they've always confronted this experience in a fragmented space, they cannot attain the unifying perspective I've been trying to sketch out here. On the contrary, most
of them react to such suggestions with nausea and scorn [*ils la
vomissent haineusement*] . . . With a great burst of laughter they
lead their dupes into the debacle into which our whole civilization
is melting."[91] The context of this vituperation is that Vigée is attacking the deconstructing commentary of Olivier Revault d'Allones,
who interpreted Abraham's leaving home in obedience to God's
command, as a choice, which defines the Jewish condition-to-be as
one of endless *difference*, wandering, and uncertainty.[92] Abraham's
departure happens to be a central motif in The Zohar, important
enough to our cabalist, Vigée, for him to say to deconstructors,
through d'Allones, hands off!

On the Christian side, a subtext of Jean-Luc Marion's thought
has been the intimation that discursive modernity is the latest
chapter in the story of idolatry. [93] What bothers Marion and his
allies—who like especially to say that "the Bible is not a text"—
about deconstruction is that it tends to dissolve the notion of *distance*, upon which a "spiritual" Christianity is based. Just as
deconstruction in literature tends to conflate the reader and the
writer in favor of an aleatory process, so in theology it would con-
found gods and worshipers by suspending indefinitely the question
of just who exactly created whom.

The French cabalist scholars, indeed, among whom we may count
Idel in one of his contemporary avatars (since he publishes in French,
English, and Hebrew), are determined to let no postmodern notions
carry the sacred writings very far into the lay realm of the fortu-
itous. That Barthean author, for instance, who has to be elided,
withdrawn, or "die" so that the text can be delivered up as an object
of contemplation for the reader, would be sheer effrontery to name,
according to Idel, in connection with Cabala. Idel, citing Paul Ricoeur
as representative of a "textualist" school of thought that would surely
comprise Barthes, Blanchot, and Derrida, maintains that such a
disembodied literary approach and qualification would be irrelevant
for scripture, and a fortiori for cabalists: "The act of 'writing' was, in
rabbinical thought and especially in Kabbalah, the act of revelation
at Sinai, in which there were present not only those Israelites living

at the time but the souls of all the following generations. Thus, the readers were not at all 'absent from the act of writing,' nor is God, the Author, 'absent from the act of reading,' as Ricoeur describes the double eclipse [of author and reader]."[94]

Here it seems to me that Idel is resisting conclusions that his own research, for instance in the proto-Surrealism of the "subject dissolving" Cabala of Abulafia's "assault on language," should point to. In so doing he is denying the very process that Cabala was created to convey, by making of it simply an adjunct to Torah and therefore requiring the same awe, reverence, and respect; yet Cabala, whose status, we need to be reminded, is nothing like dogma, is nothing if not the notion that everything written, including Torah, is merely *text*. Cabala then, is simply a way of looking at Torah, and everything else, itself above all, as only inscribed, and therefore fleeting. Cabala will grant of course that a true text exists, but one that is knowable only before creation or after apocalypse. For all practical purposes Cabala means us to wonder about everything, in fact, by putting even the holiest things in question, to preserve that faculty of wonder, or what Rudolph Otto in our century called "the numinous." An author, even if one is willing to be found, anyway, never just *signs* a cabalistic text, which is then regarded as definitive, simply because the text continues to be modifiable, as well as subsidiary to the *voice* or oral supplement and accompaniment. Whatever is cabalistic is always in process and to be continued, where everything depends anyway on the outcome of the ritual, alphabetical, sexual, mental action that has been enjoined and the spirit in which it is carried out.

Rather than resolving this issue one way or another it might be more useful and interesting to conceive that the cabalistic author is neither dead *nor* alive. After all, whatever their resemblances, The Zohar, because of its intentions of theurgy and theosophy, is not an exact equivalent of literary works that are conceived thoroughly in the spirit of aesthetic modernism. While in connection with the latter it may make sense to elide the author in favor of other entities like process, text, and discourse, with Cabala it would seem more natural to say that we neither guard nor dispense with an author. A third way, between a traditional author-focused approach and the more current text- and discourse-centered one, and one more relevant to Cabala, which likes no either-ors, preferring rather the both-ands, might be a rhizomatous, "nomadilogical" style, as evoked by Deleuze and Guattari, most notably in *1,000 Plateaus*, sequel to *Anti-Oedipus: Capitalism and Schizophrenia*. In the seminal earlier book, which emerged from the French May 1968, they had developed a structuralist-depersonalized theory they called *schizanalysis*, trained on the anonymous fluxes of desire and energy. This therapy, also promoted at the time by the "sanity of madness" approach of R. D. Laing, was meant as a weapon against the stifling tyranny, exercised in the name (Oedipus, Freud) of psychoanalysis, of subject, identity, personality, family, and state. This schizanalysis in *Anti-Oedipus* evolves into a rhizome-analysis in the later *1,000 Plateaus*.[95]

A rhizome, or rootstalk/rootstock, is a more subtle and invisible entity than the plant or tree above it, tending more indefinitely toward horizontal proliferation rather than a marked and marking verticality. Texts-as-rhizomes eschew, accordingly, privilege, hierarchy, credit, and visibility of point and situation, existing namelessly as lines, vectors, and speeds. Nor does a rhizome deign to present or represent a world, which trees and plants have always done; nor does it mean, symbolize, or signify, but rather underlies, accompanies, and parallels events, in the sense of being merely another level in a world made only of levels, or one in a thousand "plateaus." A plateau, by definition, is always in the middle of something and between two others, in other words equally above, below, and between.

The rhizome is equally an antigenealogical factor, since neither does it stand for or extend anything that would have preceded it, nor is it ever going to stand up and be counted (upon) as anything's antecedent. Rather than matter for memory, the rhizome is much more a matter of forgetting, both of its provenance and what it leads to. According to this logic of the rootstalk, then, being noticed, known, remembered, found, famed, discovered is simply a dam in the stream of the amorphic process that stops and tries to hold onto that which should be released. The rhizome merely forms, performs, transforms, effectively a result of some coalescing needs, voices, desires, energies—or of the lines they took. Significantly Deleuze and Guattari's rhizomatous, nomadilogical schizoanalysis defies the very idea of enunciation as an *individual's* statement.[96] Texts are created by mechanisms that turn out to be collective, a matter of the multiplicities that inhabit what winds up being ascribed to a person. An individual's signature on a work then represents a mask, ideology, and strategy that an hierarchical society needs to guard its privileges and perpetuate its appropriations.

The subject, however, has a way of living on, if only as "denied," so all the more strident for having to defend itself. Consequently, although one can argue just how practical, especially beyond the realm of experimental modernism, such attacks on the subject have been, an area where it might be seemly to deploy them might be that of *mystics*, or mystical discourse, traditionally ego-defying, and a fortiori, mystical writing. This application of subject- and author denying insouciance to the study of mysticism has been, indeed, the special province of Michel de Certeau, Lacanian "to the letter," and frequently cited also by Deleuze-Guattari. *Anti-Oedipus* and *1,000 Plateaus* are works that, in fact, like The Zohar, defy you to define its subject, or even to conceive very clearly of its author(s). That author, for example, neither substantial nor totally absent, that Deleuze and Guattari have fashioned, is a dual signature that is responsible indifferently for the text, it being functionally irrelevant where one begins and the other leaves off. Instead of dividing the work into chapters or sections they worked on everything together, relaying each other throughout, often even after five lines or so. So, in their books we have a central ideological statement of their generation, a kind of topical Zohar and summa of radical-anarchist modernity, coming through a fused voice that is more and different than the sum of two individual styles.

From a schizoanalytical-nomadilogical point of view, therefore, the question of Who wrote The Zohar? could seem empirically nugatory, in other words, somewhat of a sideshow or distraction (since everything serves a purpose, somehow). For the book, and especially anything like the cultural event this Zohar became, represents the articulation and incarnates the energies of a certain setting and conjuncture.[97] It would be the height of absurdity to list Moses de Leon as the author on the title page of any edition of The Zohar, however scientific, and nor have I seen such a monstrosity (among, for example the enormous variety of the thirty-four printed editions Scholem lists in *Bibliographica Kabbalistica*, from 1558–1927), for whatever its accuracy it would be clearly not in the spirit of the work.

De Leon, then, would have been expressing the "multiplicities" of his own epoch by assigning authority to a renowned, legendary, community figure of one thousand years ago, inventing, reviving, recreating the Aramaic to go along with its reborn author. For what was coming through with The Zohar, as in modern times, with Deleuze and Guattari, James Joyce's *Finnegans Wake*, or Beckett's "unnamable" words, was just that something or someone else, demanding by reason of its originality and quality to be listened to, in a language that we feel we've heard before but don't quite know what to think of or even what to call.

For the rhizome all languages, peoples, nations, religions, societies, groups, classes, or what we call such, are *false* anyway, representing certain political priorities, tyrannies, and usurpations. A *flux* of contagion, permutation, and proliferation normally *trickles* through such dams and separations as are meant to channel and control it, while sometimes, under special circumstances, assuming the dimensions of a *flood tide* of difference that can impact on life for centuries. Such indeed seems to have been the case with The Zohar, which meant that both de Leon's queer Aramaic as well as his half-angelic ben Yohai were heard, read, and observed in the caves of Safed, Syria, where cabalists were walking out to be near them three hundred years after their first reappearance.

The One and the Two Many

Cabala conceived as antigenealogical rhizome, however, only engages it on a certain level or plateau. Nothing prevents us from exploring the direction of genealogy, as long as we were not following its path as if it was the only road to truth. On the level of this nonprivileged genealogical strata, then, we may observe that it is certainly no mere coincidence that the *ain soph*—or unknowable withdrawn kernel, source, and creator in Cabala—is reminiscent of Aristotle's idea of the Deity as the primal cause and unmoved mover. On the other hand the theory of the *sefiroth*, or emanations progressively corrupted as they descend more closely to earth, would connect more to Plato, according to whom existence can only represent a diluted and sullied essence.[98] This dual heritage and deployment of some of the basic attitudes of the fathers of Western

Philosophy has also played its role in the endurance of Cabala. Through its Aristotelian heritage of primal unknowability Cabala could respectably remove itself from answering every difficult or impossible ethical or empirical question. Alternatively, a Platonic quality could come into play when, ineluctably, it becomes a question of whether one can stay in touch with one's ideals and hopes in a world that demands compromise. A Cabala that is challenged or in difficulty, then, could always fall back on this incipient Platonism, according to which the real is only an attempt, more or less successful, to approximate the ideal—one that, like the Sun in the Allegory of the Cave, is more knowable than tolerable anyway.

However this marriage or comingling of Aristotle and Plato, though a convenient one also—as is inevitably the case with partners so different—made for a certain permanent, if fecond, instability. The separation between its Aristotelian removed creator and the progressively (or regressively) more earthly realm of the Platonic emanations seems at once so drastic and yet so basic that the specter of Dualism would always accompany Cabala, a "sleeper" that could come alive during apocalyptically revolutionary times, as later in the Renaissance, and one that eventually was to play its part in reducing the role of Cabala in mainstream religious practice, Christian *and* Jewish (while opening it up, maybe, as recently, to literary-critical exploitation).

In Cabala, the *ain soph* represents the withdrawn and uninvolved, Aristotelian image of the deity, which has been left behind by the Platonic *sefiroth*, whatever descends to play, be, or otherwise more or less literally fuck with man. Indeed the creation of the physical universe from the *ain soph*, beginning time "at the beginning," is purely an effect of the *sefiroth* that have always already emanated. Even on the level of creation and emanation a certain tradition has it that the very words of the divine (scripture) are secondary, if not superfluous. All has already been said and effected by the descent into matter. Scholem quotes, in this regard, an eloquent letter from Franz Rosenzweig to Martin Buber about this kind of Cabala-before-words that regarded the hearing of the *aleph* or first letter of the first divine utterance on Sinai, when God said "I" as the full accomplishment of divine purpose and its human reception: "The only immediate content of revelation . . . is revelation itself, with *va-yered* (he came down) it is essentially complete, with *vayedabber* (he spoke) interpretation sets in, and all the more so with 'anokhi' (the 'I' which pronounces the Decalogue)."[99]

We should conceive also that this "descent" has taken place for reasons essentially inscrutable but certainly beyond any realm of supernal volition, which, as Spinoza was going to demonstrate so strictly, always is a matter, in one form or another, of wishful thinking and projection. *To will*, indeed, would be a condign declination from the divine dignity of the unknown and unknowable, withdrawn behind the line (of possible cognition, responsibility, or answerability, which is where Spinoza was to locate the deity, whom we could therefore love only intellectually), kernel not even of a secret, because an undiscoverable one. So, for example, when The Zohar exuberantly claims something that Mallarmé might have delighted in also—that the world was created for the sake of THE BOOK, or Torah—this provocative reasoning relates to the level of the emanations, not to that of the absolute, which would be above, beyond, or beside willing or not willing, much less giving reasons for such. In this sense of mysterious, unknowable beginnings, Cabala has been inspired by Aristotle's version of creation, specifically his "unmoved mover" or causeless cause. However Cabala does not need to follow Acquinas's Catholic development of Aristotle, whose purpose it was to heal the breach between creator and world by a kind of faith or fiat, in his insistence on a panoptic or "watcher" system, that of a "creator continuans," or of a God who is involved and who cares about a world, even after it has been created.

For whatever consolations, guarantees, or notions of divine presence Cabala affords turn out to be images, or, at best, temporary prospects, through the workings of the deconstructing mechanisms of the text as well as of the judgment-and-reflection-baffling effect of its moral paradoxes and ambiguities, not to mention its wilder theories of reincarnation, Sabbath-cosmic copulations, messianic exemptions from ordinary standards, letters come alive, or apocalyptic world time cycles. The Zohar, for example, likes nothing better than to challenge a reader who thinks he has understood something: "The Torah releases one word, and comes forth from her sheath ever so little, and then retreats to concealment again." Whatever, indeed, "Torah releases" only amounts to a word that would relate to one of the three grades of soul, *neshamah, ruah, and nefesh*, corresponding, in descending supernal order to *spirit, mind, and sense*, so that an interpretation is likely to be valid for one soul and catastrophic for another—while, since we contain all three of them, error may be conceived as being at once consequential and ineluctable. The Zohar, equally, is insistent on our envisioning the "Two Aspects of God," a transcendent and an immanent one, the "larger and smaller countenance," respectively, essentially the *withdrawn*, Aristotelian *ain soph*, or primal, unknowable Cause of Causes and the Platonically engaged, increasingly sullied world of the *sefiroth*. Yet we are urgently required also not to distinguish between the two aspects but to conceive of the Gods of Plato and Aristotle as if they are one, something philosophers have never succeeded in (Leibniz maybe aside, but he was able to think of death itself, which he called disorganization, as a form of life): "Why then were the Israelites chastised?" The Zohar wonders, before answering, "The reason is that they made distinction between these two aspects in God." Israel's punishment, in keeping with the demon or spirit of analogy, was certainly Diaspora, for they were separated and scattered just as they had separated and scattered a transcendent cause and immanent one. Equally, just as there are two aspects of God there are two aspects of Torah, an outer and an inner, that we must keep in mind simultaneously, because "the tales related in the Torah are simply her outer garments,"[100] which introduces a *structural* insecurity, since epistemologically we are "condemned to the choice" of depending on our faculties. Yet by the mere fact of our perception all that we could know or understand would be "outer garment," tales of Torah as well as the stories told about them by prophets and cabalists. The rule of Cabala is already that the secret revealed is immediately reconstituted as another order of mystery anyway. In short, the readers are defenseless and infinitely vulnerable to zoharic prescriptions, proscriptions, and enjoinders, whereby they are urgently required to know what by the rules of the game must elude their grasp, or what, by definition, would have turned into another conundrum by the time they think they have got a clue.

All of this points to the ineluctably verbal and rhetorical nature, intrinsically labile and ultimately nugatory and vain, of all we (are obliged to) rely on. The very Zohar itself, essential text of the movement, for instance, was regarded by one of its foremost sixteenth-century interpreters and disseminators, Moses Cordovero,

as explained by Idel (hostile only to *modern* deconstruction), as
being merely a lower and lesser rung on the ladder of Cabala, the
upper rungs of which involve an ascent into the wordless: "In the
eyes of Cordovero ... the Kabbalah can be seen as a graded system
containing two levels: 1) the lower level, consisting of the Kabbalah
of the *sefirot*, which is derived from The Zohar, and 2) the higher
level, the ecstatic or 'Prophetic Kabbalah' of Abulafia."[101] Inescapable, in Cabala, is the notion that in *this* world and *this* time, at
least, we are not dealing with substance, essence, or reality but
with appearances, hypotheses, and directions on a compass that
changes whenever we move and turn, which, of course, we must. A
real God, or beginning absolute principle, would be forever withdrawn from the affairs of this world—as Spinoza, cabalist in this
way, as Leibniz noticed in dismay,[102] was to insist later so eloquently.

Since it was not put in the position of having to follow Aquinas
in his rescue of the Aristotelian creator, Cabala worked against the
logocentric implications of Acquinas's caring-willing-intervening God,
or Christianization of Aristotle. This *present* deity would not have
allowed any iota of existence that the "tyranny of the logos" did not
inhabit. Thereby Cabala was more loyal to the *infinite*, as well as
to an element of freedom (from control, for possibility) and indeterminacy that Aristotle allows precisely by hinting at its and our
limits. For the scholastics every patch of the cosmos would be occupied, filled with the plenitude of a single idea and system; but for
Cabala, though the universe can be known through visions and
other peak experiences it cannot be secured and established once
and for all, knowledge being something we work up to and fall
away from, something that needs be corrected, maintained, restored,
overcome, and bypassed. This is yet another cause of this curiously
esoteric Cabala's wide-ranging appeal for the Renaissance. Cun-
ningly and carefully, Cabala harmonizes conflicting currents by
respecting and preserving the insights of both Aristotle's empirical
modesty and Plato's visionary ambition, beyond the church's determination, soon to be relayed by the nascent reachings of a developing world capitalist economy, to absorb everything under the
control of a single universal system.

2

The Secret of Agrippa

T he first internationally known Christian student of the
Cabala was Pico della Mirandola (1463–1494). Legend has
it (fact and fiction are intertwined in these matters, like
good and evil in Cabala) Pico saw a copy of Moses de Leon's *Zohar*
sometime in the early 1480s and immediately became enraptured
with cabalistic ideas, to the point that he succeeded in persuading
the Pope of his time, Sixtus IV, of the importance of having de
Leon's text and other cabalistic works translated into Latin. There
is some evidence that this work was begun, but there are no surviving texts to prove that it made much headway.[1] Pico adapted
cabalistic ideas from the works he read, and circulated some very
provocative statements about them which he called, bluntly, "Cabalistic Conclusions." Basically these "conclusions" involve an attempt
to adapt cabalism to Christianity. Pico was very much involved in
trying to rescue the church from what he felt were the limitations
of Aristotelian-Acquinian dogmatism; and he thought, along with
Marsilio Ficino (1433–1499) that Platonic, "inspirational" theories
of creation more nearly coincide with Christian faith than the syl-
logistic reasonings of scholastic philosophy. Partly because Cabala,
in what it imagined as its golden-age beginnings in the second
century A.D., at the start of the definitive Jewish exile, subsequent
to the first-century revolts against Roman rule, was part of an

intellectual atmosphere suffused with Platonism and also because Cabala was coming to be more widely known at the same time as the Neoplatonism of the Renaissance was gathering force and believers, Pico and some others felt that its ideas, methods, and attitudes were highly consistent with the kind of Christianity they wanted to see flourish.

The antipodal attitudes of the Franciscans and Dominicans well demonstrate how conflicting factions within the church received the advent of cabalism. The Dominicans were rigidly Thomist in outlook, whereas the mystical Franciscans eagerly adopted Neoplatonic modifications. The Dominicans condemned the cabalist works as they emerged, and started crossing over into Christianity in the late fifteenth and early sixteenth centuries (as they had also urged the extirpation of the Albigensian heresy a few centuries earlier), whereas the Franciscans welcomed them. Johannes Reuchlin (1455–1522), a major German figure involved in the Christianization of the Cabala in this period, and very much influenced by Pico, saw his work condemned and his own books, even, barely escape burning by the Dominicans.

Pico was convicted of heresy by an ecclesiastical court that was especially convened for the purpose, showing that cabalistic thinking was taken seriously enough to be regarded as a threat. This condemnation, however, was far from unanimous. Indicating also a respect for Pico and the currents of thought he was trying to promote and foreshadowing an ambiguity that was to accompany the reception of Cabala in the Renaissance, he was allowed full liberties of speech at his trial. In his defense Pico mentioned that the Christian doctrine of the "messiah-who-shall-return" could very easily be substituted for the "messiah-who-shall-come" of the Cabala. Pico suggested that the cabalistic techniques of scriptural exegesis—*notorikon* (abbreviations), *gematria* (letter numerology) and *themurah* (anagrams) could just as easily be applied to deriving a Christian message from the Old Testament. Pico's "Cabalistic Conclusions," for which he was indicted, were part of a work called *Nine-Hundred Conclusions* that he published in Rome in 1486. Pico wished to defend his conclusions against all comers at the University of Paris that same year, but he was prevented from doing so by the condemnation for heresy that intervened. Other Christian doctrines that Pico reported at his trial, which he felt were proved by Cabala, were the mystery of the trinity, the word-made-flesh, and the divinity of Jesus.

One of the judges who had declared him guilty published at Rome, in 1499, a resumé of the evidence against Pico. This was Pedro Garzia,[2] Bishop of Ussel, and he did this partly to protect himself, since Pico was soon *cleared* of the charge of heresy by special papal dispensation, even after an ecclesiastical court had convicted him.

Pico's Conclusions

A. E. Waite translates and reproduces all of Pico's "Cabalistic Conclusions,"[3] and I will cite a few of them, with explanatory and exploratory comments:

XV: Unless the letter HE had been added to the name of Abram, Abra*h*am would not have begotten.

This bit of zoharic arithmetic, according to which the "h," fifth letter of the Hebrew alphabet, is *the* letter of generation, seems to have been one of the most widely disseminated cabalistic commonplaces of the Renaissance, turning up, for instance, very prominently 150 years later, in the *fifth* chapter of the mischievous Sir Thomas Browne's *The Garden of Cyrus*, a book about the number *five*.[4] Here Pico is combining a Platonic theory of correspondences with cabalistic numerology in regard to events in the "lower" world. The realm of scriptural *words* constitutes an ideal realm, of which the earth is a copy. Therefore any alteration above is reflected by a corresponding one below.

XIX: The letters of the name of the evil demon who is the prince of this world are the same as those of the name of God—TETRAGRAMMATON—and he who knows how to effect their transposition can extract one from the other.

A cabalistic-gnostic theme of the inseparability of good and evil in *this* world is clearly in evidence; rather than something to be discarded and avoided, evil here is regarded as a way to the divine.

Coyly it is implied also that it can be the other way around: good, for instance, proud of itself and complacent, doesn't even have to turn into an evil—it *is* already.

XXX: No angel with six wings is ever transformed.

Waite turns to the nineteenth-century mystic, mage, and occult popularizer, Eliphas Lévi, the Abbé Louis Constant, for an interpretation of this conclusion, and just about as anomalous: "There is no change for the mind which is equilibrated perfectly." I think the secret of this passage, and also what makes Constant's abstruse explication finally sensible, is that stasis, calm, and security are, mystically speaking, *negatives*. Humans, motivated and restless because of structural weaknesses and inaptitudes, may attain god-like powers of metamorphosis, while surpassing those intermediary spirits that are the angels, trammeled and static because of their very perfection and completion. This would be consistent alike with the attitude of zoharic sages, who typically humor and indulge the angels who are sent to guide them, as well as with Pico's notions of unlimited human potential as announced in his celebrated *Oration on the Dignity of Man*.

XXXI: Circumcision was ordained for the deliverance from the impure powers wandering about.

The study of the Cabala is a type of circumcision (Old Testament infant "baptism," in Christian typology), in a sense that it demarcates its students as belonging to a circle that unholy thoughts and demonic instincts cannot penetrate. Permeating The Zohar is the idea of the constant presence of evil, all the more dangerous for being invisible:

The moment a child is born in the world, the evil prompter straightway attaches himself to him, and thenceforth brings accusations against him, as it says, "sin coucheth at the door" (Gen. IV, 7), the term "sin" being a designation of the evil prompter, who was also called sin by King David in the verse: "and my sin is ever before me" (Ps. LI, 5). He is so called because he makes man every day to sin before his Master, never leaving him from the moment of his birth till the end of his life. But the good prompter first comes to man only on the day that he begins to purify himself, to wit, when he reaches the age of thirteen years. From that time the youth finds himself attended by two companions, one on his right and the other on his left, the former being the good prompter, the latter the evil prompter. These are two veritable angels appointed to keep man company continually. Now when a man tries to be virtuous, the evil prompter bows to him, the right gains dominion over the left, and the two together join hands to guard the man in all his ways. [*Zohar II*, 134]

Circumcision would then be the physical and symbolic recognition and anticipation of the role of evil in the world, and, accordingly, of the *respect* we owe it at all times. The result of this awareness would ostensibly be the protection of the subject, as at the end of the passage above it is suggested that right and left, or good and evil, work *together* to guard the cabalist. Childhood, and presumably everything natural, instinctive, and primitive, equally, are seen to be defenseless against evil, showing the high premium Cabala places on the importance of intellect: before an "age of reason" we are presumably unable to conceptualize the idea of a malign being, hence, the reason it has its way with us. Circumcision then plays the part of the antinatural, the premeditated, the aware, against the vulnerability of youth, and is a permanent reminder that the world is not to be accepted *as is*.

XXXV: No spiritual things descending below can operate without a garment.

The garment of God is the Bible, the Word, which must be "seen through," with the help of Cabala, if we are to know God as well as we can. On another, Platonic level, the body is the garment of the soul.

XXXVIII: As fear is outwardly inferior to love, so love is inwardly inferior to fear.

Here a cabalistic style works as a receiving eye to invert the perceived notion, or in Nietzschean terms, "transvalue" it: fear, and the narcissistic instincts of self-preservation to which it is allied, is only apparently baser than the ostensibly altruistic love. A more intense cogitation might situate fear as above love, in the sense of reflecting a categorical call of duty, or a higher one, than gentler feelings. The effect of such mind-twisting images, as with Cabala in general, is to enjoin and oblige a work of rewriting and interpretation, in an attempt to defy a subject's complacency and conditioning, in preparation for a revelation, readiness for which has much to do with a calculated, "docta," in the language of Nicholas de Cusa, ignorance. Cabalistically, sterness and mercy work together on the sefirotic tree, above which two Hebrew names of God, *Elohim* and *YHVH* (Tetragrammaton) suggest severity and charity, respectively. Routinely, however, in Jewish worship one affirms, finally, that Elohim and YHVH, fear and love, are somehow one. Other frequent synonyms for these divine qualities would be "justice" and "charity," while how and if they work together, and how fairly, has been the subject of much debate, from talmudic times to our own. Lévinas, for instance, relying on a talmudic commentary on how divine mercy and justice can be conciliated on that severest of holidays, Rosh Hashonah, or day of repentance, remarks that the *justice* comes before the judgment, the *mercy* afterward. However accurate this is phenomenologically, since all are born to die, many have thought it would make more sense the other way around! K's sentence, in Kafka's *Trial*, it may be recalled, has already been passed by the time he gets to talk with his kindliest interlocutor, the priest in the penultimate chapter. I regard the priest's famous fable, definitive for Kafka's work and for our time, "Before the Law," as fundamentally a text of charity, restoring to the protagonist a sense of dignity that the unarguable process of the *Trial* had drained from him, giving him, finally a say, even if an empty (literary) one. [5]

XLI: Every good soul is a new soul coming from the East.

There are so many imponderables here as to almost defy hermeneutics. That the Cabala was influenced by Eastern traditions and texts, beyond the more direct Gnostic-Dualist-Manichean link, is frequently mentioned, but somewhat vaguely and more as a matter of analogies than direct influence. Patai's suggestions are intriguing, however: (1) an ancient connection between Alexander's armies exposure to Indian sculpture, and some controversial sexual motifs we may regard as proto-cabalistic in the Temple(s) of Israel; (2) Indian influence, by way of Arab culture, which had spread to the Indus river by the time of the inception of Cabala, which could have brought Yoga to Abulafia's ecstatic Cabala (through Sufism) and Hindu-Tantric notions (sacral copulation, reincarnation) to de Leon's theosophical one.[6] Cabala is a tradition whose openness to other teachings is a matter of system, but which therefore involved a potentially threatening syncretism; The Zohar itself often seems anxious about "new" things whose provenance is unorthodox, even if the contributions correspond to cabalistic attitudes. As for Tantrism, for example, cabalistic notions place sex in the realm of the sacred; and, like Zen Buddhism, Cabala likes to "enlighten" its acolytes in unexpected ways that place a premium on novelty and surprise: the Bible, for example, never means what you think it means, what it only says. When a certain Cabala becomes Christian also in the Renaissance, it obviously relates to this issue of reaching out beyond the received and the perceived, into a typological (Christ-predicting) meaning for Old Testament "signs," together with its attendant dangers and challenges, all of which explains a hesitating but fascinated ambivalence toward it. What seems exciting about this statement is a sense of action and process, Cabala maybe being the "new soul" that has just come, in movement, changing things, bringing light (from the East, where the sun rises) and life, a new dawn and a sense of things not being the same as they were before, but also of an ancient prerogative restored to its rightful place.

Reuchlin's Art

The background of John Reuchlin (whose trouble with the Dominicans we have touched on above) in the texts and traditions of cabalism was much wider than that of his predecessor-contemporary, Pico.[7] In spite of his extravagant enthusiasm, Pico, of cabalistic texts, really knew only some manuscripts, including possibly that of The Zohar, that were brought over to Italy by Jews fleeing Spain. In particular there was a zoharic commentary by a

Platonizing Italian Jew, Manaheim de Recenati, which was enormously influential on Pico and doubtless had much to do with Pico's Neoplatonic interpretations of The Zohar and the ambition and conviction with which he expounded them. In other words, Pico's Cabala, awesomely original, interesting, and ambitious as it was, in keeping with everything else this amazing Renaissance genius touched on in his short life, generally has the reputation of being somewhat indirect and second hand, learned through critics and scholars without benefit of much consultation of authentically cabalistic works, or only a fleeting one. Pico's is a highly subjective and poeticized Cabala. John Reuchlin, however, was knowledgable in both Torah and talmudic commentary, probably the first non-Jew to make Cabala so completely his own. Inspired by Pico's revelations, Reuchlin responded rather like a humanist scholar than a poet and dreamer: he made it his business to turn himself into an accomplished Hebraist, attaining a degree of proficiency that enabled him eventually to publish a Hebrew grammar for beginners in a language he did so much to promote in the first place. Being more of a scholar than a philosopher, Reuchlin wasn't concerned with using the Cabala in order to validate a philosophy of his own, as in Pico's case, whose Platonic bias probably motivated his discovery of Cabala.

Reuchlin was well informed in all three of the major cabalistic currents that were present in Western Europe for a few hundred years before the actual emergence of cabalism in print (through Pico, his supporters and detractors) in the fifteenth and early sixteenth century. These are the schools of: (1) Isaac the Blind (fl. 1190–1200—doctrines of emanations and metempsychosis); (2) Eleazer of Worms (fl. 1220—number and letter symbolism); (3) Abraham ben Samuel Abulafia (1240–1292—fusion of practical and theoretical cabalism)[8]

Abulafia, almost an exact contemporary of de Leon, had nevertheless a much less theosophical turn of mind; he turned away from the type of abstruse speculations and prophecies characteristic of The Zohar toward the realm of theurgy and personal transformation, perhaps Cabala's first great popularizer. One of the students of Abulafia as well as of de Leon, whose approaches he apparently attempted to conciliate, Joseph Gikatalia (1247–1305), had an enormous impact on Reuchlin. Gikatalia had synthesized and developed techniques of scriptural exegesis, which occupied a central place in Pico's Cabala also, that could locate the spirit of the letter in those multifarious, interconnecting, and intercorrecting ways of *gematria*, *notarikon*, and *themurah*.

Gematria is the art of numbers, according to which every Hebrew letter has a number assigned to it keyed to its place in the alphabet. Thus, since Genesis starts with a *beth*, second letter of the Hebrew alphabet, the first word of the Bible being in Hebrew bereshith, "God's Arithmetic" of creation, to employ the terms of an English writer who was a student of Christian Cabala, was *dyadic*,[9] or based on even numbers, the two being assigned to *beth* as second letter of the sacred alphabet, connoting also the duality and impurity of existence as opposed to the unity and oneness of divine essence. The "one" in Cabala represented that aspect of God withdrawn beyond the line of possible knowledge, the impenetrable, unsayable mystery and core, or *ain-soph*, while the "two" stands for the descended or manifest and emanated world of *sefiroth* and existence, impure but thereby knowable. Significantly, the opposition of these first two numbers which begin or "already are" everything, inherited also from a Pythagorean-Platonic tradition, is a numerological theme that, far from unique in Cabala, also shows up widely in Renaissance poetry and philosophy.[10] Accordingly, the two always represents an ineluctable but necessary decline from the heavenly perfection of the one, in the sense of the "fortunate fall," or sin without which there is neither world nor progeny. Thoroughly in the spirit of this cabalistic numerology is the dichotomy Spenser establishes between two of the first women we meet in *The Fairie Queene*, Una and Duessa. The *first* represents authentic Christian truth, the *second* its Catholic distortions. A corresponding distinction is conveyed by Spenser in the numbering of Book *One* of his epic for the otherworldly virtue[11] of Holiness, and Book *Two* for the worldly virtue of Temperance (since *here* is where we are tempted). Duality, alike in Spenser and Cabala, as currently for Jean Baudrillard,[12] tends to stand for fascinating but dangerous aspects of experience that relate to appearance, seduction, and simulation.

Probably another reason for the affinity of Cabala with literary styles in the Renaissance was that, as Alaister Fowler has demonstrated,[13] texts of the period could be profoundly numerological, and in subtly pervasive ways, a "hidden dimension" that is frequently lost on the modern reader. A particularly stunning example of this is Christ's decisive intervention in the Chariot, or mystical doomsday weapon that forces the Satanic legions out of heaven, thereby preparing for the "fall" of man on earth. This *occurs at the exact center*, counting by lines, of Milton's *Paradise Lost*, which according to Gunnar Quarnström, thereby deploys a "numerically symmetrical structure."[14]

However when we move from a symbolism of numbers to one of letters, our focus moves from the literary toward the scriptural text. *Notarikon* would be the name of this science of abbreviations; thus every letter of the Tetragrammaton, the name of God, YHVH, stands for one of the dimensions or worlds that name represents. Another, more literary example would be the four letters (in Hebrew) of one of the most frequent and serious words in Cabala, PARDES, meaning "garden" or "paradise." Each of the four letters (in Hebrew) corresponds to a different exegetical level for the interpretation of scripture: literal, allegorical, moral, prophetic—as also for Christian theology. Notorikon was a significant validating technique for Cabala, which, to be sure, needed to exploit the full explanatory potential of every approach to establish a basis in *Torah* for its mystical visions, which, as often as not, leave the literal letter of the law far behind or below. Cabalists also practiced a fusion of these techniques, as in the special aura of number 32, symbolic of 32 paths of wisdom available for humanity, and obtained by combination of the 22 letters of the Hebrew alphabet with the ten emanations or *sephiroth*.

Themurah, lastly, was a technique for shifting letters around so as to supply a desired conclusion with the required basis in sacred texts. Cabalistic exegetical and hermeneutic styles demanded exactly that peculiar force or will, a *volo*, which, as suggested by de Certeau about the mystical discourse in the Renaissance, *meant* to cooperate actively in the creation of meaning and thereby partake in a demiurgic enterprise of self-fashioning. This *volo* involved two kinds of action and determination. The first of these would be a will-*not*-to want, or an indifference to the socially conditioned objects of desire, earthly love, family, property, and works. This is a kind of "circumcision" that separates the subject from the world as flatly given or inherited (what Eckhart called *gelassenheit* or "coolness"). The second stage of this *volo* involves a will which then constructs another identity on the basis of an ideal of the self-to-be-realized.[15] *Themurah*, among exegetical styles, was an open door and invitation to this *activity* of the enthusiast, for whom truth had to be created on the basis of a coded anagram of divinely supplied letters. The allusion to *themurah* is explicit, for example, in a manifestly Christian-cabalist passage from another English writer of the period, William Camden, anxious to find the name of Mary disguised in Old Testament language: "If profound antiquity, or the inventour may command an invention, this [anagram-*themurah* method] will not give place to many. For as the great Masters of the Jewes testify, Moses received of God a litteral law, written by the finger of God, in the two tables of the ten commandments to be imparted to all, and another Mysticall to be communicated only to 70 men, which by tradition they should pass to posterity, whereof it was called *Cabala*. Which was divided in *Mercana*, concerning only the sacred names of God, and *Breshith*, of other names, consisting of Alphabetary revolution [movement], which they will have to be Annagramatized, Marie resolved made, *Our Holie Mistress*." Camden, however, very much of a searcher, is more interested in exploring a reality than guaranteeing it; so he cautiously floats his conclusions by referring to another tradition of Biblical commentary, that of Talmud, more empirical than Cabala, according to which, presumably, such extrapolations might be less justified: "But whether this *Cabala* is more ancient than the Talmudical learning, hatched by the *curious* Jewes (as some will) about 200 years after Christ, let the learned consider."[16] This author's unease with cabalistic styles of exegesis and thought, his efforts at distance and irony at the same time he has resorted to them, is typical of the Renaissance reception in general. On the one hand such methods could be useful and relevant, on the other there was something unnerving and dangerous about them that forced one to be alert to the possibility of deception. Camden, for example, just can't stay away from the fascinating debate on the question of the antiquity and authenticity of the Cabala, whose styles, nevertheless, he found obviously quite helpful. In the locution "hatched by the curious Jewes" there is more than a pejorative hint of cunning evil and calculation, as well as of Camden's almost involuntary ambivalence (although in the parenthesis that follows he also is careful to mention that there is no unanimity is these matters anyway); for *curiosity*, now encouraged, was still thought of as a *sin* in the Renaissance, following Eve's inability to resist hers.

The two major cabalistic works published by John Reuchlin published were *The Wonder Working Word*, in 1494; and *Cabalistic Art*, of 1517. These two books really span the heart of the career of the most accomplished Christian Hebraist of the epoch, while showing the depth and constancy of his commitment to Cabala. In *The Wonder Working Word* he lists the names of God and identifies Hebrew as the holy language, also recounting the roles of the ten *sefiroth* and identifying the "miraculous," or wonder-working word of his title as no less than the Tetragrammaton, YHVH, following Pico in his emphasis on its power. The later book reflects Reuchlin's deeper probings into the mysteries of Cabala in the twenty years that had intervened. One of his purposes, Reuchlin declared, in writing *De Arte cabalistica* was to present his side of a controversy that he was engaged in with the Cologne Dominicans, who were intent on destroying all Hebrew texts. Reuchlin, in a spirit of compromise, was willing to let them burn the Talmud (a tradition of commonsense commentary, often antithetical to the spirit of Cabala anyway), but insisted cabalistic works be spared, since, he maintained, they validate rather than refute Christian doctrines. Apparently also, perhaps in the spirit of openness and toleration characteristic of Renaissance students of Cabala and to save them from the censor's wrath, Reuchlin listed many Hebrew works as cabalistic that have not the slightest relation to Cabala except the language in which they were composed. Since Reuchlin's books are *the* primary source for all serious Christian study of Cabala in the Renaissance, his list was a source of some subsequent confusion as to what exactly makes a text cabalistic.

As Cabala becomes more widely known, anyway, there is a parallel degrading or blurring of its image, as the term *cabalist* often seems synonymous with magician-trickster. This devolution certainly becomes more pronounced in another major figure in Christian cabalism of the sixteenth century, Henry Cornelius Agrippa of Nettesheim (1487–1535), who, however, was a serious student of Pico and Reuchlin, as well as showing some familiarity with The Zohar. Nevertheless, it might not be appropriate to get too excited about "distortions" of a Cabala that itself is often so wildly imaginative and innovative in its interpretations of scripture, "deviations" (e.g., its apology for evil, apocalyptic messianism, sexual theurgy) that orthodox religiosity, Jewish and Christian, has often bitterly resented and opposed. For an ideology, also, in which the ultimate truth is unknowable and secret, one appearance or image may be functionally equivalent to another. Perhaps most dangerous of all would be the one that seems most nearly adequate, thereby simulating the capture of a truth that remains by definition elusive. As we have seen, certain fissures of problems of authority, attribution, and indeterminacy run all through that keystone text, The Zohar, which is the rocky bed upon which Cabala's reading of Torah rests. So Reuchlin's errors, well meant or not, are not merely *mistakes*, but well within the parameters of a tradition in which vagueness is very much part of the message.

In *De Arte cabalistica* Reuchlin also expands on ideas expressed in his first work *De Verbo Mirifico* on the importance of a "divine mathematics" in understanding scripture. Here he supplies clear expositions of the very influential cabalistic exegetical techniques, dwelling, for instance, at length, on numerical symbolism (*notorikon*)—finding mystical the *50*, a cabalistic number called that of "the gates of understanding," more having to do with a threshold experience of sudden illumination than a gradual journey to knowledge on the *32* "paths of wisdom." The very quantity of possibilities conveys a sense of the latitude and generosity of the tradition as well as the difficulty of ever fulfilling its program comprehensively, with a corresponding toleration of others. The finality of total transparency to the divine remains a theoretical possibility, but also highly unlikely. According to Reuchlin's sources, indeed, no man has mastered *all* 50 gates of the understanding, with the stakes being, for having passed through them all, total knowledge of God: Moses only opened *49* of the gates of understanding, which is why he was barred from the holy land.

Compared to the more pagan mood of Pico, Reuchlin remains more firmly the Christian, albeit a kind of reformer. With Pico, one feels that the Catholic twist he gave to Cabala was more of a screen behind which he could unleash the soaring energies of his Neoplatonic imagination; but, Reuchlin, whom A. E. Waite accuses of futility for trying to "read Christian dogmas into the written word of the Kaballah,"[17] perhaps because the opposition had become more suspicious, resolves everything very quickly into Christian patterns, as if he was able to advance Cabala only by limiting and confining it.

Cabala between Freud and Jung

This openness and seemingly infinite suggestibility of Cabala made not only for a certain salutary confusion that was very much a tradition but also for connections to other heterodoxies, experiments, and modifications of the Renaissance. We have seen a little how Pico was able to fill his Neoplatonic sails with cabalistic breeze— and convince at least a few well-placed others he was going in the right direction. A striking aspect of Reuchlin's "art," therefore, is that, building on a precedent for innovation of Pico's Neoplatonic Cabala, he ambitiously adds an alchemical dimension to it. For Reuchlin, as for C. J. Jung[18] in our own century, the alchemical search was a metaphor and symbol of mental and spiritual purification, transformation, and healing, a question of turning the dross matter of an everyday life into the gold of an inner truth. Whether Jung is dealing with Gnosticism, Alchemy, or the *I Ching*, the outer search is always a metaphor of inner progress. Quite the opposite was the case for Freud, for whom the inner state was displaced into outer events and behavior, not so much as symbols, as for Jung, but as symptoms. Their famous disagreement was therefore certainly over a matter of substance, not purely a result of egos in conflict. For Jung, Psychoanalysis would be a modern avatar of the ancient timeless project of the occult sciences—Alchemy, Hermeticism, Gnosticism—passing through the alembic, or purifying fires of which would result in a world- and self-transforming revelation. On the other hand, for Freud psychoanalytical therapy could only be an individual's courageous but doomed attempt to cope in himself with what was essentially incurable in the world and society. This was, is, and will always be that fundamental disharmony, disproportion, and alienation of men from each other and their cosmos that Spinoza (with Nietzsche in his eventual wake) insisted on facing. This cold universe of Spinoza and Freud would correspond, in Cabala, to the withdrawn kernel of unknowable creation. Whereas the aspiration of Jung would more connect, in cabalistic theosophy, with the level of the *sephiroth*-emanations, where knowledge, integration, and harmony, though high on a mountain, are still within the reach of the hardy climber. Once up there we may equal or surpass the very angels; but then, in relation to the secrets of creation and the mysteries of the primordial divine being, or *ain-soph*, what even do the angels know?

What the mystic, magician, or cabalist is creating in this new self, as represented by an alchemical gold of transformation, alike for Jung and for Reuchlin, is only the catalytic first step in a process whose issue is essentially redemptive. Such a discovery would be only the beginning of metamorphoses that potentially transform humanity, in a two-tiered process, for this gold of discovery and dissemination. For Reuchlin, according to Blau: "Cabala is a way of transforming external perceptions into internal perceptions; these into imagination; this into opinion; opinion into reason; reason into intelligence; intelligence into mind; and mind into light which illuminates mankind."[19]

Agrippa's Open Secret

Three sixteenth-century Italian-Franciscan monks were important in synthesizing and publicizing the doctrines of Pico and Reuchlin. These were J. P. Crispus, Franciscus Georgius, and Archangelus of Burgo Nuovo. J. P. Crispus attempted to carry on the Platonism of Pico, in the direction of a possible syncretism between conflicting elements in the church. Georgius, whose work was going to be widely influential for more than a century, published an outright cabalistic poem in 1529, *De Harmonia Mundi*, in which he uses the ideas of Pico and Reuchlin and also tries to establish a connection between the cabalists and the Pythagoreans. Archangelus is best known purely as a defender of Pico. He wrote two books in defense of the latter's "Cabalistic Conclusions" and a third that is an exposition of the concluding chapters of Reuchlin's *De Verbo Mirifico*.

As an example of the penetration of Cabala into political, ecclesiastical, and literary arenas of the period, none is more vivid than a very long poem, really a miniature epic that a French Franciscan, Jean Thenaud, dedicated in 1519 to Francis I, who had commissioned the work—which was entitled quite bluntly, *La Saincte et tréscrestienne cabale*. This poet's Cabala is mostly inspired by Pico. Tactically, its function seems to have been to attempt to move the church away from Dominican Thomism by means of the Neoplatonic doctrines that Pico found so plentifully in the Cabala. Blau prints some selections from it, which has come down in manuscript, adding also that this would be only the *tip of an iceberg* of similarly inspired writings, one of many examples of "the vast amount of manuscript material, spread over the libraries of Europe and America, which would indicate a far greater diffusion of cabalistic knowledge and speculation than can be proved from the printed literature."[20]

After Reuchlin, the most important sixteenth-century Christian student of the Cabala was Henry Cornelius Agrippa Von Nettesheim.[21] Agrippa was lead to Cabala by Reuchlin's *De Verbo Mirifico*, and as early as 1509, as a young man of 22, copying the mystical precocity of Pico, he had delivered a public exposition of Reuchlin's work. In 1510, while he was staying at Dean Colet's house in London, he was involved in a dispute with a Johannes Catilenet, who had attacked Agrippa's interest in cabalism as being heretical. So when, later that year, Agrippa submitted a major work, *On Occult Philosophy*, to the abbot Johannes Tritheim for his inspection and comment, Tritheim, while encouraging Agrippa in his occult and cabalistic studies, advised him to postpone publication of the book, due to the furor that was being aroused against the Cabala by the same Catilinet who had disputed with Agrippa in Colet's house.

On Occult Philosophy, finally published in Latin in 1533, is divided into three "books," the first of which takes up the idea that Agrippa seems to have borrowed from Pico (who in turn likely took it from Recenati's commentary on de Leon's Zohar) of a division of the cosmos into three corresponding realms: the material, the intellectual, and the celestial. To these three realms, Pico, in accord with his idealistic humanism, had added one of his own invention, that of *man*, which, however, Agrippa discreetly dropped, possibly because that would have entailed a special status and dignity for the human that might have offended an existing social hierarchy. Agrippa's overall emphasis, while holding onto the notion of Cabala as a mystical way to absolute knowledge, slides also into a more "handbook" dimension of its earthly usefulness. This is a tendency we have seen at work before in the practical though more innocent (of material incentives) theurgic-meditative cabalism of Abulafia. This approach to Cabala is still current today, both on the level of "cults" and, more aptly I think, *in the use of the metaphors of zoharic thought to decry and define our current fantasies of instant power in our own manipulated worlds*. A good example of the latter would be Sol Yurick's far-ranging essay, *Metatron*, where the "wonder-working" words of Renaissance cabalism are considered as anticipations and forerunners of a compulsive but finally delusory "magic" of modern technology.

Indeed, by the end of the first book of *On Occult Philosophy* we find Agrippa blatantly suggesting the feasibility and implying the desirability of magic by means of the enunciation of Hebrew letters and formulas: "There are, therefore [in the Hebrew alphabet] one and twenty letters, which are the foundations of the world, and of the creatures that are, and are named in it, and every saying and every creature are of them, and by their revolutions receive their name, being and virtue . . . hence voices and words have efficacy in magical works, because that in which Nature first exerciseth magical efficacy is the voice of God."[22]

This is not at all to underestimate the variety, density, sincerity, and authenticity of Agrippa's profoundly influential and important studies, lectures, and writings in and about the "dark sciences" of the Renaissance—Hermeticism, Neoplatonism, Magic, and Cabala, with forays into religious reform and a kind of incipient feminism—concluding, weirdly, in a kind of knowledge-weary skepticism that inspired the passionate refutation of Michel de Montaigne's longest essay, "The Apology of Raymond Sebond." The work that Montaigne and his generation was so concerned about was not, however, so much the blatantly manipulative *Occult Philosophy*, which the influential Jean Bodin had already discredited in *La Démonomanie* of 1580, but another by Agrippa that embraced a stance that was even more disturbing than Agrippa's magical and cabalistic divagations. This was the awesomely comprehensive and all-condemning *On Vanity*, published in Latin in 1531, translated into English and French and very widely circulated by the end of the sixteenth century (comparatively well known ever since and probably most readable for moderns because most urbanely polished, not to mention "grinningly funny" of Agrippa's major works). In this iconoclastic text, Agrippa, writing in 1526, apparently in a period of poverty and disillusionment, seemingly rejects the kind of arcane studies that had been his life's work and created his fame and/or notoriety, retreating to a position of pure fideism of faith and grace instead, and cynical especially about any chance that mere intellect(s) could probe the mysteries or grant the powers that seemed so accessible before. Here, however, as seems natural if not linear, the sin comes *after* the repentance, for 1533, or two years after the rejection of the lures of Cabala and related occult styles, saw finally the publication of Agrippa's blatantly magical *Occult Philosophy*, originally written in 1510 but which, as substantial additions prove, he had been rewriting ever since.

Charles Nauert amply documents Agrippa's continued interest in such matters well beyond the epoch of his "retraction."[23] Nauert interprets, indeed, *Of Vanity* to be more of a purification and control of magic and heterodoxy than their rejection. Since Nauert's emphasis is more on the beginnings of science than the ends of magic, for him, Agrippa, as a forerunner of methods of hypothesis and experimentation, liked to explore the possibilities for thought that were unfolding so vertiginously in the Renaissance, even if here the possibility Agrippa was exploring was that thought had no possibilities. Whether magical or empirical, Agrippan "science," together with his retraction of same, was considered far from innocent during the Renaissance and long after. It was considered incriminating, for example, that Urban Grandier (burned alive, 1634), accused of bewitching and seducing the nuns of Loudun, was acquainted with the works of Agrippa. It was surely no coincidence, also, that the woman most deeply touched or corrupted by Urbain, Sister Jeanne of the Angels, was given, during her moments of Satanic transport, to uttering names of cabalistic entities or spirits.[24]

At the very beginning of *The Vanity of Arts and Sciences*, as his book was called in an edition of 1694, Agrippa seems eager to dispel a suspicion that he must have recognized had gathered around his name. He let us know in no uncertain terms that there is a cabalism that no longer commands his respect, that espoused by those who suppose "that Science . . . enables them to translate themselves beyond the limits of Humanity, even to the Celestial Seats of the Blessed."[25] The problem for Agrippa here with progress-promoting styles is not in the techniques themselves but in the inherently mischievous and malicious nature, apart from a few rare exceptions perhaps, of the creatures who employ them. Some- one who trusts to such methods in the area of religion becomes, therefore, in Agrippa's eyes, what he calls "a perfidious Cabalist," a hopeless person precisely because "there is nothing more deadly than to be as it were rationally mad." However cabalism is merely one of a vast range of discredited avenues, in a list that follows on an absolutely *brutal* allusion to a strangely cynical myth, perhaps not so far fetched, of the ancient gnostic sect of Ophites, or serpent worshipers, according to which the original *inventors* were the sons of Cain:

There were no other Inventors of Arts than Men themselves, yet were they the sons of the worst generation, even the sons of *Cain* . . . If men be therefore the Inventors of Arts, is it not said, *Every man is a lyer, neither is there one that doth good*? But grant on the other side, that there may be some good men; yet follows not that the *Sciences* themselves have any- thing of virtue, anything of truth in them, but what they reap and borrow from the Inventors and possessors thereof. For if they light upon any evil Person, they are as hurtful as a perverse *Grammarian*, an *ostentatious Poet*, a *lying Historian*, a *flattering Rhetorician*, a *litigious Logician*, a turbulent *Sophister*, a *loquacious Lullist*, a *Letterist Arithmetician* [gematrian?], a *lascivious Musician*, a shameless *Dancing- master*, a boasting *Geometrician*, a wondering *Cosmographer*, a pernicious *Architect*, a *Pirate-Navigator*, a fallacious *Astrolo- ger*, a wicked *Magician*, a perfidious *Cabalist*, a dreaming *Naturalist*, a Wonder-feigning *Metaphysician*, a morose *Eth- ics*, a treacherous *Politician*, a tyrannical *Prince*, an oppress- ing *Magistrate*, a seditious *People*, a *Schismatical Priest*, a *superstitious Monk*, a prodigal Husband, a bargain-breaking *Merchant*, a pilling *Customer*, a slothful Husbandman, a care- less *Shepard*, an envious Fisherman, a bawling Hunter, a plundering Souldier, an exacting Landlord, a *murderous* Phy- sician, a poisonous *Apothecary*, a glutton-Cook, a deceitful Alchymist, a jugling *Lawyer*, a perfidious Notary, a bribe-tak- ing Judge, and a heretical and seducing Divine. So that there is nothing more ominous than Art & Knowledge guarded with impiety, seeing that every man becomes a ready Inventor, and learned Author of evil things. If it light upon a person that is not so *evil* as fooling, there is nothing more insolent or Dogmatical, having besides its own headstrong obstinacy, the authority of learning and the weapons of Argument to defend its fury; which other fools wanting are more tame and quietly men."[26]

A likely effect of such an avalanche or assault on all conceivable notions, attitudes, and styles, except a self-erasing one of total suspicion, was to move, or "exile" the reader from belief in the connection between sign and referent, with the former becoming correspondingly autonomous and intransitive. Such endless lists as these, whether in The Zohar or in Agrippa, seem to end not because of any real closure or conclusion, but out of fatigue and despair, because the author has run out of words, it being as impossible to say what one means as it would be to give up trying. Enumerations and lists are intrinsically frustrating, according to Paul Zumthor, for whom "any enumeration errs either through being too much or too little." For Agrippa, as for the great French rhetoricians of the sixteenth century who preoccupy Paul Zumthor, his *style* becomes *what* he is saying: "At least, intrinsically, insofar as available structure, accumulation always produces a double effect. Lexically, it valorizes at once quantity and the concrete, in opposition to pure abstract qualities: it names things, calls them to existence, *hic et nunc*, juxtaposes them, in their disarray; without coordinating them, it engenders thereby something like an excess of reality that corrodes verisimilitude. It is for this reason that Bakhtine counts it among the carnavelesque figures. Syntactically . . . the syntagmatic tie attaches to another non-cumulative element; it disperses, separates, dismantles . . . A descriptive discourse is reduced to a series of dissociated unities, accumulation demanding of the world that it be able to be said,— but that it be said outside of all 'common sense'."[27]

Any alchemy of the word, then, as far as Renaissance rhetoric is concerned, would rather be a work of deconstruction and decomposition than creation or accomplishment. Agrippa's *On Vanity*, therefore, would correspond to this advanced stage of the process or work whereby, paradoxically, only by the *destruction of the laboratory* can the experiment proceed or hope to succeed. Zumthor calls this phase, the throes of which, according to him, French literature and European culture was passing through in the late fifteenth and the early sixteenth centuries, a "time of illusion" or "jonglerie," which is when "The signifier, become available, claims its autonomy... However, under the cover of the old system, what is aimed at is no longer transmutation of matter, but rather its decomposition, for from the decomposed universe there will emerge, possibly, finally the philosophical gold. Through matter thereby the spirit [l'esprit] is liberated, which redeems it by breaking these ties [between signifier and signified]: this poetry, just like the Great Work, and in the same sense, is an 'art of love'."[28]

Agrippa, however, is not really abandoning Cabala, even in this "book of renunciations," just perhaps a certain practical-magical cabalism, with which possibly he felt he had been overly identified. For, indeed, cabalistic metaphors and figures permeate this text, which as it proceeds becomes in fact more affirmative and straightforward while losing none of its edge of bitter sarcasm. This cabalistic vocabulary, which allows him to be positive without ceasing to be critical and provocative, tends to emerge whenever Agrippa tries to be specific about the kinds of attitudes he approves of. Accordingly he extols, in a chapter called "Of the Cabalists," *after* a lengthy refutation of the self-same cabalistic-numerological exegetical styles he himself had became famous for promoting, a sort of primordial wisdom or Cabala beyond words: "For there being most high mysteries and therefore they are not written, nor to be written; but to be kept in silence among the Wise Men, who are to reserve them in the most secret parts of their Hearts."[29]

Nor is Agrippa's tone mocking in the least as he enunciates the *founding* narrative of Cabala, that is the episode of Moses' experience of a dual vision on Mt. Sinai: a lesser one that was outward and external, though dramatic and spectacular, because product of the face-to-face meeting, the other a prophetic vision, based on Moses' weirdly privileged glimpse of "another side" of God, a hidden part that becomes the basis of a cabal for all future ages: "Moses enjoyed both these visions, as the Scriptures witness. Of the first, we read that *Moses* saw God *face-to-face*. As to the other, we read what God spake therein: *Thou shalt see my hinder parts*.

And by the means of this later vision *Moses* made a Law, instituted Sacrifices and Ceremonies, built a Tabernacle and other Mysteries, according to the most elaborate exemplar of the whole world, comprehending all the secret works of God and Nature therein."[30]

Of Vanity, far from a refutation of Cabala, more likely was an attempt to disseminate a higher form of it. Agrippa's Christ himself seems very much the cabalist whose mission it was to turn what had become a hieratic, esoteric teaching into an egalitarian, accessible, and ultimately revolutionary one. A universal Christian *cabal*, or knowledge of the word of God, was meant to relay a more restricted Jewish one, according to which only a single people were to be privileged. Here Agrippa is in harmony with a generalization of mystical experience that was to have such awesome consequences in the next century in the mass-appeal messianic movement of Sabbatai Zevi, and also in the English Puritan Revolution of Levelers, Diggers, Ranters, and Fifth Monarchists. An expression, contemporary with Agrippa, of this marriage of mysticism and insurrection was the extirpated Münster anabaptist-communist episode. Thomas Münzer, charismatic leader of the Peasant Revolt and inspiration of the coming Münster "New Jerusalem" (1534–1535), forerunner of all modern revolutionary utopias, was executed in 1525, at the age of thirty six. Agrippa composed *Of Vanity* in 1526. The threat of Anabaptism obviously had a powerful effect on the imagination of the period, and long after. We find Thomas Nashe's lumpen "gentleman traveler," Jack Wilton, alluding with much irony to Agrippa's fame as magician-conjurer,[31] execrating the Münster movement at length, seventy years later in *The Unfortunate Traveller* (published 1594), for its assault on social order, property, and hierarchy.[32] Nevertheless the excesses involved in the extirpation of the "heresy" led even a personage as cynical as the narrator of the novel, Jack Wilton, to abandon, in disgust, his military career: "With the tragical catastrophe of this Münsterian conflict did I cashier the new vocation of my cavaliership. There was no more honourable wars in Christendom."[33]

Surely the defiance of Agrippa's *On Vanity* Christ, his warnings against the pretentions of any privileged access to the divine, would go along well with the insousiance toward hierarchy of an Anabaptist revolutionary, as well as imply the willingness to act on such class-challenging convictions: " 'Ye are not to think that it [insight into divine mysteries] belongeth onely to divines, but to every one, man & woman's, old & young; so that everyone, according to the space & capacity given to them, is bound to have knowledge thereof . . . ' Christ commanded his Gospel to be preached to all creatures throughout the whole world; and this not in the dark, *not whispered in the ear*, not in private chambers, not to some particular Doctors & Scribes; but openly, upon the house tops, to the people, to the multitude . . . For this cause, Christ chose his Apostles not Scribes, not Doctors, not priests, but unlearned persons of the vulgar people, void of knowledge, unkillful, and Asses."[34]

Agrippa's advice to look rather at the bottom of the social ladder for sanctity is in accord also with cabalistic attitudes. The mule driver who is an angelic *illuminati* in disguise or heavenly visitor is indeed one of the characteristic features in Cabala. Such a type is in fact one of the basic narrators in The Zohar, which likes so frequently to gather its wisdom from the unlikeliest sources. In a lengthy section, called *Sava*, or *The Old Man*, a donkey driver reveals himself as a great cabalist, which means, essentially, a heavenly visitor in earthly disguise.[35] A humble exterior is sure clue, zoharically, to inner sanctity and rank. The eighteenth-century cabalist and founder of modern Hasidism, the Baal Shem, was supposed, accordingly, to have spent decades hiding his light while exercising the profession of wagon driver and pretending to be an illiterate.[36] This same cabalist passion to look for the extraordinary in the seeming ordinary has been expressed in modern times no more intensely than in the stories of Bruno Schulz: "Where is truth to shelter, where is it to find asylum if not in a place where nobody is looking for it: in fairground calendars and almanacs, in the canticles of beggars and tramps?"[37]

Hardly haphazard, therefore, is Agrippa's direct allusion to cabalistic Hebrew-mystical sources for his burlesque defense, in a hilarious Shandean chapter that comes close to concluding his book, "Digression in Praise of an Ass," against the self-accusation of blasphemy for having called an Apostle an ass. Cabalistically it turns out that calling someone an ass, in fact, a beast that was born and bred only to carry and to serve, is the very highest praise: "But lest anyone should flatly acuse me that I have called the Apostles Asses, it will not be from the purpose to discourse the Mysteries of the Ass. For this Creature the Hebrew Doctors expound to be the

Hieroglyphic of Fortitude, Strength, Patience & Clemency: and that his influence depends on *Sephiroth*, that is *Hochma*, which signifies wisdom."[38] Lurking not far away surely are other "asinine" echos and resonances: a gnostic-Egyptian *asinus portans mysteria* [mystery-carrying ass], as well as Balaam's speaking ass in scripture. The moral of all this could be, as Dogberry proves in *Much Ado About Nothing*, "be careful whom you call an ass"! Impossible, in this connection, to leave untouched Agrippa's baroque association of Cabala with Moses' glimpse of what his translator calls, euphemistically, after the discreet King James version, "the hinder parts of God"—which makes calling the Apostle "God's Ass" high praise indeed!

Agrippa and His Shadow

Agrippa's skeptical mood differs from that which Montaigne was to adopt fifty years later principally in that it was more urgent, radical, and exigent, demanding of the reader not only a renunciation of the complacencies of received knowledge but also what might amount to implicitly insurrectionary "acts of faith" that risk disturbing and provoking established hierarchies. Montaigne's answer to this kind of extremism was to pose, coyly, the skeptic's question to himself as to the basis for his very doubt: How do I know that I don't know? For Montaigne and others, who wanted to think of Agrippa as a libertine cynic and dabbler, his recantations, as well, surely as his prior cabalistic "magic," were the strategies of a desperate atheism that therefore stood urgently in need of response and qualification. Already in his century, Agrippa, indeed, was being stereotyped and parodied in some of its most illustrious works: Agrippa is assigned by Thomas Nashe's Jack Wilton, whom we've met before as the enemy of Anabaptism, the role of tour guide for the Earl of Surrey in Germany, where his job is to conjure up wax-museum visions of "Erasmus, Sir Thomas More, Thomas Cromwell and Charles V, as well as the famous vision of the fair Geraldine who appeared to Surrey."[39]

Well before then Agrippa had turned up as the confused and muddle-headed astrologer, the cuckolded Herr Trippa in Rabelais's *Tiers Livre*,[40] and also as the model for Marlowe's Doctor Faustus, in the play by the same name in which Agrippa is even alluded to once directly in the context of damnation:

> Tis magic, magic that hath ravished me
> And I, that have with subtle syllogisms
> Gravelled the pastors of the German Church
> And made the flowering pride of Wittenberg
> Swarm to my problems as the infernal spirits
> On sweet Musaeus when he came to hell,
> Will be as cunning as Agrippa was,
> *Whose shadow made all Europe honor him.*[41]

This "shadow of Agrippa," which represents *conjuring of spirits and demons* in the text, also may stand for a controversial association of the extravagant goals that were defined by the occult sciences with an intrinsically amoral technology that was meant to realize them. Essentially this doubt typically thrown on the reputation, achievements, and intentions of Agrippa has to do with a question, now more urgent than ever, of a disproportion between human knowledge and wisdom.

What shadows our knowledge is the suspicion that our catastrophic century has brought closer to conviction—that it doesn't make us any wiser. Quite the contrary, it makes destruction, in all its subtle guises, so much easier. This shadow falls also over Goethe's *Faust*, as more recently over Thomas Mann's novelistic reworking of the Faust legend, *Doctor Faustus*. Contemporaneously with Goethe, it was from Agrippa's *Occult Philosophy* that Frankenstein, in Mary Shelley's novel, claims to have "received the fatal impulse that led to my ruin."[42] For Goethe, also, that same iconoclastic Agrippa who attacked the value of all knowledge in *On Vanity*, a reading of which triggered an intellectual crisis in his youth,[43] was as alive and disturbing as the magical one that was seeking for special powers and dispensations. In Goethe's creation of the character of Faust, indeed, the cynical Agrippa of *On Vanity* and the blatantly cabalist one of *Occult Philosophy* come or work together in a supernal-infernal-harmony-cacophony. Faust's renowned inventory of "useless knowledge" that opens his first scene in Goethe's play, motivates, indeed, the recourse to the occult strategies that eventually backfire on the protagonist.

This ambivalence in occult studies generally and Cabala in particular, especially here as it comes through Agrippa, between truth and power and the temptation to conflate the two, or to define the latter in the personal terms of limitless aggrandizement, had caused a devolution frequently of the image of cabalist as someone who goes to extraordinary lengths to achieve ordinary things. So Marlowe's Agrippan Doctor Faustus performs the miracle of obtaining grapes in December,[44] forerunner certainly of the overwhelmingly trivial pursuits and outlets of the miracles of modern technology, going nowhere ever faster. What protected the integrity of the earlier Jewish masters of Cabala, as well as their Christian acolytes, was their "outsider mentality," that is, the intrinsically exilic and marginal nature of their project, essentially, as mystical discourse tends to be, turned inward. Even when there were social consequences and repercussions they did not need to judge themselves by the world's increasingly secular standards, but just be able to occupy some sheltered corner of it. On the other hand, someone like Agrippa was a mystic, magician, and cabalist *as well as* many other things: legal scholar, university professor (always, however, as was Paracelsus, hired on the temporary and vulnerable basis we call *adjunct* today), and world-traveled and invited lecturer. He, therefore, was expected to, and did in fact, take positions on the crucial political and ethical issues of his day. Such an individual must have been prepared to bear the brunt of some powerful contradictions as well as challenges. It is asked of such a person, for example, that whatever truths he has garnered from his arcane researches be translated quickly into the social terms of power and efficacy. For Cabala, and its proclaimed fidelity to the "word" of God was not and could not be, with Agrippa, Paracelsus, and their experimental generation the only loyalty and focus, when there was so much else that had to be taken into consideration. There were provocative trends of the time that had to be harmonized and reconciled: Dualism, Alchemy, Astrology, Numerology, Pythagoreanism, Neo-Paganism and Stoicism, as well as Christian-Erasmian Humanism. Exigent also were the immediately pressing concerns of the Catholic establishment with the Protestant challenge (pressed *also* by its "Radical Reformation"-Within-the-Reformation) looming up very visibly, so that everything said of significance tended to take sides, with all that implied in terms of security, not to mention very real risks of annihilation.

The imperatives of an increasingly secular-materialistic society and a capitalist order that establish *their* community on the basis of an individual's ability to command strength and resources, as well as cunning and calculation in their disposition, cannot be ignored, or not for long, *if* the promoters of any "new" approach, however idealistic, are to endure. In such a practical world all transcendental styles of understanding, devotion, and cultivation inevitably are called upon to observe a bottom line of the immanent needs and strategies of the moment. Cabala, as were other occult styles in the Renaissance, was called upon to fulfill the very material needs they were created to nuance and transform. They were summoned to play a universal competitive game, to become that edge sought by an individual to come out ahead in a struggle for predominance that our culture reads as survival. That in this process of transmission, promotion, and communication, something would be lost is evident. According to the doctrine of correspondences, for instance, that is intrinsic to the Cabala and that the Christian Renaissance received from zoharic and other sources, as well as from Neoplatonism, Alchemy, and Hermeticism, a modification in one realm is a modification in all; but it is the particular, if understandable impatience and distortion of magical methods to assume that the realms can be manipulated, monkeyed with, therefore, at will. In this incipient "culture of the instant" it is taken for granted that a new costume, mask, or disguise, a new power or gimmick is equal to elevation, height, and sublimity. Quite otherwise, in the *occult traditions* that open up the possibilities of a transformation, changes are produced much more slowly, more a matter of years, decades, lifetimes—as in Henri Bergson's renowned metaphor for "creative evolution"—the cube of sugar in the cup of tea: you have to *wait* for it to *melt*. Any enduring development, alteration or "epiphany" depends, first of all, on the attainment of a state of inner readiness and on an exhaustive, patient, and demanding preparation, study, and action, and *not* on the quick compulsive performance of a ritual or pronunciation of any formula.

For better or worse, Agrippa's *Occult Philosophy* seems to have become a part of the cultural vocabulary of the West by 1550, and all indications are, by the number of editions and frequent references to it in other works, that it was well known for at least the three ensuing centuries; but, as we have seen before, the price of popularity seems often to be loss of authenticity, to the point where what remains of the awesome energy, variety, and erudition of Agrippa's efforts to expand the mind of his public seems to be a

mere defiance, purely, of any and all authority, holiness, sacredness, or tradition. Agrippa, the mage who aspired to the heavens
had become the condign atheist and scoffer, anxious to drag all
others down to hell to keep him company, in a process whereby the
Neoplatonic, Hermeticist, cabalist priest or rabbi becomes identified
with the lowest form of exploiting magician, debunker and trickster, and one whose motivation is all too human. In addition, the
name of Agrippa in particular seems to be associated by the end of
the sixteenth century with a kind of libertinism, that, for instance,
of the French *forts esprits* who saw all religious and social systems
as being subservient to power relations. From this point of view
cabalistic notions and figures were seen to be more mystifying than
mystical, the cabalists being merely the cunning manipulators of a
religion they themselves believed in only to the extent that it was,
as Karl Marx was to call it a few hundred years later, "the opium
of the people." For example, the works of Henoch Clapham (fl.
1600), a once popular, if now deservedly forgotten, religious author
of the period, are replete with pejorative references to cabalism
that habitually point to the worldly motivation behind its transcendental claims; thus, a libertine character he calls, simply, an "atheist" suggests cynically the iconoclastic intent behind any "fancy"
scriptural hermeneutics, in a pamphlet-dialogue published in 1608,
in London: "Tut, the writers of the scriptures were very politick
men. The summer [commentator] of *Tragus Pompeius* notes Moses
to have been a very politick Captaine, and Joseph a notable Magician, who well know that such an itchie people as *Israel*, would
never be kept under, but by propounding some forms of Religion."[45]

Such a clumsy parody of cabalism's ideas and intentions is, of
course, a gross distortion and misrepresentation of the complexity
and seriousness of Agrippa's thought, which is obviously being
targeted here, more or less personally. It might be said, indeed,
that, far from defining things in rigid categories and dismissing all
opposition to them as naïveté, Agrippa floated or problematized his
whole occult system by publishing its retraction even before it appeared in print. Cabala, for Agrippa, is the farthest thing from
dogma imaginable. Instead, it is something that changes and grows
as one's understanding does and therefore can be applied to the
dynamics and mutability of everyday life, as in his original adaptation of zoharic exegesis to the momentary requirements of the

feminist controversy. There is no finalized form for Agrippa's Cabala, any more than there is one for the other arcane objects of his passion and interest, which remain, instead, merely a series of intriguing conjectures, suggestions, hypotheses, and possibilities.

If, for example, in Book One of *Occult Philosophy* he is being rather literal and tempting about the magic and power of (Hebrew) letters, by Book Two he has advanced to the more abstract dimension of a cabalistic numerology, or *gematria*, challenging his student in a different way, who always must move on and up or leave the ship, as Agrippa once does himself, with *On Vanity*, as suspicious as the magic it had renounced. Here again, even in abandoning, he is far from definitive. Agrippa's availability, flexibility, and curiosity are in evidence not only within texts but from work to work, always reaching out to the works and experience of others—a notable example of which is how he is able to keep learning from Reuchlin's pioneering dedication to and study of the Cabala. *Occult Philosophy*, composed in 1510, circulated widely in manuscript for the more than twenty years before it was published while Agrippa and others thought about its message and what its audience might make of it. The Third Book, therefore, of this work, as published in 1533, has opened up to receive the intervening results of Reuchlin's deepening knowledge of cabalistic sources in their original Hebrew, published in the latter's *De Arte cabalistica* of 1517. Agrippa therefore borrows extensively from Reuchlin's later studies for a discussion of the subtleties and science of the Tetragrammaton or name of God. Nauert, who has compared the 1510 manuscript of *Occult Philosophy* with the 1533 published version, remarks the vastly expanded range of cabalistic references and allusions in the later text, which he attributes both to Agrippa's ongoing receptiveness and the intervening appearance of Reuchlin's second book on the subject.[46]

Whatever Agrippa's modifications of Cabala tradition, and they sometimes seem to be substantial, unquestionably there is a humor and a deferral in his presentation of it, a plenitude and variety of quotation and authority, and a tentativeness that is very much in the spirit of The Zohar. A flagrant departure from zoharic precedent was, for instance, Agrippa's *De Origine peccato* [Original Sin], a treatise of 1518 in which the fall of Adam and Eve is described as having been sexual. Nauert cites this as possible evidence of

Agrippa's lack of acquaintance with The Zohar.[47] However this judgment might be qualified in view of the context. Agrippa was serious enough as a student of Cabala for something so salient as zoharic "sacred sex" not to have escaped him; but here I think, instead, Agrippa's momentary motivation was strategic and conjunctural, in the sense that he liked to shake, provoke, and disturb, assailing his readers where they live, as it were.

Adding to this impalpability and availability is the very quality of Agrippa's style or rhetoric, whereby we are often unsure to what extent the author is in accord with or is taking distance sarcastically, ironically, or academically from the opinion or text cited, of which there are myriads. The page typically takes on the quality of a list of erudite allusions and references, as if what was intended was a cultural morass of options through which the readers are forced to create their paths. Agrippa's style of rhetoric, with its provoking-confounding effect was not, of course rare in the period, when what was new was not only print but also the kind of reader and reading publication would bring, and as a matter of fact, this "anxious style" was preceded by a century-long evolution of literary attitude from the idea that words reflect truth to a suspicion that language could only deceive. From the point of view of the later product of what Paul Zumthor calls "an exilic type of culture," that reader who believes most in what the words are merely saying would be the one who was the most profoundly duped: "In a culture that is globally classifiable under the integrated type, intertextuality functions as a process of elimination of ambiguity, implying the conviction that specific truths are possible; in an exilic type of culture, this function is inverted (process of 'lying', no specific truth is conceivable). The European 15th century, and my rhetoricians eminently, are situated in a historical moment where the first type begins to fall into the second . . . From which [result] the apparent incoherence of behavior and discourse, the predominance, by turns, of a desire for integration and of a desire or constatation of exile." It is not surprising equally that this "rhetoric of exile" has a natural interest in and affinity with the occult and mystical ideologies and texts, including Cabala, which were starting to find a wider European audience at the end of the fifteenth century. Zumthor mentions specifically, in connection with the style of his rhetoricians, the texts of Agrippa, as part of a "wave from the East" that started with "hermetical writings . . . that crossed from Italy to Greece as early as 1462, and were known in France by 1494. In 1505 Henri Estienne published the *Pimander* [a basic Hermetic text of ancient provenance] [bound] together with a dialogue of the cabalist Lazzarelli, procured by Lefevre d'Étaples; 14 years later Jean Thenaud[48] dedicated his cabalistic treatise in verse to Francis I." [49]

Agrippa has understood all too well how to create a zoharic insecurity whereby the reader, while admiring much, would likely be at a loss to recognize what exactly is being recommended and in what spirit. What Agrippa had to say about Cabala as well as other occult currents had as much to do with provoking, exciting, and stimulating his contemporary audience as relaying a "truth" that could, by its very nature, never exist in any finished version. In fact, it was very likely this very principle of uncertainty and indeterminacy, of limitless possibility that resulted, in some cases, through an understandable if regrettable impatience, in the premature closures and pejorative stereotypes his entire project was quickly subject to and has continued to be up to our own century.

The Two Laws

That very basic and founding Cabala notion of the two laws, one given to Moses as a written text, or set of commandments, the other the oral tradition, spoken in his ear, or Cabal, allows Agrippa this room to move from position to position as the time and inspiration require or invite. By its very nature an oral communication has no final form but always invites a following one, especially when compared to the relatively stable aura of the inscribed or written. However, a practice of writing, of research, whose model is the evanescence, the aliveness of the verbal, necessarily reminds one of its contingency in the moment of its being set down. This notion of the room allowed by the idea of the two laws, oral and written, of Moses, endemic to Cabala, seems to have taken root quite early in Agrippa's consciousness. In a book he published in 1515, *The Threefold way of Understanding God*, Agrippa's purpose is to define a syncretic area where all faiths converge in terms of this binary model of Mosaic reception. Just as a Jewish Cabala could stretch the holy letters of Torah into shapes that could cover the contingencies of the present, a Christian Cabala would find its way around texts and dogmas that were obstacles to the realization of the Renaissance ideals of humanism and syncretism. Cabala could provide a prestigious and hallowed example of an alternative, a bypassing, transcendence, an overcoming, in short, an *aufhebung* of the literal, the traditional, the assumed. This had the potential of sweeping all received wisdom aside, including ultimately, as in the later recantation of Agrippa, *itself*. Meanwhile, the notion of a primordial Mosaic polysemy would work its modifying magic on the prejudices of religious monosemy, insisting otherwise that "even the Gospel, like the Mosaic law, has one meaning on the surface for the more simple, another in its core, which has been separately revealed to the perfect."[50]

It is only fair, then, to admit that however debased, altered, or distorted his image was in popular and/or literary works, where it has served seemingly as a marker or warning as to the limits and dangers of certain kinds of unusual, secret, or unapproved knowledge, the thrust of Agrippa's project and career was toward awakening and maintaining a sense of the novelty, power, wisdom, and relevance of human possibilities, especially as they relate to the mystical traditions, *Cabala* very prominently among them. Indeed, it was through him that Cabala left the mystic's cell or scholar's study and entered vigorously into the arena of the socially controversial, a secular area beyond the earlier theological debates on the question of relative orthodoxy. Beyond the wild, if surreal and fascinating, Neoplatonic divagations of a Pico, the monkish eccentricity of that rare and stubborn Christian Hebraist, Reuchlin, it was Agrippa's treatment and communication of the subject, its wide and open mindedness, susceptibility to modification, wit, humor, and erudition that brought Cabala into the public domain and kept it there for so long. Therefore what Waite says about Agrippa seems quite fitting, especially in view of the way he has been underestimated over the centuries: "It is to him that we owe the first methodical description of the whole Kabbalistic system ... and his three books, entitled *DE OCCULTA PHILOSOPHIA*, are practically the starting point of Kabbalistic knowledge among Latin reading scholars of Europe."[51]

Agrippa's advance over those who influenced him was due to his imagination, flexibility, and nerve in exploring a vein of esoteric lore or hidden history that had been uncovered by the international dissemination of Cabala, in order to deal with some of the concrete issues of the day. He, for instance, gave a new dignity to the Renaissance debate over whether there was still a place for magic in the dawning world of empirical science, by establishing continuity between magical philosophy, practices, and ideals and the cabalistic precedents. So, for a significant figure in the theosophical and Neoplatonic revival of the seventeenth century, Thomas Vaughan, Agrippa is very much an anchor and a master, especially at the beginning of Vaughan's dazzling and dangerous "mystical career" that combined poetry and alchemy with Cabala.[52] *Occult Philosophy* was how one came to know of such things, a vast panoply of an area of knowledge that supplied generations with its introduction to realms of study and efficacy that provided alternatives both to traditional religious authority (scholastic Aristotelianism) and customary epistemological methods (deduction from the authority of unexamined premises), and thereby provided inspiration and precedent for its readers to venture on their own.

Agrippa's texts remained, indeed, strangely open and fluid for their readers—the way we have seen the writings and ideas of Cabala have always been—who then felt free to experiment with them. In Vaughan's case Agrippa's Cabala seems to have been pulled into two directions, first "upward" toward providing a vocabulary of an ambitious, far ranging mystical speculation and aspiration, then "downward," toward conjuring and magic powers, which is also very much a part of the Agrippan legacy. In a bold misreading of the "master," Vaughan added to his 1665 edition of the *Three Books of Occult Philosophy* a *Fourth Book*, discovered shortly after Agrippa's death, but which, because it amounted to really a manual of practical magic, had been almost universally regarded as spurious. This discourse of magic was a very different thing in the seventeenth century, after Bacon and Descartes, than in a sixteenth-century London fresh from the visit of Giordano Bruno. Magic, and the idealism it became allied to, with the Cambridge Platonists,[53] was now a protest and a rebellion against the scientific trivialization of humanity, conveying a message of integration and synthesis against the increasingly dominant spirit of fragmentation and analysis. Thomas Vaughan and the Cambridge Platonists were willing to utilize heterodox methods to deal with orthodox issues,

that is to descend from the heights of Platonic-Pythagorean speculation into the social arena. In this they very much followed in the
footsteps of Agrippa, who liked nothing better than to deploy
magical-numerological speculation in order to clarify mundane
issues.

A good example of this "descent" of Agrippa's Cabala into the
area of empirical issues and problems was Agrippa's clear, if theoretical, feminism, at a certain point in his career, which we've
touched on a few times. His treatise on this subject, *Female Pre-
Eminence*, first composed in 1509 reached a wide and sympathetic
public during the Renaissance; it had been translated three separate times into English by 1670,[54] once even into heroic couplets.
Here Agrippa deploys a wide range of cabalist ploys, strategies,
and arguments in praise of women, who emerge not merely as
men's equals but easily their betters. First of all, picking up on a
remark that occurs in The Zohar, or, perhaps having noticed it in
summaries or commentaries of that book that were circulating,
woman's very name, *Eve*, in numerological terms, is closer to the
Tetragrammaton, or God's, which approximates her *more nearly*
than man to the divine. Secondly, the very meaning of her name
indicated a relative elevation over men, since Eve means "life,"
while Adam merely designates the lowly earth out of which life is
to come. Thirdly, she is the last, most recent, therefore the most
perfected, "latest model," of God's creations, *and* the only one who
was born in Paradise. Paradise, "Pardes," or *Garden* in Hebrew, it
bears repeating, is a word of profoundly cabalistic resonance, each
letter of which conveys a different exegetical-existence level. Through
their studies, actions, and devotions the cabalists are said to make,
temporarily, a Paradise on earth, to which God likes, periodically,
to come and sport among his faithful. Woman, who was created
there more newly is the way of fastest access to the numinous, as
if always afterward there is nothing between her and the divine,
whereas *she* stands between man and the world above.

These hyperboles, though supported by cabalistic learning, are,
of course, an obvious response and reaction to the calumnies of
women that were a solidly entrenched Judeo-Christian doctrinal
and polemical tradition, blaming her initially for that first exile
and expulsion from Eden; and a dialogue-argument between mi-
sogyny and feminism was a familiar topic in Renaissance debate.

However, Agrippa is surely deeply enough imbued in Cabala for us to sense behind his provocative and dramatic exaggerations on the superiority of the female the prestige of the *Shekinah* figure, feminine emanation of the divine that is a specific contribution of Cabala and The Zohar to an awakening of esteem for women in the Renaissance. If, indeed, the cabalist worshiped and studied with men, so as to produce the charming force that would attract the visits from above, it was, on the other hand, *only through the woman* that a divine presence could be experienced and lived at its maximal intensity—and that only through the passage and challenge of sexual intimacy. This is contrary to the constitutional mysogyny of a certain Christian-Platonic tradition, already solidly established in the Renaissance, which climaxes in the nineteenth century in the witty disdain of a Kierkegaard or a Baudelaire for the woman, according to which, by the very fate of her fluxes and fertility, she is considered to be baser, more earthly and material than man. *Quite the contrary*, according to cabalistic logic, as relayed by Agrippa: for woman, created in Paradise and *above* the earth, from a walking, standing, upright being (*man*, made of earth *himself*), is therefore of a finer, more gossamer matter. Therefore, she is always already closer to Heaven, or does not have as far to go.

It is symptomatic also that when Cabala, as here through Agrippa, becomes engaged in worldly issues and arguments, it seems to seek out those points where social relations and hierarchical arrangements are at their most molten, fluid, and questionable, ushering in an "anxiety of the new" with all the authority of an ancient but dormant wisdom. Cabala always connotes motion, both in the way a past is conceived and the way a future is anticipated. It is, therefore, a great reformer, originator, innovator, and challenger; but, uncannily, on the supposed basis of *what has been*, a hitherto hidden promise that is only waiting for the right moment and preparation to emerge in the dazzling light of day. Even in its portion in the Renaissance debate about magic, Cabala incarnates this principle of a reinvention of the past as a structural basis of the future. In a very substantial way the idea of magic conjures up what is most ancient and primeval in human instinct and prehistory and fulfills the timeless wish, which began to come under suspicion in the Renaissance but which, like an obsessive dream, just won't disappear from our archaic unconscious, that of an integrated, caring cosmos. On the other hand, as a practice and an attitude, the meaning of magic is to place the potential for change, alteration, and improvement in human agency; it shares with science, as much a collateral paradigm as one that it prepares the way for, a refusal to accept any condition, even mortality, as final and definitive. Science and magic both equally give to man a responsibility and a duty of *self*-realization.

Cabala as Fad

Cabala shared both with an ancient magic and an incipient science a sense of limitless effort, dynamism, and restlessness. Like magic it incessantly seeks a cure for the illness that is existence, whose symbol and metaphor is the Jewish exile and diaspora. Like science, its method is one of curiosity, hypotheses, experience, study, and action. The very notion of an *oral law*, one of the *exact meanings* of Cabala, that controls, checks, or modifies a written one, constitutes it as a *science* of the question and putting into question; and the profound affinity of Renaissance thought with this unlikely "secret" and non-Christian tradition is based on its floating or problematizing of received knowledge, always subject to being challenged and transformed on the basis of a correcting notion. Small wonder that a thinker as independent as Agrippa, for whom there was no such thing as the unthinkable (except for the unthinkable), was willing to align himself for so long with Cabala, and even to define his career thereby, for the latter obviously was a system that allowed him to stay open to the imperatives and calls of the moment while maintaining also the ideal vision of a transcendent goal as a constant presence and pressure in existence. This balance of mutability and stability allowed by Renaissance Cabala accounts also for the *passion* with which that subject is studied, followed, and promoted during the period, which constitutes, at least until recently, a buried, repressed, or maybe "denied" chapter in our intellectual history, which it has nonetheless helped to compose.

    This is a point made brilliantly, comprehensively, and convincingly by François Secret in *Le Zohar chez les kabbalistes chrétiens de la Renaissance*. Secret had, however, been preceded in his enthusiasm by Adolphe Franck, in the nineteenth century, through his *Kabbale ou la philosophie religieuse des Hebreux.* For Secret, Joseph Blau, whose *Christian Cabala* is the standard work we have been citing often in these pages, had ignored the results of his own extensive findings by dismissing the Cabala as a mere fad: "The authors who are presented here started an intellectual fad," Blau had decided already by the end of his first chapter, drifting into alliteration as if to speed Cabala away by making it sound as light as a jingle, "The fad flamed flickered and finally faded."[55] Blau, also, according to Secret, simply did not go deeply enough into the basis for certain very *dubious* conjectures of his. For instance, Blau *assumes* that there was only a very minimal acquaintance with or interest in original Hebrew Cabala texts in the Christian Renaissance, since the major one, The Zohar, was not published in Hebrew until the middle of the sixteenth century, and, as a matter of fact, not even in Latin, and then only partially, until late in the seventeenth century. However, Secret points out that not only were Latin anthologies of extracts, summaries, and commentaries from and about The Zohar circulating extensively in print and in manuscript by late in the fifteenth and early in the sixteenth centuries, but knowledge of Hebrew was not so rare, and was commonly regarded as very desirable and useful, for instance as a tool in Reformation and Counter-Reformation controversy. Indeed, by the middle of the sixteenth century, lengthy sections of The Zohar, comprising its all-important commentaries on Genesis, had been translated *twice* into Latin (the second time because the projected publisher was unwilling to return the original manuscript) by that strangely stubborn French Hebraizing Christian mystic and cabalist, Guillaume Postel. Postel had already published a Latin translation of a shorter, earlier, but essential cabalist text, the *Sefer Yetzirah*, or *Book of Formation*, which was in print for at least one hundred years, until it was supplanted by a retranslation. Postel's zoharic translations have turned up recently in manuscript collections that Secret consulted (printing also extensive passages in his book), and none other than the greatest authority on Cabala in modern times, Gershom Scholem, has *confirmed.* Blau should surely have taken the existence of these enormous surviving translations of The Zohar into account when he came to his conclusions about the essential superficiality of the influence of Cabala in the Renaissance, especially since he himself, albeit discreetly in a note, mentions the discovery of Postel's *Zohar* and that Scholem had verified its authenticity.[56] Apart from this stunning revelation, Secret fills in some other gaps in Blau's account: students of Reuchlin, not remarked by Blau, who continued collecting and commenting Hebrew Cabala texts until well into the seventeenth century; evidence that major philosophical figures like Leibniz and Pascal were very well informed about Cabala. Secret likewise deepens the history of Christian Cabala from the other direction, at its beginning, which Blau considers being Pico, in the last decade of the fifteenth century. Secret shows, to the contrary, that by Pico's time there was a solidly established group of Christian adepts and experts on Cabala, including those almost-legendary nomadic promoters of the occult who had adopted the names of Flavius Mithradates and Paulus Heredia.[57] A Mithradates is also mentioned by Scholem (who calls this mysterious person Guiglemus Raimundas Moncada) as having completed a manuscript translation of an important pre-zoharic cabalistic-gnostic text, *The Bahir*, or *Book of Brightness*, which was then consulted by Pico in 1486.[58] This *cabal* was mostly centered in Spain, prior to the expulsion of the Jews in 1492. For instance, a Spanish Christian cabalist by the name of Pedro de la Caballerio was circulating in 1450, or forty-six years before Pico's notorious "Cabalistic Conclusions," an important theological treatise called *Zelus Christi* (and about which there was still enough interest 150 years later to justify a new edition), which refers systematically to The Zohar as an anticipation of Christianity.

Cabala seemed especially useful as the link, the cement between competing ideologies and a bridge of understanding and communication. Guillaume Postel, whose obsession with The Zohar was legendary, or should have become so, was notable also for an enthusiastic syncretism, typical of other Christian cabalists like Agrippa, that led him once to journey to Constantinople in order to present his case for joining Christianity and Islam. Postel became an accomplished Hebraist and adept in Cabala while still remaining within the Christian orbit, therefore still capable of affecting his culture from within. This Christianizing potential of Cabala in the Renaissance is not to be underestimated. There were several quite dramatic conversions of Jews of rabbinical stature to Christianity that were attributed to their studies of Cabala, including that of Paulus Ricci, who translated an important text by the thirteenth-century Spanish cabalist, Joseph Gikatilia, *Sha'are Orah* (Gates of Light), into Latin and who was prominent also for his other cabalistic publications as well as for his support of Pico. Strangely I know of no conversions that worked the other way, from Christian to Jewish by way of Cabala, with the possible exception of Jean Bodin.[59] Cabala, indeed, as we've noticed in relation to Postel, may have allowed some very demanding Christians, of the type of Agrippa or Paracelsus, to (seem to) stay within their religion, avoiding a "fall" into atheism or agnosticism. Its explanatory potential and exegetical resources and variety could provide for more flexibility than orthodoxy could allow. The Zohar, for example, could accomodate an otherwise daunting Machiavellian moral relativism that went along with an incipient separation of states from the absolutes of religion, by its assigning "this world" to an "other side" of evil that must be conciliated and respected if it is ever to be transcended. Cabala and its associated styles of textual analysis and extrapolation would allow the space for compromise and adjustment that was missing within more narrowly Christian limits.

Often spared, because of their presumed Christian meaning, from even the fires of an inquisition that consumed all other Hebrew texts, Cabala's writings could serve as an open channel to a world of wisdom and a set of rules at variance with the times. So, for example, Cabala could give a new dignity and use for magical strategies that Christianity had always been suspicious of, if not opposed to. On the other hand, standing in the way of scientific progress could be the barrier of the authority of Scriptural literalism the metaphorical hermeneutics of Cabala could bypass. Or Cabala could provide a vast new repertory of information, approaches, and arguments about practical issues of concern, as an alternative to the familiar Christian vocabulary. It was a way of reflecting and deciding differently about things without necessarily embracing the possible insignificance and likely futility of marginality. The cabalist could find evidence in the Bible that the Christian did not suspect was there but would have to respect, as we have noticed from Agrippa's strategy of scriptural allusion and numerological exegesis on the question of woman.

In this sense Agrippa's very retreat from Cabala, or from a certain kind of "cabalistic magic" in *On Vanity* is in the spirit of a tradition for which nothing is exempt from challenge, negation, and exception: without the ability to demur, what would our affirmations be worth anyway? Surely such a station of halt and reflection in the progress of a thinker as exigent and restless as Agrippa was both necessary and ineluctable, if the mystical research he staked out early in life was not to be hampered by his very reputation for competency at it. The recantation of *On Vanity* was then required in order to prevent the notion of progress on the "road to the absolute" from becoming a matter merely of the technology of transportation. What looks out at us from this stopping place and prospect that is *On Vanity* is the face of a truth that does not change, not that mutability would be totally excluded. However, what would alter would be the relative *clarity* of the image of truth, which sooner or later would become obscured. The truth, when it is clear, is conveyed and expressed by moralities. These are, as everyone suspects or knows already, ends of youths, friendships, loves, talents, interests, passions—reminders and rehearsals for the crowning finish of life itself. This truth is always already there, entire, complete, and pristine at every instant we are not, in one way or another, asleep—our function in life probably being nothing more glamorous or essential than, in one way or another, to wake ourselves up, and each other.

Cabala as Beginning

It is, indeed, the combined influences of habit, routine, fear, and other endemic factors having to do with the necessities of survival in authoritarian society (and all societies are tyrannical, whatever the degree and style, demanding first of all *obedience*) that are the causes of this clouding of the clarity and cogency of this vision of "things as they are." The function of the new, for the mystic or any other searcher, is then to restore and reinhabit this lost moment, to make us all starters again, equal in our vulnerability and our aspirations: paradoxically the purpose of the new can only be the old, to make it new and entire again. There is a naïve wisdom in beginning, in learning merely to recognize our first *letter*, that is beyond the accumulated knowledge and privilege-connected accomplishments of the erudite.

This assumption is basic to The Zohar, one of the most signal innovations of which, according to Scholem, was to emphasize the spiritual value and wisdom of poverty,[60] a virtue conspicuous for its absence in much of mainstream Judaism, for instance Maimonides' *Guide to the Perplexed*.[61] This humility, according to which pretension to knowledge and accomplishment is necessarily a form of blindness in an existence in which we are all constantly beginners, was one of its most effective strategies in its attack on intellectual pride and arrogance and its attempt to float certainties by bringing them back to what we already know and have forgotten. This recalls also a Platonic doctrine of reminiscence which it seems to have been the affair of Cabala to incorporate into Judaism:

> The very first thing taught to children, the *Aleph Beth*, transcends the comprehension and the mind of man, and even of the higher and the highest angels, because the Holy Name is concealed in the letters. A thousand and four hundred and five worlds are suspended from the point of the *aleph*, and seventy-two holy names traced in their full spelling, which uphold heaven and earth, upper and lower beings, and the Throne of the King, are suspended along the stroke of the *aleph*, while the mystery of Wisdom and the hidden paths and the deep rivers and the ten Words all issue from the lower point of the *aleph*. From this point *aleph* begins to extend into beth, and there is no end to the wisdom that is here inscribed . . . On one tiny letter are suspended thousands of thousands and myriads of myriads of delectable worlds. [*Zohar V*: 74, 143]

Equally, Agrippa's *On Vanity*, in its systematic declamation on the futility of all pride in learning, would remind us that however far we've gone we haven't gone far enough if we haven't gotten back to the moment of beginning, if we've lost sight of our end, which was also our origin. Cabala's self-defining notion of an interlocking, interdependent, oral and written law is surely an effective framework in which to emphasize a "correction" like this, by bringing down the linear accumulation of letters, words, and texts to a matter of the sudden insight and revelation of the humility (and glory) of the instant. This reminder is supplied by the breath or "spirit" whispering in our ear and making us see the letters differently. Correspondingly the arrogance and materiality of the instant, its self-proclaimed entirety and sufficiency, is checked by the existence of the written letter in all its living past, as a succession of a multitude of such instants, each with its insight and truth that comment on our present moments.

Connected to this founding idea of the oral and written law that was to allow its Renaissance students so much room and flexibility in adapting and applying their learning was also another set of oppositions that was basic in Cabala. These were the polarities of the secret and the open, the hidden and the revealed, the unseen and the visible. There are all kinds of nuances involved here too: some things are secret because they are impossible to say, some because they are not wise to say, some because they cannot be known. Then there are also secrets that may come to be known in time, when either they need to be and/or one is ready for them—like the Cabala's myth about itself, according to which it was initially hidden and now, in regard at least to certain parts or aspects of it, it is more or less of an open secret (though what it *really* means might still be undisclosed). Most confounding of all, what about a secret that cannot be revealed in words, through, say, the limitations of language itself? For example, the very concept of action itself might imply a domain beyond articulation, a "leap," as Kierkegaard has called it, that speculation (Hegel) could never make from within its own system. The sexual moment, so central to Cabala, is doubtless one of these secrets verging on the unsayable, for which all descriptions are functionally distortions. Relevant also to this problem of the secret and the project of its manifestation are the philosophical investigations in our own century of Ludwig Wittgenstein, who wondered (publicly, privately?) about the very possibility of a private language, for anything in words, and a fortiori written ones, belongs *by definition* in the public domain: even a coded language, meant to be understood only by the writer, is keyed on some systematic basis and potentially readable.

Generally also in these oppositions, for Cabala, that which is *secret* seems to be *more significant* than that which is not, except perhaps on the very highest levels: "Moses knew the Holy Name, as it is both disclosed and undisclosed, and attained to an insight to which no other man has ever attained" [*Zohar V*, 57]. It is important, however, not to separate the secret from its contrary but to realize that what is manifest is there to protect, preserve, and even convey what is not. This is the drift of Pico's "Cabalistic Conclusion" XXXV: "No spiritual things descending below can operate without a garment," which could well have been a précis of a zoharic commentary on *Psalm CIV*, 4: " 'who makest thy angels into winds' . . . For the angels in descending on earth put on themselves earthly garments, as otherwise they could not stay in this world, nor could the world endure them. Now, if thus it is with the angels, how much more so must it be with the Torah—the Torah that created them, that created all the worlds and is the means by which these are sustained. Thus had the Torah not clothed herself in garments of this world the world could not endure it. The stories of the Torah are thus only her outer garments" [*Zohar V*, 211].

It is interesting that Spinoza, writing in the seventeenth century, duplicates this argument exactly; for him the stories of the Bible need to be taken in the spirit of the prophets attempting to communicate the principles of Divine Law, or of an enlightened morality to the passionate masses that need things to hold on to. Even though for Spinoza the Biblical narratives were masks for an ethical and political message, not a theosophical one, I think it is a safe assumption that it was partly the precedent of cabalistic styles of exegesis that inspired his "scandalous" (for Jews and Christians alike)[62] deconstructions of Scripture.

Naturally such a strategy, deciding on the necessity of appearances while maintaining that the essence lies elsewhere, would make sense for a "community" without a country that has had to make exile a way of life and whose land has been a portable territory of sacred texts and an even less substantial oral tradition, or *cabal*. In a world that belongs to the other, always the demonic evil, though an inevitable one, what one *is* cannot be said, or be said openly. Here the hidden, the silent, and the unrecognized tend to be more meaningful than the open, spoken, and seen, but lean on the latter for their endurance: for the rule of exile, and all the more compelling if it is life or reality itself which is exile, is that to be *noticed* is to invite destruction. This theme of the precession, the superiority of the unknown over the known, the inner over the outer, on which it nevertheless depends, is so common in The Zohar as to be *endemic*; it might even be said that this is what the book, and a fortiori Cabala, is about, or *is*, purely and simply. For The

Zohar purports to be the secret history, one whose hiddeness is reconstituted on different levels as soon as it is revealed, of Torah. This is a secret, furthermore, impossible to glimpse in the full light of day, which is why *midnight* is its favorite hour, and available, unlike the Ten Commandments, engraved in tablets for all to see—only fitly, through flashes, metaphors, symbols, interruptions, visions, or through what Kierkegaard and Baudrillard after him have called "the method of indirect communication."

Kierkegaard introduced the concept of indirect communication as *the* strategy of his aesthetic or pseudonymous works.[63] This "charming" style Jean Baudrillard has described recently, in situationist (Guy Debord's *Society of the Spectacle*), post-May 1968 terms, as a paradigm and model for the resistance of seduction to a quantifying, *identifying* culture of production.[64] Kierkegaard, finally, of course, no kind of joker, meant this indirect communication seriously, that is, to be characteristic merely of a lower, aesthetic dimension, while for the more advanced ethical and religious ones, a more direct edifying style was in order. On the other hand, for Baudrillard, heir of Nietzsche and an existential generation from which other worlds have vanished, it is indirect communication that assumes the stature of an ideal or becomes an end in itself. From a Platonic-Kierkegaardian-Hegelian point of view then, Baudrillard would be *twisting in the wind* of some kind of shadow realm of matter, while perhaps Agrippa of the surprising *On Vanity* would be transcending this tempting but insufficient phase of indirect communication by abandoning metaphor and gimmick in favor of the more direct simplicity of cynical (to the world) fideism.

The Paradox of Secrecy

Another vivid example of this polarity—intertwining of what The Zohar likes to call "the undisclosed and the disclosed" is its account of the two wives of Jacob, Leah and Rachel. Why, ask the zoharic masters, was the woman Jacob loved best, Rachel, buried by an open road, while Leah, who was really foisted on him through her father Laban's pagan trickery, enjoys the full honors and recognition of burial beside her husband? "Seeing that the patriarchs were privileged to be buried in the cave of Machpelah with their wives, why was Jacob buried with Leah and not with Rachel, who was the "foundation of the house"? The reason is that Leah bore more children from the holy stock. R. Judah said, "Leah used to go out every day to the highway and weep for Jacob when she learnt that he was righteous, and prayed on his behalf, but Rachel never did so. Hence Leah was privileged to be buried with him, while Rachel's grave was set by the highway. The esoteric reason, as we have affirmed, is that the one typifies the disclosed and the other the undisclosed" [*Zohar II*, 316]. We may remark here the recourse to the explanatory potential of an "esoteric" reason, by definition more authoritative than the outer or exoteric reasons with which the commentary begins. This priority of the hidden over the manifest, the latent over the only apparent, can be remarked elsewhere in The Zohar even in the realm of the inorganic metaphors, especially those of precious metals, that the book likes to use to convey this dialectic of the seen and unseen. For example, in what follows we hear praise of the "shut-in gold" we can only imagine, while being invited to disdain, the kind we can hold in our hands and see: "What, now, is the difference between the two kinds of gold? The higher gold is in the symbol of the closed mystery, and its name is Zahab sagur, 'shut-in gold', that is, pure precious gold (I Kings VI, 20, 21), shut off and hidden from all, concealed from the eye, which has no power over it, but the gold below is more revealed" [*Zohar IV*, 21].

Secrecy is not only recommended in The Zohar, but also *enjoined*, for it likes to be clear also about the risks involved, whatever the prospects of temporary gain, of revealing secrets to others who have no right to know and can only use the information to damage or destroy its purveyor. A good example of the imperative of nondisclosure are the sanctions on the indiscretions of otherwise praiseworthy behavior of the otherwise illustrious King Hezekiah, ruler in some of the glory days of ancient Judea. He, giving into an impulse of vanity, had allowed outsiders [actually, Babylonian visitors], called "idolatrous nations," a glimpse of the Holy Ark and Tables of the Ten Commandments. The consequences of the indiscretion go way beyond the individual (as a matter of fact he himself is spared them) to affect, disastrously, his family and nation:

Hezekiah sinned in exposing the mysteries of the Holy One, blessed be He, to the view of idolatrous nations. God therefore sent him, through Isaiah, a message saying: "Behold, the days come, that all that is in thy house, and that which thy fathers laid up in store until this day shall be carried to Babylon, etc." (Is. XXXIX, 6). Through his sin in disclosing that which should have remained hidden, opportunity was given to the other side [i.e., the *K'liphoth*, or shells, the sinister forces that avail themselves of every opening to contaminate and draw sustenance from any sacred region—translator's note] to obtain dominion over it. For, as explained already, blessing rests on that which remains undisclosed, but as soon as it is disclosed the other region obtains scope to exercise dominion over it. It is written: "All that honored her despise her, because they have seen her nakedness" (Lament. I,8). [*Zohar II*, 267–68]

Openness, which our culture, at least *openly*, is inclined to be favorable to, is here the very definition of sin, especially where the thing revealed is of a nature that should have remained a concealed mystery. Nevertheless, existentially, there is and always has been a permanent pressure on the hidden to come out into the light of day, for to be human, in contradistinction to being God, as Spinoza defined it so succinctly and irrefutably, is to be unable to assimilate one's essence to one's existence: "The existence of God and his essence are one and the same thing . . . The Being of substance does not appertain to the essence of man—in other words, substance does not constitute the actual being of man."[65] Here Spinoza's God of unknowability and difference recalls that God of Cabala, which is called the Ancient Holy One, equally separate from all possibility of contact, relation, or knowledge. However, for Spinoza, there would be no *other* way of seeing God, except an illusory one (which he calls "dreaming-while-you're-awake"), no divine emanations, from an intermediary realm like that of the *sephiroth*, to attenuate the severity of this system. What Spinoza asked of the philosophical worshiper is an intensity of devotion and the love that is equal, or even superior, since disinterested, to that of the rewarded one. This is the "intellectual love of God," an *amor intellectus dei*, without the reward of a divine descent or any other sublime company.

All this is well and good, yet however secret, subtle, and undemanding and invisible one would like to be in one's prayer, we are inevitably brought out by a world whose recognition of us is just about as necessary as is air. One's survival is contingent on forces and persons external to oneself. By very definition one must be able to be found, located, and defined. This necessary emergence, however, exposes the individual to aggression equally from external sources. One also has a motive in exposing one's secrets to public gaze, as well as those of one's group, because of the chance that others might see things similarly too, which possibly would extend and enrich whatever the content one was keeping secret was, or else disarm an opposition to it. The other side of this vulnerability is a probable loss of authenticity, as the secret is shared by ever greater numbers and loses its tone and quality. There is a tendency, in any case, for a reconfiguration of the secret, as each new opening leads to new disillusionment—and this has been very much the "secret history" of Cabala. As disseminated, for instance, in what Scholem calls the "heretical Cabala" of Sabbatai Zevi and Nathan of Gaza in the seventeenth century and Joseph Frank and others in the eighteenth century, that "secret of evil" that we have so often cited as being intertwined with good is reconstituted as a mystery in itself: "In order to liberate the hidden sparks from their captivity, or to use another image, in order to force open the prison doors from within, the Messiah himself must descend into the realm of evil. Just as the Shekinah had to descend to Egypt—the symbol of everything dark and demonic—to gather in the ten fallen sparks, so the Messiah too at the end of the ages starts on his most difficult journey to the empire of darkness, in order to complete his mission."[66] In the urgency and desperation of this escalating process of incorporation of the demonic into the morality of everyday life, the idea of the harmony of evil and good—the way, according to a metaphor that is frequent in Cabala, our right and left hands work together is *dropped* in favor of a plunge into the extremity of evil, on the other side of which presumably good is waiting: "Not before he has reached the end of his journey will evil disappear and redemption extend to the external world . . . It is as if an anarchist rebellion had taken place within the world of Law. The reaction went so far that in certain radical conventicles acts and rites were practiced which aimed deliberately at the moral degradation of the human personality: he who has sunk to the uttermost depths is the more likely to see the light."

Sabbatai Zevi's notorious conversion to Islam, which defined his movement finally, and Joseph Frank's tyrannical and sexual excesses are two examples of what I am calling this reconfigured secret. Frank's followers tended to convert to Catholicism, Zevi's to Islam; but these conversions were, of course, not sincere, in the sense that some illustrious Jewish scholars and rabbis converted to Christianity by way of their own Cabala early in the sixteenth century. The purpose of the later converts instead was, by joining and strengthening what they looked upon as an evil empire, to bring about a new beginning after an apocalyptic end of things-as-they-are, which, according to messianic prophecies, won't change until they can get no worse. The outward actions, therefore, of such perverse enigmas as Zevi and Frank, presumably, were meant to be read the way the cabalist was asked to read Torah, looking for the hidden symbolic content behind the often (childishly?) manifest one. The problem here is, as we may recognize in our own century, beyond a certain point of intensity evil has passed, beyond any conceivable dialectic of hidden and manifest, into the realm of the horrendous and simply unspeakable: how to articulate, bring into our dialectic, use as passage to any "light" the evaporation of 90,000 human beings in 9 seconds, not to mention the work of the ovens, or the less dramatic but even more sure polluting of our planet? These are secrets we don't know about because we cannot stand knowing.

Until, however, this escalation of the problematic of evil in the seventeenth and eighteenth century, now exponentially pushed, through the power of technology, beyond the limit where Cabala or any other paradigm can account for it, what we had been dealing with were the dynamics of a system of perpetual movement whereby the hidden needs to surface, as if for air, but then needs to resubmerge, as if for protection. The undisclosed and the disclosed are in constant progress toward each other. Betrayal, at all events, is already included in the very notion that something must be kept secret, as in the fact of revelation there is implied a rule of secrecy that is being temporarily suspended.

We may remark also how the historical creation, development and manifestation of Cabala is connected with this pattern of thrust into a world from which it simultaneously or subsequently is forced to recoil. The pressures to share that "secret gold" tend, at times, to become irresistible, especially when, as in the Renaissance, it seems widely adaptable to other cultures and religious styles. Cabala then goes on exhibition, as it were, but thereby prepares the way for its own retreat, since a *shared* secret is, by definition, no longer one, on the way to being by proliferation no longer a *cabal*. Anything interesting, original, provocative, threatening has been lost in the vulgarizations and compromises of the processes of dissemination. Society sees anything new, anyway, as a danger—either of a rival hierarchy or as contestation of its order. Its enemies, by surfacing, are only marking themselves for either elimination or incorporation. In the latter case the alternative has ceased to exist as a distinct entity, with its own difference or secret. There is, finally, if one is going to be faithful to one's inspiration and truth, no alternative but to take to the road of exile again. Thereby one has started that whole infernal or, really, all-too-human cycle again, from secret to manifest and back to secret again; but at least one hasn't become complacent, stopped or been stopped, and there may be "intimations of immortality," or at least some ecstatic moments on the way.

Meanwhile, one communicates, but *indirectly*—one doesn't impart all of one's knowledge, or not anyway in terms so unmistakable as to leave no room for retreat. One relies on stories, metaphors, examples, anecdotes, exegesis—and, at a certain point, when one's accumulated reputation and accomplishments become too onerous a burden to bear, then, in the sight of all, one sheds the whole weight and is suddenly light and secret again. Such may account for some of the turnings in the "secret" career of Henry Agrippa Von Nettesheim, someone who had become *identified* very solidly in the public mind with Cabala (and other occult traditions) and was therefore more or less obliged to a public recantation—as a mask behind which he could continue to pass along on his once-again-hidden path.

Bibliographica Kabbalistica

An annotated, critical commentary and selective
search of sixteenth- and seventeenth-century texts,
mainly continental

The principal work for the study of the Kabbalah is The *Zohar*, which is
written in a very lofty style in the Syrian language. All other Kabbalistic
writing are to be regarded as merely commentaries on The *Zohar* or extracts
from it.

—Solomon Maimon

Although Agrippa, Reuchlin, and Pico are some major names
associated with the dissemination of Cabala in Europe of
the Renaissance it is impossible to give an adequate idea
of the true scope of this movement through them alone. An annotated and critical bibliography of works that either cite, or discuss
Cabala will, I hope, indicate how really widespread the cabalistic
and/or para or pseudocabalistic concepts, mentality, and terminol-
ogy were in the Renaissance. By conflating these more or less
faithful renditions of Cabala I mean to stress that they would nev-

ertheless remain on the same continuum of meaning, while conveying a similar indeterminacy.

Intrinsically cabalistic is the notion that any attempt to render
the essence of things, including even a hallowed scriptural one, can
only be a more or less misleading approximation and distortion.
This floating of the signifiers of truth and falsity is one of the ways
that Cabala anticipates a Nietzschean modernity, beyond the consolations of good and evil. Cabala, even at that vague and controversial point of its inception, is already a discourse that proclaims
its own unreliability and infidelity, its ineluctable betrayal of itself,
in the very substance, whether written or oral, through which it is
revealed. The blatant paradox of its open secret is that the hidden
that is revealed is no longer a mystery, but for that very reason
remains one.

The bibliography that follows concentrates on continental examples, though a few English items have crept in too. I plan to
emphasize England particularly in the final chapter. I call this a
"critical" bibliography because, where possible, I try to relate the
work to aspects of Cabala we have already been commenting. I've
set up this chapter, generally, in descending order of how much I
have to say about the listed items. I begin with a thematic section,
"Topics in Cabala," where my comments tend to be relatively extensive, with the texts arranged chronologically under each theme,
according to the date of publication of the first work of the author
listed. The next two sections, which I call "The Dissemination of
Cabala," and "Cabala as Motif," are strictly chronological. Here I've
tried to list the items as briefly as possible, but in the original
languages, where I could locate them, to give a sense of Cabala's
cosmopolitanism, an aspect of its syncretism. The reader will find
fuller data for each entry in the general Bibliography, where also
the English translations of these challengingly abstruse titles, from
a number of languages, living, dead, and obsolete, are my own
responsibility (or Lynn Thorndike's).

A word is in order about style: often I use the title as a jump-
ing-off place, following a trail of associations to relevant, sometimes much more recent places. So, for example, in "Saint Teresa's
Castles and Kafka's," I leap from Garzoni's *Universal Castle* (1585)
to Kafka's *The Castle*. Other times, I prefer to "back into" a subject,
as for the most notable and comprehensive collection of Christian

cabalistic texts of the Renaissance, Pistorius's *Cabalistic Arts* (1587), in "Mainstream Cabala." Here I approach my subject through the lens of a Lurianic Cabala (which Pistorius ignores, although or because he was contemporaneous with it), as represented in an important anthology of about a century later, Knorr Von Rosenroth's *Kabbala Unveiled* (1677–84). Pistorius's Cabala was that already classic Christian one, as it came up, especially in the first half of the sixteenth century, through Pico 's acolytes—Reuchlin, Georgius, the Ricius brothers, and Galantino. Von Rosenroth's authors rather would have approached these classical Christian cabalists in the mood of the dramatic Lurianic modifications that eventually put Cabala on a collision course with destiny, culminating in the messianic-apocalyptic Sabbatian episode and apostasy, and its ambiguous and controversial aftermaths. They would have looked into the earlier cabalists, generally more anodyne, serene, and confident (of their orthodoxy), for anticipations that corresponded to their own priorities and (sometimes revolutionary) ideals. So if I sometimes scant diachrony it is because, in my own order of priorities, it seemed more important to me to focus on what Cabala *meant* than what it *was*.

Topics in Cabala

Radical Cabala

Lodovico Lazzarelli (1450–1500), *Crater Hermetis* (1505). This was a mysterious text that circulated widely in the Renaissance, by an author who apparently belonged to a circle of Hermetic occultists. *The Crater of Hermes* was apparently bound with another more illustrious work, since Nauert mentions it "as an adjunct to that edition of the Hermetic *Pimander* which Agrippa probably used."[1] This *Pimander* was a classic of occult literature that started circulating in Greek in the third century A.D. under the august pseudonym of Hermes Trismegistus, then was translated by Ficino late in the fifteenth century into Latin for a European audience. Hermetic Philosophy, which, as a matter of fact, Agrippa lectured on in 1517 in Italy, had numerous points of congruence with Cabala. First of all, an assumption of a pristine or oral tradition, necessary complement of scripture, is common to both; secondly, both assign a powerful role to magic in the life of the adept, a point that Nauert emphasizes:

> The enlightened soul, the soul which had attained a true understanding of God's revelation, would not only regain mastery over its own body but would also win power over all nature. Thus the study of the Cabala and the hermetic literature led into the study of magic . . . It was precisely this power over nature which Adam had lost by original sin, but which the purified soul, the *magus*, now could regain. This magical knowledge had long been associated with the Hermetic tradition; and while the main current of medieval Jewish cabalism had been hostile to any such attempt to associate mystical illumination with magic, yet the cabalists had firmly believed that the enlightened soul did possess great power. They had not been entirely free from the corrupting attempt to make use of this knowledge for magical practices.[2]

Blau's opinion was that Lazzarelli's *Crater of Hermes* must have been written by 1494, since it was dedicated to Ferdinand of Naples, who died that year.[3] Nauert calls Lazzarelli flatly a "Hermetic enthusiast and fanatical occultist,"[4] but finds, interestingly, that his influence on Agrippa was considerable, since *The Crater of Hermes* was certainly a source for zoharic and cabalistic allusions in a number of Agrippa's texts. According to Nauert, Lazzarelli's belief in the *real* (motivated) rather than a conventional connection of words with objects, and also his emphasis on the importance of the Magus, or guide, show up also in the general system of Agrippan magic. Nauert mentions in this connection a prolonged residence in Italy that intervened between the original composition (c.1510) and the revision (c.1530) of Agrippa's *Occult Philosophy*. Absent from the first, unpublished draft, Lazzarelli is definitely quoted in the revision (published in 1533) though *not mentioned*. That Lazzarelli was rather ignored than forgotten is suggested by Agrippa's having overlooked his presence elsewhere in his work also, as remarked by Nauert:

> Unacknowledged use of *Crater Hermetis* is apparent in the *Dialogus de homine* [*Dialogues on Man*, 1515–16], a fact which

suggests that the thought of this fantastic millenarian, Lazzarelli, was current in the circles at Casale Monferrato among whom Agrippa was living when he wrote the *Dialogues*. The general influence of Lazzarelli may be traced in the increased emphasis which Agrippa gave to the Hermetic writings during his residence in Italy. While Agrippa's *De Occulta Philosophia* always stressed a mystical illumination of the soul, his contact with the thought of Lazzarelli may help explain why the theme of spiritual regeneration received a more thorough treatment in the revised version of his treatise on occult philosophy. Lazzarelli put much stress on the regeneration of the soul under the tutelage of a spiritually illuminated master, and also on the power of the *magus*.[5]

The presence of Lazzarelli in Agrippa is, furthermore, a matter of verbatim citations by the latter of the former, as well as allusions to identical passages in The Zohar, which, given its huge dimensions, could not be mere coincidence. Agrippa's omission of the name of Lazzarelli (given also that Agrippa is an inveterate name dropper, his books sometimes seeming like just annotated lists of them) may be related to Lazzarelli's reputation as a radical promoter of the power of magic in the pursuit of individual self-realization, a demiurgic project that could appear, in a strictly Christian context, as pagan and demonic. Since the onus of suspicion on Agrippa was already heavy enough for him to have postponed publication of *Occult Philosophy* for almost twenty-five years, it would seem reasonable that he would disguise his use of a source that, nevertheless, was quite fascinating and useful to him, as Lazzarelli obviously was to Agrippa's esoteric entourage in Italy. Lazzarelli's provocative *Crater*, however, in all the glory of its pagan antinomianism and hedonism surfaces just a few years later, when it is unabashedly avowed in the neoplatonic-hermeticist-cabalist circle constituted in Italy of the 1520s by Egidio da Viterbo and Pietro da Galantini. Paradoxically, at least in pre-Counter Reformation Renaissance, the closer we come to the Pope the more unorthodox, pagan, and magical religion can afford to become!

In summary, *The Crater of Hermes*, which evidently was resorted to cautiously by some, like Agrippa, who were profoundly affected by it, and proudly proclaimed by others, nevertheless illustrates the latitude, toleration, and experimentalism of a certain very strong and stubborn current of mystical-religious ideology of the early sixteenth century. It was able to make its iconoclastic and demiurgic statement without worrying too much about Christianity, belonging rather to a surviving and vital pagan or Neopagan tradition, and involving, ambitiously and unapologetically, a celebration of "forbidden" knowledge, in its explicit recourse to conjuring magic and angel-summoning, personage-creating ritual, which it dignifies in terms of its sublime goal of regeneration of the soul— maybe a sort of *Naked Lunch* of the Renaissance, affecting all, and at least for a generation, avowed by few.

Pietro di Galantini, *De arcanis Catholicae veritatis* (1518).   Galantini was a renowned Jewish convert to Christianity by way of Cabala, the purpose of whose *Arcane Catholic Truth*, as is obvious from the title, was to show others the same "truth": Judaism before Christ *was* Christianity, as a cabalistic reading of scripture will demonstrate. The other more recent books in the extended title includes The Zohar, whose antiquity Galantino coincidentally disbelieves! Included in the above book is a summary of a text on the Hebrew *Shema Israel* prayer by Paulus Heredia, a nomadic Spanish Christian Cabalist whose impact on Pico was profound. Galantini was that rare kind of scholar who knows his sources' sources. According to François Secret, Galantini practiced also the mysticism that he preached: he thought of himself as an "the Angel Pope,"[6] a curious messianic entity first mentioned by the twelfth-century prophetic theologian, Joachim of Floris, and whose doctrines, like Cabala, attractive as well as threatening to many, and at one time officially condemned, still had an enormous impact on religious life in the later Middle Ages and beyond. Windelband mentions Joachim of Floris's *Eternal Gospel* in connection with a messianic-apocalyptic eschatology that would make it natural that one could be, as was the case in the Renaissance, in the circle of Egidio da Viterbo and Pietro Galantini, *at once Joachimist and cabalist.* According to Windelband Joachim had announced the completion of a process of transformation of external into internal, of time into timelessness, that had only been promised by the early Christian fathers: "the 'pneumatic gospel' of Origen was asserted to have here attained reality, the period of the 'spirit' to have begun."[7]

Galantini belonged to a group of esoterics that gathered during the 1520s around another very important cabalist of the Renaissance, Egidio da Viterbo. Marjorie Reeves remarks that "Egidio collected Joachimist prophecies as well as cabalist mysteries and gathered within his household a group of humanist scholars in Greek, Hebrew, and eastern languages who studied prophecies as well as linguistics."[8] Galantini's book was popular, as the numerous editions from three countries indicate. Especially well known were his "excerpts" from The Zohar, which were still respected well enough to be translated from his Latin into Italian by G. M. Vincenti for a book published in Venice in 1659, *The Messiah is come, explained and proved by stories from the Hebrew in 100 lessons.*[9]

Finus Hadrianus, In Judeos flagellum. Venice, 1538. *Scourging the Jews* isn't really the antisemitic diatribe its title might suggest it is, but rather the kind of "lesson," if a slightly patronizing one, that a parent might administer to a child out of love and concern. Book 9 of this book is taken up with Cabala, and proclaims that it will be about "What the human race was like, and the state of knowledge when the Jewish cabalists were teaching, and what their contributions to knowledge were."[10] Secret treats this work as a real intertextual nexus and example of the influence of Cabala. Begun in 1503 and written in 1510, but not printed until 1538, its publisher, Daniel and Sons, added marginal references to Galantini's important work, which had appeared in the meantime. Secret also notes that Fini quotes what was to be a very famous excerpt, *on the subject of the sephirotic tree,* from *The Bahir,* a pre-zoharic cabalistic text that had already been quoted by Marsilio Ficino, Florentine neoplatonist, in *On Christian religion* of 1474. This same passage from *The Bahir* was to reappear in various works connected with Cabala from the Renaissance up to the eighteenth-century: G. Postel's *On the Harmony of the Earthly Sphere,* of 1544; M. Neander's *Sanctae linguae erotemata* [Erotics? of the holy language], of 1556; F. Tasso's *Twenty familiar arguments on the coming of the Messiah,* Venice, 1585; M. Vivaldus's seventeenth-century edition of *Zeal of Christ,* which was written around 1450, in Spain by Pedro de la Caballeria (sic); Joh. Salomon's *37 Demonstrationes,* Francfort, 1660; Christian Schoettgen, *Hebrew and talmudic hours,* Dresden, 1742.[11]

Scholem, who, early in his career, thought *The Bahir*, or *Book of Brightness*, indispensable enough to translate it into German, has also commented extensively on it, especially in *The Origins of Kabbalah*.[12] *The Bahir's* is a Gnostic presence that pervades also Scholem's magisterial *Major Trends,* where it was introduced as "the oldest Kabbalistic text, the highly obscure and awkward book *Bahir*, which was edited in Provence during the twelfth century."[13] Unlike The Zohar, according to Scholem this *is* a compilation of older texts of various provenance, particularly Gnostic, which emphasized the separation of the realms rather than their correspondence. The later Zohar would relate rather to a comparatively modern element of Jewish Neoplatonism, and was predicated, on the other hand, on a harmony of the realms, or, in Agrippan terms, a Natural Magic. Scholem further suggests an analogy between *this* Gnostic aspect of Cabala represented by *The Bahir—and* the Cathar or Albigensian heresy, which developed and was extirpated in close proximity to it. The latter has been credibly identified by Runciman[14] as an extension and survival of the ancient Manichean dualism, for which the division of the cosmos into a Good and Evil principle is basic.

Other ways in which the Cabala of *The Bahir* connects with this Christian heresy is in the doctrine of *gilgul*, or reincarnation of souls, which is only rarely present in the later Cabala of The Zohar, where it seems to work as an ultimate rationalization, for instance, for earthly inequality when all others fail. *Gilgul*, or reincarnation, was likely to have been ultimately of Eastern origin, along with the Manichean-Gnosticism of the medieval Albigensian Dualism (called also the *Bulgar* heresy) as well as that of *The Bahir*. Equally the symbol of the mystical-sephirotic tree that was to be so influential seems to have been introduced in *The Bahir*, but this tree is not necessarily the symbol of organic unity and connection, as would seem natural to suppose, for what it represents is rather the separation of the branches as well as the discrete layers of its bark: "All the divine powers form a succession of layers and are like a tree."[15] Another Gnostic element generally thought to have been introduced into Cabala by *The Bahir* is the doctrine of the Shekinah, or feminine divine, a concept of pagan provenance that early found a place in Jewish mystical movements, while leading a parallel life in the Christian Dualist Heresies, equally inspired by pagan-Gnostic sources.

As might emerge from the summary above, *The Bahir* is rather a compilation and smattering of provocative ideas—some of which were to germinate in other forms later—than a consistent theological treatise. Like The Zohar also, but even more credibly, The Bahir is pseudepigraphical, that is, as if from a previous time and by someone prestigious, which added to its fascination and to the diversity of uses and contexts in which it could be applied, as well as to the ways it could be understood—all of which accounts for the stubborn presence, which Secret has so diligently inventoried, all through the Renaissance, of this slight but significant and apparently awe-inspiring text.

Guillaume Postel, *Abrahami patriarchae liber Jezirah* (1552). This is a Latin translation of an original Hebrew cabalistic work dating from the early Middle Ages, brief but revered and immensely influential. Like The Zohar, and in keeping with a self-effacing cabalistic style, this *Sefer Yetzirah,* or *Book of Formation,* sometimes called *Book of Creation,* is pseudepigraphic, or attributed to a Biblical (in this case Abraham) or otherwise "holy" character, but even more patently so. Nevertheless I don't think it has ever been close to being decided as to who the real author was, as was certainly the case with The Zohar, assigned, especially ever since Scholem's definitive analyses, very confidently to Moses de Leon. The authority claimed by this work is immense, however, and in a way, outranks zoharic Cabala, since the Abrahamic revelations predate and predetermine the Mosaic ones that are assumed by de Leon as coming through by way of ben Yohai. Waite, who tends to scant Postel's contribution, admits somewhat grudgingly that, indeed, "Postel connects with Kabbalism by the great fact that he discovered and made known in the West that celebrated BOOK OF FORMATION which contains some of its fundamental doctrines."[16]

The *Sefer Yetzirah* is distinguished in Cabala for being the first known source for the doctrine of the ten *Sephiroth,* or Emanations. This text, whose authority and influence was so redoubtable, nevertheless was very succinct and schematic: in no version does it exceed 1,600 words. Postel accompanied his translation of it with his own extensive (according to Waite, very fanciful) commentary and his translations of other commentaries on it from the great Cabala generation of thirteenth-century Spain. The focus of the

Sefer Yetzirah is emphatically on cosmology and cosmogony, with particular attention to numbers. The *Ten Sephiroth*, which it introduced, for instance, combined with the 22 letters of the Hebrew alphabet yield the corresponding 32 number of the Gates of Wisdom that is to be thematic for Cabala. The influence of this book was felt especially on the side of a practical, theurgical, and therapeutic Cabala—for instance an "ecstatic" one of Abulafia in the thirteenth century, which emphasizes a correspondence of the *Sephiroth* with parts of the human body rather than on the more philosophical-theosophical, messianic, and utopian side of The Zohar and the sixteenth- and seventeenth-century interpretations of it. Wherever thereafter it is a matter of the mystical manipulation of numbers and letters, or of magic pure and simple, the *Sefer Yetzirah* is not far away. It is mentioned, for instance, by the Neopagan-pagan Hermeticist Lazzarelli in his *Crater of Hermes*,[17] published in 1505 along with the Hermetic classic, *Pimander*; and it is important too for Peter Bongus's widely known *The Mysterious Meaning of Numbers* of 1585, and therefore played its part more or less directly in the numerological style of poetry that the researches of Alastair Fowler and others have uncovered as being a formidable, now much neglected or ignored, element in Renaissance poetic practice. Its impact is apparent on Agrippa, whose name, justifiably or not, already in the Renaissance, and of course after, was synonymous with a controversial "practical" cabalistic methodology, involving schematized rites, rituals, formulas, and incantations. It seems suitable that Postel, with his reputation for demiurgic energy and extravagance, should have attached his name to this text, while his extensive work on The Zohar had to wait until recently for legitimization.

A primordial *Sefer Yezirah*, of course, floats sublimely above such blatantly magical applications, especially in the pursuit of very mundane ends. Waite, for instance, agrees with what he says is the opinion of its early students who "regarded it as the head and source of Kabbalism";[18] and one doesn't have to read very far in Scholem to notice that he considers it, together with The Bahir and The Zohar as one of the three fundamental texts of Cabala, and probably the most *basic* one, in the sense of a foundation on which the rest is built.

Nevertheless, Scholem also conveys a sense of uneasiness with this text, even with its immense prestige and influence, relating to possibilities of abuse that are not as evident for the two others, perhaps because of their greater obscurity, ambiguity and complexity. Abraham Abulafia, a thirteenth-century contemporary of de Leon, whose Cabala, which seems to place the sacred within reach of the individual without the preamble of a lot of literary edification, was effectively derived from The *Sefer Yetzirah*, was also, according to Scholem, very much aware, in the temptation of a "spiritual luxury," of the possibility of abuse of the *power* it accessed: "He [Abulafia] warns against the use of the Book of Creation for the purpose of creating to oneself—in the words of the Talmud—a fat calf. They who want this, he says bluntly, are themselves calves."[19]

The fact that the Christian cabalists of the Renaissance were more likely to know this book than other Hebrew originals may have been more than a matter of its brevity or seeming clarity, but could have had something to do with its apparent practical possibilities. As for the imperatives of *typology*, or requirement of finding Christian messages and prophecies in Old Testament texts [*then*, novelty had to be related to Christian paradigms, as *today* education needs to be linked to employment] of Christian Cabala generally, the choice of this text over others must have been a result also of certain contexts and priorities of the period. We may understand, for instance, Johannes Pistorius's selection of Christian authors rather than Jewish to expound Cabala, in his very important anthology of 1587,[20] to be more than a matter of mere ignorance or nonavailability of sources in Hebrew or in Latin translations, but also a question of decision, interpretation, and choice; the research of François Secret has brought out that The Zohar was far from the secret for the Renaissance that Joseph Blau makes it out to be. Likewise the wide dissemination and impact of the *Sefer Yetzirah* in the Christian Renaissance needs to be accounted for also in terms of the mood of those who translated, read, and used it, their fascination with individuality, power, and freedom, together with the invention and discovery of tools that would put these in the reach of ever greater appetite for transcendence. This might reasonably be seen as consequence, in Walter Benjamin's terms, of the elimination of the aura of the numinous, which went along with the progressive elimination of the connection of craft to individual product in a nascent industrial society of interchangeable-because-identical objects. Following Benjamin's famous model, technology's function is to restore what technology has ruined, the way the invention of cinema was meant to restore contact with a sensory world from which industry had separated the workers; and what technology could be more immediately available than the letters of the alphabet and the numbers of the fingers on the hands? It was only in the seventeenth century, finally, with the distinctions then made ever more strictly between magic, astrology, and religion on one side and experimental science, astronomy, economy, and politics on the other, that Christian Cabala is ready to turn toward the arduous mystical path of the zoharic texts and away from facile sephirotic or numerological equivalencies with Christian paradigms and/or worldly ends. Ironically but not surprisingly, Cabala's survival becomes problematic, however, at that very moment when its more authentic message, as well as more challenging texts and implications, seems to be emerging, as if it needed its disguise in order to continue to be (hidden).

Giordano Bruno, *Cabala del cavallo pegaseo* (1585).   This evidently not-earthbound *Cabala of the Horse Pegasus*, was a work published in Italian, simultaneously in Paris and London, where it connects with a proselytizing, very influential and controversial trip to England by the nomadic-syncretic mystic idealist, Giordano Bruno. This stubborn Renaissance genius and heretic, burned by the inquisition in Venice in 1600 for refusing to retract, was deeply imbued with Cabala, as well as with Neoplatonism, Hermeticism, and Alchemy.[21] An adventuresome and courageous spirit, he traveled and lectured widely all over the continent and in England. According to Denis Saurat,[22] his contacts in London with Edmund Spenser or his friends, are reasons for a significant presence of Cabala in that poet's works: the Sapience figure in the "Hymn to Heavenlie Beauty," for instance, too sexual to be a Mary figure and too sacramental to be a Neoplatonic Goddess of Eternal Wisdom, is a seemly avatar of the cabalistic *Shekinah*.

In a more general way, the numinous and commanding but wise and nurturing female figures that represent Queen Elizabeth in the *Faerie Queene* would owe something to the awe and respect in Cabala for the principle of the feminine, tantamount to the form God's presence takes on earth. A generation later, the baroque extravagance of Donne's lament over the early demise of a young woman, "The Second Anniversary," who somehow represents all order, symmetry, and purpose, might make more sense as an elegy over a "wasteland" or abandoned terrain of an earth no longer hallowed and consoled by this feminine avatar of the divine, or Shekinah of the Cabala. The passing of the two Elizabeths that Donne was conflating, both the Queen and the late Ms. Drury, have left the world desolate, as if abandoned by heaven and therefore subject to the purposeless energies of secular science and politics (Donne's decried "new philosophy"). Later, in Milton's *Paradise Lost*, indeed, the figure of the feminine has evolved, analogously with the gnostic urgency of Cabala of the later Renaissance, whereby the darker Lilith relays a brighter Shekinah. From being that "link with the divine" she could be in Spenser's *Fairie Queene*, she's transformed by Milton into inlet to the demonic, ambiguous, if anguished pretext for a "fortunate fall"!

Julius Conrad Otto, *Gali Razia* (1605).[23]   The *Gali Razia* was a problematic but very widely disseminated Renaissance addition to the canon that suggests that the Jewish Cabala was evolving, in some very provocative ways, even as its Christian students were trying to adapt their religion to it. This radical supplement to the Cabala doubtless contributed to an atmosphere of urgency in which a Catholic establishment foe like Mersenne undertook to oppose the whole movement,[24] shortly after the above work became available in Latin.

In *Major Trends*, first published in 1941, Scholem mentions an extremely radical, visionary, innovative, and mystical but controversial work, which he calls the *Galli Razaya,* as having been written by an anonymous author, in Hebrew, in 1552, in the context of its promotion of the doctrine of *gilgul*, or transmigration of souls, which then becomes increasingly important in Cabala.[25] Scholem ascribes what he thinks of as this un-Jewish idea to a situation of *exile*, which by the middle of the sixteenth-century, sixty years from the Second (or Spanish) Diaspora, would appear definitive and which would therefore require an ever more elaborate metaphysics: One was returning in some kind of history, if not in *this* one. In a later book, *Sabbatai Sevi: The Mystical Messiah*, first published in Hebrew, in 1957, Scholem emphasized a different aspect of this work, which he conjecturally attributes to an Abraham ha-Levi Berukhim, whom he calls "one of the most striking figures in the community of the devout in Safed who greatly influenced its ascetic and devotional practices." Scholem here stresses the attention of the *Galli Razaya* to the problem of evil, which as we have seen, is already handled with a good deal of nuance and concern in The Zohar. The particular problem that the *Gali Razaya* sets for itself is the frequency with which great figures of Jewish history take up with non-Jewish [therefore evil, from the other side] women: "The cases of Judah and Tamar, Joseph and the wife of Potiphar, Moses and Zipporah, Samson and Delilah, Boaz and Ruth, Josha and Rahab . . . and others suggest a mysterious relationship between Israel's saints and heroes and the 'other side' that requires explanation."[26]

This *Gali Razaya* escalation of the question of evil beyond the zoharic handling of it seems to be in the direction of its normalization, or its *banality,* to use the term Hannah Arendt invented for the "mystery" of the holocaust. For The Zohar, evil was ineluctable but the recourse to it is still exceptional, recommended at those rare times when the stakes are very high, as in the cases of Jacob and Esau, or Samson and the Philistines, when what was being decided was whether a people would be monotheist or pagan. From zoharic toleration of evil, through the *Gali Razaya*'s acceptance of it to the Sabbatai Zevi's, and *a fortiori*, Joseph Frank's later embrace of it, in whose hands it becomes *enjoined*, we may trace a progress of this tendency to include ever more frankly dubious behavior within the realm of the good. The concept, for instance, of the "holy fraud," or "redemption through sin," ancillary and explanatory in the older Cabala, becomes increasingly important in the newer. As the social and historical situation require ever greater energies of dissimulation, it ultimately becomes the essence of Cabala practice itself: the true cabalist,[27] as Zevi did himself, converts to what they considered the religion of the other side: Islam.

Cabala as Anathema

Jacob Hochstraten, *Destructio Cabbalae* (1518). *De Cabala an toleranda* (1519). Scholem lists both of these "smearing" works, *The Destruction of Cabala* and *Should Cabala Be Banned?* as being tracts against Reuchlin,[28] specifically the latter's *De Arte Cabalistica*, which was published in 1516, arousing opposition of the Cologne Dominicans who, in a spirit anticipating Tridentine intolerance, were opposing Hebraizing trends in Christian philosophy, theology, and practice. Hochstraten was part of the Dominican reaction to Reuchlin's well-known admiration for the Hebrew language and Hebrew texts, around which there developed the continent-wide Pfefferkorn controversy that eventually was to involve even the Pope, as well as many of the major figures of what was soon to be the Reformation in the first few decades of the sixteenth-century. Heinrich Graetz provides a magisterial analysis and overview of this fascinating controversy between the Dominicans, on the one hand, and the Hebraizing reformers and cabalistic "fellow travelers," on the other, really an overture to the Reformation and Counter Reformation alike.[29]

Joseph Pffeferkorn was a Jewish convert to Christianity who was trying to make his reputation by advocating the suppression of Hebrew-language texts, especially Talmudic ones, although his suspicions extended also to Cabala for their supposed opposition to and mockery of the tenets of Christian faith. The context of this dispute was that a certain "Hebrew chic" had developed as a strategy of reformers against existing Catholic hierarchies and practices that they were attempting to modify; and the discrediting of Hebrew texts was accordingly natural among those who wanted to reply to these challenges. Even Martin Luther, who later in life adopted an anti-Semitic attitude, at the time of the Pfefferkorn controversy lent his support to Reuchlin's Hebraism; and Hebrew remained a significant and signifying element in the radical wing of the Protestant Reformation right up to the time of Cromwell, when a process started that eventually led to the readmission of Jews, who had been expelled from England in 1290.

It is not wise, however, to conceive of the Christian response to Cabala as being completely predetermined by the differing life styles of the religious orders. A prevailing notion, which has been solidly reinforced by Blau, has been that the hard-headed "empirical" Dominicans staunchly opposed Cabala, or indeed anything very subjective, especially mystical in matters of faith, whereas the "dreamy" Franciscans tended to welcome such developments. Blau, for example, establishes this dichotomy very seriously,[30] stressing, as he does, finally, the intrinsic restrictions—beyond which Christians would not venture—to the spread of Cabala in the Renaissance. For

Secret, on the other hand, this distinction proves to be an unsafe generalization, which many exceptions qualify. He attacks Blau even on *this* limitation of describing the Christian Cabala as essentially Franciscan. Like Blau's other notions about the ultimate narrowness of the scope of Cabala it was simplistic. Secret points out that there was both sympathy and opposition to it within both the Dominican and Franciscan orders. Cabala adepts were present even in that most *practical* of Counter Reformation creations, the Jesuits![31]

Benedictus Pererius, S.J., *Adversus fallaces et superstitiosas artes* (1592). In this tract, *Against Fallacious and Superstitious Arts*, Pererius admits, nevertheless, the legitimacy of "natural magic," essentially a practical application of a doctrine of correspondences promulgated by Neoplatonists such as Nicolas de Cusa, but he denounces the "demonic" ambitions of what he calls "cabalistic or astronomical magic"[32] to manipulate the cosmos and reality at will. Pererius's arguments against Cabala have been borrowed from Agrippa's *Vanity of the Arts and Sciences* of 1530,[33] where, however, as we have noticed, the refutation was very ambiguous and, as a matter of fact, far from definitive. Pererius's indecision regarding Cabala, whose "natural magic" aspect he accepts, reflects Agrippa's anguish also, as well as that of the epoch. What was in question, then, was not so much the power and energy of new or revived systems of understanding and knowledge as their direction and purpose. Interesting also is the author's Jesuit affiliation; at the time of this work's publication the Society of Jesus has been in existence for about forty years, and is in a period when its empirical attitudes, emphasizing work in and on the world, are being widely disseminated, attracting both followers and controversy.

De Certeau, a modern Jesuit himself, made of this struggle between worldly effectiveness and inner truth and authenticity very much of a leitmotif of his book, *The Mystic Fable*, whose theme was the very vital challenge mystics were able to pose, within The Society of Jesus in the seventeenth-century, to its increasingly secular and worldly policies; and this protest was made in the name of some of the same values for which the Jesuit order were founded. The annihilation, or reduction, of this "opposition" marked then for *mystics* [as a discourse] the beginnings of its end and a prelude to its modern devolution into a marginal phenomenon, tolerated merely because it is no longer significant enough to persecute. The increasing stridency, shrillness, anguish, exile, alienation, and sheer "sickness" of these seventeenth-century outsiders' voices, as they come through de Certeau's sympathetic text, convey a sense of the desperation of a message that it will soon no longer be possible to hear, because there will no longer be a place in this world to receive it.

The Jesuits hadn't so much rejected the interiority of holiness as deemphasized it, according to one of the founding mottoes and strategies of the order: "To leave God for God." This means to approach God rather through service in this world than to revel in the spiritual luxury of communion with the divine. The mystic opposition within the order took the position, however, that worldliness had gone so far that the divine was lost sight of entirely.[34] Coincidentally, Secret documents a history of Jesuit sympathy and scholarly interest in Cabala, which then would be a *mystics*, in de Certeau's language, like related currents of Hermeticism and Alchemy, that the Jesuits could not so much deny epistemologically as oppose strategically. Secret cites, among others, especially Cornelius à Lapide as a Jesuit-Christian cabalist.[35] Lapide published a cabalistic book in 1532, while the Society of Jesus was created in the 1540s, so presumably Cabala was an interest he took *into* the Order, leaving one to wonder whether others did so also.

Antonio Zara, *Anatomia ingeniorum et scientarum* (1615).   In Zara's *Anatomy of Skills and Sciences*, Cabala is totally "trashed" as a debased and superstitious practice, analogous to chiromancy and the divinatory practice of the gypsies.[36] Specifically this seems to have been one of the more strident of some works that we have listed (and there must have been many more) whose opposition to Cabala, and related religious, mystical, or magical styles was a matter of program and polemic. The number, popularity, and intensity of these tracts, spread over a period of nearly a millennium (basically 1200 to the present) testify to the fascination and the attraction of the doctrines they attacked, as well as to their strength and durability. We need only recall Heinrich Graetz's furious repudiation of The Zohar as "the book of lies," which inspired very largely Scholem's rehabilitation of Cabala, to be reminded that the struggle was not between religions but rather between mysticism (and all it implies in terms of challenge to social hierarchy) and orthodoxy *within* religion. Complicating the situation there was certainly ambivalence on the part of some authors who never seemed to be able to make up their minds on what exactly to think of the Cabala, some parts of which were to be condemned but other aspects valued; and also, through a practice of intellectual honesty whereby the opponents ideas were explained—so that the reader could understand what it was exactly he was being asked to reject—the more serious critiques (such as Mersenne's) tend to be very informative about what they are against. We owe much of what we know about Renaissance Cabala, as well as of other provocative currents of the time, to its opponents: this was an age in which the physical extirpation of the "heretic" and his or her writings was far from unusual; but what they stood for, and frequently scrupulously exact citations from, or summaries of, their texts would live on in the words of their enemies. Christians, however, were already old hands of this strange respect they pay to their opponents: for almost two thousand years (or until the findings in this century of original manuscripts in Egypt) basically *all* we knew of the Gnostics came from the scrupulous and comprehensive writings of the Augustine and Iraneus against them.

Of course, other attacks on Cabala are prominent among the works inventoried for this chapter. Although I have not really researched much beyond 1700 in any organized way, even a glance at any comprehensive survey like Scholem's *Kaballah*, will confirm that the polemic continues well into the eighteenth-century and beyond. We can notice this in the struggle between Rabbinical and Hasidic Judaism, not to mention the scandalous factor of the converting (into Catholicism, Islam, or just into Moravian families that kept up an underground loyalty to the Apostate) Sabbatian cults, then into the nineteenth and twentieth centuries (when it's still rife, and with a novel dimension added to its acrimony, internecine violence in Israel). At about the time of the Enlightenment, Judaism had already become a more complicated matter. A perfect paradigm of this complexity may be the illustrious Moses Mendelsohn, who made himself at home in both German and Jewish culture. A more confusing example is provided by Solomon Maimon, cited at the beginning of this chapter, who started out a cabalist and ended up as a child of the Enlightenment, making profoundly original contributions in philosophy that earned the respect of Kant and Lessing. Maimon also composed confessions similar in spirit to Rousseau's, before drinking himself to an early and very secular death in a Polish nobleman's castle!

Fittingly. these sequels to a Renaissance polemic over Cabala survive in an ongoing debate on how much of Scholem's rehabilitation of Cabala, particularly in its Sabbatian version, to accept, as well as an even more difficult question of what, if anything, one can or should do about it. For, as Harold Bloom would not be the last to admit, given the rigors of his reasserted "Western canon," *not everyone can be Kafka*; and to that, surely, Stanley Fish would want to add, "amen, and it's a good thing too!"

Mainstream Cabala

Cornelius à Lapide, *Commentaria Bibliorum Chuonradi Pellicani* (1532); *In Pentateuchum* (1618).   This Conrad Pellican (1478–1556), in Lapide's title, was an important Christian cabalist who had copied texts by Postel and a Dutch orientalist, Gerard Veltwyck, the latter an ambassador of Charles V who had written a critique of The Zohar and Cabala.[37] The importance of Lapide's *On the Pentateuch* was implied by Maren-Sofie Rostvig's citing this book of his as a popular source for Renaissance notions about number, and one that relied on traditionally respected authorities in support of its decisions. Here, "Philo Judaeus, St. Augustine and Bede are invoked in support of the view that there are 6 days of creation for symbolical and arithmetical reasons."[38]

From the paragraph-long extended title of *On the Pentateuch* (see Bibliography), it would seem indeed that Lapide was as much a cabalist as one could be and still count oneself as a Christian. The Cabala allusion is clear in the mention of Simon ben Yohai, primary narrator, as well as listed author of The Zohar. For Lapide, indeed, Simon ben Yohai comes off as being a kind of apostle of Christ. Lapide mentions also in the title that he was basing his exposition on texts that appeared in Latin translation in Galantini's popular book *Of Arcane Catholic Truth*, containing excerpts from The Zohar, which went through numerous editions all through the sixteenthth century. Anchoring his text in orthodox typology, whereby the Hebrew mysteries are seen as supports for Christian faith, in addition to linking his work to the respectable authority of Galantini would surely qualify Lapide's as mainstream Christian Cabala.

Johannes Pistorius, *Artes cabalisticae* (1587). This very popular, varied, and lengthy tome of Latin translations, *Writers of the Cabalistic Arts*, was surely, if there was one, the Norton Reader of Cabala of the Renaissance. It was an anthology of what must have seemed to Pistorius as the most important or most accessible (and appealing) cabalistic texts. More volumes were planned, but this is the only one definitely known to have appeared. Nevertheless, there is probably no more important or influential publication on Cabala in the Renaissance, especially from a Christian (however, Lutheran-Protestant) point of view, than this book, which Blau even claims flatly was one of the most popular and widely read religious documents of the late sixteenth and seventeenth centuries as well as a major conduit for the diffusion of Christian Cabala in English literature.[39] What probably qualified its "hegemony" finally was the publication of Knorr Von Rosenroth's later translations of extensive sections of The Zohar, as well as other works in Hebrew on Cabala, into Latin, published in 1677 and 1684, in two volumes, as *Kabbala Denudata*. *Kabbala Denudata* made undeniably evident, as was *not* the case for Pistorius's earlier collection, largely devoted to *Christian* cabalists, Cabala's *Hebrew-Jewish* provenance and inspiration—whatever other currents fed into it or Christian developments it prompted or allowed (since Rosenroth too was as Lutheran, as was Pistorius, and as eagerly interested in converting the heathen, whether Jewish or Catholic).

Two very important sixteenth-century Jewish figures, for example, not yet widely enough known to be in Pistorius's 1587 collection but amply present in Rosenroth's book of 1677, were Moses Cordovero and Isaac Luria, the second of whom has been the most important name in Cabala between Moses de Leon and the present. Cordovero and Luria were at the heart of the mystical group of cabalists who had gathered in the city of Safed in Syria, out of which had come the enigmatic and controversial *Galia Razia*. Cordovero was most notable for being the author of *Pardes rimmonim* [A Garden of Pomegrantes], first published in Cracow in 1591. *Pardes*, or "Garden" in the title of this book, renowned for its beauty and intellectual clarity and rigor, represent the style of exegesis, typical of Cabala, whereby Torah should be understood on four different levels—each one corresponding to one of the four letters of the word Garden as it is written in Hebrew: (1) literal; (2) figurative; (3) moral; and (4) mystical [secret]. Cordovero seems to have succeeded in creating an Acquinian-type synthesis whose purpose it was to solve paradoxes that The Zohar was just as content to let stand as such; for instance, Scholem mentions particularly a conflict between theism and pantheism that Cordovero's formula "God is all reality, but not all reality is God" was meant to answer.[40] Cordovero, therefore, is responding to an increasing exigency in his century for systematic thought (Harold Bloom calls him blatantly, perhaps not overstating the matter, "an early structuralist"), while continuing also to represent a mystical way or alternative.

Isaac Luria, Cordovero's later contemporary, who emphasized relevance, pedagogy, and explanation, did much to popularize and disseminate cabalistic notions; but the level on which he carried on his activity is very different from Cordovero's. If the latter aimed at making mystical ideas pass muster with the intellectually demanding, the former, more of a charismatic leader and visionary, pitched his appeal on an emotional level. Luria was no great writer or academic, a trait he shared with the later notorious leader, Sabbatai Zevi, and his ideas were spread, beyond his immediate circle and time, basically by texts by his indispensable disciple, Hayim Vital. Luria's seems to have been, quintessentially, an exilic mysticism—gnostic, visionary, utopian, therapeutic, and practical, and keyed to an era when any actual return to a real place for the "chosen people" was increasingly to be excluded: one was to find one's paradise here and now, or never. Luria's mysticism was therefore of the "ecstatic" variety, and his theosophy accordingly stressed an urgency in a situation about which a zoharic Cabala had been more desultory and relaxed. To account for the reality of evil, which an earlier Cabala tended to rationalize by conceiving it as a Neoplatonic emanation, from a design or kernel that still remained benign (evil being the illusion, because we cannot see the end for which it was allowed), Luria developed particularly the doctrine of *Tsimtsum*, or withdrawal of the Creator from his creation. A Lurianic world is one that has been abandoned by the divine and left on its own (overwhelmingly evil) inclinations. Central to this ideology specifically was a concept of a primordial "fallen world," which was expressed in a metaphor that was going to be very crucial for a later heretical Cabala, that of the Breaking of the Vessels, whereby darkness, evil, and disorder were unleashed upon the cosmos. For Luria, this permanent crisis, far from being cause for resignation and ataraxy, rather requires the permanently urgent alertness, anguish, and work of repair or *tikkun*, this mission filling his followers with a sense of purpose and duty, or maybe of a desperate optimism.

A different, more ominous path had been traced, however, but one based on similar assumptions by the morally experimental *Gali Razia*, which seems to have come out of Luria's circle—that of embracing and maximizing the fallen condition of evil and participating in it so as to bring on apocalypse and a new order; and this tendency, from being exploratory and tentative, becomes explicit in the Sabbatian Cabala in the seventeenth century. It is fascinating, nevertheless, that these currents of an evolving Cabala that surface for the Latin-reading European audience, together with more classic passages, in Rosenroth's translations of 1677, *Kabbala Denudata*, tend to be expressed as commentaries on the still commanding *Zohar*, which, as we have stressed so often, is basically a commentary on Torah; so that what we are dealing with in sixteenth- and seventeenth-century Cabala comes down to being interpretations and commentaries on what already was an interpretation and commentary.

It should be remarked also that the Renaissance Christian appropriation of Cabala, characteristic, for example, of the anthology of Pistorius of 1587, would appear, in the light of contemporary theory especially, to be far from the flat *mistake* that scholars even as qualified as Blau and Waite are inclined to think of it as; Secret's recent studies have revealed that the Hebrew sources, and in their original language were far from hidden in the period. That mysteriously stubborn enthusiast and syncretist, Postel, for example, well before 1550, incredibly, according to Secret, may even have *retranslated* a massive manuscript version of The Zohar that an editor claimed to have lost. Another documented project of substantial translation of The Zohar was that of Egidio da Viterbo, which Secret alludes to together with Postel's: "A version [of The Zohar] produced for or by Gilles de Viterbe, who very likely was collecting material for the edification of his own works, is a collection of often lengthy extracts of an incomplete Zohar. The version that G. Postel produced, however, in the intention of publishing it, comprised the entire first section of commentary on Genesis. His editor, J. Oporin, having failed to publish the work, and dying without having returned the manuscript, Postel recommenced a translation, which he might even have finished."[41]

Whether or not Postel ever completed an entire translation, as Secret thinks likely, the version he sent to Oporin has, in our century, been *found* in a manuscript collection; and Secret prints extended excerpts from it, in Postel's Latin, in *The Zohar and the Christian Cabalists of the Renaissance*. This "rediscovered" translation of Postel is somewhat a mystery in itself. In the massive study which he published in 1929, Waite, whose bias is against Postel and Christian Cabala generally, which he sees as interfering with an esoteric-mystical message that comes across more effectively from Jewish-Hebrew sources, mentions its existence as if it were merely a vague rumor: "We have seen that tradition refers also to his Latin translation of the ZOHAR, for which Franck [major historian and analyst of Cabala of the nineteenth century] sought vainly in the public libraries of Paris."[42] Fifteen years later, however, Blau mentions that "This manuscript, long hunted and by many writers suspected of being mythical, was discovered by Perles in the Munich Stasbibliothek as Cod. Lat 7428 (Genesis). Perles's discovery has been verified by Scholem."[43]

Yet Blau, suspicious (or more likely *divided* on the matter) of Cabala, of whatever variety, and seemingly writing out of a tradition of nineteenth-century Jewish positivist scholarship that, reacting to what it considered the "excesses" of heretical Cabala, had little patience for mysticism anyway, minimizes this discovery— consigning it, as Waite did *his* distrust, to a footnote. Blau, who had announced his conclusion near his beginning that Cabala was only a Renaissance fad, had based his argument very largely on the period's lack of access to The Zohar, which the discovery of this item would call into question. Finally, Blau dismisses the matter entirely by commenting that Postel's Zohar had not been printed anyway: "Had the translation of The Zohar on which he worked been published, he might have merited even more consideration."[44]

All of this is not very convincing, naturally, to Secret, whom rather it seems to infuriate, *especially* as one of Blau's major concerns has been to establish the wide dissemination of manuscript material about Cabala, compared to which what was published was only "the tip of the iceberg," in a period when print was not as common or indispensable a passage as it is today. Blau, indeed, seemed to be writing against his own conclusions when he refers to "the vast amount of manuscript material, spread over the libraries of Europe and America, which would indicate a far greater diffusion of cabalistic knowledge and speculation than can be proved from the printed literature."[45] Blau, Secret objects, skirts the issue of other projects of translation and collection of Hebrew texts, for instance, that of a student of Reuchlin's, a J. A. Widmanstadius, who was "one of the epoch's great collectors of cabalist texts,"[46] whom Blau ignores or simply does not know of. Equally Blau will *not* recognize Postel's seriousness and dedication as a scholar of Hebrew. However, the section of The Zohar Postel had translated and which *survives*, that of the commentary on Genesis, would fill the first two volumes of the five-volume English translation of Sperling & Simon and run to well over six-hundred printed pages.

Whatever Blau's convenient doubts as to the accessibility of Hebrew in the Renaissance, certainly C. Knorr von Rosenroth, one of the last great names in Christian Cabala of the Renaissance cannot be faulted for lack of acquaintance with the Hebrew originals of the works he translated for his anthology of 1677–84. Nevertheless, he seems to have been very clear in the ample explanatory statements and documents he appended to his work (for instance, correspondence from Henry More, English Platonist, poet, and important Christian Cabalist) that he felt that the outcome of his labors would be to convert the reader to Protestantism. Rather than being the result of a misunderstanding, ignorance, or confusion, the Christian interpretation of Cabala appears to have been a result of a more or less deliberate choice. The Hebrew classics apparently were well within reach of many scholars, either in the original or through translations, extracts, summaries, and abstracts, circulating in print or manuscript and, of course, through the verbal interchange of an age when the technology of reproduction was far from taken for granted. The Zohar and other cabalistic texts had made already their own ineluctable "misreadings" of Torah, in order, for instance, to fit scripture into the changing needs and expectations of a definitively "exiled" generation. By insisting on locating in the Cabala a cause for Christian faith the Renaissance was only continuing on this path of ingenuity, whereby intention, need, and spirit is valued over literal letter and law.

The Canon of Pistorius

The texts included in Pistorius's influential collection of mainly Christian responses and adaptations of Cabala were:

1. *Reuchlin's* De Verbo Mirifico *and* De Arte Cabalistica

2. *P. Riccio's* De Coelesti Agricultura

This influential Jewish convert to Christianity, by way of Cabala, was an eminent associate of Eugenio da Viterbo's occult studies group. Paulus Riccius had a brother, Augustinus, also a cabalist, who apparently had an impact on Agrippa when the latter was in Italy. P. Riccio's *Heavenly Agriculture* was first published as a series of shorter tracts in the second decade of the sixteenth century, but it comprises about half of Pistorius's massive tome.

3. *Leo the Hebrew's* De Amore

Waite is unhappiest with Pistorius over the inclusion of this item, in which he sees practically no cabalist element. This work, which was enormously popular, seems to have isolated a certain sexual element from Cabala, and added to it a bit of Romantic sentimentality.

4. *Archangelus de Burgo Novo's* Apologia

This was a well-known defense and exposition of Pico's doctrines, published about the middle of the sixteenth century. Archangelus, like Pico's other allies, tried to clear the daring philosopher from the imputation of heresy. Although Pico had been formally cleared, one of the judges who had voted to condemn his conjectures, a Peter Garzia, wrote subsequently explaining why he thought his decision was just. Deemed most outrageous by Garzia and those who had voted Pico's condemnation, apparently, was the cabalistic conjecture he had offered that "nothing so proves the divinity of Christ as magic and Hebrew Cabala," thus claiming a priority for his occult approach even over the hallowed Christian theology, as practiced by such as Saint Thomas Acquinas. Archangelus tried to cope with such well-founded accusations by reasoning that Pico did not mean his magic Cabala to compete with Theology but accompany it, since the business of the latter would be to establish a system on the basis of a revelation that it was up to the former to *prove*. Interestingly, for Archangelus and many other Renaissance acolytes of the occult, cabalistic magic assumed the dimensions and role that we might today ascribe to experimental science. The republication of this text, along with other related ones (Reuchlin, Riccio) this late in the century show how deeply imbued cabalistic studies still were with Pico's Christianizing "magic".

5. R. *Joseph's [Gikatila]* Sha'are orah

This was the *Gates of Light*, the Hebrew-language cabalistic work which reached the widest audience (in Latin translation) in the Renaissance. Gikatila was an important late thirteenth-century contemporary of de Leon and Abulafia, a part of the generation of the golden age of the Spanish Jewish Cabala. His book appears here in Riccio's translation, in the introduction to which the latter had composed a systematic presentation of aspects of Cabala in sixty-six separately numbered items, a "digest" that became a standard Renaissance source in the sixteenth century and, through Pistorius, was going to be useful for at least another one-hundred years.[47] The prestige of Gikatila's *Gates of Light* may be adduced from the fact that it, alone in Pistorius, was included (in Riccio's translation) in Knorr Rosenroth's later anthology.

6. The Sefer Yetzirah *or* Book of Formation, *listed as* by *the* Prophet Abraham.

This essential cabalistic text, just a few pages long but crucially important and an absolutely founding document, expounded the mysteries of creation and *introduced* the doctrine of the emanation of the sephiroth. It appears here in Postel's translation, which had been in print since the 1550s. The *Sefer Yetzirah* is probably the most extensively commented short work in the history of Cabala, both Jewish and Christian.

Waite's opinion is that, whatever its popularity and the intrinsic merits of the writing, Pistorius's collection is basically spurious, at least as regards "The Holy Kaballah."[48] For him, in addition, it is a very serious drawback that there is very little representation of texts translated from the Hebrew. Strictly speaking, this is not true, since Gikatila's *Gates of Light*, translated from the Hebrew into Latin by Riccio is a very significant inclusion and Waite himself mentions that the *Sepher Yetzirah*, an awesomely influential short treatise composed sometime from 300 to 600 A.D., but habitually ascribed to Abraham, "father of the Jews," is also present; but Waite may have felt, and justifiably, that given Riccio's systematic Christianizing introduction to *Gates of Light* and the brevity of the *Sefer Yetzirah*, however sacrosanct, they were meant more as a token of Jewish inspiration for Cabala than as any substantial recognition of it. Waite's severe reservations about Pistorius's version of Cabala were, of course, well founded; and an underlying purpose of his own book, *The Holy Kaballah*, was to redress the errors and confusion resulting from the Christian appropriation of the Cabala in the Renaissance. Two of the authors included in Pistorius, Leo the Hebrew and Riccio, Waite identifies, disdainfully, as having been *converted* Jews. Yet conversion in the Renaissance was often a complicated issue, frequently related more to survival than sincere conviction. According to Graetz,[49] Leon Abrabanel-Medigo, the Leo the Hebrew whose *Dialoghi d'amore* Waite finds so confounding, was no convert, although his children were being raised as "sham Christians" in Portugal at the time their father was writing in Italy. Even for Graetz however, for whom lack of Cabala would not constitute a weakness, Leo's poetry was philosophically related more to Greek than to Jewish culture and was, accordingly, more appreciated by Christian than Jewish readers. Probably there was no more popular work by a Jewish writer for the Christian public in the Renaissance, since Graetz cites an astonishing five editions of it in the space of a mere twenty years.

Waite's objection, that converts or those whose mentality is very close to Christian are not the best situated to represent Cabala, is perhaps overstated, since those who know both sides might have an advantage stemming from a knowledge and intimate connection with both Christian and Jewish, as well as other religious, philosophical, or cultural traditions. The Cabala that the Christian Renaissance responded to so extravagantly and in so many dimensions—philosophical, literary, medical, theological, political, sexual—certainly was problematic. However, the Cabala *of* the Renaissance was the one they invented, the one they took and could handle from the sources that were available and that their conjuncture allowed and enjoined. Much the same suspicion over a Christian distortion, anyway, would pertain, unquestionably, to the evolution of the Jewish Cabala, for instance that of the school of Safed, in the sixteenth century, with the introduction of the very unsettling theories of reincarnation and the hints of the "holy sinner" life style that was to impinge so radically on the later history of the movement.

Carolus Montecuccolus, *In cabalam introductio* (1612).   Blau identifies Montecuccolus, author of this *Introduction to Cabala*, as a follower of Pico. Montecuccolus had begun his book by citing, with great enthusiasm, Pico's "Cabalistic Conclusion," the one that most outraged Garzia and the other judges who voted against him, worth repeating because it surely became the *leitmotif* of Christian Cabala in the Renaissance: "There is no science which makes us more certain of the divinity of Christ than magic and cabala."[50]

This sentence, bolder, more irritating, and unacceptable (since thereby magic takes epistemological precedence over theology), even, than the other wild "conjectures," was condemned with Pico's other "conclusions" as heretical, the same year, 1486, they were pronounced, but not decisively enough to keep them from being repeated widely in the ensuing centuries and therefore from surfacing as quasi-scriptural here well over one-hundred years later. Very much of a Christian cabalist in the already traditional mode of Reuchlin and Georgius, Montecuccolus seems to have been somewhat of a cultural phenomenon of precocity, like his forerunner Pico, dying even younger (at 19), and composing this comprehensive treatment of Cabala at eighteen. An equation he constructs between the first three cabalistic *sephiroth* and the Christian trinity would seem to be representative of the kind of "mystical mathematics" the delegated Catholic opponent of Cabala (and other heterodoxies), Marin Mersenne, felt obliged to enter the lists against nine years later with his *Questions on Genesis*. This Trinitarian interpretation was not, interestingly, always to be a province merely of Christian Cabala but was to be also a widely debated and provocative element in the Jewish polemic that raged around the Sabbatian "heresy" and its aftermath later in the seventeenth and well into the eighteenth centuries (and beyond). The concept of the trinity provided, as a matter of fact, a tempting way of solving, philosophically, the problem of filling a gap between a withdrawn, inscrutable creator and a creation that connotes some involvement and presence. After the model, therefore, of the Christian trinity of *Father-Son-Holy Ghost*, a threesome will be more or less discreetly promulgated by eighteenth-century Sabbatians of *Ain Soph-Demiurge-Shekinah*, in a development that for Rabbinical Judaism seemed appallingly tantamount to an utter rejection of monotheism.

Jacques Gaffarel, *Abdita Divinae Cabalae Mysteria* (1625); *Codicum cabbalisticorum quibus est uses Iannes Picus* (1651). Scholem remarks that an edition of the first book came out in Amsterdam in 1676, and a French translation by Samuel ben Chesed in 1912.[51] Thorndike indicates that Gaffarel wrote other books on the Cabala, while mentioning that in *The Hidden Mystery of the Divine Cabala* the author "replied to the attacks of George of Ragusa and Mersenne."[52]

Gaffarel's theory, in the second listing (an index of manuscripts used by Pico in his studies of Cabala), was that Pico relied heavily for his knowledge on the summaries and commentaries of Menahem Recanati, his Jewish tutor, rather than original texts in Hebrew. This is a crucial issue, at least in the history of Christian Cabala, given such impetus by Pico's energy and extravagance. Pico is a major source for Agrippa and others in transmitting Cabala, so by establishing that he relied on second-hand knowledge, Gaffarel, whether aware of it or not (since, in the earlier work he had been defending Cabala), is weakening the whole movement at its root. As Blau sees it, "the point made by Gaffarel in the seventeenth century . . . [was] that the major source in Hebrew cabalistic literature for the conclusions of Pico was the Bible commentary by Menahem Recanati. It is important to mention this only because Menahem's commentary is not an original work but a simplification of The Zohar. Pico's source may be said, therefore, to be a watered-down version of the cardinal document of the cabala."[53]

This kind of depreciation, if that is what it was, probably played a part in Blau's disillusioning conclusion, announced early on, as the fundamental superficiality of Cabala for Christians. Curiously, while Blau's negativity has gone, to my knowledge, unchallenged or unremarked in English-language scholarship, there is some very well-researched *opposition* to it by François Secret, in French. For Secret, Cabala is rather a major event in the history of ideas, and as we have noticed before, he has called Blau to account for denying this, citing vast areas, for instance, of pre-Pico Christian Cabala that Blau ignored, as well as his underestimation of the French peripatetic mystic and syncretist, Guillaume Postel, whose translation of The Zohar he doesn't seem to want to know about. Blau indeed, seems to be himself in continuity with a nineteenth-century tradition of Jewish scholarship, represented by Heinrich Graetz, which was outraged by "excesses" committed by Cabala in the seventeenth and eighteenth centuries, weird currents, like those of Zevi and Frank, whose strategy was to maximize earthly evil so as to bring on a new world. It is interesting, indeed, how very important the context and intentions of the particular scholar is in deciding about these things. A. E. Waite, whose esteem for Cabala is very high, finds in Gaffarel's book support for an *entirely* different conclusion than Blau. For Waite, the index mentioned by Gaffarel in his title, which seems to have been some kind of commented table of contents to The Zohar, *proves conclusively* that Pico was working from an original, whereas for Blau it meant simply that the index, which he must have consulted in Recanati's commentary, was all he knew of The Zohar. Waite further goes on to mention that in the early twentieth-century French translation of The Zohar by Jean de Pauly the Gaffarel-Pico-Recanati index was thought reliable and helpful enough to attach to the text: "The manuscripts purchased by Picus represented the identical work which has been known for six centuries and over under the name of SEPHER HA ZOHAR. An index of the codices acquired by him was published in 1651 by the French bibliographer Gaffarel, and in the only full translation of the ZOHAR [Jean de Pauly's French] into a living language its installments are appended to the various sections. There are innumerable mistaken references, but the index reflects the text; what is missing in items referred to one section may be found sometimes in another . . . there is no question that the treasures of Picus are those which we know under the distinctive name of ZOHAR."[54]

Cabala and Philosophy

Leo the Hebrew, *De Amore* (1535). Cabala in Leo the Hebrew's widely known book *On Love* has had the reputation of being a matter of image rather than substance, blending into a genre of Neoplatonic love poetry, with a tincture of mysticism—accounting for its popularity, in several languages, during the Renaissance and after.[55] Waite is of the opinion that this work, therefore, did not merit its place in Pistorius's definitive collection: "There is only one direct reference to the Kabbalah in the whole three hundred folio pages which the dialogues occupy in Pistorius."[56] Waite notices, however that this text shares, nevertheless, a certain sexual attitude in common with Cabala, both in regard to the world, because in it "however much love is transcendentalised in the dialogues, it is always sexual, as it is throughout the ZOHAR," and relating to heaven, where God is divided into knowable and unknowable aspects. The experience of sexual congress would remain the primary metaphor for the fullest possible realization of mingling with that part of the divine that can be *known* (taken in the Biblical sense of carnality), passion taking precedence over intelligence. Although we cannot understand the divine intellectually, we can and must combine with it physically, in an act rather of transcendental copulation than transcendental meditation: "This Book of Love and its Mysteries moves forward to deeper things, when the knowledge of God is presented, as regards language and images, under a transcendentalised sexual aspect. God is loved in proportion as He is known, and as He cannot be known entirely by men, nor His wisdom by the human race, so He cannot be loved as He deserves, for such an exalted sentiment transcends the power of our will . . . This felicity does not consist in the cognoscitive act of God . . . but in the copulation of the most interior and united Divine Knowledge . . . Such copulative felicity with God cannot be continuous, however, during our present life."[57]

Amos Comenius, *The Labyrinth of the World* (1631). Constantinos Patrides refers to the indebtedness of this idealistic and internationalist Baconian educator for his cosmic hierarchies to Pico's *Platonic Discourse on Love*. Comenius was the author of many pedagogical texts, as well as this mystical confession, which tries to locate the divine in what it calls, in its subtitle, "The Paradise of the Heart." Comenius's Reformist versions of Neoplatonism were apparently a factor in the formation of John Milton's poetics of justification (of divine order). Comenius conceptualized what he thought of as a seven-fold pattern of levels that are linked by the toils of educators and the efforts of poets, but these seven are really only a more nuanced version of Pico's *three* harmonious and corresponding realms, that same cabalistic arrangement of the three worlds of the elementary (physical), the intellectual (mental), and the celestial (spiritual) that was adapted from The Zohar (or a précis or index of same). [58]

It is tempting to conjecture how neatly Spinoza's three-rung epistemological ladder, of just a little later in the seventeenth century—composed of (1) "sensual" imagination; (2) reason; (3) intuition—fits into this tradition of hierarchical, if corresponding, realms. In common with Cabala and the Gnostic and Platonic notions it was transmitting, Spinoza opines an increasing solitude as one rises to a higher level and thereby experiences the refining process of *conversion* (a modern ironic avatar of which would be Kafka's "Metamorphosis"). On the lowest plane, that of imagination—which Spinoza calls also, pejoratively, merely "opinion"—confusion and ambiguity is maximal, where anyone's word is as good as anyone else's since one is subject here to a necessity which can always be canceled by a greater one. This is expressed through the contradictions and inherent futilities of one's own and others' desire, most of the torment over which lies precisely in an ineluctable if unreliable illusion than one can or should do something about realizing one's wishes. This lowest level would correspond in Cabala to the ordinary condition of *irrational* (which Spinoza calls pejoratively also, in a usage that should dismay us, "imaginative") humanity, threatened, tempted, and assaulted constantly by the double-bind fantasies and seductions of evil, called "the evil prompter." Spinoza's next highest plane, the *rational*, is the one that only an earthly elite can hope to inhabit, or just a few individuals in some of their best moments; nevertheless, its consolations and guidance are humanity's best defense against the disorders and "sad passions" or fears and hopes of the delusionary imagination. This rational rung seems close to Cabala's intellectual plane, whereby study of sacred texts and dialogue with the masters is in itself a protection against exposure to cosmic (external) and psychological (internal) elements that one is inevitably racked by on the lower rung.

This emphasis on security in the soberly cerebral motivates a suspicion, alike in Spinoza and Cabala, of somatic states generally, whether that of sleep, dream, or of bodily functions and gratifications. Spinoza, indeed, likes to qualify error as a state of "dreaming while one is awake." Cabala is, however, while cautiously so, more sanguine than Spinoza about the possibilities of unconsciousness: at the same time as one is defenseless against suggestions from below (lustful, most usually) one is also, hopefully, correspondingly open to the ameliorating influence of those from above. Samson and David, for instance, were great (sexual) sinners but also great achievers.

The highest level, the *intuitive*, for Spinoza is the one that, suitably, he seems to say least about. What is involved here, beyond the rational, is the remarkable "intellectual love of God," separated from all narcissism, egoism, and interest; and because there is nothing earthly to attach knowledge of it to, there is equally no language in which it can be expressed or known. This level of the intuition of Spinoza would be that of the unknowable mystery of Cabala's *ain soph*, or irrefrangible, hard kernel of the divine, withdrawn behind the line of conceivable human perception or intellect, a beginning from which the rational as well as sensual-irrational-imaginative planes have emanated, while yet remaining cold, entire, and apart. It was precisely Spinoza's ultimate intuition of the unconcerned and uninvolved divine that constituted for Leibniz the cabalism he would try to correct: for the latter, quintessential philosopher of science, the unknowable as such did not exist, only the not yet known, or more exactly, the not yet understood.

Joseph de Voysin, *Disputatio Cabalisticae* (1635); *Observationes in prooemium Pugionis fidei* (1687). As explicitly mentioned in the extended title of the first book, *Cabalistic Disputation*, Cabala here is meant to coalesce with Platonism.[59] This is in the tradition of the European and Christian adaptation of the Cabala, commencing with Pico's Neoplatonic interpretation of Recanati's commentary on de Leon's Zohar, in the last quarter of the fifteenth century, and reaching an apogee with the mystical rendering of the cabalistic ideas and styles common among the Cambridge Platonists in the last half of the seventeenth century. Secret mentions that Voysin was a source also for Pascal's acquaintance with Cabala, specifically through the second listing, which would be his prefaced edition of Ramon Martin's *Pugio fidei*.[60] This *Sword of Faith*, a testimony to the importance of Cabala among Christians centuries before Pico's fancy for it, was composed late in the thirteenth century. Martin was a Spanish Dominican with a special competence in Hebrew, someone who was apparently very well able to use cabalistic styles of argument and exegesis in support of Old Testament typology.

Graetz was never less an impartial historian than when he wrote about Martin, whom he calls "the first man in Europe to sharpen weapons of learning for the contest against the Jews. Raymond Martin wrote two books full of malevolent hostility against Judaism whose very titles announce that the prison cell and the sword were to be employed against its adherents. They are called *Bridle for the Jews* and *Dagger of Faith* ... Although Raymund Martin's 'Dagger of Faith' was neither sharp nor pointed ... yet it made a great impression because of the amount of learning displayed therein."[61] That four centuries later Martin's *Sword* was still in the Christian arsenal speaks for the ongoing relevance and effectiveness of cabalistic methods in so crucial a matter of conversion. Voysin's edition of this work was not published, however, until well after Pascal's premature demise (1662), so presumably the influence was exerted through his earlier book, *Cabalistic Disputations*, published in 1635, or through personal communication between these two seventeenth-century French "mystics."

Pascal's renowned fideism, whose "heart had its reasons," would find only confirmation in a Cabala that became increasingly attached to faith as it evolved. Faith, of which Cabala seems to demand a greater quantity than did a less mystical, rabbinical Judaism, becomes an even more important factor in the Lurianic sixteenth-century modifications. These require the cabalist to believe in a primordial and cataclysmic Breaking of the Vessels, inviting a permanent duty of repairing them. Faith, then, becomes all the more ineluctable when the later followers, adherents, or sympathizers of Sabbatai Zevi (which, *before* the apostasy, whatever the subsequent denials, comprised, more or less intensely, with rare, if important, exceptions, just about the whole Diaspora) and his prophet Nathan of Gaza, are asked to believe all the more blindly after the betrayal. In the Jewish tradition, of course, miracles have occasionally happened, but, seemingly as a last resort, and usually accompanied by tangible signs and events that made it easier to accept them, as well as warnings not to count on more. Alternatively, a certain rational vein, from Maimondides (who said the day of miracles had passed with the Second Temple) to Mendelsohn and Graetz, would prefer to do without them entirely, if at all possible. Sabbatai, on the other hand, has been one of the few important figures in Jewish history who has been commonly compared to Jesus; and this has been at least partly because of the credibility he was able to inspire, on a basis more of charisma and eloquence (the former his, the latter Nathan's) than rationality. Unquestionably this "faith" factor played its part in the drift of Cabala away from traditional Judaism in its recent history as well as a certain affinity it has always had for Christianity, which believes, following an early father, Tertullian, "because it's ridiculous" (credo quia absurdum est). For the Christian adepts, as well as their Sabbatian counterparts, of "negative capability," as the English Romantic and very platonist poet, John Keats, was later to define the ability to resist an "irritable reaching after facts," material evidence is rather in the realm of doubt than faith.

Cabala as Medicine

Johann (of Nidde) Pistorius (1546–1608), *De vera curandae pestis ratione* (1568). In this *True Rational Cure for the Plague*, Pistorius undertakes to expound the "miraculous" medical uses for Cabala. A little bit later on, opposing this presumption, a Jacob Heilbronner, ostensibly parodying Pistorius's vocabulary in the title of his own polemic, *A Magical and Cabalistic Method of Curing Every Disease*, which he published in 1601, attacks Pistorius especially for his "verbal prescriptions", based on the theory of the healing power of certain magic words and formulas. According to Thorndike, "Heilbronner has found this magical book which Pistorius wrote while practicing medicine, in which he asserts that there is a power in words and names to cure diseases, and talks of a ladder of angels, three horizons, and the Cabala of the rabbis. Heilbronner declares that all pious men believe that good and holy angels of God lend no aid to magical and theurgical incantations, characters, words, names and letters, even the *Tetragrammaton*. The inference is that Pistorius has been for many years an associate of the demons."[62] Thorndike assumes also that Heilbronner was really attacking here a later book of Pistorius, the extremely important anthology of cabalistic texts of 1587, but found it easier to make his points against Pistorius's confessed interest in the application of Cabala to medicine.

Worth noticing here also is this challenge to the forays Cabala is so often tempted to make into therapeutics, which amounts frequently, of course, to treading into someone's medical or theological territory, or both. Equally interesting is that the strenuous counterattacks often allow the validity of Cabala in a field other than their own. The historical context of these "games of tennis" is that a medieval synthesis and theological unity had been irremediably fractured but no new order was yet decisively in place, though there were many hints as to what it would be like (technological-scientific-materialistic-secular). One therefore wasn't sure if one were living for heaven or for earth, or if one could or should do both. Mere health, as physical well being, for instance, seems to become an important factor in the Renaissance, an adjunct of the rising philosophy of power, which always requires material force and energy. This accounts for the sudden relevance of medicine and styles of treatment and authority as well as the inception of what William James was later to term "healthy mindedness" in religion, with Jesuit and related religious movements that were trying to stay relevant to more secular circumstances. Another response to the same set of urgent circumstances came out of the mystical currents, including Cabala, which either tried to reestablish transcendence in immanence, through an ideology of Natural Magic, or to redignify sickness and exile as ramparts against secular power, behind which intimacy with the divine could still occur. However, because of the fragmentation of cultural, political, and religious authority, lacking was any final or decisive key, word, or structure, hence the obsessive, incessant search for one, the recourse also to the stake and pillory as means of dealing with opponents who could not be convinced by more civilized means. By the middle of the eighteenth century, of course, the battle is over: the mystics are now "tolerated," since they no longer constitute any kind of rival order or menace: health, power, material vitality, and visions of prosperity are to be the reigning masters. Such a "final solution" would eventually create the consensus necessary to propel the other, whoever that turned out to be, outside of the arena where words are treated seriously. Any opposition from now on must go under-ground, into dreams, art, the unconscious, jokes, substance-or-oth-erwise-induced "visions," nomadism, psychosis, seduction. *On the surface* one can henceforth fight the enemy only with their own weapons, in other words, by going over to them.

Until the great modern states started filling this "vacuum of the Renaissance" at the end of the seventeenth century, what was missing was a commonly shared set of values that could act as an instance of last resort; so such "debates" went on endlessly in an atmosphere of Renaissance plurality, insecurity, and ambition. Heilbronner's lack, for instance, of solid empirical grounds from which to attack Pistorius's cabalistic-Paracelsan medical magic is apparent in his resorting to the example Thorndike paraphrases above of "good and holy angels of God" that would be opposed to such diabolical techniques. On this childish level, of course, of whose angels are better, the debate could and did go on indefinitely, only to be interrupted from time to time by equally inconclusive perse-cutions and executions, for instance, as recounted by de Certeau, a certain "Pierre de Lancre, royal councilor at the Parliament of Bordeaux, a 'disciple and imitator of Montaigne,' told how he had sentenced to the stake hundreds of these 'magicians,' among whom he included both the *alumbrados* [Spanish mystics who claimed a special divine illumination] and the Rosicrucians."[63]

Thomas Liebler Erastus, *Disputationum de medicina nova P. Paracelsi* (1572). This *Disputation on New Medicine* is a critique of the abuses of Paracelsan cabalistic "medicine," the very notion of which to this apparently empirical author, seems to be a flat absurdity. On the other hand, it is significant that the ideas of Cabala are considered to be otherwise salutary and worthy of respect. Thorndike's paraphrase brings out the tension of this characteristic ambivalence about a doctrine that, at once, attracted and repelled: "Erastus approves of the cabala if it is limited to anagogical and symbolic interpretation of the Bible. But if it attempts to work wonders by concepts, words, characters, figures, prayers, and observance of hours, it is nothing but detestable magic and he is surprised that so sound a scholar as Reuchlin put as much faith in it as he did."[64] Aside from the fact that the whole matter of truth and falsity is ambiguous for a doctrine according to which falsity is intrinsic, this defensive separation of Cabala into true and false approaches is, of course, perfectly understandable from the point of view of its reception; but it should be pointed out that, apart from its abstract theosophical conceptions, Cabala does indeed attempt to work wonders by enjoining specific behavior and rituals. Without its mystical theosophy, cabalistic magic becomes just another means of exchange in the world, but, like Marxism, Cabala is (was?) a theory that cannot do without a practice. A critique like Erastus's seems to be quite typical in its ambivalent appreciation of the virtues and dangers of Cabala. Although his recommending a separation of an a ideal from a practical Cabala is understandable, it is contradictory also, since what it does is to sever the premises of Cabala from its conclusions, through fear of contamination of the higher ideals by a world that looks only for results. If Cabala, thereby, is rendered harmless it achieves this by way of insignificance. It has been denatured, truncated, neutered, and is, perhaps, farther from itself than if it was subject to the outright distortion of mumbled formulas and instant magic; because in the latter is kept at least the theory, if not the noblest conceivable practice, of an organic connection between higher and lower realms.

Henry van Heer, *Spadocrene, hoc est fons Spadanus* (1614).   This *The Eunuch's Fountain of Sterility* was a very intemperate but surely typical attack on the Paracelsan-alchemical-cabalistic methods of Johannes Van Helmont (1577–1644), probably the most influential figure in mystic medicine (Thorndike's phrase) of the first half of the seventeenth century. Windelband calls Johannes Van Helmont (not to be confused with his son, Franciscus Mercurius [1618–1699], who carried on in his father's footsteps, even publishing many of the elder Van Helmont's works posthumously) one of the most important of the numerous pupils of Paracelsus. Windelband explains that, together with Boëhme and other Platonists, he resisted the new "mechanical" principles for explaining soul and body, of Hobbes, Spinoza, Descartes, and Leibniz, holding fast instead to a traditional vitalism (concept of soul and body as qualitatively homogenous entities, energized by a vital force or entelechy, which can be affected and modified through occult techniques). Marjorie Nicolson agrees thoroughly with Windelband on the importance of Van Helmont, adding only: "His genius was recognized and acknowledged by his generation in that ironic fashion of theirs—by long imprisonment and condemnation for heresy." [65]

Cabala, in the Van Helmonts and the Cambridge Platonists, was an ally in this resistance to Cartesian Cogito—rationalism and the mind-body dualism it fostered, defending a vision of human integration against the threat of an incipient scientific fragmentation and mechanical reduction—protecting, at least some and for a while, against both the terror of the stars and that of the atoms. Alternatively Cabala could function, for instance, in the conciliating idealism of Henry More, who was long associated with the younger Van Helmont, as a bridge between an otherwise starkly contradictory Cartesianism and Platonism. For More, Cartesian dualism was tolerable, even desirable, as the most current (cabalistic) metaphor or mask in a continuing progress of revelation.

The Van Helmonts adapted their Cabala to the experimental mood of the day by making it more gestural and physical. This practical aspect is evident, for instance, in the elder Van Helmont's cabalism, in a treatise he wrote based on a bizarre idea that Hebrew characters for letters represent primarily the physical motions of the mouth and tongue used to produce the sounds. [66] Thus it is not only the words that have the Paracelsan "magic operative force," but, more importantly, the very position of the organs of speech, whether any sound comes out of them or not. The Van Helmonts, who like the other vitalists were trying to deal with the "reality" of Cartesianism, were also important for their influence on the seventeenth-century Cambridge platonists: Thomas Burnet, Ralph Cudworth, and Henry More. The elder Van Helmont's influence on the Cambridge Platonists was certainly reinforced through his son, Franciscus Mercurius's connection (in the formal capacity of physician) with Anne Conway (1631–1679). Franciscus's bond with the Lurianic-Lutheran Cabala, which was of a dramatically apocalyptic nature while not shy of the subversive (of orthodoxy, whether Christian or Jewish) notion of reincarnation, of Knorr

Rosenroth was one that was organic and intimate. Rosenroth, translated the works of the elder Van Helmont into German as well as a book by the younger that extended (his father's) cabalism into the uncanny experimental domain of an invention of a sign language for the deaf. Both Rosenroth and Franciscus had studied Hebrew intensely in Amsterdam, where they knew each other, and Franciscus was to participate significantly, if anonymously (maybe having observed the rewards of his father's fame) in the *Kabbala Denudata* anthology of 1677–1684, while serving, through his stays in England as an intermediary between More and Rosenroth. Coincidentally, it is this Christian cabalist, Knorr Rosenroth, who later translates Sir Thomas Browne's compendious summa *Vulgar Errors* into German, and into the same language More's influential treatise *Immortality of the Soul*. A theological work by Rosenroth that explains cabalistically *the* portion of the Bible that the visionary English seventeenth-century probably found most fascinating, *Genuine Explication of the Visions of the Book of Revelation*, was published in English translation in 1670, or just about the time, through the younger Van Helmont, the name of Isaac Luria is becoming a more familiar one in England.

Anne Conway was the lifelong confident, correspondent, and Platonic Love of Henry More, probably filling the kind of role in his "life of the mind" that was Princess Elisabeth's for Descartes. Although her correspondence and conversation would have sufficed, a manuscript that she left behind, which was edited into a book by More and Van Helmont, *The Principles of the Most Ancient and Modern Philosophy*, place her among the most important Christian cabalists of the seventeenth-century. The "most ancient" philosophy is Cabala, while "modern" can mean only Descartes, so difficult yet so necessary for these visionaries to come to terms with; so as Nicolson comments: "Her attempt in her treatise was to suggest a way of thinking which should include the most significant features of Cartesianism, amplified and corrected by what she believed to be the complementary system of the cabbalistic philosophers . . . her desire is not therefore to go back to the past; but—like many other seventeenth-century cabalists—to find a way of thought which should make consistent the Christian religion and the new science of the century." How she manages this is through the insertion into the appalling Cartesian separation of the mind and body, which had resulted in the latter's becoming nothing more than a machine, or a mechanical principle, the cabalistic notion of a plurality of souls (or minds), only one of which would be so alienated. These hermeneutic acrobatics seem positively Leibnizian, in the sense that they find a dignified place for everything. Indeed, Leibniz, who had heard of Anne Conway through Van Helmont was enormously impressed by her and, in fact, winds up alluding more to her than to More, in his *Nouveaux Essais*, as a representative of the idealist-vitalist current.

Anne was the revered Aspasia-Mary of a mystic circle of poets, philosophers, cabalists, doctors, alchemists, and even scientists, including Franciscus Mercurius (who was all of those things and a few more), that gathered around her in her country estate, at Ragley, where a prolonged illness (something like a twenty-year headache) kept her for decades. This "community" seems to have been a kind of Christian cabalist equivalent, at least in spirit, of the Jewish-mystic City of God of Safed. Sheila Spector, basing her justified hyperbole on Nicolson's edition of the Conway letters, says, in her recent annotated bibliography of Cabala, flatly, that Conway was "Considered one of the greatest female thinkers of the seventeenth century," listing a cabalistic work by her, published posthumously, and three cabalistic texts of Franciscus Mercurius Van Helmont.[67]

Obicius, Hyppolitus. *De nobilitate medici contra illius obtretatores* (1619). In *On the Noblility of Medicine against Its Detractors*, Obicius, citing Pico and his sixteenth-century proponent, Archangelus de Burgo Novo, defends Cabala as an authentic magical art that has its uses also in medicine;[68] thereby he situates himself in the tradition of Paracelsus and Chamisso, or those who were applying a practical Cabala to the problems of the body. It's curious that, for a sublimely transcendental ideology, this very earthly terrain of the body was where the fight over Cabala was often engaged. Some, for example, while disallowing its more grandiose claims, of union, or "copulation" with the divine, allow for its medical usage; others felt that the latter was a derogation and distortion of the message of Cabala. This surely resembles the quandaries of H. C. Agrippa, as we have described them in chapter 2. Agrippa certainly felt pulled between the two poles where he seems to sway back and forth: on the one side were the claims of a rare if difficult access to sublime possibilities and effectiveness; while on the other there was the need to respond to the demands of his generation, increasingly articulated in the secular terms of power, health, and survival (his own, most immediately, given the contingencies of the life of a man of letters of the sixteenth-century, forerunner and prototype of today's rootless and vulnerable intellectual).

Complicating this issue also is the question of correspondences or analogies, certainly intrinsic to Cabala in the connection it established between a spiritualized matter and a materialized spirit; for Cabala as for mysticism generally, problems of the body are never far away: "What is the body? Mystic discourse is obsessed by this question,"[69] as de Certeau has commented acutely; however this was a different, more sacral body, before it was handed over to production, medicine, psychology, prison, conditioning, and education. De Certeau suggests even that the discourse of *mystics* vanished because it no longer had any material to work with, once the body had been "claimed" by grossly material values associated with production.

In what sense are we to conceive of the body? In paring our toenails are we worshiping the numinous? In some essential portions of The Zohar it is very much a question, indeed, of God's toenails and worse. The Zohar as well as Torah, which it comments, is very much preoccupied with our bodily parts and what we do or don't do with them. Unquestionably the Cabala was useful to the Renaissance in exalting or at least giving a good or better conscience to pleasures of the senses by supplying them with a religious aura and thereby confuting some internalized obstacles to "progress". Within the strictly Jewish ethos even Cabala had to overcome an ancient proscription, which Maimonides (1135–1204) had recently reinforced, against representing the deity anthropomorphically, on its way to its own worshipful use of the flesh. The role of a theorist of "seduction" like Jean Baudrillard, maybe, isn't so different today from this reassuring function of Cabala. A justification for Baudrillard's philosophy of ineluctable simulation is elimination of a certain residual hesitancy toward cultural evolution, all the more formidable if the direction of that evolution is toward meaninglessness. A thesis of an early book of Jean Baudrillard's, well before the fascinations of seduction or simulations of virtual reality, was that the role of publicity in our culture is not so much to sell or even tell about the product, *but rather to ease our guilt*, hung over from a Christian asceticism that went along better with an earlier phase of Capital, at consuming it.[70]

Cabalistic physicality may, in this spirit, be read as one of the ways the Renaissance used to reinvent a past to which a present could believe itself faithful. Possibly this "excusing" potential could lead all the way over to another decried Renaissance current, libertinism. Blocking the way from Cabala, and other similarly challenging occult styles that tend to sacralize the physical, to libertinism, which finds redemption enough in the physical itself, such was the purpose of Montaigne's most serious and extensive essay, *The Apology to Raymond Sebond*. This work was a response to the challenge posed by the logical aporias of Agrippa's *Vanity of the Arts and Sciences*, which had traced vividly a trajectory from experimental, far-ranging mystical-cabalistic exploration to the blind alley of a skeptical fideism. This fideism was presented by Agrippa as the only possible recourse to accepting the implications of the vast but illegitimate power afforded by a skilled frequentation of the occult. For Agrippa, occult studies were in league with and finally tantamount, in titanic pride, to empirical sciences. In such an atmosphere of universal irony and suspicion, for Agrippa and his acolytes (John Dee, Theophrastus Bombasus Paracelsus, Thomas Vaughan) "everything is permitted," even as *Vanity* had the effrontery to recommend, *blissfully ignorant faith*!

However, if there was one thing Montaigne, a true man of the West, would never *resign* it would be intellect. His remedy, in this desperate extreme, was to float Agrippan-Cusan "ignorance" (*docta ignoratio*, or learned and intended stupidity) on the seas of its own thought: *for how do you know you do not know*? Ironically, Montaigne is appalled at the ethical vacuum that yawns when the demiurgic demonism of occult ambition ends in the total abandonment of mind, with a corresponding reduction of the human to the status of animal or even object. This is *irony* because Montaigne's ultimate tendency is to desert the ethical anyway, by referring it indefinitely to other scenes, where all behavior, no matter how shocking or unusual, is considered acceptable—as in his famous allusion to "the other side of the Pyranees," there where what is bad here is good. Agrippa, on the other hand, in much the same manner as

Montaigne, of a display of "total learning," or enough to dissuade anyone from anything, holds on all the more tightly to those things he does know, pointing the reader beyond words, while Montaigne's has been referred to other words, works, customs, and winds up not even sure what not knowing means, not even *sure* progress is such a bad thing.

Nevertheless, there is a connection, maybe even a causal one, between the specter of libertinism and a cabalistic-medical-theurgic "floating of the signifier" that both Agrippa and Montaigne exemplified as well as warned against. The same relation holds between Libertinism and Cabala as between Magic and Science, both of which imply a willingness, drive, and instinct, however hampered or disguised, to experiment beyond the realm of good and evil, or all moral parameters, in the interests of the always-further reaching out of an indomitable, unteachable will to power. From this point of view, that of impatience with all limits and incipient violation of all boundaries, Science is the Magic of our time, as Magic was the Science of yesterday.

When Cabala became a messianic movement in the seventeenth century, which occurred ineluctably under the pressure of events and rising expectations, when there was no longer time or patience for human and divine bodies merely to *represent* each other, they were pronounced, by Sabbatian fiat, as having *become* each other. From that point on, it became impossible, catastrophically, for a body to be or do wrong, in a world from which abstention could mean only loss and lack of faith. Libertinism and Cabala come together, in fact, during this period, when Cabala offers its banner of hope to the masses, at a time when Holy Land and Holy Body can only become literal, both to be attained, reached, touched, inhabited through adding an eleventh commandment, *which was to disobey the first ten*, onto the Decalogue! Later one Frankist-Sabbatian cabalist, Baruchiah Russo (Osman Baba), even recommended, for instance, turning the thirty-six acts of sexual union and incest the Bible forbids into positive commands.[71] This libertine quality becomes even more evident as Cabala goes into its eighteenth-century exile-within-exile of anomalous cults and even popular movements, that, responding to a quintessentially modern demand for "ecstasy now," then spread over Eastern Europe—for instance, most scandalously, in the ritual promiscuity of the

Frankists and related sects like the Greek-Turkish Dönmeh of Saloniki, who followed Sabbatai into Islamic apostasy.

Saint Teresa's Castle and Kafka's

Tommaso Garzoni, *La Piazza Universale* (1585). Scholem cites this work as containing an extended disquisition on Cabala.[72] Garzoni's *Universal Fortress* was apparently widely known in Europe. Surely it is no coincidence that it was later translated into German by that same mysterious seventeenth-century writer, H. C. Grimmelshausen, whose fascination with religious dissidence and anomaly is known to every reader of *Simplicissimus* and who published a short novel, "The False Messiah," about Sabbatai Zevi in 1675, or shortly after the notorious apostasy.

The word *fortress* is used frequently in mystical literature—in the idiom of Saint Teresa, for instance—as a metaphor for *interiority,* interchangeable also with castle. This architectural metaphor is very prominent, for example, in Saint Teresa of Avila's masterpiece, *The Interior Castle* (1588). This text, according to Catherine Swietlicki, was just about the acme of the Spanish Christian Cabala of the Renaissance.[73] Swietlicki, not the first to notice the impact of Cabala on the great Spanish mystics, does a comprehensive and credible inventory of correspondences between zoharic "mansion" imagery and Teresa's many-tiered fortress or castle that seems too exact to be just coincidence. It is significant that Teresa, Luis de Leon, and Juan de la Cruz were all of Jewish *converso* descent; but Teresa, not very erudite, was likely to have absorbed her Cabala indirectly through folk motifs and instinct and also by instruction of the more learned Juan, with whom for years she was in daily contact.

Equally there are unquestionably mystical echoes in the title of Kafka's *The Castle.* The alternation, for instance, of pristine clarity and deep, murky obscurity as ways in which the strangely urgent nomadic Land-Surveyor glimpses the Castle are thoroughly in the tradition of the fitful nature of visionary experience, or even parodies of same. Additionally, Shekinah and Lilith figures are absolutely strewn through Kafka, especially through the three novels, often interchangeable, or hard to tell apart, as they tend to be on the lowest of the ten sephiroth, *Malkuth* or World, of Cabala. Certainly there is an air of symbolic vagueness, urgency, and indeterminacy about these "women" of Kafka—with a hint of sexual mysticism about them, as if they were necessary and ineluctable links and connections to the numinous (Law, Castle, Amerika), or alternatively, the fastest way from its terrors and challenges.[74]

The structurally interminable nature of Kafka's texts, the traps, futilities, and quandaries they pose, would well exemplify a motto from the ancient text, the *Pirke Abot*, as profoundly awakening as anything in the Jewish mystical literature: "You are not required to complete the work, but neither are you free to desist from it." A dialectic and dialogue of the hidden and the open, as Kermode, for instance, expounds it in *The Genesis of Secrecy*, would correspond very well to the desperate mood of this motto as also to the teasing indeterminacy of zoharic styles of exegesis and commentary: "Parable . . . may proclaim truth as a herald does and at the same time conceal truth like an oracle . . . We glimpse the secrecy through the meshes of the text, but what is divined is what is visible from our angle. It is a momentary radiance, delusive or not." The appeal to authority, for Kermode's Kafka, as it was in The Zohar, is as dubious as it was ineluctable. Before Kafka's Law we are "hot for secrets," while all the same, ruefully, "our only conversation may be with guardians who know less and see less than we can." As Kermode notices also, although we are given a number of variously plausible explanations for the prolonged and likely vain wait of K. before the Door of the Law, which was "there only for him," there is no single meaning for this allegorical adventure or lack of same, no one way in which it can and must be understood.[75] K., we may assume is Everyman, or Humanity, with no choice but to wait to see what we are living for. Equally we must assume that there must be a reason, but beyond that, and, of course, that "momentary radiance," which depends however on senses that Kafka trusted about as little as Spinoza, we know only that we know nothing, and not even that!

That Kafka himself was a more or less desultory student of Cabala has become familiar enough to have become almost a commonplace. For instance, writing in introduction to the American translation of *Amerika*, it is rather the cabalistic background that is taken for granted by Klaus Mann than Kafka's immediate social circumstances, which need to be specially stressed: "His vision of

The Trial and *The Castle*, in which the invisible Power hides, was influenced, not only by the esoteric wisdom of the Cabala, but also by his own experiences as a minor functionary of the ancient Austrian Bureaucracy."[76] More baroquely Angelo Maria Ripellino speaks of the atmosphere in which Kafka came up, reminiscent of alchemical "magic Prague" that the English polymath-hermeticist-cabalist John Dee and his counterfeiting, by then earless younger alchemist colleague, Edward Kelley, sojourned in memorably, if enigmatically, as guests of Rudolph II, King of Bohemia, late in the sixteenth-century. Kafka's Prague was suffused with a kind of *Eastern European-Jewry chic*, perhaps of the kind that turned Scholem, against the grain of his assimilationist family, toward the mysteries of Cabala, or at about the same time, according to Bakan, aroused Freud's curiosity about The Zohar. Ripellino mentions, for instance a "Jiri [Langer], friend of Kafka, student of the Cabala and psychoanalysis and author of poems in Hebrew."[77] Kafka's connections with this Eastern European Cabala have recently been the subject of a book-length monograph, by Karl Erich Grözinger.[78] Grözinger scants, however, the kind of urgently messianic-revolutionary and gnostic Cabala that Scholem (and Benjamin) found in Kafka, in favor of a more mellow-sentimental (maybe more livable) Hasidic one. For Benjamin and Scholem, Kafka was somewhat of a meeting place of minds that were drifting apart, especially in the thirties— Benjamin toward a secular if messianic Marxism, Scholem toward a mystical-philosophical Zionism. Kafka became a neutral ground where literature and mysticism could meet on the terrain of Cabala.[79] Kafka was, as they could agree, one who created his literature out of the whole cloth of the cabalist paradox of the ineluctable betrayal involved in a revelation of the hidden, which somehow still remains a mystery: *before the law*, as impossible to obey or know as to abandon.

Harold Bloom has reinforced his idea as to the protomodernism of Cabala in general and The Zohar in particular with a specific focus on Kafka as cabalist. The name of Bloom's recent little book *The Strong Light of the Canonical* reflects an approach to Kafka through the style and mood of a messianic-gnostic Cabala as pronounced by Scholem in some powerful but enigmatic and uncharacteristically prophetic statements from the thirties, "Ten Unhistorical Aphorisms on Kabbalah." The tenth of these Bloom has paraphrased and partially translated as follows: "Kafka, un-knowingly, secularized Kabbalah. His writings therefore have for Scholem as for Benjamin and others 'something of the strong light of the canonical', of that perfection which destroys"[80] These ten "Unhistorical Aphorisms" of Scholem, subject of a searching essay-commentary by David Biale,[81] are a bit of a mystery in their own right. They constitute one of the few occasions on which Scholem expressed himself directly, leaving aside his usual scholar-historian's objective stance. Complicating things, at least for a wider public, is that they have not been, to my knowledge, published in English, due to copyright or other restrictions. Biale reproduces these very dense and frequently obscure, not to say esoteric fragments in their original German, which he then paraphrases and expounds.

Biale states flatly that: "Scholem saw in Kafka's writing . . . a modern form of Kabbalah. Like Nietzsche's aphorisms, Kafka's parables are characterized by ironic twists and reversals . . . By making daring use of counterfactual conditionals, Kafka explored alternative interpretations of biblical and other classical stories . . . It was this ability to explode the conventional reading of well-known texts and reveal their secrets that must have reminded Scholem of the Kabbalah and made him see in Kafka a kind of neo-Kabbalist."[82] Scholem claims, in any case, that Kafka's would have been a he-retical Cabala, an extension and continuation, on literary grounds, of the confused struggles of the Sabbatians to realize eternity in time, while putting into question—not to mention being ready to abandon in the interests of this higher goal—all ethical or religious orthodoxy and normativity. Idel and some qualified others[83] have, as a matter of fact, suggested analogies between, say, Umberto Eco's concept of the "open work" and the composition of The Zohar, or Breton's Surrealist approach to language and the style of Abraham Abulafia, late thirteenth-century cabalist; but Scholem's notions are of a different order of extravagance entirely. We are left to conclude, happily or not, without the Sabbatian revolt there would have been no Kafka (as, in another domain and sense there also would have been no Zionism), which, given the centrality of Kafka to modernism in literature, means there would have been no Borges, Blanchot, Pynchon, Bruno Schultz, not to mention figures like Jerzy Kosinski, I. B. Singer, and Romain Gary, generally less innovative in style, but who make explicitly of the occult more of a statement about their world. Or, approached from another direction, would such a project as that of *Finnegans Wake*, to reinvent a language, been even remotely conceivable had not cabalists of sundry varieties, Christian, Jewish, heretical, unwitting, not dared first to *rewrite the Bible*? If, indeed, as Bloom and Blanchot have intimated, the original sin, cabalistically speaking, had something to do with *writing*, then the repairing of a shattered world, thereby performing a *tikkun*, might very well involve more of the same fortunate fault through which we fell the first time.

It's surely no coincidence, then, that Scholem's culminating, tenth aphorism ("Kafka, unknowingly, secularized Kabbala . . .") focuses on writing, through a statement about a writer's writer, Kafka, if there ever was one, that is aimed at another for whom writing was everything, Walter Benjamin. Benjamin, who had published an essay in which, according to Biale, he had denied "the theological problem of the inaccessible Law (*halakah*) which Scholem held was the key to understanding Kafka's *Trial* and the parable 'Before the Law.' He [Scholem, in response] wrote to Benjamin 'Kafka's world is the world of revelation, yet from that perspective in which revelation is reduced to its Nothingness (Nichts).'" Biale's cabalistic gloss for this Nichts is "the divine abyss that stands between the mystic and comprehension of the hidden God. Here the paradox of comprehending the incomprehensible, which characterized the historical Kabbalah . . . became fully apparent, as it only could from a secular viewpoint," citing also Scholem's resolution of this quandary, from this same letter of 1934 to Benjamin: "The unrealizability (*Unvollziehbarkeit*) of that which is revealed is the point at which . . . a correctly understood theology . . . and the key to Kafka's world come together," which is tantamount, the way Biale's sees it, to Scholem's having concluded that: "The realization of revelation in the medium of the historical tradition is necessarily inadequate and even paradoxical . . . This was the problem for the Kabbalists and it was also the problem, in its most acute form, for Kafka."[84]

This interesting debate over whether of not there is "theology" in Kafka, and of what kind, needs to be seen also in the context of the lifelong argument between Scholem and Benjamin over the relevance of mystical insights and vision to the problems and duties of modern secular life. It would not require too great of a leap of the imagination to regard Benjamin, brilliantly gifted also in stunning reinterpretations, as the kind of "heretical neocabalist" that Scholem makes Kafka out to be. One more turn of the screw Harold Bloom has made and remade, of course, turns Scholem himself into this strange breed also. Today's cabalist is, accordingly, all the more so one for not knowing it, or at least not letting on he or she does. This kind of mystic, as cabalists have always done, but a fortiori, more so in this age that is dominated by secular values, would hide what he was about, exacting that kind of ironic revenge on reality Kierkegaard liked sometimes to imagine, while finally rejecting the notion as too absurd, a Christ who would never admit to who He was exacting on the world. Ultimately such a hallowing would remove Benjamin specifically and literature generally from the onus and task of furthering a social-revolutionary praxis, at least in any strictly materialistic sense, by connecting them solidly to higher, more visionary and ennobling ends. That paradox, which Scholem found to pertain to historical Cabala, seeing it also as the essence of Kafka, in other words of the exemplary literary art of our time—that is, *that the truth is both unrealizable and incommunicable* (while continuing to tease us with the certainty of its existence, since it is the bedrock on which even our doubt is based) is attenuated, nevertheless, and made *livable* by the glimmer of a possibility of coming closer to it, even if in a fragmentary and incomplete manner. Meanwhile the very notion of ineluctable insufficiency, defeat, and failure, become subject to a kind of Nietzschean *amor fati*; while they imply, on some level at least, if only that of idea and aspiration, their *affirming* opposites, against which they can be measured and be found wanting. In fact it is this very incompletion that serves as reminder, thorn, and provocation to work toward (re)discovering all that is missing. In life, it is the direction we work in, not whether we get there, that finally matters. Meanwhile the nerve and indomitability required constantly to face a structurally guaranteed frustration would be a quality in Kafka, and by implication modern(ist) literature and art generally, that we may allow ourselves to call cabalistic.

The Mystery of Numbers

Peter Bongus, *The Mysterious Meaning of Numbers* (1585). Coincidentally, and from a perspective that is not so different than the cabalist, Bongus's book has surfaced in the context of Alastair Fowler's revelations as to the "lost art" of Renaissance numerological poetry—findings that have brought out the philosophical implications of the subtly mathematical structure of major poems by Spenser, Milton, Donne, and others.[85] Bongus carries on a tradition that had its pagan origins in Pythagorean number mysticism, continues with Pythagorus's Syrian-Neoplatonic biographer Iamblichus, crosses over into Christianity most notably in the works of St. Augustine, especially as interpreted for the Renaissance by Cassiodorus. As explained by Rostvig: "The fact that editions of Cassiodorus' work appeared at Antwerp in 1566 and at Paris in 1579 and 1589 may explain why the late 16th century theologian, Petrus Bongus, quotes so often from Cassiodorus in his systematic survey of the symbolic meaning of numbers. Cassiodorus was, in turn, following St. Augustine's theory on the logical coherence of the Holy Ghost's ordering of the Psalms."[86] Bongus's work first appeared in Latin in 1584, as *De numerorum mysteria*, and by 1617 had gone through five editions.

Blau cites Bongus as a follower of Pico, mentioning that he systematizes Pico's doctrines into a science of numerology.[87] This is representative of a certain current of mathematical Cabala of the Renaissance, out of which came Francis Meres's *God's Arithmetic* of 1597, and also William Ingpen's *The Secret of Numbers* of 1624. Both Ingpen's and Bongus's books are part of a useful inventory Fowler established of what he called "arithmological publication," in the Renaissance, which "obliges one to suppose that even comparatively esoteric number symbolisms then aroused more interest than some modern writers unfamiliar with the period are willing to believe. Giorgio's *De harmonia mundi* and Bongo's *Numerorum mysteria* both went through several editions, the former being also translated into French. In English there was William Ingpen's *The Secret of Numbers* (1624). And many popular encyclopedic, hexameral [ordered according to the six-day week of creation], or magical treatises had sections on number symbolism: St. Augustine's *De Civitate Dei*, Macrobius' *In Somnium Scipionis*, Valeriano's *Hieroglyphica*."[88]

Windelband ingeniously makes the connection, suggested also by Cassirer, of the link between this Neoplatonic and Pythagorean numerology and modern science, though very definitely from the point of view of the progressive model of the latter, inevitably denying to this "number mysticism" the dignity of a substance and meaning of its own. This image of the occult sciences as the forerunners of the empirical kind thoroughly imbues also Lynn Thorndike's monumental diachronic encyclopedia, whose title, *History of Magic and Experimental Science*, establishes an order that is more than mere coincidence. The recent structuralist paradigms of such as de Certeau and Lacan, have found instead in mysticism a discourse that is a response, opposition, and resistance to the hegemonies of science and secularity, instead of their mere denial. Before this structuralist reevaluation the scientific systems, with their attendant, mostly hidden, hierarchies, abuses, and inequalities, could be preceded honorably only by such styles as could be shown to have led up to them, or to have made them possible. This was how the "magical" approaches could be defended against a total positivist rejection of them. "Primitive religion," for instance, even for someone as openminded as Freud, could only be a way station in the eventual scientific cure of neuroses, and a way of shedding light on their etiology. Correspondingly, even such a sympathetic account of the "dark sciences" of the Renaissance as Hiram Haydn's *Counter-Renaissance* made extensive use of this "magic leading up to science" argument.

This progressive model is inevitably present in Windelband, writing in the 1890s, or very much the heyday of an optimistic Neokantianism. Nietzsche had, of course, been eloquently objecting to the dangers and complacencies of this "confidence," but, ahead of his time, he naturally wasn't very well heard, and when he finally was, it was only to be catastrophically misunderstood by the National Socialists. Accordingly, for Windelband, numerology represents an advance over subjective epochs of mystical "participation". This epoch was that of an organic continuity and unity with the universe, in the sense that Lévy-Bruhl was to use the word, yielding eventually to the relative objectivity of a gestalt of "spatial forms" and "number-relations," which *in turn* will lead to modern science. Magic is prescientific for Windelband because it involves the imposition of structure and pattern (no matter what kind, *any design* being considered progress over none at all) on what was before regarded as having to be suffered as a destiny: *"herein lies one of the most important preparations for the origin of modern natural science. The Book of Nature is written in numbers; the* harmony of things is that of the number-system. All is arranged by God according to measure and number; all life is an unfolding of mathematical relations ... The procedure of the world brought forth from God, from the construction of the Trinity on,—as, for example, in the attempt of Bouillé[89]—is again to be conceived as a process of the transformation of unity into the number system. Such fantasies were followed by men such as Cardan[90] and Pico. Reuchlin added further the mythological creations of the Jewish Cabala."[91] Hyam Maccaby has commented in a similarly progressive-positivist vein, meant certainly to counter Graetz-type accusations of obsolescence and obscurantism specifically on a connection between Cabala and modern science:

> The Enlightenment itself owed more to kabbalistic and neoplatonic occultism that to common sense ... Indeed, the rise of modern science ... owes much to the Kabbalah. Normative Judaism ... kept its gaze on this world and dismissed cosmological speculation with the talmudic injunction against asking "what is above, what is beneath, what was before, and what will be hereafter." The Kabbalah, turning its gaze from earth to heaven, produced a daring cosmological scheme of soaring range, precursor of the vast schemes of modern astronomy and atomic physics ... the Kabbalah was concerned with hidden *forces* in the universe and with the possibility of harnessing and manipulating them; this has been the key concept of modern science and the secret of its power. So it was paradoxically the irrationalism of mysticism, rather than the rationalism of Talmudism that turned out to have more in common with the ultra-rationalism of science.[92]

Not surprisingly it was Nietzsche, who, just about contemporaneously with Windelband, anticipated and likely helped to create a structuralist-synchronous paradigm for the occult and science. He found them to be not so much parent and offspring as fellow siblings, descended from a common source for each in a *Faustian* drive for knowledge and power. The fact that Gnostic-Manichean energies seemed thoroughly relevant to Nietzsche is plainly apparent in the provocation to the assumptions of a Western progressive rationality involved in his having made the historical-legendary founder of Dualism, Zarathustra, the speaker in what was as close to a systematic philosophical statement as Nietzsche ever came, *Thus Spake Zarathustra*. Uncannily, also, in a passage in *The Joyful Wisdom*, the scientific drive for total knowledge and control is conceived as springing from that same appetite for power that inspired magical and occult manipulatory systems. Science, therefore, far from having made magic obsolete, is merely its latest avatar! Or to put it in the terms, say, of Sol Yurick's *Metatron*, technology would be the Cabala of our day. Surely ironic, then, is the italicized rubric, "Prelude to Science," in the following aphorism, which would seem rather to say that science is a form of magic rather than something merely made possible by it: "Prelude to Science:—Do you believe then that the sciences would have arisen and grown up if the sorcerers, alchemists, astrologers and witches had not been their forerunners; those who, with their promisings and foreshadowings had first to create a thirst, a hunger, and a taste for *hidden and forbidden* powers?"[93]

What seems to be a diachronic model here, of the link between occultism and science, should not, however be confused with a privileging of the latter, as I think is the case with Haydn, Windelband, as well as Maccaby (in his reading of Cabala). Behind Nietzsche's apparent diachrony, however, lurks a cynical and sinister synchrony, according to which he would attack science's privilege by wondering what it is that it is a prelude to, locating rather the "will to power" as the primordial factor, for which science is simply the temporarily dominant expression, because, whatever its liberal veneer, it is a crueler, more savage, deadly, and unscrupulous form than magic. Anticipating things just a little bit, but in an escalation Nietzsche very clearly predicted, whereas before we might have taken a century or so to burn a few thousand witches and/or heretics, now we can and do evaporate 100,000, who have been "saved" by modern medicine just for that purpose, in nine seconds. It seems to me also that de Certeau and Yurick, who I have been citing as students and critics of the link between mysticism and modernity, share rather in this Nietzschean mistrustful and ironic synchrony, rather than in any confident, because redeeming, diachrony. They do this by way of the very questions they put to the science that mystics are supposed to have led up to.

The Dissemination of Cabala

Paul Ricci, *In cabalistarum, seu allegorizantium eruditionem isagoge* (1514); *Portae, Lucis (sic). Hec est porta Tetragrammaton* (1516). The earlier book, *On Cabala, or Digest of Erudite Allegory*, was a systematic, Christianizing introduction to Cabala, really the first comprehensive exposition of the subject of the period, still important enough for Blau to have translated it and included in its entirety in *The Christian Cabala*. Ricci, a Jewish convert, whose cabalistic studies, ostensibly, drew him into Christianity and into his subsequent and enthusiastic work of dissemination and propagation, is a cornerstone of the Christian Cabala in the Renaissance. At the other end of the century Ricci's efforts were to fill more than half of Pistorius's defining if not definitive collection. In sympathy with the mystical flights of Pico, Ricci was also a conscientious scholar and translator, whose connections to the intellectual and political life of his time were also very solid: he was a friend of Erasmus and also personal physician to Emperor Maximilian I. Blau's opinion is that he unified the scattered dogmas of cabalism and saw it as a "way of life" rather than merely an eclectic philosophy.[94] The second listing is Riccius's popular translation of Gikatila's thirteenth-century text, *The Gates of Light* (which, in the Latin, Riccius seems to have used as a pseudonym, Light Gates), apparently one of the Latin translations from original Hebrew works that *were* widely available in print in the Renaissance. It was republished, for example as part of the Pistorius anthology of 1587, about half of which was devoted to texts written or translated by Riccius, grouped under the title of *Celestial Agriculture*, accompanied by the first mentioned work above, *In cabilistarum*, a widely known and appreciated systematic introduction to Christian Cabala. Almost a century later Ricius's translation of this classic work of Gikatila is still very much alive, since it was the *only* Pistorius text carried over into the Knorr Rosenroth anthology of 1677.

Franciscus Georgius, *De Harmonia mundi totius cantica tria* (1525). Georgius is one of the hard core, (composed also of Archangelus de Burgo Novo and J. P. Crispus) of sixteenth-century Franciscan defenders of Pico. His *Harmony of the World* is a work of *incalculable* importance for the dissemination of Christian Cabala in the Renaissance. Alastair Fowler calls this book, in another but related context, "one of the most significant arithmological treatises of the Renaissance."[95] The influence and popularity of this book is a constant leitmotif in the texts of Frances Yates, who has done so much to bring about an awareness of occult contexts for Renaissance thought and culture. Yates accords, for instance, a place of honor to Georgius in spread of cabalistic consciousness through the great Elizabethan generation of Dee, Sidney, Spenser, Shakespeare, and Marlowe. Widely known in Latin, *Harmony of the World* was also translated into French in 1578 under the auspices of the mystical French royal House of Valois. This was part of a strategy, according to Yates, rooted in the occult, of religious syncretism that provided the logic and motivations for a provocative important proselytizing visit to England of Giordano Bruno (then attached to the French court), whose echoes were to resound for decades. Interestingly the impact of Georgius crossed even the lines of the genres and was felt in architecture, as it has been substantiated that his sephirotic schemes were instrumental in creating the design for the Church of San Francesco della Vigna, in Venice, early in the sixteenth-century.[96]

Georgius's very ambitious *Harmony of the World in Three Cantos* was a long religious-philosophical poem whose purpose is to demonstrate the unity of all fundamental philosophical systems, with a good deal of emphasis on Cabala and Pythagoreanism particularly. This work follows through on the syncretizing aspects of Pico's idealism. Blau, insisting as always on minimizing Christian Cabala, finds in Georgius, as he had for Pico, only "slight knowledge of cabala,"[97] a statement to which Secret takes *enormous* exception for Georgius, as he had for Pico. First of all Secret mentions the presence, in *De Harmonia mundi* of a very ample cabalistic bibliography that will be an resource for Agrippa and also Egidio da Viterbo, whose esoteric group included Galantini. Secret also notes with dismay Blau's omission of another work of Georgius, called the *Problemata*, which he says is absolutely "stuffed with Cabala," and also points out that one of the most prominent seventeenth-century opponents of Cabala (and of anything resembling mysticism in general), a Père Marin Mersenne, had taken Georgius's work seriously enough to single it out, in the title of his treatise, for a refutation aimed at the whole movement.[98]

Caspar Peucer, *Commentarius de praecipuis divinationum generibus* (1553). Peucer, author of this *Commentary on divinatory methods*, is an *opponent* of the Cabala, but is much impressed by the ingenuity with which it treats the symbolism of numbers.[99] In spite of this fundamental opposition, we may note an evident indecision on this matter of Cabala, which teased so many of his contemporaries and which, finally, he can neither entirely denounce or really approve of either. Very *tentatively*, it seems to me, he promises to discuss, in the extended title, on the subject of divination, "to what extent divine authority as well as physical principles are represented theirin," about which we can assume that they must be so somewhat. Here he adds, nevertheless, apotropaically, that he will provide also "a discovery of diabolical arts and imposture." Blau's ample quotes from Peucer[100] confirm this ambivalence fully: On the one hand, Peucer condemns the aspiration to worldly power through manipulation of letters and syllables, which he regards, even when effective, as of demonic provenance. On the other hand, Peucer is quite pleased that cabalistic numerological formulas are able to confirm that the events of Christ's passion and assumption are anticipated at the time of creation, through the prophetic magic of scripture. Worth noting, surely, also is the evident popularity of this text, symptomatic that Cabala was the subject of a good deal of intellectual conjecture and interest, apart from the enthusiasm of its faithful acolytes or the denunciation of its orthodox opponents. First published in the Faustian (or Lutheran) city of Wittenburg, it resurfaces in a French translation in Paris, in 1584, not long after the translation there of Georgius's by-then classic of Christian Cabala, *Harmony of the World*. Subsequently there was another edition, in Latin, from Frankfurt, in 1593.

Guinther of Andernach, *De medicina veteri et nova* (1571). Guinther apparently was well aware of the Paracelsan or "magical" approach toward the medical arts. He takes a tolerant view, as is obvious in Thorndike's paraphrase of his medical opinions: "Guinther... alluded to remedies sought from the cabala, demons and idle superstitions, and notes that some say that so long as a cure is effected, it makes no difference whether God or the devil is responsible for it."[101] Cabala here seems to scrape by, barely, on the basis of a loophole for the demonic doctor. Among his other talents (certain kinds of prognostication) the devil in the Renaissance was remarked for his skills in medicine, which probably had something to do with why Jews, barred from other fields, were often tolerated or even respected, as physicians.

Pierre Le Loyer (1550–1634). *Discours, et histoires des spectres* (1586, 1605). After deprecating a distorted identification in the Renaissance of Cabala and Magic, Blau cites Le Loyer as being someone who could appreciate the distinction, and "who understood and illustrated the valid techniques of cabalistic science, used as a means of developing the allegorical sense of the Scriptures. The cabalism which is met in combination with magic is, he maintained, different and a product of degeneration."[102] Thorndike, equally has high praise for Le Loyer, noticing that he skillfully presents the "views of Jewish rabbis and cabalists and Moslems on the essence and origin of the soul," as befits "one of the most learned Frenchmen of his time."[103]

Philip de Mornay, *Trewness of Christian Religion* (1587). De Mornay [1549–1623] was a prominent Hugenot statesman, theologian, and advisor to Henry IV, who founded the first Protestant academy in France, at Saumur, in 1599. De Mornay's text, very widely disseminated and in several languages, contains an entire chapter that expounds Cabala according to the idealistic theories of Pico della Mirandula; this book also makes a number of other allusions to Cabala, including a very prominent one in his "Preface to the Reader."[104] An illustrious battery of translators, Sir Philip Sidney and Arthur Golding, the former being the premier poet of his age, the latter an eminent scholar (responsible for English version of Ovid's *Metamorphoses*), show the esteem with which de Mornay's thought was treated, as well as demonstrating that the English golden age literary generation of the 1590s—Spenser, Marlowe, Shakespeare, and Chapman—certainly had some access to cabalistic notions, distilled through Pico, de Mornay, Bruno, and others.

Julius Sperber, *Kabbalisticae precationes* (1600, 1675). According to Scholem, Sperber here mentions Buddhism in connection with Cabala,[105] another illustration of the syncretism the latter could facilitate. The republication after seventy-five years of the century of these *Cabalistic Prayers* shows the stubborn persistence of cabalistic style in the seventeenth century; and the place where it re-appears, Amsterdam, one of the centers of Sabbatian "heresy," was certainly still trying to digest the astounding news of the apostasy of the messiah, a few years earlier; hence maybe a reawakened interest in pre-Zevi devotions in a city that had been inundated with countless editions of Sabbatian tracts, many from the pen of Zevi's prolific and articulate "prophet," Nathan of Gaza.

Isaac Beeckman. *Journal tenu de 1604 à 1634.* Thorndike indi-cates that Beeckman, in what is now a standard reference work for intellectual life in the seventeenth century, discusses the methods of Raymond Lully (Spanish Catholic philosopher, mystic, and theologian, 1235–1315) as being distinctly related to the Jew-ish Cabala.[106] Lull, who was an immensely prolific writer, really a library all to himself, was the confluence of many mystical and occult currents; while "Lullism" was an interpretive science dis-tinctly related to cabalistic numerological, alphabetical, and anagrammatical styles of exegesis. Lull's dates place him, indeed, in what we have described as the golden age of Jewish Cabala in pre-Diaspora Spain, contemporary with de Leon's composition of The Zohar and Abulafia's ecstatic practice and wanderings. To these we should add what were to become Gikatila's widely circu-lated and translated (by Ricius, eminently, in the early sixteenth century) writings that established a middle ground for Cabala between the poles of zoharic theosophy and Abulafia's practical-ecstatic theurgy. The mere existence of Lull's and others' Chris-tian Cabala in Spain hundreds of years before it started up in Italy, for François Secret, helps him establish that, contrary to Blau, Cabala was not just a novelty that Pico picked up on to give a little substance to his Neoplatonic visions of universal mystic syncretism. Instead it was already, by the time Pico found it, a well-established, if still provocative recourse many had taken in the conciliation or harmony of tradition and authority with the imperatives of a changing epoch.

Ioao Bravo Chamisso, *De medendis corporis* (1605). According to Thorndike, in this book about healing, Chamisso "saw no more reason for denying the efficacy of literary elements, when properly ordered as in the Cabala, than for denying the marvelous force of the magnet."[107] One of the most frequent applications of Cabala during the Renaissance was in the medical arts. What was involved was the manipulation of the letters in the holy Hebrew alphabet as a way of treating ailments or enhancing certain qualities, Cabala lending itself to such practices also because of its multilevel emphasis on the body, both human and divine—compensating for the hallowed Christian renunciation or denial of it. Also, medicine and Cabala have in common the fact that the individual, through his hygiene, discipline, and habits, intervenes with and tries to alter a natural course of things. This is a point that Windelband makes very cogently about Theophrastus Bombastus Paracelsus (1493–1541), renowned if not notorious for his use of secret formulas in the arts of healing: "Physicians especially, whose vocation demanded an interference in the course of Nature and might seem permitted to expect special advantage in the secret arts, showed an inclination toward these magic arts."[108]

Strozzi Cicogna, *Palagio de gl'incanti* (1605).   For this eight-volume encyclopedia of magic, or *Palace of Enchantment*, which appeared originally in Italian but was published the very next year in Latin, a cabalistic framework is provided in the intention, announced in the extended title to treat things according to a threefold perspective. These amount, really, to the triune worlds of Cabala: celestial (divine), spiritual (mental), and elementary (physical). With this well-disseminated and respected text we may witness a phenomenon of a certain merging of heterodoxy and orthodoxy. This author, who was an eminent citizen of Vicenza, according to Thorndike a "noble, theologian and doctor of laws" and his city's ambassador to Venice, is unquestionably mainstream in matters of religion, suggesting that whatever strange styles he explores or explains must come under the category of the acceptable. Cicogna is notable apparently, not only for his quality of introducing difference but also for his facility or ability at providing a common home for the occult heterodoxies. In his work there is, for example a profound sense of the *interpenetrating* of Cabala and Astrology, as suggested by Thorndike's casual précis: "Cicogna discusses the Cabala somewhat and attributes to the rabbis and cabalists the doctrine that angels rule the signs of the zodiac and four elements, and that nine choirs of angels correspond to the celestial spheres."[109]

Cabala doubtless could provide a relatively friendly terrain for astrology, harried on the one side by a purifying Protestantism and a stricter post-Tridentine Catholicism and on the other by the indifference of rational empiricism. Astrology had to walk, additionally, a razor's edge between the heresies of fatalism that would make the Christian choice nugatory and that of a hyperbolic free will that accords to humans the demiurgic prerogatives of the divine. With Cabala the main problems of coordination with the prevalent Christianity were not so thoroughly structural as with astrology, but having to do with issues, easier to conciliate, of its Hebrew provenance (since, after all Jesus was some kind of Jew, plus the Torah could be read prophetically, etc.). The fact is that *all* divinatory styles were both much in demand and very much under attack all during the Renaissance. There must have been some good reasons, nevertheless, for their being retained for so long, and, indeed, although no longer in any official capacity (since the Reagan years), they are, of course, still with us. Windelband, accordingly, provides a useful comprehensive rationale for this insistent presence of divinatory systems, where Cabala was so prominent, in the overall universalizing tendencies of Renaissance culture: "Astrology, with its influences of the stars upon human life, the interpretation of dreams and signs, necromancy, with its conjurations of spirits, the predictions of persons in the ecstatic state.—All these elements of Stoic and Neo-Platonic divination were then in most luxuriant bloom. Pico and Reuchlin brought them into connection with number-mysticism; Agrippa of Nettesheim adopted all the skeptical attacks against the possibility of rational science, in order to seek help in mystical illuminations and secret magic arts."[110] However, Windelband is certainly being a bit sanguine about how well occult styles worked in a climate that was also, especially after the Council of Trent, increasingly hostile and suspicious. The ambiguities and double binds of Astrological Magic, in its efforts to conciliate its ambitions and energies with orthodox Christian practice, on the other hand, are well in evidence in D. P. Walker's survey of *Spiritual and Demonic Magic, from Ficino to Campanella.* Walker defines as *acceptable* a divinatory magic, which he calls *subjective*, according to which the individual is restricted to receiving influence from the position and movements of the stars, but as clearly *beyond* the pale, what he calls a *transitive* or *objective* magic, according to which the person, having absorbed the influence of the stars then goes on to transform (or even generate) other beings. Ficino, for example, would just barely stay on the safe side of things, though it took a lot of diplomacy on his part and just plain good will on the part of others to keep him there; whereas someone like the Neopagan, demiurgic hermeticist Lazzarelli (with Agrippa, Bruno, and Campanella in his titanic wake) would have crossed clearly over the line.[111]

Anonymous, *Bericht eines Cabalisten Über die 4 figuren des grossen Ampitheatri Khunradi* (1608). This is an unsigned appendix to Heinrich Khunrath's *The Secret Light of Magicians and Philosophers*. Thorndike lists Henry Khunrath (1560–1605) also as the author of a compendious encyclopedia of the occult, or the *Ampitheater of the Only True Eternal Wisdom*, of 1609. Khunrath, as emerges from Thorndike's paraphrase, seems to manifest a typically Renaissance alternation of suspicion and attraction to Cabala and other "magical" styles: "All sciences not acquired from God or divine magic, or the Christian cabala by prayer and tears are furtive waters and not perfect gifts from the Father of Lights. Khunrath lists as handmaids of true wisdom the Cabala (*not however that literal vulgar Jewish variety*, but far superior theosophy), magic, physiognomy, metoscopy, chiromancy, the doctrine of signatures of all natural things, alchemy, astrology and geomancy... An alliance of alchemy and cabala is also urged, and seeking the secret of the philosopher's stone not from the writings of gentile philosophers but from holy writ."[112] Symptomatic here also is Khunrath's structural distrust of a *Jewish* Cabala, taken to be perverted by a crassly materialistic magic, while a Christian sort would be abstract, elevating, and spiritual. Cabala, to become usable *gold*, needs to be cleaned of its Hebrew *dross*. This is, of course, a characteristic reading of Plato, from the early Church Fathers to Hegel, Kierkegaard, and beyond, placing Jews in a lower realm or cave of appearances.

Oswald Croll, *Basilica Chymica* (1609). Croll was an enthusiastic adherent of Paracelsan-cabalistic medicine. In the first sentence of Thorndike's paraphrase we may remark a sense, pervasive in Cabala, of the influence upon each other of the human and divine: "Men possess magnetic power over the stars, just as the stars influence them. Besides the magic of Paracelsus, Croll adduced that of most ancient Cabalists of the Hebrews and their three worlds."[113]

Christophorus Lauret, Hazoar temporis Messiae (1610).[114]   This *Zohar in the Time of the Messiah* is another example obviously of Christian cabalist extravagance or "misprision," since even those who believe that Simeon ben Yohai created The Zohar have never placed him earlier than the second century A.D. Strictly speaking there could have been, even assuming its ancient provenance, *no* Zohar in the time of the Messiah, unless, of course, it was "in the air." Worth remarking also, in the title, is the matter-of-fact transcription of the Hebrew-Aramaic name for The Zohar into Latin, which might go to support Secret in his insistence that texts of Cabala, in their original language, were not so inaccessible as Blau claimed they were.

Claude Duret, *Thresor de l'histoire des langues* (1613).   Scholem indicates that this work contains a description of the holy books of the Cabala and also a summary of their contents.[115] This important but probably overlooked text may be taken as an example of the penetration of Cabala into the learned discourse of the Renaissance. Taken in its widest sense as a theory of the mystical provenance and destiny of words, Cabala here is *nevertheless* assumed as something one has to know about to understand the history of language. Secret, who, as a matter of fact, did his thesis on Duret, adds, more recently, that "this book reproduces the most important passages of the Christian Cabala" and is, indeed, the first "Bibliographica Kabbalistica!"[116]

Anonymous, *Adumbratio Kabbala Christianae* (1614).[117]   An obviously proselytizing and typological text, taking advantage of aspects of Cabala that were frequently seen to be in harmony with Christianity: for example, what was taken to be an occasional allusion to resurrection (which might have been a surfacing rather of the Indian idea of reincarnation); the feminine divine, Shekinah, or Bride of God figure—taken as an avatar of the Virgin Mary, as the final link of what was presumed to have been a Jewish trinity of Ain Soph, Demiurge, and Emanation, whose purpose was to anticipate or ready the world for the Christian one of Father, Son, and Holy Ghost; and then, throughout Cabala , a kind of New Testament gentleness combined with an apocalyptic mood that treats this world as a passage, ordeal, or testing place.

Jacob Boehme. *De Signatura Rerum* (1621). Waite suggests a connection between the "Virgin Wisdom" that figures so prominently in the philosophical mysticism of Boehme and the concept of the Shekinah.[118] Boehme is, generally, one of the Christian mystics most commonly assumed to have been deeply influenced by cabalism, and also probably *the* one whose influence on literature has been most profound. Cabalistic ideas are funneled, for instance, through the theosophy of Boehme, then pass (by way of Swedenborg) into the highroad of English mystically tinged poetry, the "ways" of Blake and Yeats.[119]

Johann Ernst Burggrav, *Introductio in vitalem philosophiam* (1623). Burggrav's *Introduction to Vital Philosophy*, as is apparent in the extended title, part of which I have reproduced in the Bibliography, is a book very much in the Paracelsan mode of vitalist-alchemical-cabalist medicine. Vitalism was a doctrine that established a strict continuity between interpenetrating realms of existence. Therefore, altering a balance or affecting the order in a higher realm would impact on a lower, or the other way around, if one wanted to treat "the sick society." Illness, accordingly, would not be dealt with directly but through repetition of sounds or manipulation of elements that resound through the cosmos on a certain level, which change then redounds through all of creation. In Burggrav's Paracelsan scheme of universal relevance and influence, Cabala is a fundamental connecting element, providing, as it were the ladder on which the various rungs or levels can be located and "repaired," thereby strengthening the soundness both of the particular and the general (of the rung and the ladder). Another way of conceptualizing this is to conceive that Cabala is that force that enables the powers, fates, and energies of a heavenly astrology to come down to earth, where a vitalistic medicine can prescribe or proscribe on its basis. Thorndike sensitively pinpoints this *crucial* linking role for Cabala in this scheme: "The Hebrew Cabala is made responsible for the doctrine that all the virtues of the stars and celestial ideas are received by the moon, and thence passed onto inferior matter."[120]

Significantly the *moon*, really a cabalistic leitmotif, is the relay station that converts this astral-astrological current or energy, too pure or intense for immediate usage, into such diluted states as

makes it accessible down here. The moon's importance as a cabalistic symbol was based on its correspondence, because of its "constant mutability," to an analogous lability in letters, always yielding
one to another. To each letter there is additionally an associated
sephira, or realm in a world of emanation that would further channel the energies that stem from a (now) too remote astral source.
The moon assumes its necessary inferiority, according to cabalistic
legend, at the time of the *exile*. This can be either (or both) a
philosophical-symbolic Lurianic *withdrawal*, which predates and
even *causes* creation, or a more literal and ethnic alienation, commencing with the destruction of the Second Temple. Before this
exile the light of the moon was equal to that of the sun, while
afterwards it had to become much dimmer, more "reflective," symbolizing the lessened, filtered knowledge which is all, in our currently "fallen" state, we are capable of.[121]

Marin Mersenne, *Quaestiones in Genesim* (1623). Mersenne is a
Catholic opponent of the Christian Cabala. Just as there was a
descent, from Pico, of those who favored Cabala, so the opposition,
which caused Pico's "Cabalistic Conjectures" to be condemned as
heretical when they were first offered, was and remained surely as
stubborn. Peter Garzia, Bishop of Barcelona and one of the judges
who condemned Pico's notions as heretical, replying to Pico's subsequent Papal exoneration, published, in 1499, the first substantial
refutation of the very idea of a *Christian* Cabala, attacking with
particular annoyance the proposition that "magic and Cabala are
the surest evidence for Christianity." It was to Garzia, that
Archangelus of Burgo Novo was answering (see Bibliography) in
his important subsequent defense of Pico.

Whereas Garzia attacked Cabala as a violation of orthodoxy,
Mersenne will see it rather as an offense to reason. Mersenne is
interested in "converting the heathen" (*the* Christian argument for
Cabala), but rather through ontological-philosophical proofs, and
certainly not at the price of irrationality that Cabala seemed to him
to demand. Interestingly he is quite well informed on that which he
opposed. In selecting Genesis for scrutiny Mersenne is locating himself quite relevantly in the field of cabalistic conjecture, since Genesis, or *Bereshith*, is very definitely the book of choice for The Zohar,
by far more extensively commented than any of the others.

Mersenne found Cabala to be simply not serious enough to be Christian. In his "informed" decision to reject Cabala as a serious option he anticipates the scholarly distance Blau takes from his mystical subject three centuries later, which he *pre*-judged to be "a fad that flickered." Indeed Blau *cites* Mersenne as evidence in support of the general drift of his own research, which was, while discovering its wide dissemination, to downplay the significance of Cabala in the Renaissance. Blau, however, neglected a factor that might have qualified his reliance on Mersenne for his notions about Cabala. Catholics, especially after the Reformation is in full career, might tend to regard Cabala as a Protestant plot and consider Hebrew texts, of whatever pretension of consistency with the New Testament, with suspicion; whereas the Protestants would be more likely to exploit such "authorities" to show how the church had perverted its own pristine message. Mersenne, obviously a spokesman for some kind of religious establishment was taken seriously indeed. In addition to the book that Gaffarel published a few years later to defend the orthodoxy of Christian Cabala, Mersenne also provoked the English mystic, cabalist-alchemist, and budding Rosicrucian, Robert Fludd, into issuing a massive manifesto of theosophical-hermetic-neopagan protest and apology.[122]

Athanasius Kircher, *Oedipus Aegyptiacus* (1623); *Mundus Subterraneus* (1663–1665) *Arithmology Concerning the Hidden Mysteries of Numbers* (1665). Kircher was a Jesuit intellectual, maybe resembling in his range, depth, and impact the Jesuit structuralist and (Lacanian) analyst of mysticism, Michel de Certeau, in our own times. Kircher was certainly one of the most accomplished and gifted figures of the century, as well as, evidently, being a great communicator. He was interested in everything eclectic, unusual, occult, and strange, a critic, theologian, scholar, and priest; and he wrote an important compendium of the occult based on a metaphorical geology of mining, *Underground World*, published in two volumes between 1663 and 1665. Additionally he was a scholar with a point of view, very much that of the Christian cabalist, where he was not above a bit of originality too. He has been cited, for example, as being the first to identify the cabalistic Adam Kadmon, an embodiment of the total integration of the earthly and the godly, with Jesus.[123] Thorndike, who collected some of the same strange material for us that Kircher assembled for his century, stresses rather the latter's "scientific" impartiality than his Christian cabalism, which he apparently was able to be discreet about also. Thorndike finds Kircher exceptional precisely in his "setting forth the superstitions of Gnostics, Arabs, and Hebrews, magic amulets, Pythagorean Cabala, and the wheel of life or death, without approving of them."[124]

Waite, more committed to the occult than Thorndike, sees Kircher, instead, as a participant in and promoter of the mystical energies he inventories. He refers to Kircher's massive survey of the occult underground, for a theory of Natural Magic, according to which "things seen are a counterpart of things unseen." This connects, for Waite, to Philo's Platonic articulation of the "existence of an archetypal world," by way of a maxim of correspondences that Kircher had cited: "There is no herb on earth to which a certain star does not correspond in the heaven." This is, for Waite, exactly the *essence* of Cabala: "The whole theory of Natural Magic is embedded in this doctrine. Compare ZOHAR, one might say passim, for it is a recurring doctrine."[125] Waite remarks also that in an extended passage in *Egyptian Oedipus* of 1623, Kircher explores and comments the fundamental cabalistic numerological "magic" of the 32 paths of wisdom. This he rather presents not in the sense of vulgar manipulation but in the syncretic spirit of the classic way of holiness toward the secrets of knowledge "by which the holy men of God may, as Kircher observes, after long toil, long experience of divine things and long meditation thereon, penetrate to the concealed centres."[126]

Johannes Bitaudus et al., *Fourteen Theses in Opposition Alike to the Paracelcists, Cabalists* (1624).   These theses, however, were *censured* by the Sorbonne and suppressed by the Parliament of Paris in the same year they were published, showing that Cabala, commonly grouped together with other heterodoxies of the Renaissance, was a matter of heated controversy, the outcome of which probably depended very much on the particular political and religious climate. From Thorndike's summary, it appears that these statements were unacceptable by reason of their boldness and novelty, in apparently attempting to combine an Aristotelian perspective with a magical Paracelsan-cabalistic one.[127]

Philippe D'Aquin, *Interprétation de l'arbre de la Cabale* (1625). This *Interpretation of the Cabalistic Tree*, with drawing of same, is an exegetical work, but probably, because in the vernacular, aimed at a combined learned and popular audience. If the moon was, for Burggrav, a cabalistic representation of man's fallen condition and the reflected light that was the best he could hope to enjoy on earth, the tree rather symbolized a condition of connection to some original sources of strength and meaning. This would be a sephirotic tree, that is made of a trunk and branches stemming or emanating from the unknowable ain soph, seed or kernel. This tree is most usually pictured inverted, that is growing down, from roots in heaven toward the earth, precisely that sephirotic tree that The Zohar takes as the "tree of life," which is one of its most frequently recurring images.[128]

Revealing also is the claim in the extended title that the work has been derived from *Hebrew* language sources, which, judging from the research of Secret, seems quite likely; or even if the texts were Latin translations, the mere mention of Hebrew shows that language could suggest something of the authority and awe of the numinous for a Renaissance reader.

Johann Caramnel Lobkowitz, *Cabalae Totius brevissimum* (1643); *Cabbalae Theologicae Excidium* (1657). Scholem mentions that the former book, *A Brief Explanation of the Whole Cabala*, of 1643, presents the Cabala favorably in relation to an occult science of anagrams,[129] an approach which also William Camden had taken in *Remains* (1614). We may take Lobkowitz as a paradigmatic case of an ambivalence, which we have remarked also in Camden and other authors, in the reception of Cabala in the Renaissance. In the fourteen years that intervene between the appearance of the first and the second book, *The Overthrow of Cabalistic Theology* of 1657, Lobkowitz had turned evidently into a determined opponent, maybe even a *furious* one. This *Overthrow* served, curiously, as an introduction to a *Hebrew* translation—the purpose of which should surely make us wonder—of Thomas Acquinas's *Summa Contra Gentiles*. Was this version for the sake of Jewish converts who would perhaps know Hebrew rather than Latin, or did putting Saint Thomas into Hebrew lend his text (cabalistically, maybe reason for Lobkowitz's angst) a certain aura of sanctity?

Iohannes Stefanus Rittangel, *Liber Jezirah* (1652); *De Veritate religionis Christianae* (1699). This is the second important Renaissance translation of *the Sefer Yetzirah,* so influential for the thaumaturgic or magical side of Cabala. Perhaps it is not only coincidence that it was published *exactly* one-hundred years after Postel's version appeared. From the little essay comprised by its extended title, however, we may measure an intervening development of a more empirical spirit. While Postel's perspective was Catholic-mystic-syncretic, Rittangel, like his contemporary, the cabalist anthologist Christian Knorr von Rosenroth, was resolutely Lutheran-Protestant, therefore less inclined to the visionary aspects of mainstream Cabala as it "ascended" from Pico. This is a distinction that I think impacts on the relatively empirical attitude of Rittangel. Whereas Postel's title had affirmed flatly that the text was by the Biblical Patriarch Abraham, Rittangel's merely says it was ascribed to him (the Rabbi Abraham, whose commentary is included, is surely a contemporary). Likewise the Rittangel title is specific about the type of contribution the book made, in terms of the introduction of the thirty-two cabalistic paths. Nevertheless, as made perfectly clear in the statement he makes in the extended title of the later book, *True Christian Religion,* to the effect that Jewish Cabala *is* the true Christian religion, Rittangel's perspective is as resolutely typological (regarding the Old Testament as a sort of New Testament in disguise), as Postel's was one-hundred years earlier, if less magically so. This I think shows how ineluctable this "misprision" was—even for scholars like Postel and Rittangel, with easy access to Hebrew originals and Jewish sources.

Andreas Sennert, *Dissertatio Peculiaris de Cabbala* (1655). Windelband mentions Sennert,[130] author of this *Special Discourse on Cabala,* as promoting, in the tradition of Eckhart, Bruno, Boehme, and Campanella, a kind of mystical-empirical atomism whereby the smallest element of the universe contains and exemplifies the largest and vice-versa. This amounts to, in the words of Campanella, a Natural Religion, or de facto conversion of the everyday into the numinous—parallel with a Natural Magic promulgated by such as Agrippa and Paracelsus, also inclined to see a miracle everywhere, and very much in the spirit of a certain wondrous and wonder-working (Reuchlin) cabalistic word.

Caspar Schott, *Magia universalis naturae et artis* (1657–1659); *Physica Curiosa* (1667). In the first book, a gigantic work in four volumes and twenty-six hundred pages, there are numerous but seemingly respectful allusions to Cabala, while in the second there is a systematic attack on it, as paraphrased by Thorndike: "Without reason or authority the cabalists suppose some connection of sympathy between letters and syllables and heavens and intelligences."[131] Possibly the negative reaction is connected to the promulgation, at the same time as its publication, of the controversial "heretical Cabala" of Sabbatai Zevi, self-appointed messiah and apostate to Islam—according to whom 1666, by sacred computation, was going to end an old world and usher in a new one. At all events, for anyone interested in the subject it would seem impossible for Cabala, Christian *or* Jewish, to be exactly the same after Zevi as before.

Johann Steidner, *Jüdische ABC Schul im Buch Yezirah* (1665). A clear allusion to the Trinity in the extended title of this strange primer, *The Jewish Alphabet School of The Sefer Yetzirah,*[132] places the work squarely within the current of Christian Cabala. Possibly, because of the prominence of the Trinity in the title, this is a Catholic interpretation of that basic cabalistic text to compete with the Lutheran, Rittangel's version. The *Sefer Yetzirah,* which had been republished in a new translation into Latin by Rittangel in 1652, by reason of its enigmatic brevity and the multitude of versions, commentaries, and points of view it had embraced, seems finally to be more suitable for the purposes of (urgent—reason why the work is written in German?) conversion than the more discursive and philosophical zoharic texts, which would require seminars that could run on for decades just to grasp what the issues are, much less to decide what to do about them.

Johann Christoph Steeb, *Dulcedo de forti sive Elixir* (1673, 1675); *Coelum sephiroticum Hebraeorum* (1679). About the earlier book, *Elixir of the Brave,* of 1673, which was popular enough to be reprinted two years later, Thorndike notes that Steeb attempts a synthesis of Alchemy and Cabala, showing again how readily and regularly the latter could serve as a metaphor or illustration of the other dark sciences of the Renaissance, crossing into other mystical styles as easily as it and a fortiori, its 'heretics' crossed into other religions. This potable gold, that one could and some doubtless did *drink*,[133] was a heady brew made of equal portions of Alchemy and Cabala, a combination whose origin was Paracelsus. Cabala and Alchemy were joined in the Paracelsan "technology" that was either brought over to Bohemia by the occult missionary, John Dee, whose "medium," Edward Kelley, was official alchemist at the court of Rudolph II, or discovered by him there. In the seventeenth century Thomas Vaughan, twin brother of the Platonist poet, Henry, very much identified with this cabalistic alchemy. Vaughan claimed to have rendered gold from dross matter by the time he was twenty-three, but later perished inhaling toxins during an experiment in which he tried to duplicate these results.

After some evident juggling between heterodoxies, Cabala, in Steeb's later book, emerges as the dominant metaphor or key that organizes and explains all the other mysteries, truly the Queen of the Occult (and all other) Sciences. Thorndike calls this book, bluntly, "A Sephirotic Heaven purporting to derive new principles of medicine, chemistry, astronomy, astrology, botany, zoology, anthropology and other sciences from the most ancient Hebraic truth through the gates of intelligence revealed to Moses." *The Heavens of the Hebrew Sephiroth*, on the other hand, with its tamely pedagogic and academic extension, "revealed through the Mosaic gates of wisdom, explained from the most ancient Hebrew truths," seems nonmessianic-eschatological, considering the apocalyptic developments taking place in the Sabbatian-heretical Cabala with which it is contemporary. Possibly it is part of a post or para-Sabbatian reaction. Significant in this recall to ancient texts is the prominence of the most hallowed Jewish figure, that of Moses, the allusion to the most typical of cabalistic metaphors, that of the thirty-two gates of wisdom, *and* the assurance, warranted or not, that Steeb's ideas stem directly from Hebrew-language sources, Hebrew being mentioned *twice* in the single sentence of the extended title. The purpose of all this appeal to sacred authority was possibly to restore and redefine a more classical Cabala as an antidote to the wildly provocative surmises (including that of an imminent end of the world, believers in which were expected to leave for Jerusalem and await it there), whose apocalyptic logic conveyed implied or direct revolutionary challenges to prevailing social hierarchies.

Adam A. Lebenwald, *Von des Teufels List und Betrug in der Hebraer Cabbala* (1680). This *Hebrew Cabala as the Devil's Cunning and Fraud* apparently is a new edition of one or more of the eight tracts Lebenwald printed in the 1580s in Salzburg. Lebenwald, as is obvious from the title, libels or smears Cabala, though Thorndike mentions that he defends Paracelsus,[134] perhaps because the latter lay claim to practical (the bottom line of rendered gold, always able to excuse the sinner) not spiritual efficacy; and so he might not have come as much into competition with established religion as Agrippa, Pico, and Reuchlin certainly did, whether they meant to or not. The evidently intemperate nature of the attack plus the language of the German vernacular suggests also that Cabala had obviously a popular appeal, and for a *Christian* public also. Christians are warned against Cabala here as very much a kind of Jewish plot, maybe in the antisemitic spirit Communism was sometimes to be considered a few centuries later. The pejorative allusion to *Hebrew* shows the other side of the *sacer* coin, here a guarantee of Cabala's *demonic* nature; whereas, elsewhere and concurrently, it was rather an assurance of its *divine* provenance and effect.

Speaking of the devil seems always to have been an exercise in Renaissance semiotics, which may open up for us a positively dizzying Barthean perspective. Typically mention of the devil, demons, or demonism in the title of any text dealing with cabalism in particular or the occult in general is surely means that it is a rejection, usually a vituperative one, of Agrippan magic. The first of these, and a book that set the pace for an anti-Agrippa and anti-Cabala backlash, threatened and probably inspired by the very success of the styles it was opposing, would be the important if apparently somewhat incoherent *Démonomanie*, published by Jean Bodin, in French, in 1580. The bias of Bodin's book, which defined Agrippa and the Cabala for which he stood in *demonic* terms, is very much the basis of another important marking in this tradition, partly because of the elevated social place of its author. This was the *Daemonologie*, by James VI of Scotland, soon to be James I of England, published in English in 1587. James's book essentially rejected any claim of Agrippan Cabala, whose most distinguished contemporary representative was *John Dee* (whom James did not need to mention, for the house and legendary library at Mortlake of Dee—away at Prague, communing with spirits—to be sacked), to be considered as a serious and acceptable medical, philosophical, or religious recourse. A Christian Cabala had soared so proudly with Pico, Reuchlin, and Agrippa at the beginning of the sixteenth-century, and then went on to float sublimely on the wings of the Hebraizing Guillaume Postel's zoharic midcentury dreams of universal mystical syncretism (which was to include not only Jews and Christians but also Mohammedans), to finally reach an apogee in the idealizing impact of figures like Dee and Bruno on the English literature of the Age of Elizabeth. Yet by the beginning of the seventeenth century, it has become clear that the existence of Cabala, however interesting and challenging, and often very relevant, especially in times of revolutionary or eschatological unrest (or both), was to be a marginal and dubious affair, that of a determined, if highly qualified and motivated, underground.

Cabala as Motif

Anonymous, *Opusculum de Auditu Kabbalistica* (1518, 1578).[135] We may remark here the application of Cabala to empirical matters, in this *Short Essay on Cabalistic Phonics*. This is contemporaneous, at the time of this text's first appearance, with Cabala's parallel devolution, with Agrippa, or at least the part he was known or notorious for, into worldly magic and manipulation. Interestingly this work, which announces itself as "quite small," was important enough to reissue sixty years later, at about the time Georgius's, *Harmony of the World*, which sets the tone for Christian Cabala of the entire sixteenth century, was being translated into the French vernacular.

Symphorien Champier, *Prognosticon Libri* (1521). Symphorien Champier's career as a writer and a publisher seems to be somewhat of a paradox as well as an example of Renaissance ambivalence on the matter of heterodoxy: ostensibly hostile to the Occult it seems that he could write and publish about nothing else. *Prognosticating Books* begins with a section, "Prophets," in which you can sense the confusion of a mind that no longer knows what or if to believe. Here Pico the cabalist's authority is paramount, but Pico, as everything else, has become so much a matter of interpretation. Champier, anyway, is all over the map and back again, as he "considers the Hebrew Cabbala, natural magic against which he says Pico finally turned, poetic fury, the causes of pestilence, storms, sterilities and other scourges, which like Francesco Pico he ascribes to divine wrath rather than to the stars."[136] Whatever his confusion or skepticism Champier (1471–1537) obviously related to a *very* esoteric group of cabalists, mystics, and neoplatonists, one which we have met through one or another of its members who gathered at the court of Francis I of France. Jean Thenaud, known to us already for his long cabalistic poem, which remained in manuscript, also dedicated to Francis I, was also very much a part of this circle. Close by, too, was Lefevre d'Étaples, who had published the radical pagan cabalist and hermeticist, Ludovico Lazzarelli's *Crater of Hermes*, equally offered to Francis I, bound along with the recently discovered *Pimander*, supposedly composed anciently by the Thrice Great Hermes (a kind of hermetic equivalent to the cabalists' quasi-legendary Simon ben Yohai). Champier published also the mystical *Theology* of Asclepius, who was a disciple of Hermes Trismegistus.

Joannes Elysius, *Satis metuendi diluvii verissima liberatio* (1522, 1523). In this *Most True Liberation from the Fearful enough Flood* the author appends a section to the end of his work, which he calls the "Elisian Annexes," wherein he discusses natural magic and the Hebrew Cabala.[137] This *Most True Liberation* is one that is anticipated by this essentially *astrological* essay, whose purpose was prophylactic, that is, to warn of inundations threatened by an anticipated conjunction of stars, under the baleful and very watery sign of Pisces, that was supposed to take place in February of 1524. This conjunction had been impending since 1499, when an eminent prognosticator, a Johann Stoeffler of Justingen, had made people aware of it, in a popular almanac. In a panic that the catastrophe impending might be a "universal deluge," over fifty books and twice as many editions were published in the next quarter-century, in a pace that picked up, approaching frenzy, as the dreaded date approached. Cabala, as we have noticed before in remarking how well it coincides with Alchemy, was the kind of style that could act in concert with other occult remedies and perspectives. While other styles, particularly astrological, would appear to be more orthodox and reliable, in times of danger another raft or sail is always welcome. I suspect, additionally, it was sometimes a very much *needed* recourse, compensating for the essential fatalism, for instance, of Astrology, according to which one was passively *acted upon* by the stars. There was, as a matter of fact, a more aggressive version of Astrology, one connected with a very ambitious but also questionable *ars notoria*, according to which one conjured the presence and powers of angelic beings associated with stars. Such doings, however, were highly problematic (risky—one *burned* for even being suspected of such, and not always, like Faust, in one's own fire!) because of the claim to demiurgic stature by those who dared to practice them.

Cabala was a theory that held a promise of *actively* reversing an astrological influence, from the person to the stars, and back to oneself and others, while minimizing the risk of falling into the heresy of claiming a god's creative powers. For one thing, it may have been likely that one could get away with using the metaphors of cabalism for *participatory* styles of divination that could come under the charge of heresy if one used astrological figures. Cabala was, by reason of its exotic Hebrew provenance and essential novelty, a less familiar and everyday terrain than Astrology, where the parameters of how it could and did impact on every aspect of life, political, theological, even judicial (the place of the stars at the time of arrest, confession, or inculpation could be a factor in determining guilt or innocence), were under constant debate, challenge, and rearrangement.

Nicolaus Peranzanus, *Vaticinium de vera futuri diluvii declaratione ex intimarum mathematicarum cabalisticarum* (1523).   This *Prediction of a Flood and Determination of the Last Days of the World from the Intimations of Mathematicians and Cabalists*, published in Ancona, is concerned with the same floods, anticipated because of the starry conjunction expected the next year, as were the subject of Elysius's work. Cabala in both is linked to a strategy of predicting and preventing natural catastrophes. The tone, nevertheless of Peranzanus's work seems a little more elevated than Elysius's. For one thing, Peranzanus is anticipating the "universal deluge," unlike Elysius who was content with warning of just plain high waters. The imminent end of everything means "no time for nonsense," so triggers eschatological and apocalyptic reflections, a theme Thorndike picks up on: "After defining [what he considers] a flood [caused by supernal agency], Peranzanus cites various opinions as to the beginning and even more as to the end of the world. We are given the views on this last point of the cabalists."[138]

It seems paradoxical (since Jews were supposed to be the materialistic ones) to me how readily Cabala becomes magically "practical" in Christian hands, whereas for Jewish cabalists (whether zoharic-theosophical, Abulafian-yogic, or Safed-utopian) it rather floated more above mundane affairs, a realm of the leavened and impure they thought best left to the obscure if ineluctable workings of the "other side." We have to wait until the amulets and spells associated with Hasidic developments of the eighteenth century for a similar devolution, a worldly aspect that motivates, for instance, Scholem's significant denial of the authenticity of Hasidic Cabala.

Worth noticing here also is the evidently mystical nature of Renaissance mathematics, conflated, in the extended title, even with Cabala. In a preface addressed to the Bishop of Castellamare, Peranzonus talks of his intention to handle mathematics as if he were about to enter a holy ground, one shared not only with Cabala but with Astrology. He apologizes, in Thorndike's paraphrase, for having "ventured to direct his mind to the most sacred and almost divine science of mathesis. He further advises the bishop to pay no attention to the opponents of astrology." Just as it is now accepted that modern chemistry has roots in alchemy, so mathematics may connect us directly to a rich and very *literary* tradition of numerological speculation, from Pythagoras, through Renaissance metrics (Spenser, Milton), through its theosophical adventures from Blake to Yeats, by way of Boehme, Swedenborg, Blavatsky, and the Rosicrucian Cabala of S. L. G. Mathers. This circle ends fittingly where it began, in the palandromic number-and-letter-juggling strategies and games of Georges Perec and the post-Pataphysician French OuLiPo group. These, indeed, are *more* than reminiscent of the language-and-digit play of the great French rhetoricians of the early sixteenth century, whose practices also were related to cabalism, an association that emerges very clearly in Paul Zumthor's analyses of the literature of the Late Middle Ages and Early Renaissance.

Federicus Iadertinus, *Febres, de humana felicitate ac de fluxu maris* (1528). This work, *Fever, Felicity and the Tides*, published in Venice, five years after the last two flood-obsessed tracts, is a conservative and it seems somewhat hysterical defense of Astrology, especially in its medical applications, against all comers. The claims of Astrology to preeminence and the author to excellence in it come *first* in the extended title (see Bibliography), perhaps an indication that these claims are being seriously challenged. Among the heterodoxies Astrology is at once the one that is most comfortably ensconced, yet also, for that very reason, the most clearly threatened. Iadertinus wants first of all to reject a nascent empirical medicine (which, in a protomodern spirit would explore an essentially physical etiology for illness) and reaffirm the efficacy of an astrological one, which, of course, "involves taking into account both the hour of the patient's nativity and the time when the sickness began." Those same astral forces that rule the person, of course, rule the tides, so illness as well as inundations can be predicted and ostensibly averted or avoided by understanding their configuration. Iadertinus rejects, however, as insane, pretentious, or even heretical any other occult recourse than the astrological. Cabalistic or alchemical approaches to medicine are treated by him as altogether unacceptable, which may show how uncomfortably close they could come to certain interests and investments that were already so tightly connected to Astrology.

This may reveal also how tormented, dubious, and *crowded* the whole terrain of occult heterodoxy, which had expanded precisely in response to a demand for it, was becoming in the Renaissance, as if the church could put up with just so many of these "illegal immigrants," whose sin was to remind the astrologers that they were once outsiders too. While for others Cabala could ease the strains between Christian orthodoxy and Astrology, for this author it could all too easily be *mistaken* for it. We may be assured, according to Iadertinus, that Astrology is thoroughly Christian, only as long as we *stop* there: "Nor could pursuit of the cabala render us blest, which end could be attained only through the orthodox sciences."[139] That Astrology flirted with heresy should not blind us to the fact that the greater scandal and outrage for the church would be the outright *denial* of Astrology (although there were evident dangers in predicting the demise of Popes and suchlike). Savanarola, the arch enemy of Astrology, it should be recalled, was *burned*; while Pico, who had so offended the orthodox with his provocative Cabala and "sacred magic," never even had to recant and would, as a matter of fact, have lived to see his own exoneration had he lived just a few years longer.

Leo Suavius, *Theophrasti Paracelsi philosophiae et medicinae universae compendium* (1568). Things get very modern, complicated, and ambiguous with this Paracelsan acolyte and eminent translator of and authority on occult texts, Leo Suavius, whose "other self," Jacques Gohory, apparently wrote much more skeptically about these same mystical matters in French. Suavius was Leo's (no doubt he was a Leo) name when he was being mystical and a Cabala enthusiast, something that is very much a factor in this book on Paracelsus, inventor of that mysterious medicinal mélange of Cabala and Alchemy. We may sense, even through the distance of Thorndike's paraphrase, a certain Neopagan energy, relating to the iconoclastic, "god-making" current, or Radical Cabala, of Lazzarelli and the Hermetic *Pimander*, radiating, especially from the word *Olympian,* in this *Compendium of the Philosophy and Medicine of Paracelsus*: "For magic, cabala and the use of images many authors are cited, in especial Tritheimus in his *De Septem Secundadeus* [On the highest bliss]. Another work by Trithemius, the *Steganographica*, is defended against the criticisms of Bovillus and Wier as well as censure of Cardan . . . For Suavius man is a microcosm with a star within him as an Olympian spirit that tears away the veil and makes possible the cabalistic art."[140]

Suavius, as a later acolyte of Tritheim, would connect also with Pico's Cabala, especially as it came through to England and Western Europe so notably with Agrippa. It was, indeed, *Tritheim* who enthusiastically approved of Agrippa's *Occult Philosophy*, which he got to see in manuscript in 1510, although he advised a delay in publication until the public was better prepared—which Suavius's unquestionably has been! One did not rest comfortably in the Occult in his day, if indeed one ever has, being maybe a style or mood one rather floated on, tried out, experimented with, than believed in any permanent way. For seven years later, in 1575, we find Suavius signing his real name, Gohory, like Milo Minderbender in *Catch 22* contracting to destroy and preserve the same bridge, to an attack, in French, against the alchemical-cabalistic principles of

Paracelsan medicine he himself had defended so loyally as Suavius. It should be added, maybe to excuse Suavius/Gohory or explain their changes, that retraction and/or disgust with one's past seem to be an integral part of the occult-cabalistic life style. Of the three great names of Christian Cabala of the early Renaissance, Pico, Reuchlin, and Agrippa, only Reuchlin remained committed unquestionably. Pico, as a matter of fact, subsequent to his cabalistic divagations and claims, fell under the influence of the reformer Savanarola and wrote what was going to be a definitive attack on Astrology, which would be, in the way Ficino (who also wrote somewhat against the Astrology he so obviously practiced) and Pico understood it, very closely connected to Cabala, to crown his weirdly meteoric career. Peter Garzia, who published a book in the last year of the fifteenth century to brand as heretic Pico's *mystic* Christian Cabala, also had to take it upon himself to defend a legitimate Astrology against Pico's *rationalist* assaults. Agrippa's reversals were confusing and ambiguous also. However, one could even call his denials of Cabala, as I have tried to do, "cabalistic." Then, of course, there's Kafka, whose work has something to do, I hope we have been able to show, with Cabala, who wanted his work to be destroyed, which wouldn't have meant he never *wrote*.

   Cesare de Evoli, *De divinis attributis quae Sephirot ab Hebraeus nuncupata* (1571).   This very popular *The Divine Attributes, Called Sephiroth in Hebrew*, first published in Prague, wants to teach its reader a little bit of the "language of God" before the book has even been opened. Scholem counts three more published editions of this book in the next eighteen years, all originating in Venice.[141] The *places* of publication here speak volumes too. Prague would have been the magical center of Europe. It was there that Dee and Kelley went a little later to be court wizards for Rudolph II (Dee overreached himself in presuming to counsel the king, but the more down-to-earth medium, Kelley, became official alchemist). Of Italian cities, additionally, it was probably Venice, because of its bordering and maritime situation, at this time, that was most open and tolerant of mystical heterodoxy in religion, a factor undoubtedly Giordano Bruno, underestimating the authority of Rome (where he was burned in 1600), trusted too much in his decision to return there from his heretic's exile.

Antonio Piccioli, *Rapiti Renovati* (1587). The "rapture" in the title of this *Renewed Rapture* is to be taken, not as selective postapocalyptic survival but in the pejorative sense of a combination of rape and enchantment, maybe a parody or caution against the extremes of the baroquely sexual mysticism of Saint Teresa's piercing by the "arrow of God," caught *in flagrante* stone by Bernini. Thorndike identifies Piccioli, indeed, as another of the numerous opponents who felt it necessary to warn the public, and it seems increasingly in the vernacular, against the dangers and temptations of Cabala: "He rejects cabalistic methods of dealing with numbers, letters, diacritical marks, lines and points."[142]

Johann Georg Godelmann, *De magis veneficis et lamiis recte cognoscendis et puniendis* (1591). Godelman follows up on Jean Bodin's influential *Démonomanie* of 1580, which argued that Agrippan-cabalistic magic was demonic in effect, inspiration, and provenance. For Godelmann, however, while witchcraft was to be eschewed, the advantages of a "natural magic" approach to things were too evident to be totally ignored. A respected physician, Johann Wier (as a matter of fact, once a good friend of Agrippa's), for example, a generation before Bodin, had also worried that occult remedies and cabalistic styles were, in their Paracelsan avatar, becoming outrageous. Wier, in an influential book, first published in 1564, *Demonic Wonders*, which went through many subsequent editions, including a popular abridged version, *She-devils*, of 1584, established limits for magic, defining and defending a natural or benign form as against a demonic or malign. This Natural Magic, once cleansed, was also allowed *vast* areas of legitimacy and efficacy, which Bodin's attack of 1580 then threatened to abolish. Godelmann's purpose was to establish a middle ground between the outright negations of Bodin and the excessive room allowed by Wier. Accordingly, he fundamentally accepts the principles of Natural Magic, on the basis of the Platonic-Christian doctrine of correspondences it grew out of, but he very definitely turns against the exotic Paracelsan alchemical-cabalistic blends and remedies. Curiously a constitutional anti-Semitism in Godelmann seems to help him keep a magic he wants, while averting one he regards as unsafe or heretical. The thinkers and practices he regards as unfit all seem to have delved into Cabala, which he regards as structurally unsound by reason of its Jewish, therefore demonic provenance, a *stain*, which, however Christian or contemporary it pretends to be, just won't wear off. According to Thorndike, he "classes the Jewish Cabala, *whether old or new*, as a species of incantation. His attitude to Jews is indeed very hostile. He wonders that there are Christian princes and republics who put up with and defend this blasphemous and magical people.' "[143] Curiously, Cabala here seems to serve as a winnowing device to keep Magic on the safe side of orthodoxy.

Cesare Riviera, *Il magico mondo de gli heroi* (1603).   This was evidently a popular (reprinted at Milan, 1605) and enthusiastic guidebook to the worlds of the occult. Riviera's most important sources are Trithemius, Ficino, and Khunrath, while his heroes here are Hermes and Orpheus, communicators of formerly hidden knowledge or explorers into forbidden and dangerous underworlds, or Renaissance versions of them like Agrippa and Paracelsus. The "magic world" is none other than the fifth essence of Alchemy. Cabala here is very much of a motif among these mystical styles, while "cabalists," whom Riviera prefers to treat *en masse*, absolutely haunt these pages.[144]

Pietro Maria Castiglione, *Admiranda naturalis* (1622).   This book of Castiglione's, *Natural Wonders*, adopts and adapts what amounts to an Ideology of the Occult, as promulgated by Riviera's *Magic World of Heroes*, into the practical world of medical remedies. This can be seen even in the fuller title of Castiglione's book, which advertises a cure for kidney ailments. Castiglione cites Agrippa's *Occult Philosophy* respectfully, and is favorably disposed also toward astrology and divination, while his attitude toward Cabala, even through Thorndike's paraphrase, seems close to reverential: "The Cabala has been admired almost through eternal ages. It is very difficult to acquire, and other sciences are prerequisite and a natural ingenuity. But it does not require knowledge of the superstitious arts."[145]

Francisco Torreblanca, *Daemonologia sive de magia naturali* (1623).   *Demonology or On Natural Magic* is by a Portuguese monk who is trying to map the same precarious middle ground between the damning rejections of Bodin (who respected the power of magic but thought it all evil) and the tolerance (once the absolutely malign was excluded) of Wier for heterodoxy. This is the same terrain of compromise, outside of which Cabala fell, that we have seen Godelmann delineate. A clue as to the latitude to be allowed in this work to the demonic would be in the respectably academic suffix, "ology" which follows on "demon" in the title, quite different in connotation than the "mania" Bodin had appended. Torreblanca is no friend of Godelmann, however. For Torreblanca, Godelmann's very denial of the demonic is *demonic* itself, in accord with the familiar axiom that the devil's subtlest ruse is to suggest he does not exist. If I have understood Torreblanca's rather convoluted logic correctly, the demonic is inseparable from Natural Magic, which for him is acceptable, as long as it doesn't become too extravagant and ambitious, *which*, however, has been surely the case for the high-road of cabalistic-alchemical theurgy, as traveled by such heretics as Agrippa and Paracelsus. Cabala, interestingly, serves here as the same kind of defining moment for Natural Magic as it did by way of the structural anti-Semitism of Godelmann above. Cabala, for Torreblanca, as it was for Godelmann, is irremediably corrupted by its Jewish provenance and quality, which allows him to totally disallow its Christian version. Torreblanca very accurately strikes at the heart of Cabala, Christian or Jewish, when he denies that words can have the kind of demiurgic power that Reuchlin, Paracelsus, and Pistorius attribute to them, insisting also that "the Cabala is an invention of the devil [certainly, here, the Jew], as are the *ars notoria* [summoning angels] and *ars Paulina* [magical manipulation of words]."[146] Torreblanca's position has its ironies, however, which may even amount to a kind of "denial" or "anxiety of influence," since that very Natural Magic, to which he reserves a large portion of legitimacy, is at least partly a product of the same cabalistic mentalities he won't acknowledge. Additionally his very nuanced notions about the interpenetrating and balancing of good and evil seem consistent with traditionally cabalistic ideas as we find them in The Zohar and The Bahir, as well as the Lurianic, soon to be Sabbatian modifications. Thorndike even remarks that that precious distinction, established so authoritatively by Johann Wier, and which even survived Bodin's bold challenge to resurface in Godelmann, between a diabolical and a natural magic, just about *dissolves* in Torreblanca, who has "jumbled together natural and diabolical magic almost inextricably."

Wilhelm Schickardt, *Bechinath Happeruschim* (1624). The title is a German transcription of the Hebrew for *Inquiry into Exegesis.* Scholem indicates that a lengthy section of the above work is about Cabala.[147]

Andreas Tentzel, *Medicina Diastatica* (1629). A "diatastic" approach to medicine, was one, I believe, that focused on the intestines and involved a cabalistic-alchemical approach to treating them that tapped the subtle but powerful energies that have often been thought to accompany death (for instance, prophetic powers, as in John of Gaunt's "This blessed isle" apostrophe-curse on England in *Richard II*). *Indicated*, it appears were substances whose efficacy had been discovered by Paracelsus, which were, in fact, human remains or *mumia*. At the time of death a separation of the realms (physical from spiritual) occurs, each of which, preparing for the "leap," had accumulated a maximal amount of force. The Paracelsists considered it possible to capture these energies in these particulary intense forms so as to make them usable and tonic for the living. Cabala, therefore, enters into Tenzel's medical magic through its notions of the interpenetrations of realms of life and death. Tenzel relies on a specifically Christian Cabala also for its mystical-typological equation of the birth of Adam with the "birth and death" of Christ, as symbolized respectively by the Edenic Tree of Life and the Cross.[148]

Laurens Beyerlinck, *Magnum Theatrum* (1631). Theater, as in "All the world's a stage," is a familiar Renaissance metaphor for the cosmos. This particular book is an enlargement of Theodor Zwinger's sixteenth-century encyclopedic survey *Theatre of Human Life* (1565, with three more editions, all enlarged, by 1604). Beyerlinck's bias, as was Zwinger's before him, was resolutely antioccult. It seems symptomatic, however, that in Beyerlinck's version (he had changed a topical into an alphabetical order) he found it necessary to attack many more of the magical practices and theories than had Zwinger, as if the appeal of such recourses had rather *grown* than diminished in the meantime. Thorndike notices "new articles on amulet, antichrist, apparition, arcanum, benediction, cabala, ceremony, fascination . . . incantation, incubi, and maleficium."[149]

Father Juan Nuremberg Eusebio, *Occulta Filosofia* (1633).   Eusebio, a Spanish Jesuit, follows in the discreet footsteps of such as Wier, Godelmann, and Torreblanca in his intentions of rescuing a certain Natural Magic by eliminating from its domain some suspected or dangerous elements. Here again, Cabala falls very definitely on the side of the forbidden and is called, in fact, a "vicious science."[150] This is the same terrain of compromise, outside of which Cabala and everything Jewish fell, that we have seen Godelmann survey. If one wanted to keep what the Jews brought one had to exclude the Jews, plus rename or not mention Cabala. This couldn't have been an easy trick for Eusebio, who, indeed, calls his book after Agrippa's *Occult Philosophy*, whose lineal connection to a Cabala of Hebrew provenance, through Pico, Reuchlin, Riccio and others, was so manifest.

Mathias Bernegger, *Orationes Duae de Cabbala* (1640).   As well as being listed by Scholem for these *Two Orations on Cabala*, Bernegger is mentioned by Thorndike as a correspondent of Kepler (whose physics certainly had mystical aspects, as did Newton's) and translator of Galileo. Bernegger had translated the latter's *Dialogues on Two Systems of the World* into Latin (published in 1635). Some letters Galileo sent to Bernegger, which he meant to be appended to that work (they arrived too late for that, however), in which he maintains that one should not always read the Bible *literally*, sheds some light on the reasons why a scientist might look to someone who was versed in Cabala, likely as a buffer against the threat of the accusation of heresy. Cabala is surely based on the notion that Scripture was never meant to be read *only* literally.[151]

Theodor Hackspan, *Miscellanearum sacrorum . . . accesit ejusdem exercitatis de Cabbala Judaica* (1660).[152] It's notable here that in what is obviously a collection of general commentary on sacred matters, Cabala figures so prominently in the title. From this we may conclude that Cabala was also something that people were curious enough about to make of it somewhat of a selling point for

texts that may have been very largely concerned with other matters. People evidently felt that they should know something about
Cabala, while also being cautiously concerned that they should be
able to trust the competence of their teachers of so delicate and
possibly dangerous a science.

Jean Baptiste Morin, *Astrologia Gallica* (1661). This book em-
ploys cabalistic metaphors and figures to justify Astrology. In
Thorndike's paraphrase, Morin explains how "God made the division into twelve signs corresponding to the natures of the planets
and the twelve houses, and revealed this to Adam . . . by way of the
Cabala."[153]

Martin Schoock, *Physica caelestis* (1663). The cabalistic astrology of Morin's, however, makes no sense for Schoock, whose major
intention in *Celestial Physics* is to draw the same kind of line
between what is acceptable and unacceptable in Astrology that
writers like Godelmann, Torreblanca, and Eusebio wanted to draw
for Magic. As for the latter, it is Cabala that helps Schoock, nega-
tively, to establish his distinctions. He, accordingly, rejects decisively that aspect of Cabala that most impacted on Astrology. This
was the concept of the "celestial alphabet," which associated letters
and stars, as conceived by mystical inventors like Paracelsus, Postel,
and Fludd, all of whom Schoock alludes to before pronouncing their
efforts "vain and idle."[154]

Candido Brognolo, *Alexicacon* (1668). This work, which was
published in Venice in two large folio volumes, whose extended title
goes on to explain it is "about evil and evil spells," seems to have
been a kind of compendium of information needed in order to practice magic or avoid its effects. Brognolo, however, is stridently anti-
Cabala, which he attacks not only for its intrinsic demonism but
because he thinks its conclusions are not consistent with logic and
common sense.[155] We may assume, as is the case with other malign-
ing publications, especially those aimed at a popular audience, that
the fact that it is necessary to warn people (again and again) of its
"dangers" is an index both of Cabala's appeal as well as the threat
many saw lurking behind it of social and religious iconoclasm and
disorder.

Caspar Knittel, *Via Regia ad Omnes Scientias et Artes* (1682).   What Knittel here calls "the Cabala of the Hebrews" is very much a station on this ambitious *Royal Road to All the Sciences and Arts*, published initially in Prague and reprinted five years later in Nuremburg. Scholem notes that Cabala is especially prominent in a section called "The Hebrew and Pythagorean Arts of Universal Knowledge."[156]

Johan Henning, *Cabbalalogia* (1683).[157]   I'm not sure if this work is a parody or is reverently in the spirit of a Hebrew and Old Testament-oriented Christian Cabala. The latter seems, however, to me to be more likely, since it describes itself, in its extended title as "a brief introduction to Cabala through ancient Jewish rabbis and poetic examples." Through the coinage, "Cabalogy," which I have never seen before or since, Cabala is probably—as when the study of demons is called "Demon*ology*"—being presented as an academically respectable discipline.

François de Monceaux, *Disquisitio de magia divinatrice et operatrice* (1683).   This *Disquisition on Divining and Operative Magic* is taken up, in large measure, what must seem to us as a bizarre science that was all the rage for awhile, that of *alectryomancy*, or divination through the call of cocks, probably an important factor in many people's lives before the invention of the alarm. Monceaux also includes here a comprehensive survey of the various sorts of divination of his time, arranged alphabetically. In this list Cabala figures prominently, and Monceaux focuses particularly on its semiotic aspects as he explores the occult implications of the concept, originated anciently by Pythagoras, and perpetuated by Pico, Reuchlin, Agrippa, and Paracelsus in the Renaissance, of the magical "internal force of words." He describes this position while rejecting it insightfully as the fundamental message and idea of the Cabala.[158] Perhaps we may opine that, before Cabala "goes underground" in the eighteenth century, after its Sabbatian embarrassments and ineluctable retreats before science and technology (which monopolize thenceforth the realm of the miraculous), it dives first into the animal realm, as if the voices of the prophets and mystics could only be tolerated in the crowing of the first cock of the day, when we are half dreaming anyway!

Cabala as Reincarnation

Franciscus Mercurius Van Helmont, *Two Hundred Queries about The Revolution of Souls* (1684). Franciscus Mercurius, whom we have met before as the faithful cabalist son of his Paracelsist father, Johannes, marks I think a desperate and dramatic climax and limit in the Christian Cabala of the Renaissance. Franciscus is very obviously a contemporary of Sabbatian apocalyptic Cabala and apostasy, resorting also, on the Christian side, to his own sort of imaginative and even scandalous remedies, although of a more theoretical sort. As documented amply by Marjorie Hope Nicolson (through her edition of Anne Conway's correspondence) and Sheila Spector, in her annotated bibliography, the Cabala of the younger Helmont was evidently a powerful influence on the ideas of the Cambridge Platonists. Henry More, the most distinguished and respected figure among the Platonists, already was deeply imbued with cabalistic notions, ideas, and styles, practically the leitmotif of his theology of justification, which he called, referring to literal, allegorical, and moral interpretive levels of scriptures, his "three-fold Cabbala." More will insist, in thoroughly characteristic zoharic fashion, for instance, that a literal reading of Genesis is tantamount to Atheism. He writes, for instance, to Anne, Countess of Conway, in 1653: "I have according to my promise sent your Ladiship my 3 fold Cabbala [*Conjectura Cabbalistica*, which he had just published]. I am very sensible how much this story of the Creation, by being insisted upon in the most literall sense, has furder'd Atheisme in the world." The More-Conway fascination with Cabala can be followed (starting with Nicolson's index, which only lists the more extensive allusions) throughout their correspondence, which is then given focus around 1670 when through Van Helmont they start participating in the preparation of the important translations of The Zohar and cabalistic commentaries Knorr Von Rosenroth is going to start publishing in 1677. Von Rosenroth seems to have been eager to secure More's collaboration for his collection, seeking his advice, through correspondence and by way of Van Helmont who traveled back and forth from England to the continent, maybe mainly for that purpose. The subject of Rosenroth's coming anthology is a constant theme of discussion, anticipation, and excitement in the Christian cabalist circle, formed by More, Anne Conway, and

Van Helmont in England in the 1670s, just as if they were an advisory editorial committee. It was at More's suggestion for instance, through advice that had been offered by his fellow Cambridge Platonist, Ralph Cudworth, who obviously knew his Cabala, that Von Rosenroth decided to add Riccio's translation of Gikatila's *Gates of Light*, which alone was kept from the earlier Pistorius collection, to his anthology. The Von Rosenroth-More correspondence becomes itself a substantial portion of the second volume of *Kabbala Denudata*, of 1684.[159]

What this Cabala of F. Van Helmont adds to the one already in place, through More and his acolytes, is the support and structure of its direct provenance from the doctrines of Isaac Luria. We know just about to the exact date of the arrival of this Lurianic Cabala in England through a letter More wrote to Anne Conway on February 5, 1671: "I have sent you two Cabalistical papyrs together with my Notes, and if your Ladiship desire a copy of those papyrs your Ladiship sent me from V Helmont [who was staying at the Conway estate], I will make my sizour transcribe them for you . . . I had with me to dinner last Sunday, our professour of the Orientall languages, and another Doctor of Divinity well versed in the Rabbins, and a bishops son of Suedland, well skilled in that learning, and a Jew . . . and as for that Isaac Luria whose commentary in MSS. Peganius [alias for Knorr Rosenroth, whose letters to More concerning the projected publication of *Kabbala Denudata* had been carried to England by Van Helmont] sayes he has to helpe him to understand the Zoar, the Jew told me that they hold that Isaac Luria to be the most knowing man of their cabbala of the Jewes Nation."[160]

A paradox of pedagogy as old as Plato is that we can only learn that which we are ready for, so, in some sense, know already. More and his generation, accordingly, had already given that preexistence-apocalyptic-revolutionary Lurianic turn to their Cabala before they ever heard of Luria, which is why his teachings were so welcome as soon as they became aware of them. Likewise for Milton he didn't need to know of Luria for his ideas about Cabala to be turned in a Lurianic direction by the radical exigency, that of saving and healing a fallen world, of his times. Neglecting these conjunctural factors I think invites a fall into the trap of literalism. Werblowsky, for instance, I think is short sighted in arguing, in

"Milton and the *Conjectura Cabbalistica*," that whatever Cabala there is in Milton would be of the (more anodyne) pre-Lurianic sort, since Milton's knowledge of the subject was owing to More's *Conjectura Cabbalistica*, which was published in 1653, much before Luria was known in England.

The Lurianic modifications that rose out of the purist sixteenth-century school of Safed, were dramatic indeed. Luria assumed a primordial Breaking of the Vessels, with a correspondingly cosmic urgency of *Tikkun* or Repair of them. In Lurianic Cabala also an idea, likely of Indian provenance, of *gilgul*, or transmigration of souls, became much more forceful and prominent than it had ever been before. While, on the Jewish side, these Lurianic ideas of apocalyptic *repair*, or messianic reincarnation, evolved, in a century's time, into a revolutionary and political Cabala of the Sabbatians, on the Christian side, that same explosive mixture turns into a very original, novel, and speculative Cabala of F. Van Helmont and the Cambridge Platonists. As a matter of fact among the latter, a version of reincarnation, the theory of the preexistence of souls, had been already been circulating discreetly, but nevertheless causing some scandal. Although one of its advocates, George Rust, in a pamphlet published in 1660,[161] took care to cite Origen, preexistence has never mixed very well with Christianity, which found it generally impossible to conceive that Christ could have come to earth in any other avatar than that of one Life of Jesus. Illustrating the essentially foreign provenance of such an idea, another acolyte of reincarnation, Joseph Glanvill, called his book, published anonymously in 1662, flatly *Light from the East*.[162] Neither Rust nor Glanvill signed their works but because both were adoring student-disciples of Henry More his influence was immediately (and rightly, since he had suggested the notion to them) suspected. Nicolson, citing More's letter to Conway on the flurry at Cambridge caused by Rust's anonymous pamphlet, leaves no doubt: "'It is a book,' he said, 'that hath witt and learning in it, but our Vice Chancellour lookes upon it as a dangerous book, and therefore did in some sort censure it in the Consistory.' The radical opinion for which it was principally condemned—a belief so old that in that generation it had become daringly new—was More's favorite idea of preëxistence; and indeed so consonant with Rust's were Glanvill's ideas that the *Lux Orientalis* and Rust's *Discourse of Truth* were later published together, annotated by More. The seed which Henry More had sown had fallen upon fertile ground; the dragon's teeth were becoming armed men." Some of these wild seeds had also fallen in foreign soil, for we find More, in a letter to Anne Conway of 1670, saying about Van Helmont's first visit to him in Cambridge, fresh from Holland: "He inquired much for a little book of prae-existence (which I perceive was that of Mr. Glanville)."[163]

The *Two Hundred Queries* of Franciscus Mercurius is indeed nothing less than a systematic attempt to adapt and adopt these seemingly very un-Christian (or even un-Jewish) theories of reincarnation to the urgencies of a Cartesian rationality, also very much of the moment, so was perhaps a last ditch attempt to save Cabala, even at the cost of possibly risking the turning of it into something like a philosophical version of Sabbatian mystical heresy. Although Luria is not mentioned specifically in the text proper, a nameless translator's enthusiastic preface makes that lineage crystal clear, by alluding to an upcoming project, if this meets with favor, to render another work into English. This is a book that the translator mentions was composed in Latin a few years earlier, called *A Discourse on Souls Taken from the East and Adopted from the Works of Isaac Luria, Called the Eagle of Cabalists.* Anonymity both of translator and author were seemingly *de rigeur*, in such provocative surmises,[164] but Scholem positively identifies Franciscus Mercurius as the "anonymous" author of an important tract, *Cabalistic Adumbrations of Christianity*, in Knorr von Rosenroth's *Cabala Revealed* anthology of 1677, whose novelty precisely was its incorporation of specifically Lurianic motifs and texts. Scholem adds specifically that Mercurius was a major conduit of Cabala to the Cambridge Platonists, Henry More, Ralph Cudworth, and Thomas Burnet.[165]

Reincarnation indeed is able to answer many of the questions and find ways of solving the conundrums and the quandaries posed by such proponents of Natural Religion and critical-historical reading of scripture that had gathered around the name of Spinoza and been carried on in the spirit of Descartes. That injustice for instance that cried out to logic and to Dante of damning those born before Christ's latest coming is resolved definitively, if one allows the validity of such speculation: Those that disappeared before getting the opportunity will simply return and receive one very good one sometime between now and apocalypse. This is indeed, according to our ingenious Mercurius, why the world didn't end on Good Friday of the year of the Crucifixion: "Is it not probable that the very Reason, why the World was to last so many hundred years after Christ's Resurrection, is, that all those Souls, that had lived formerly in the world, and dyed without Repentance, before *Christ's Death*, should again live in the World, and have full time given them under the Gospel-dispensation, to repent and be saved?"[166] Another apparent Scriptural solecism that Cabala was meant to solve is the manifest lack of fairness in the unreliability of rewards for good or evil conduct. The Zohar, for example, likes to reassure us that the reason why the good so likely go hungry, naked, and worse in this life is because they are living for another life, and vice-versa for the well-off evil, who live only once. Mercurius is, however, defending scripture against a much more severely rigorous and "scientific" assault than such notions, even converted in Christian terms of a more sublime Heaven, can parry. *Revelation* 13.10, for instance, specifically affirms: "He that killeth with the sword must be killed with the sword." To the evidence that speaks for itself that those that live violently often die peacefully in bed, Mercurius is able, through reincarnation, to respond that such will perish violently in a future life.[167] Just as, for Mercurius, we have more than one life, so there has been more that one world; and he relies on a traditional cabalistic exegesis that there was another world, one of Creation, that existed prior to the one that Adam (Christ) was ushered into, which was, pejoratively, a World of Faction, which in its turn may not be the last either. Inconsistencies in one realm are to be, or were already, ironed out in another. Interestingly, it is at this very sensitive and speculative point in his argument that Mercurius alludes to Judaism, which I think he had been rather trying to be discreet about—insisting, for instance, in his extended title, how very *Christian* reincarnation would turn out to be. It was, in fact, the ancient Jews, in collusion somehow with Pythagoras, who first became aware of this succession of worlds and lifetimes. This Greek-Jewish awareness was in fact true Christianity, *avant la lettre*. For Mercurius, indeed, *Christ* himself is not exempt from reincarnation, a truth that encompasses persons, worlds, *and* gods: Christ enters in the Torah in the shape of the prophet Elias, returns in a newer testament as John the Baptist, where He also comes out as himself, *but* will come again (for the *last* time) to collect such early souls as will have to return between the third and fourth manifestation.[168] Mercurius implies, in his calling this cyclic phenomenon "the revolution of humane souls" in the full title, that these theories deserve the kind of credibility then increasingly if belatedly accorded to the *revolutions* of the stars of Copernicus, who had dared to so dignify the movements of the stars in the (eventually) world-changing work he published in 1543, *De revolutionibus*. The hidden analogy is a good one: If stars go around, why, indeed, not souls? Answering this question is surely impossible, but merely posing it makes it easier to understand why Christianity (up to and including Milton) went by Ptolemy for so long.

Mercurius is too serious a theologian, too well descended and connected intellectually not to be aware how deeply challenging this is to the very essence of Christianity, which was rather consti-tuted specifically in denial and refutation of such cyclic theories as reincarnation, eternal return, and repetition. A constant theme of the early church fathers was to anathemetize such "futility" as pagan. Such notions would make of Christ's passion and crucifixion, in the eyes of Iraneus or Augustine, a ludicrous and derisory spec-tacle, to be staged an infinite number of times before a distracted audience, much as Shakespeare was going to say about the assas-sinated Julius Caesar, and therefore turn the basic event of the Christian calendar, which is linear and finite, into repertory the-ater. From the serious, unalterable, irreversible mood of a sub-limely unique passion, cosmic cycles usher us instead into that virtual world, now so familiar, of the "society of the spectacle." Mercurius does concur with, respectfully, or at least pay lip service to, the classic Christian critique of cyclic paganism.[169] However, by taking his reincarnation from Lurianic,[170] therefore ancient (as Cabala and The Zohar was then assumed to be) Hebrew, rather than Indian sources, Mercurius is evidently trying to Judaize and eventually Christianize the theory. He also manages, through some spectacular exegetical-hermeneutical acrobatics, the absolutely stun-ning feat of *combining* the extensions and infinities of cyclic rein-carnation with the unique chance for redemption, which in Christian-existential terms, by definition, can come *only once*, maybe the metaphysical equivalent to the mathematical miracle of squaring the circle. He does this finally by putting a *cap* on return, by intimating that Christ's next one will be the last! Reincarnation and Redemption, are, however, too disparate to be married ultimately by fiat, even one as clever, urgent, and obviously well intentioned as this. Finally, however, the conflation of linear Christianity with cyclic Paganism would collapse under the weight of its sheer absurdity, a testimony to how far gone, desperate, or drunk you have to be to see the line and circle as one, or lines, as it were, going in circles. I think, rather, what is confessed here by the very extravagance of these remedies is the exhaustion of Judeo-Christian religious systems, confronted by the unprecedented imperatives and conjunctures of our incipient technological-industrial-commercial and very secular age. The great Western monotheisms have by the end of the seventeenth century so declined in relevance that even the twistings and innovations of an idealistic mysticism, one of the major avatars of which is *Cabala*, is unable any longer to rescue them. Surely when we start to talk about future incarnations, all that can mean is that our past lives are no longer germane to the ways we have to live this one. Among irreconcilable contradictions, none could be more *spectacular* than this Vedic-Hebrew-Christianity Mercurius creates by merging reincarnation and crucifixion. Its idealistic visions of cosmic syncretism fragmenting into fantasies, Cabala has lapsed or evolved into imagination, dream, and ingenuity—all synonyms for what we mean today by *text*. Cabala has taken refuge in realms, in other words, where impossibility is no disqualification, in the caves, palaces, and ghettos of *literature*, where, if at all, we may look for it today.

4

The Kiss of the Spouse, Cabala in England (1497–1700)

The first evidence we have of the dissemination of cabalistic ideas from the Continent into England is in the work of the English humanist and educator, John Colet,[1] whose *Two Treatises on the Hierarchies of Dyonisius*, of 1497, were written after Colet had returned home from a two-year stay in Italy. There evidently he had come into contact with cabalism through a study of the works of Pico. In the *Two Treatises* Colet reproduces a page from Pico's *Apologia*, which he had prepared in his own defense for his trial for heresy of 1486; and he also refers to the translation of cabalistic works, from Hebrew into Latin, undertaken by Pope Sixtus IV at the request of Pico. From a letter Colet wrote to Erasmus in 1517 we also learn that he was interested in Reuchlin's *De Arte Cabalistica*, since he complains to his distinguished correspondent that Erasmus had sent a copy of Reuchlin's book to John Fisher, Bishop of Rochester, but not to himself.[2]

In a sermon this same John Fisher delivered in 1521, he uses and explains the word *cabala* twice, adopting the bifurcation in religious history between an oral and a written tradition and calling the oral tradition "the cabala." Another example of the penetration of Cabala comes from the annals of courtly education: Giles de

Gaez, court librarian for Henry VII and Henry VIII and tutor to Princess Mary, completed, probably in 1532, for the young princess, an introductory course in French conversation. In one of these lessons he refers to the fact that "the cabylysts doth make fyftie gates that they name Intelligence." Blau's opinion is that this might be an indication that the Cabala was by then fairly well known, since this seems to be a rather recondite allusion.

Later in the century Cabala is still a recognizable element in intellectual vocabulary, as Everard Digby, whom Blau graces with the title of "a minor English philosopher," promotes cabalistic ideas, derived from Reuchlin's *De Arte Cabalistica*, in a book called *Theoria Analytica*, which he published in 1579. Cabala is also mentioned in a work by Henry Howard, Earl of Northampton, *Defensative Against the Poyson of Certain Prophecies*, of 1583.[3] In this book, which I consulted in the *Short Title Catalogue* [of books published in English between 1475 and 1640] photocopy collection, Howard tells the story of his encounter with a certain Brocada, whom he calls "a cabalist at court," who claims to have predicted the fall of Antwerp through a literary technique. What should make the student of divinatory arts of the Renaissance suspicious of heterodoxy or worse is the claim to accuracy in *dating* specific events. Although prediction of the future had attained a certain measure of grudging acceptance, even in the posttridentine church, as well as in the more various and diverse strands of the Reformation, the pretension to exact knowledge of things as they concern individuals was widely regarded, when reliable, as heretic and demonic, or otherwise as simply fraud. This is the much-needed rationale, for example, according to D. P. Walker, for Tommaso Campanella's defense (1636) of a "good" astrology against Sixtus V's general Bull (1586) against divination: "The Council of Trent had condemned only those books on divinatory astrology which claimed certainty and precision of prediction infringing free will."[4] The attribution, therefore, to a cabalist of such precision would be an indication of a certain corruption, by this point in the century, of the image of Cabala.

Cabala, Shakespeare, and The School of Night

As we have had occasion to notice in the matter of the reception of the Cabala of such as Agrippa and Paracelsus, by this time a debased but widespread meaning of it was that of a device for divination, according to which a "cabalist" would be the equivalent of a fortune teller. This is indeed the kind of Cabala that is attacked by Antonio Zara, in *The Anatomy of Talents and Sciences*,[5] published in 1615—as well as by a host of other authors, including possibly Shakespeare, in *Love's Labor Lost*, which has been regarded as being at least partly intended as a satire against the supposed pretentious elitism of the "magic" of Raleigh and Marlowe's "School of Night." In her interesting study of 1936, *The School of Night*, Muriel Bradbrook made a case for an influence of Cabala on this mysterious association—which seemed to have existed as much, if not more, in rumor as in fact—frequenters of which were accused of atheism, heresy, and blasphemy. This influence would have come through Agrippa and John Dee, been reinforced through Bruno's visit to England (connections to Raleigh and Spenser), and become blatant through a member, William Warner's, epic poem *Albion's England*, which uses the image of a forever unknowable God in terms that identify it unmistakably as the inaccessible and remote Ain Soph of the Cabala.

Shakespeare, here, if the allusion indeed is to Raleigh's group, would be ironizing a certain clannish aspect of Cabala that otherwise was a positive force in his plays. According to Frances Yates, Shakespeare absorbed his Cabala, though probably not as directly, from some of the same sources as Spenser, especially by way of Francesco Giorgio, a Venetian Franciscan friar, whose mystical-numerological-musical schemes of universal harmony and reconciliation, worked out earlier in the sixteenth century, had an enormous impact on intellectual life in the Renaissance. Giorgio's *De Harmonia Mundi* circulated very widely all through the century, but there was also an important translation of this essential work of Christian Cabala into French published by the La Boderie brothers (well-known and connected occultists and poets) in 1578. Shakespeare's "little Latin and less Greek" certainly did not mean French, as established by the "lessons" in *Henry V*. However, Yates opines, "It is not necessary to suppose that Shakespeare knew Giorgio's work only through the French translation. He could have known of it as diffused in the Dee circle."[6] Giorgio, in turn, had based his very optimistic numerological mysticism on Pico, Ficino, Reuchlin, and Hebrew sources, the latter close to him in Venice. Giorgio's ideas, because of their reassuringly orthodox provenance, functioned throughout the century to protect cabalists from the accusation of heresy or demonism.[7] Giorgio's Cabala, for instance, conjured spirits and angels specifically as protection against demonic forces.

Cabala, according to Yates's daring "re-envisioning," would be reflected in three kinds of places in Shakespeare—first of all, in the invention of spirits, for instance those that hover protectively in *Midsummer Night's Dream*; and secondly, in images of an intermingling of earthly and heavenly beauty, as in the Platonic dialogue between Jessica and Lorenzo that concludes *The Merchant of Venice*, or that is the ultimate framework of the "joined realms" of *The Tempest*; lastly, in a certain practical and judicial harmony of qualities that is an ideal to work toward, as in the balance between mercy and justice in the famous trial scene in *The Merchant of Venice*, which Yates sees as a more or less direct rendition of the *sephiroth* as conceived by Giorgio.[8] Yates relies, for this perspective, on Daniel Banes's *The Provocative Merchant of Venice,* which she finds, however original and useful, just a little too schematic:

> He gives throughout his commentary diagrams illustrating the interactions between the characters and ends by finding these remarkably summarized and completed by the diagram of the Sephirotic Tree in which the Sephiroth are diagrammatically interrelated. Banes completes the Sephirotic Tree by adding the names of characters in *The Merchant of Venice* to the names of the Sephiroth. This is a somewhat high-handed procedure but it does lead Banes into some interesting suggestions. He sees the trial scene as a diagram with Shylock on one side, Antonio on the other, and Portia in an intermediate position. Shylock represents the Sephira Gevura or Din, JUDGEMENT SEVERITY; Antonio corresponds to Hesed, LOVING KINDNESS; Portia is equated with Tiphereth BEAUTY or MERCY who mediates between the two opposites of Severity and Kindness and attempts to reconcile them with Beauty-Mercy. Banes points out with many quotations that Mercy is not a monopoly of Christians but is enjoined in Jewish law and in Cabalist mysticism.[9]

Nevertheless, Cabala in Shakespeare, pervasive as it is, would be a much more ambiguous entity than it is in the more purely poetic and courtly texts of such as Spenser and Sidney, inevitably more dialogic, we would say today, because of the nature of his form and audience, and responding more complexly to the shifting political climate of the day, in which mystical styles were never innocent. Thus Shakespeare in *Love's Labor's Lost* will attack tactically a School of Night whose notions he otherwise very largely shared (even in the same play—Berowne's Neoplatonic encomium of Woman conveys something very close to a mood of welcome for the cabalistic Shekinah), reflecting thereby an increasingly widespread suspicion of the occult. The allusion, if it was one, to Raleigh's circle, if there was one, would come in the context of an interchange between Berowne and the King on the confounding subject of the latter's "beloved's" having a dark complexion, not associated at the time with either good looks or heavenly behavior: "KING: Oh paradox! Black is the badge of hell/The hue of dungeons, and the school of night;/And beauty's crest becomes the heavens well" [IV, iii, 249–51]. Berowne's women-worshiping speech occurs just a little later in the same scene, from which I'll excerpt just the refrain: "For when would you, my lord, or you, or you,/Have found the ground of study's excellence/Without the beauty of a woman's face?/ From women's eyes this doctrine I derive:/They are the ground, the books, the academes,/From whence doth spring the true Promethean fire/. . . From women's eyes this doctrine I derive./ They sparkle still the right Promethean fire;/. . . That show, contain, and nourish all the world" [IV, iii, 294–98; 345–50]. These renowned lines, which tie all hope of human *ascent* so tightly to the feminine in a manner that recalls in its urgency the role of the Shekinah in Cabala, were a version certainly of Count Bembo's philosophy of love (woman as the ladder to heaven or link between the domains of divine and earth), as communicated to the Age of Elizabeth, in the fourth book of Castiglione's *Courtier*, especially in Thomas Hoby's translation of 1551. It seems a likely assumption that the Italian Renaissance generation of Castiglione would have felt some of the impact, in its turn, of the widely disseminated Neoplatonic, hierarchical, and feminized Christian Cabala of the nearby Venetian Franciscan monk, Giorgio. Finally, it seems to me that woman's love as it shines through this play veers rather toward Cabala and away from Neoplatonism in its projection of an eventual marriage of the lovers (after Berowne has had his year's chance to try his wit out on the dying). From a strictly Neoplatonic perspective any ascent to the realm of ideas takes place on the other side of the carnal, which lovers need to avoid like the proverbial plague; while Cabala makes of connubial bliss rather an ineluctable passage to the absolute.

At about the same time that Shakespeare was inviting us to wonder, gently, in *Love's Labor's Lost*, about the validity of an elite's mystical withdrawal from the world, Marlowe, on the other hand, whose name had even been linked to Raleigh's mysterious group, lambasted, ridiculed, and smeared cabalistic magic thoroughly in his immensely popular play, *Doctor Faustus*, whose protagonist was none other than the notoriously demonic Agrippa.[10] In common with an ambivalence that is inseparable from the Renaissance's attitudes toward magical styles of thought in general, Shakespeare and Marlowe are understandably ambiguous about esoteric matters; and so indeed is Henry Howard, Earl of Northampton, in his *Defensative Against the Poison of Certain Prophecies*, published about a decade before *Love's Labor's Lost* and *Doctor Faustus*. There he treats Cabala with more reverence than he does the fortune teller who is supposed to be the cabalist. Howard even hints at the sacred provenance of Cabala, almost in the same breath as he brands its acolyte as a fraud. He explains, while seeming to accept its feasibility, that Cabala originally meant the "oral tradition" that was revealed to Moses at the time of the divine communication of the written law; but his mood becomes once more patronizing and suspicious when he concludes this account of his encounter with Brocada, the "cabalist at court," by counseling both the self-styled prophet and the naturally curious reader: "I advised him in a charitable sort, rather to followe the sound advice which was given to Origen, by his godly Father, not to wade any deeper in the meaning of the holy writ . . . than the playne and open sense thereof would beare."[11]

As much as trickster and magician, paradoxically, Cabala seems to represent commonly in the Renaissance a mysterious anticipation and confirmation of the "truths" of Christianity. If Agrippa, however unfairly, represents this first unpopular image of the cabalist, Reuchlin seems to embody the second and more respectable one. Blau, for instance, refers to a sermon given by a Reverend Henry Smith around 1590, in which he uses an example lifted out of Reuchlin's *De Verbo Mirifico* (republished in England in 1552), whom Blau says Smith has misinterpreted, in order to establish that the divinity of the Virgin Mary and Jesus Christ is proclaimed by the Old Testament: "Rabbi Hacadosh proveth by art cabalistical out of many places of Scripture not only that the mother of the Messiah shall be a Virgin, but also that her name shall be Mary. Like as also the same Rabbi Hacadosh proveth by the same art out of many texts of Scripture that the Messiah's name at his coming shall be Jesus."[12]

The Cabalas of the Age of Elizabeth

Although, perhaps because of the extravagant way his theories are stated and certain mystical intimations and generalizations that go along with them, Denis Saurat's ideas about Cabala and Literature[13] have tended to be treated less than seriously, I think he does make a fairly good case for the presence of some cabalistic influence in the works of Edmund Spenser. He is especially persuasive in his identification of the Sapience figure, in "An Hymn of Heavenly Beautie"—about whose unusual presence in the poem there has been much conjecture—with the cabalistic Shekinah. Saurat supposes that Spenser had either read of the Cabala or had heard of it indirectly through Giordano Bruno, who moved, and very notably, in circles frequented by Spenser's friends. Yates also assumes that the link with Bruno is likely, even probable; but Bruno, whose style was more pagan, manipulative, and Agrippan, would have found a Spenser who favored a more affirmative Cabala, that of Francesco Giorgio, the Venetian Friar whose Pythagorean-Hebraic meditations seem to have been very influential in the Renaissance, especially in the sixteenth century. It would be from the current of Giorgio that Spenser absorbed a Cabala that would generate his numinous image of Queen Elizabeth, at once the Gloriana, Belphoebe, and Britomart of the *Fairie Queene*, as Shekinah for the Israel of Britain. *The* key role in the dissemination of this Cabala of Giorgio to the generation of Spenser, Sidney, Raleigh, and Chapman was played by the catalytic Elizabethan mage, pythagorean, alchemist, and strange missionary (to the "magical court" of Rudolph II of Bohemia), John Dee. Bruno's effective and proselytizing visit to England would have been to some eclectics, poets, and intellectuals well prepared to receive him, as well as being able to put his teachings in perspective.[14]

Bruno himself published a little book on the Cabala in Italian, in London (certainly because Italy, where Bruno was burned at the stake fifteen years later, was already in the throes of its antimagical reaction), in 1585: *La Cabala del cavallo pegaseo*.[15] The "horse Pegasus" in the title relates to a version of the theme, prevalent in zoharic texts, and related also probably to a certain Erasmian "praise of folly," of wisdom coming from unsuspected places—which Bruno handles playfully, however, in connection with his very *serious* syncretic theurgy that collected some of the most powerful occult currents of the Renaissance in an imposing, challenging, and finally, for the Catholic establishment, which executed him, *insufferable* synthesis. Bruno's Cabala, as described by Frances Yates,[16] tended to be provocatively manipulative and "magical" in the style of Agrippa, that is, deriving from the numerological Pythagoreanism of the *Sefer Yetzirah* tradition rather than from the more theosophical Zohar. One senses that his ultimate allegiance was neither to Cabala nor Christianity but rather to a premonotheistic, pagan, esoteric Hermeticism, which promoted the "divinity" of man untrammeled by Christian (or indeed, Jewish) duties and guilts, somewhat in the radical-iconoclastic style of Lodovico Lazzarelli's *Crater of Hermes*, so influential—but probably more discreetly—in occult circles early in the sixteenth century. Lazzarelli's innovation, which he claimed cabalistic provenance for but which really takes him out of the Judeo-Christian context, lay in his ascription of possible demiurgic powers to a person, able, with sufficient dedication and adequate training, to *create* celestial beings that subsequently serve their progenitor(s). Actually Lazzarelli did not claim originality for the recipe of these cosmic creations but, as recounted by D. P. Walker, said that he had been taught them by "a certain Joannes Mercurius de Corigio . . . [who] appeared in Rome in 1484 wearing a crown of thorns bearing an inscription 'Hic est puer meus Pimander quem ego elegi' ['This is my son Pimander, whom I elected'], preaching and distributing leaflets; at Lyons, in 1501, wearing the same garb, he performed miracles by natural magic and promised Louis XII a son and twenty years' extra life. He was a wonder-working magus, who had himself, as Lazzarelli tells us, been regenerated by Hermes Trismegistus."[17] Lazzarelli's relation to Joannes, whom he calls his father, begotten somehow "aethereo semine" [through ethereal? semen],[18] seems to be identical to his strange siring by Agrippa Thomas Vaughan paraded later, even more miraculous, since, unlike for the earlier pair and given that cryogenics was not then an option, it would not have been possible.[19]

Bruno's synthesis of Cabala, Hermeticism, and Paganism in the alembic of his bold assertions about human potential demonstrates that Cabala, in other forms than Giorgio's reassuringly Christian and orthodox one, could also become part of a Renaissance panoply of forbidden but fascinating sciences, often warned against, indeed, as part of a series of "mistakes." As we approach closer to the seventeenth century there is, as a matter of fact, a distinct tendency to regard Cabala as suspiciously iconoclastic and potentially demonic rather than as a support of Christian hope and an aid to conversion. This development is, indeed, in full swing, by the early 1590s, at the time of Marlowe's assault on Agrippa's reputation, while the prestige of John Dee was declining vertiginously also. By the end of the century even the gentle Giorgio was no longer acceptable. A basic text that seems to kick off this anti-Agrippan movement was the *Démonomanie* of Jean Bodin, which appeared in Paris in 1580. In a few years this suspicious mood had evidently reached England, for, in a book published in London in 1584—*Discourse Upon Divels and Spirits*, a supplement to his *Discoverie of Witchcraft*, which appeared in London that same year—Reginald Scot, according to Thorndike, "opposed interpretation of dreams, augury, cabala and judicial astrology."[20] Yates connects Bodin's "demonizing" of Agrippa with the opposition to him of James VI, then King of Scotland, soon to be James I of England. The latter's book of 1587, *Daemonalogie*, was fiercely anti-Agrippan (not because James did not believe in magic but rather because he thought Agrippa's, and anything like it, was witchcraft), insisting, for example, that the spurious, "black magic" fourth book of Agrippa's *Occult Philosophy* was authentic. Interestingly James's book appears just about the time that Dee is returning from his alchemical adventures in Bohemia. One opines that if Dee had been able to be as discreet about Agrippa as Agrippa had been about Lazzarelli his reception might have been more welcoming. But by that time Agrippa, because of the climate of increasing suspicion, was a hard vice to hide.[21]

Although a manipulative-magical side of Cabala fell into disrepute a certain numerological-mathematical approach seems to have been better able to keep its innocence, especially where its promoter(s) did not pretend to be able to control or change things thereby. We may remark, for instance, that in the texts of Sir Thomas Browne, the prestige of cabalistic mathematical and alphabetical techniques is often invoked but these texts are shorn of their directly operative force, in the sense that they are assumed to have had something to do with the way the world was originally structured: for Browne they are more privileged explanatory paradigms than, as they were for Agrippa and Dee, effective rituals and necessary rites.

Cabala's ability to endure in this abstract form in Browne may be explained by the absence of any firm and reliable control for a style of thought whose trait it was rather to question authority than take its place. Cabala could lend itself readily to the imagination and the requirements, as well as the religious presuppositions, of the individual who resorts to it. Such seems to be the case with Frances Meres's *God's Arithmetic*, of 1597, whose Pythagorean title hints it to be very much imbued with the spirit of cabalistic numerology, for instance in the emphasis he places on *even* as opposed to *odd* numbers, in harmony with the Manichean-gnostic dualism of Cabala: from the fact, for example, that Adam is given a mate Meres is able to decide that two is a better number than one; and also more obscurely, but with a certain emotional logic that "addition and multiplication belong to God, but subtraction and division belong to the Devil."[22]

Meres's numerology is fanciful, however, even in a tradition that emphasizes inventiveness, for the *one*, in Cabala, as well as more generally Pythagorean and Christian mysticism, has tended rather to be the number of pristine holiness and integration, whereas the *two* has commonly represented division, separation, fragmentation, simulation, and fall, although an ineluctable and eventually a happy one. The increased patience Cabala shows over more orthodox styles, whether Christian or Jewish, for the duality of life should not be confused with Dualism, which would have been a blatant revival of the ancient worship of a principle of evil, coeval to one of good. According to Grözinger, a contemporary authority on Kafka and Cabala, "[In Cabala] dualism *always* remains subordinate to monotheism: even evil is in its own way part of God's manifestation."[23] Grözinger's purpose here was to eschew Dualist interpretations of Kafka, for instance a Marcionite-Gnostic one that would suggest the author was writing on the basis of an assumption, for which evidence both in text (and existence) would not be lacking, that the world was created and is maintained by an evil demiurge. However, I'm not so sure about the *always*, or at least that the separations between the realms are always so clear cut. For Cabala, especially in its more cataclysmic avatars the *two* can be very close to the *one*, if not intimate. Kafka may well be some kind of a cabalist, but maybe more of a Sabbatian one than Grözinger could admit. For Scholem, on the other hand, whom Grözinger cites abundantly but whose gnostic themes he seems to miss, Kafka's is sublimely our century's "turn of the screw" of a heretic Cabala.

For Cabala, ambiguity, or the *two*, is more of an earthly destiny than a principle of heavenly provenance, since the *one*, however distant, unapproachable or even indifferent, can have neither rival nor companion (even the Shekinah is God's bride only in the world of emanations, leaving him otherwise in the pristine solitude of the *ein soph*). Consistent with Cabala, therefore, is Spenser's contrast between two heroines, Una and Duessa, truth and falsehood, accorded, respectively, Books One and Two of *The Fairie Queene*. Yet, Una is never so distorted by Duessa's simulations and betrayals that she loses her clear preeminence; and, though her knight loses sight of her for a while, it is clear equally that it is the Truth of the One he has lost sight of, in falling, however ineluctably, under the spell and lure of the Two.

(H)Enoch Clapham Redivivus—Ancient Theology and the Protestant Preacher

About Cabala, where secrecy is the rule, people tended, fittingly, to be coy, even for authors where an impact is more direct, literal, and unmistakable than in Spenser. A Hebrew word for God in its title, for instance, led me to finding what I believe to be a thoroughly Christian-cabalistic poem about scripture in Henoch Clapham's *Elohim Triune, displayed by his workes Physicall and Metaphysicall, in a poem of diverse form*, published in London in 1601.[24] In the preface Clapham alludes to the cabalistic practice of interpretation of scriptures according to the holy letters of the Hebrew alphabet. Although we have already remarked on Clapham as a strident opponent of Agrippan-magical Cabala, here he seems to be a proponent, if a grumbling one, of a Christian one. This ambivalence, if puzzling, was not at all untypical of a Renaissance that agonized—for example, earlier with Ficino—over whether Astrology would fit into a Christian scheme of things. For Ficino, who organized his life around defending against the threatening "melancholy" of Saturn,[25] Astrology was just too essential to do without, so he wound up distinguishing between a heavenly and a demonic science, only the *latter* of which was to be regarded as heretical and blasphemous. Similarly, Cabala, in view of the many ways it could "come on," and the various ends it could serve—in medicine, philosophy, theology, conversion, feminism, eschatology, literature, divination, and more—would be difficult to shut out entirely. It should therefore not astound us that, after implying in his preface that he has structured his epic on cabalistic principles, Clapham pretends not to know, or need to know, very much more about Cabala, referring a curious reader, for further elucidation upon this matter, to a Iacobus Brocardus, though no individual works by this author are cited. This authority, Brocardus, to whom Clapham (who preached for an English Anglican congregation in Amsterdam) is ready to confide the soul of the trusting but curious reader, is certainly the same person that Henry Howard had treated like a fool or clown a few years earlier as *Brocarda* or "cabalist at court."

A period biographical dictionary turns Brocardus or Brocarda into a James Brocard, author of *The Revelation of St. John Revealed*, translated from Latin by J. Sanford and published in London in 1582. In the preface to his translation of this work Sanford discusses the concept of the microcosm in terms of Agrippan-Paracelsan natural magic, and in Brocard's own preface a cabalistic notion that God's "ends" are imbedded "in the beginning" is very forcefully articulated: "The beginning and proceeding of prophecie seemeth to be thus, that is the framing of the world, in the very creatures and in this worke god hath marked what he would bring to passe in the world from the first time to the last." This leads Brocard to the grounding concept of a Christian Cabala, that "Moses (and a fortiori Adam) contains Christ."

Exemplifying the manner in which cabalistic styles of exegesis could be deployed as arguments in the religious controversies of the Renaissance, in a passage which follows, Brocard, who doubtless had a Protestant ax to grind, deploys the method of *gematria*, or assigning numerical equivalents to letters in the Hebrew alphabet, to decide that the names of certain popes are the equivalents of the names of the devil.[26] Brocard also refers to the "wheel of Ezechiel,"[27] which in a Jewish mystical system, contemporary with Gnosticism, that predates and anticipates Cabala, is a primary symbol. This is the "merkabah" or chariot that is the vehicle and transport for visionary experience.[28] Brocard, whose purpose in this work seems to be more polemical than theological or philosophical, contents himself with rapid allusions to Cabala rather than offering any systematic exposition, so I assume Clapham was referring his reader to another work by the same author.

In a "Preface to the Christian Reader," with which Clapham has introduced his religious-epic poem, *Elohim Triune* (or *Trinity God*, which would amount, quite neatly, to a Hebrew motto for Christian Cabala) he is, however unwillingly or unassertively, quite specific and even a little erudite in expounding the sources of Cabala in that oral tradition, with which it had become synonymous: "The Iewes, or rather the Rabbins of the Iewes over and beside the written law of God incommended to all Israel, they bragge of a second lore or kind of learning which Moses received in mount *Sinai*, which they terme *Cabal* and the professors thereof Cabalists: in our tongue valuing nothing else but tradition and traditionaries. This (they say) was delivered by mouth onely to Moses, he by mouth to others and so on till it came to Hillel or Simon Iustis Gamaliel, and so forward till the time of their talmuds confection. Sometimes they fetch this cabalique learning from before *Moses*, making *Jacob* to prophecy upon his sonnes by that (as by virtue of this Cabalique spell, they will that Moses wrought his wonders in Aegipt)."

In a footnote to this passage, introduced under the rubric of "Apologis Archangelo," Clapham refers his reader to his source for this idea to Archangelus de Burgo Novo, a sixteenth-century Italian-Franciscan monk, who was the chief apologist for Pico's controversial Christian-Platonic rendering of Cabala.[29] Clapham's need to refer the reader to his sources does not prevent him from knowing who the right ones are. He obviously has difficulty or finds it otherwise inexpedient owning up to what he knows about "the Cabala phenomenon," something whose extravagance annoys or threatens him in some ways, while remaining useful or even indispensable in others. The concept of an oral tradition, for instance, would be helpful for someone trying to adjust religion to an incipient secular morality and economy, by allowing for exceptions to and qualifications of the written rules. However, as an English Protestant more or less distant from the Catholic Church, he could not help but be suspicious about a certain congeniality between the Papal establishment and a Christian Cabala at the beginning of the sixteenth century, a connection that he nevertheless needs to refer to, if only in a note. Next we find Clapham wondering about some of the philosophical paradoxes and quandaries connected with Cabala, as well as their political implications—even waxing a little sardonic over the contradiction of an oral tradition being conveyed, nevertheless, in texts, as he escalates into sarcasm on the ineluctably mystifying effect of any "secret" tradition:

They (Romanists) stand for the defense of this unwritten verity, as the *Cabalists* for secret learning. Yea, this is it that causeth the Fryer Archangelus so to storme at the sober Bishop D. Gurizia, for impugning Mirandulae's cabalique positions. For he seeth well, that the Cabalique and unwritten verity, they are like to Hippocrates twins, if the one die, the other cannot live after. Yet this is a wonder in my minde, and by their leaves, I will propound it for a question: Seeing this kind of learning is by them termed *Hyd, secret, not for Hogs, but for pure Illuminated spirits*; and therefore at first not written: how comes it now about that they write their unwritten stuffe, that now the vulgar sort (which they term Hogs) they shall also see and know their mysteries? In my judgement they sould have caused a great deal of less stirre in the world, if his unwritten veritie had ever been unwritten, & never talked of, but only secret among those *Familiq; illuminated Elders*.

Manifestly the Hidden

This "revealed secret" was of course a paradox that has always been one of the mysteries of Cabala,[30] one that was far from hidden from its early masters of the School of Gerona, in Spain, of the late twelfth century, whose writings attracted a very angry and influential letter of condemnation from the most respected authority on esoteric Judaism of the time, Isaac the Blind, of Provence. Scholem had discovered this important letter and reported on it in 1934.[31] As recently recounted by a student of Scholem, Joseph Dan: "The main purpose of the letter was to express Rabbi Isaac's anger when he heard that his disciples in Gerona did not keep their kabbalistic traditions secret, but talked about them openly and published books on mystical subjects. Rabbi Isaac believed that there was great danger of misunderstanding if the Kabbala were revealed to the uninitiated, and that kabbalistic secrets should not even be put on paper in the form of a book."[32]

The impact of Rabbi Isaac's disapproval seemingly was overwhelming, at least for a while; and this interdiction was obviously an obstacle that the great Spanish cabalists of the thirteenth century—de Leon, Gikatila, and Abulafia—had to overcome. Probably what helped them do this was a Neoplatonic and mystical nuancing of the idea of the secret. Spanish Jews, because of an atmosphere of relative toleration fostered by Moslem culture, were open generally to intellectual and philosophical developments in the Christian West; whereas Eastern European Jews, subjected to pogroms and crusades, tended to be more isolated. According to these subtle hermeneutics every revelation or discovery is only another "garment," layer, or level of a sublime untellable mystery, which was not a matter of (only) words in the first place. Whether or not the Truth can be known may be a point that should remain moot, but we may agree anyway that it cannot really be *told*, at least in any ordinary way. Torah itself would be only an embodiment and symbol of another Torah, which would be the authentically effective one, which nevertheless always remains anticipated, one yet to come. A fortiori, this deferral would be a mechanism that operated all the more ineluctably for cabalistic commentaries on the Torah as well as on the commentaries on these commentaries.[33]

This is a situation, overall, not without resemblance to Blanchot's contemporary version of the Mallarméan notion of a literature of the *le livre à venir*, or of a book always yet to be.[34] On another, more hallowed level Cabala's *announced* taciturnity approximates the enigmatic Eastern wisdom of that strange self-erasing statement so memorably announced by the great classic of Chinese mysticism, the *Tao Te Ching*:

> The Tao that can be told is not the eternal Tao.
> The name that can be named is not the eternal name.

The purpose of such a mind-twisting style, whether of the deeply mysterious cogitations of the Tao, the more articulated rationale of the thirteenth-century gnostic-neoplatonic cabalists (connected probably to Cusan or "learned" ignorance), or in the language of Blanchot's modernist idealism, is to remind us of the limitations of words, whose function would be more to point us in a salutary direction than to tell us what we'll find when we get there.

Most likely some concerned and sensitive exceptions to or qualifications of this rule of secrecy would have made sense to a man like Rabbi Isaac the Blind, who had gained a reputation for great wisdom. Rabbi Isaac, indeed, left at least a few important textual fragments behind also, not to mention the letter warning cabalists *not* to write. Maybe, sensing, prophetically or just cannily, an appetite for freedom here and now in an "oppressed" people, he anticipated that a secret knowledge made public would sooner or later tend to serve mundane and temporal ends that would, by adulterating its message, enter into a ruinous complicity with the world it was trying to transform. Events seemed eventually, however, to leave behind the antinomies of this debate between discretion and dissemination that becomes finally nugatory, or at least merely academic. As, with the increasingly exilic status of the Jewish communities during the Renaissance, even normal religious practice had to be dissembled—secrecy, from being a closely guarded precious exception, became a routine rule of survival. This interdiction against revelation of the mysteries ceases to be cogent in a world in which one's very religion had to be a secret. Finally, and certainly by the late sixteenth and seventeenth centuries, the mystical masters of Cabala were also expected to be popular leaders and, whether in their own name or through the efforts of their acolytes, published writers.

Surely by the time Clapham is "preaching" to his congregation of readers, in 1601, Cabala doesn't seem to be a secret to anyone, while its claim to being a hidden knowledge is made out to be either an outright contradiction or total joke. Likewise I think the popular tone of Clapham's remarks, with more than just a tinge of anti-intellectualism, always well received by any kind of general public, establish something that might not be so obvious from the writings of more rare, eminent, and talented figures, like Pico, Agrippa, and Bruno: that Cabala was a widely known, promoted, and disputed movement and that it was more than merely an eclectic philosophy practiced by a few recondite, Faustian spirits at court or in the monasteries. For Clapham was an Anglican priest, who, in fact, had also announced, in the "Preface to the Christian Reader" of his cabalistic poem, that his purpose in versifying scripture was to make the Bible more easily accessible *to the average member of his congregation*. Clapham's position is curiously, if understandably, ambiguous. As is apparent from his poem he has obviously been influenced by cabalism, ostensibly in the form it filtered through its Christian apologists of the early Renaissance, as interpreted most recently for him by this same evidently "suspect" James Brocard he has grudgingly referred his reader to for more information on the subject. However, he concludes his preface with a disavowal of Cabala and Brocard so extreme, given the cabalistic style already manifest in the title, and as we will soon see, in the contents of the poem, as to amount to what we might call, to marry Freud with Bloom, a mechanism mixed of equal portions of denial and "anxiety of influence." This would be a fear of corruption by a compelling, because internalized, foreign (or which one would like to think of as such) agency, or predecessor that has imbued one too deeply to even be acknowledged, which because its presence must be dealt with in some way, can only be denied: "This kind of learning [Cabala] I could have farced my Poem withall (making great ados about the first word of Genesis *Breshith*: examining why God begins his writing with B, why R followeth and so forward: which I know into itching ears would have been passing solations), but I think that *Iacobus Brocardus* hath therein done more than enough."

Getting Past Creation

Here Clapham is being a little sly, if not downright devious, with his reader. By introducing Cabala in a parenthesis, he is understating its importance but letting us know, nevertheless, that he has thought enough of it to become acquainted with its fundamental doctrines. Unquestionably, Cabala in general and The Zohar in particular is obsessed with Genesis, creation, and beginnings. Cabala is far from unique in its interest in beginnings, for, as Nicolson has noticed, "Bara [was]: the Creation . . . on which every important Jewish and Christian Father expressed himself."[35] However, neither Saint Augustine's *City of God*, nor Maimonides *Guide to the Perplexed* comes close to matching the obsession of The Zohar with Genesis. Fully 40 percent of the Sperling-Simon translation of The Zohar is taken up with commentary on the Book of Genesis; and, given the fact that the Cabala texts since the thirteenth century tend to be, in one way or another, commentaries on The Zohar, I think we can safely say that when we are talking about Cabala creation and beginnings are never very far away. Furthermore, there is a certain tradition in Cabala that Scholem, citing Rosenzweig, has reminded us of,[36] according to which not the act of creation is the essential but the moment *before* the beginning, the divine intention to have things start.

The cabalistic deity who is, inscrutably, ultimately, and always already only intention, would correspond, in literature, to the modernist writer who writes "intransitively," forbidding and defying understanding, as well as entry into and exploitation by systems of exchange. The nineteenth-century continental Romantics who rediscovered Cabala, and through whom even Scholem was initiated (together with Walter Benjamin, by way of the Christian cabalist, Franz Josef Molitor), were prepared already by a sentimental education, exactly that of Werther, that valued *potential* over *product*, the beginning over the end. Blanchot locates the essential gesture of modernism, which started with a certain Romantic "refusal" to write, not in the act or result of the writing process, but in the "moment before it." Blanchot's examples of this Bartelby-type gesture are the hesitancies and deferrals of the Romantic German Atheneum generation of the Schlegels, Novalis, and Hölderlin, as well as the "withdrawn" genius of the early nineteenth-century French aphorist, Joseph Joubert. The remarkable brilliance of the little that the latter actually wrote suggested a massive unwritten work, thereby anticipating what was to be the style of modernism in literature: that the process, intention, and *start* take precedence over the subject, result, and *end*.[37]

If there were one word that would suggest the mood, climate, and meaning of Cabala it might well be that first one in Torah, *bereshith*, or "in the beginning." Accordingly, Clapham subtly makes us wonder why, in a text, the Bible, if ever there was one, where every word must have been intended, the first word of scripture, indeed, *does* begin with a *B*, referring us for an answer to this and other questions we might have, to Brocard, not so disapproved of that he is not mentioned. Compounding this deviousness, there is also an element of Ciceronian *praeteritio* at work in his presentation. He is going to "pass over" cabalism, but in passing, as it were, he manages to say enough about it to at least whet our curiosity, plus convince us he knows a lot more than he will say or admit to. It becomes very quickly obvious as soon as we turn to the poem itself that Clapham's disclaimer of cabalism has been, to say the least, disingenuous. In the opening section, "The First Day of Creation," he describes, for example, some company Jehovah may have had early on:

> Nor was the thing, that was not Aelohim*,
> Triune Iehovah**, onely God in all.

Whereupon Clapham gives us footnotes explicating these names of God in a Christian-cabalistic style, essentially a *gematria*-type logic that finds in these beginnings an incipient trinity, while granting the one-ness of the Jewish God. Of *Aelohim** he says: "*[This is] the plural of Aeloha or Ael. By which plurality, Moses would lead us unto that Trinity is unity. By which word, is expressed the source of God: whereby all was made." Of Iehovah** Clapham explains: "This name expresseth the true Being of God, whereby all things have Being. It is given by Moses, first in Gen. 2.5 set before Aelohim: commonly termed Lord. But Lord is the English of Adon, which the Iewes did read instead of Iehovah: concealing this as ineffable; terming it for his 4 letters (I.H.V.H.) in Greek, Tetragraminaton." Later on in the poem Clapham discusses the characteristics of the Hebrew language and alphabet in blatantly zoharic terms that seem strikingly similar to the visionary hermeneutics of Van Helmont's occult theories of correspondence between physiognomy and Cabala, which seem to be either shared or anticipated: "Old Adam's language termeth fire (Vre)/But light caul (Ore!). First letters are the same/In Hebers tongue, Aleph and Vaf by name,/ Distinguished by sound, not by figure/Closely inferring, Fyre for cheife occasion/Of simple light, through subject ayres Invasion"[38] Especially the fourth line of Clapham's verse, which theorizes that Hebrew letters are "Distinguished by sound, not by figure," has the ring of what will be the Van Helmonts' very sound-oriented, anatomical, and medical Cabala. Thorndike's commentary on the Cabala of J. Van Helmont sheds light on the attraction of such theories for men of religion as well as of medicine, the one trying to rescue bodies, the other souls. This was based on an ability to supply answers for a generation that was eager for an explanatory principle, like that of a Cabala of letters, that was at once physically anchored and metaphysically still reassuring: "Helmont was author of a treatise on the alphabet of nature in which he held that the very Hebrew characters for letters represented the motions and configurations of the tongue and the mouth which were required to produce the sounds of letters, and that consequently Hebrew was the easiest language for a deaf and mute who also had weak sight. At first sight this may seem a harmless fancy on his part of no linguistic or scientific significance. But there was the danger that it might encourage belief in the operative and magical force of words, characters and the Cabala."[39]

In other works of Clapham that show up in the STC the impact of cabalism is also very much in evidence. In 1596, for example, Clapham published a book in London entitled *A Briefe of the Bible Drawne into English Poetry*. Along with his poem, Clapham insists on supplying his reader with a running cabalistic commentary on the Biblical action, and he is particularly informative on the subject of the names of God.[40] In 1606 Clapham published, again in London, *An Abstract of Faith Ground on Moses and Applyed to the Common Creede*, where he ascribes the Cabala not to Moses, as he seems to advertise, but to Adam. Moses was, indeed, the recipient of the *visible law*, and of *written scripture*, but Adam received the far superior, though *invisible and sacramental law* by way of the cabalistic "tree of life."[41] Here Clapham seems to be trying to outflank a Hebrew provenance (presumably Adam was uncircumcised, whether or not he was equipped with a navel) so as to establish the anteriority of a Christian Cabala. A little further on, we find him so expert a cabalist, and also *Hebraist*, that he is employing the esoteric style of *gematria* to deduce how long the exile in Egypt endured: "Jacob sayeth this in Gen 37:37 Aeredh* el-Beni abel Sheoah, I wil go downe to my sonne." Of the *Aeredh* it is duly noted: "*Cabalistically one might say that the letters in (Aleph, Resh, Daleth) in Hebrew numeration 205 they might import the time of his seeds being in Egypt, being much thereabouts so many years."[42]

In *A Chronological Discourse*, which appeared in London in 1609, we find Clapham become fairly erudite in his cabalism. We find him citing Pico and also dwelling on Ricius,[43] the illustrious convert of the early sixteenth century and the mainstay of Pistorius's popular anthology of (Christian) Cabala of 1587. Clapham cites Ricius's *De Mosaico logo mandatis* [On the word commanded of Moses] at length, while another allusion to him is accompanied with a reference to a book called "Cabal Art," surely Pistorius's collection. Clapham had been talking, as Cabala likes to do, of times of dearth and exile: "A thousand years shall the Desolation be, sayth the Talmud*," which he dutifully notes: "ut est in Paula Ricio [as said by Ricius]."[44]

Cabala was for Clapham, as for many others, a kind of an anguish, a style that he found it difficult either to accept or reject. So we are not surprised to hear at least a tinge of irony in his references to it, which sometimes, as we've remarked before, even graduates to sarcasm, as in a passage we've quoted (p. 92) from a pamphlet he published in 1608, *Error on the Left Hand through Preposterous Zeale*, aimed at Puritan-antinomian radicalism, in connection with a certain devolution in the image of the cabalist— who becomes in the popular mind a kind of Agrippan trickster. In another tract, however, which appeared that same year, *Error on the Right Hand through Frozen Securitie*, aimed at Catholicism, we find him showing off his erudition, garnered from Cabala, Hermeticism, Neoplatonism, as well as a kind of metaphysically interpreted medicine, on the subject of metempsychosis: "Read (not to mention Trismegistus, Iamblicus, Porphyry, Proclus) the writing of the great

Physicall clerks, Paracelsus, Quersitanus and others and you shall find (by plain demonstration) that every Minerall hath his life and spirit: And as the Galenists have granted the corruption of one creature, is the generation of another: so neither can this be, if so a life and spirit were not convied from the dying bodie into another. Whereupon else cometh it, that notwithstanding all sortes of daily dyings, there is yet a plenteous conservation of every creature in this kind?"[45]

The frequent cautions against excesses conveyed in the ironic mood, as well as in the titles and contents of his texts, might remind us that Clapham was preaching in the "Cabala hotbed" of Amsterdam, as head of an English-speaking Anglican congregation there. The city, in which Spain was predominant for so long, was crowded with fugitive and converted Jews, as well as marranos; these latter two categories were very important for the syncretic religious mysticism of the Renaissance. The *structural* secrecy of Cabala would have made it an especially attractive doctrine to marranos, or nominal Christians who were practicing their Jewish faith in hiding. For Cabala all faith, like the primordial creative principle, is *hidden*. Later on in the century, Amsterdam, with its inclinations toward innovation, was really the Western European center of the Sabbatian heresy. The harmony between English Puritan and Jewish millenarianism is shown by the visit to England of Manasseh ben Israel,[46] famed cabalist and chief Rabbi of Amsterdam, as Oliver Cromwell's guest, when the question of the readmission of Jews to England was being considered. In Holland, additionally, there were opportunities for contact between Jews and Christians that were no longer available in most of Europe and inexistant, as a matter of fact, in England, from which Jews had been expelled in the thirteenth century.

This was, additionally, a time when religion, far from the conservative force it has been generally thought to be in modern times, was often identified with revolution. The new historicism of Raymond Williams and Christopher Hill, for instance, has shown us very credibly that religious chiliasm and political radicalism, often went hand in-hand. There had been freedoms, for instance, claimed and taken by the Anabaptists' Münster Rebellion of the 1530s, which necessitated a bloody extirpation that was to haunt the collective unconscious of the century. As a matter of fact substantial literary traces were left as documentation of the cultural trauma this episode constituted for the Renaissance. In Thomas Nashe's *The Unfortunate Traveller*, often called "the first English novel," which was published near the end of the sixteenth century [1594], the memory of the Anabaptist rebellion sixty years earlier is still quite fresh, disturbing, and provocative. Jack Wilton, the main character-narrator meditates at length (ten full pages[47] out of a novel that is only some 120), if suspiciously, from his mercenary *(lumpen)* point of view, on the validity of those religious revolutionaries' claims to social justice and equality. Finally, however, the brutality of the genocide that ends the episode disgusts even the cynical Jack forever with a military career. Nor was Thomas Münzer, awesome inspiration of the Anabaptists, the only "Theologian of Revolution"[48] in an age that had a number of them. Thomas Münzer, executed in 1525 for the role his League of the Elect played in the Peasant Revolt, never really established any Anabaptist Religion, but merely articulated very effectively the "free spirit" principles (which had been circulating, more or less subversively for centuries) upon which the Münster rebellion was based. The leaders and really creators of the latter movement were Jan Matthys and Jan Bockelson (John of Leyden), the latter in its most halcyon days of sexual license and political-religious antinomianism (1534–1535), and still capable of scaring (children) in the form of that "specter of revolution" that haunts Halloween in a pumpkin avatar as Jack-o-Lantern.[49]

Religion, especially of the millennial, or even reformist sort, far from being the "opium of the people" Marx later called it, was in fact during the Renaissance *the* primary conduit of utopian and social-revolutionary aspiration; and this was a quality that intensified in the seventeenth century to the point that it was religious revolutionaries in England who finally leveled their aristocracy and decapitated their king. On a more purely mystical level, later in the century, about the time England, weary of radical idealism, was recalling its monarchy, the political implications of Sabbatai's messianic-heretical Cabala were quite apparent to the Turkish rulers of the time, whose fears of subversion of the social order, according to Scholem, were their main reasons in forcing the apostasy (the "messiah" was given the choice of conversion to Islam or testing his immortality against a squad of the Sultan's expert archers). There was, moreover, even allowing for the ritual accusation of license against heretics, a real connection also between sexual and religious liberation, as exemplified by the documented programmatic promiscuity of the Münster rebels. Later on, texts (for instance, by Laurence Clarkson or Abiezer Coppe) of that "Anabaptist revival" constituted by the radical segment of the English Revolution of the seventeenth century are replete with claims of exemption from the restraints of any conventional morality, especially in regard to matters of property and sex. For them, indeed, there is no such thing as sin, for which there exists the word, but as for a square circle, no reality. Yates mentions, in this spirit, that a French translation, published in 1578, of Giorgio's major book on Cabala, *L'Harmonie du monde*, was dedicated to a member of "The Family of Love". This was a secret, syncretic, and antinomian sect whose liberality accorded with the conciliatory-syncretic policy of the French royal House of Valois.[50] However fascinated, therefore, any popular preacher like Clapham was with Cabala, certainly disclaimers, warnings, and caution was very much in order. Cabala, indeed, as it evolved during the Renaissance was becoming increasingly extremist and eschatological. The knowledge and power it promised and maybe delivered were attractive but also threatening entities, which needed to be guarded against and ironized, since they, or similar talents, had been known to turn against their possessors. Marlowe's Faustus, modeled on the cabalist Agrippa, for instance, is quickly overwhelmed and disillusioned by the magic that first entranced him. The case of eschatological rebellions, like that of the Anabaptists (and others), is a little different, since they assume a social dimension from the outset and tend to be destroyed, not from within, like the errant mage or overreacher, but from without by the vested interests and ruling classes they threatened and provoked. Antinomian ideas, which would have included cabalistic ones that open up scripture and practice in novel ways, would certainly assume a portion, at least, of the responsibility for these outbreaks.

The Other John Davies

In spite of the disclaimers, stresses, and cautions they seemed to demand, cabalistic-style formulations, as in the case of Clapham, who seemed to be particularly fond of them, were widely deployed in the Renaissance, whether in philosophical and religious discourse or in medical and protoscientific texts; and of course, they seemed especially welcome to poets, always looking for new ways of imagining old things. What led me, for instance, to look for traces of Cabala in the metaphysical epic poem, *Microcosmos*, published in London in 1603, by John Davies (1565–1618) was the inclusion of the letters of the Tetragrammaton, in Hebrew, in its extended title. This poet is not to be confused with the very much more famous and frequently anthologized *Sir* John Davies (1569–1626), author also of epic-length poems on the subject of cosmic order, and an essential piece in E. M. Tilyard's important reconstruction of the survival of a medieval hierarchical system well into the Renaissance, *The Elizabethan World Picture*. Sir John Davies's world view, while sharing abstractly with Cabala a notion of correspondences in the "great chain of being" of the cosmos, according to the formula of plenitude that Arthur Lovejoy has traced through literary history, seems insufficiently sensual, concrete, and physical to be cabalistic. On the other hand there is a suggestion of Cabala even in the brief formula in which Michael Stapleton describes John Davies's poem as a "physiological and psychological Microcosmos," as well as in the language of the title of another work of Davies's that Stapleton mentions, *Mirum in Modum, A Glimpse of God's Glory and the Soul's Shape* (1602).[51]

Here Cabala is suggested generally by the idea of participation in the divine through the senses: first through vision, keeping in mind that sight of God is a rare, dangerous, and controversial issue in Scripture—unlike the God of Cabala, either personally or through his Shekinah, so much more familiar, at least in his emanations, with his acolytes; and then touch and maybe feeling is suggested in the notion of shape. Shape, additionally, echoes a branch of cabalistic studies concerned with the shape or figure of the Godhead, in the light of our prospects for knowledge of it, as explored by Scholem in *On the Mystical Shape of the Godhead*. Although John Davies does not mention Cabala explicitly it seemed to me that the text affords a few hints of its influence. For one thing the title, *Microcosmos*, summons up images of a world of natural magic and correspondences that is basic to Cabala as well as to allied Neoplatonic and hermetic currents. Cabala seems to enter specifically, at a certain point in his work, when Davies is grappling with that most difficult of questions, *Theodicy*, and until Leibniz, at least, philosophically insoluble—that is the question of the existence of evil in a divinely generated universe: or, in Davies's words, "How can the soul err if she is from God?" This is a problem, of course, that Cabala is absolutely obsessed with: vast areas of The Zohar, for instance, are devoted to explanations and rationalizations of the "evil" present in *Torah*, frequently designated, ambiguously, as a "strategy of the good," of which Jacob's fooling of his brother Esau would be the example of choice, and David's deliberate placing of Bathsheba's husband in a battle situation where he was sure to be killed, a close second. On another level that flirts with or enters into what Scholem designates as "heretical cabala," the claiming of perfection for the soul, implying the *impossibility of error*, would justify, by redefining, even the most outrageous desertion, crime, or promiscuity as somehow "good," at least in a messianic context. Such deviations, far from unique to the Cabala of the later Renaissance, were well known and greatly feared by a nascent Christianity in late antiquity, as for example in the Gnostic sects who worshiped the tempting serpent (Ophites) or who made heroes of such as Cain (Cainites) and Esau.[52]

What made the hermeneutic feats Cabala could perform on the subject of morality especially useful in the period was the fact that this reevaluation, redefinition, or, in Nietzschean language, inversion or "transvaluation," was one of the vital concerns, on many levels, of the Renaissance, starting at least with Machiavelli's moral relativism and practical cynicism. Certainly, a good part of the attraction of Cabala for the Renaissance lay in the way it was able to float received values in the interest of a higher morality, meaning, or goal. Such agonies of conscience suffuse, for instance, the theater of Shakespeare and, less bashfully, Marlowe, and their contemporaries, in which, typically, the most effective and useful political agent is also, disturbingly, the least scrupulous (Richard III, Bolingbroke, Tamburlaine). An exponential exacerbation of these kind of dizzying quandaries was likely a reason for the Puritan abolition of theater. The uncanny Jacobean and Carolingian escalation, of such as Webster, Turner, and Shirley, prepared for certainly by that most outrageous of Elizabethans, Marlowe, turns *evil* into a *good* in itself—which will correspond in later (heretically) cabalistic terms, to the Sabbatai's notorious "marriage to a whore," or his ultimate cataclysmic conversion to Islam.

For our English poet John Davies the solution to the problem of evil seems to be in a related mystical realm also, as he resorts for consolation, in his distress, to the very notion of a *cabal* or secret tradition or book in which such things are explained, while remaining closed to ordinary understanding. About Theodicy, or the science of justification Davies proclaims only: "This is the Gulfe that swallows up the soul/And quite confounds her, if she enters it:/ The secret deepe, deep *wisdome* did enroul/In that still-closed *book* of *secrets* . . . /Some so desire to *know*, that faine they would /Break through the *bound* that humaine knowledge barres/To pry it to his brest which doth unfold/*Secrets* unknowe."[53] For Davies secrecy commands awe and respect, since it implies that answers to our questions and doubts exist. These answers simply are withheld from us for our own good, or because we are not ready for them. Yet a fundamental association of Cabala with the hidden and the secret can also be a factor in the ambivalence connected with its reception.

Rules for Use

It seems that the Cabala that came to be widely known in the Renaissance, even outside of eclectic circles, increasingly suggested that danger and temptation went along with its benign, explanatory (justifying) uses, which pitfalls needed to be guarded against. To deploy a coincidentally apt metaphor, since many cabalists were doctors, it was a powerful medicine that needed to be taken with caution. So it was often lumped together with other disapproved-of styles, which supposedly incline to a derogation from responsibility and alertness, even sobriety, ostensibly because in relying on these one's will and intelligence would be alienated, and one's curiosity stymied by ready-made answers that allow for no further questions. Essentially Francis Bacon's opposition to magic, for instance, was not based so much on his doubts as to its efficacy but on his notion that working harder for results would be better for one's character. Magic, for Bacon, would be a form of immaturity, instant gratification, and inebriation. D. P. Walker cites a significant positive statement on magic that occurs twice in Bacon.[54] Since we are nevertheless dealing with Francis, not Roger, this efficacy of magic would be really a matter of strengthening the powers of the imagination—which Bacon is careful to eschew as an ultimately harmful recourse. Recent experiments in electromagnetism of brainwaves, apparently generating sufficient power to move cursors around on a screen, and which eventually would enable people to land planes through concentration,[55] may shed a different light on the claims of Renaissance magic! The power of imagination that magic can fortify, even according to the scrupulous Bacon, may have been more (or less) than merely a moral one.

Inebriation as Ascent

That renowned Kantian project of moving humanity from a minority state of authority-dependent infancy to one of responsible, independent majority is well under way in the Renaissance, which first, after classical antiquity, imagined it. On the other hand, drunkenness, divine passion, and fury, whether over love, God, politics, ideas, or art, had also its ancient privileges, honored high-priests, and ceremonies. As Edgar Wind, Jean Seznec, and D. P. Walker have pointed out,[56] some fundamental elements of Paganism live on very well in the Renaissance, in a sometimes uneasy, but still ineluctable compromise with Christianity—from Botticelli's Venus that could in no way be confused with the Virgin Mary, to the astrological decor in the Vatican, replete with Greeks gods and goddesses. Meanwhile it becomes the specific function of *allegory* to launder this "gold of the gods" so that it comes out looking clean and Christian, a process that started in the late Middle Ages already with the widely disseminated moralizations of Virgil and Ovid. This is the drift of Seznec's illuminating study, *Survival of the Ancient Gods*, where he explains that the allegorization of Virgil is in full career by the sixth century A.D. with the African grammarian Fulgentius's *Expositio Virgiliana*. In a larger, Nietzschean sense, in the great age of Greek, and a fortiori Roman philosophy, allegory already operates on the otherwise confounding immorality of the Dyonisian-Homeric impulse. Christianity simply put more strain on this process by insisting on higher standards of behavior,[57] which, unlike Judaism, it disseminated.

Yet Cabala, also, is nothing if not allegory; its fundamental role had always been to make the "truths" of religion pass muster in an age with new needs, expectations, and demands. Nietzsche's affirmation of *inebriation* as the necessary condition for art would conceivably be our own way of allegorizing and justifying the exceptions that all artists must be to the otherwise compelling tyranny of the rule of reason:

> *Towards a psychology of the artist.*—For art to exist, for any sort of aesthetic activity or perception to exist, a certain physiological precondition is indispensable: *intoxication*. Intoxication must first have heightened the excitability of the entire machine: no art results before that happens. All kinds of intoxication, however different their origin, have the power to do this: above all, the intoxication of sexual excitement, the oldest and most primitive form of intoxication. Likewise the intoxication which comes in the train of all great desires, all strong emotions; the intoxication of feasting, of contest, of the brave deed, of victory, of all extreme agitation; the intoxication of cruelty; intoxication in destruction; intoxication under certain meteorological influences, for example the intoxication of spring; or under the influence of narcotics; finally the intoxication of the will, the intoxication of an overloaded and distended will—The essence of intoxication is the feeling of plenitude and increased energy.[58]

This theme is already a commonplace in Romantic, then Symbolist poetics: as in the DeQuincey-Poe-Baudelaire connection, summed up by the latter, translator of more than the words of the first two, in the first and only rule of art: "Be Always Drunk!" This was already a familiar formula, one, for instance, prescribed by Rabelais. It was rather Nietzsche's daring and originality to lend this outrageous apostrophe the prestige of philosophical rigor, thereby, of course, allegorizing it; so that when the Surrealists descended into their dreams it was with the best of consciences. Cabala, in the Renaissance, provided its channel for fluxes of cultural energy and imagination to escape from accountability to and restriction by prevailing norms, by creating a shelter, terrain, and a territory "beyond good and evil" where one's limits would only be one's own. Certainly some of the boldest spirits of the Renaissance, among whom we may count great poets (Spenser, Milton), Goddrunk, syncretic mystics (Postel, Bruno, Pico), and a number of other strange searchers (Agrippa, Dee, Thomas Vaughan), whose studies in themselves often amounted to scandal and controversy— these tended to be drawn to Cabala, which as it evolved in ever more provocative and antinomian form in the seventeenth century attracted ever more individualistic followers.

A reformist-type text, indeed, turns up in the STC collection, which practically *defines* Cabala as inebriation, along with some other "sciences" (including, strangely, the empirical). According to a sermon, *A Diet for Drunkards* by Thomas Thomson, published in London in 1612, one becomes a cabalist, alchemist, even an empiri-cist or theological pedant, the way one goes to sleep, has a drink, or falls in love, through lapse of will, energy, and sobriety: "Those who are drunken with curiosity, are a generation of quick-sighted gentlemen, who because they would seem to see further than other men, pass further than they should in curious artes; as from true *Philosophie* to deceitful *Alcymie*, from laudable *Astronomie* to dev-ilish Astrologie and divination, from wholesome *Physike* to the uncertain experiments of foolish *Empiricks*; and from the true proportion of faith in divinitie, either to the prophane *Cabala* of Jewish *Rabbines* or to the unprofitale wrangling of subtle School-men."[59] Interestingly, also, that same caution against an excessive restlessness and curiosity justifies both Davies's pronouncement in favor of a "book of secrets," whose mere existence can quell a Faustian fervor, and Thomson's warnings against Cabala and other "drunken" methods.

Mystical Heresy and the Impasse of Desire

Both the promotion and the *prohibition* were products of the same fascinated ambivalence: as Freud tirelessly pointed out in our own times, what we desire we interdict or displace. De Certeau, as a matter of fact, as a Lacanian and structuralist historian of religion, always on the alert for analogies between psychoanalysis and mysticism, hints at "Freud's connections to the Moravian Jewish tradition, which was marked by Sabbateanism," to which he ap-pends a suitably enigmatic and provocative explanatory note: "There was a Sabbatean saying that 'the law is fulfilled by transgres-sion.' "[60] This translates, in Freudian terms, to the respect for "sin" that its prohibition demonstrates: it is *because* we want to do something that we forbid it. There is indeed some kind of Sabbatian-Frankist lineage behind Freud, however on his wife's side, and David Bakan explores the implications of this element comprehensively in *Freud and the Jewish Mystical Tradition*. Bakan's monograph is a comprehensive literary-historical study of the correspondences between Cabala, especially of The Zohar, and the life and work of Freud.[61] This was a matter, to a certain degree, of direct influence, but, more importantly, one of an osmotic absorption of a style that was very much in the air in the Jewish community of turn of the century Vienna, as also, a little later, in Kafka's Prague.

Bringing on interdiction-by-denial, *this oral component* in Cabala, and also in mysticism generally, syncretically insousciant of scripture, God Him-or-Herself-or-Neither, not to mention religion, the state, and the economy, responds to a deep need for an approving, nourishing, libidinal presence, for which we can just *be*. Mystics can perfectly well even be atheists in the sense of denying themselves the rewards, consolations, and complacencies of faith while assuming its tasks—a "higher" type of belief, perhaps, at least in the Hegelian sense. This is not to scant differences in mystics attached to particular religions—or to none—but to stress, instead, their characteristic impatience with their own religion, which they either transform or transcend or both. On the other hand, the mystics' very indifference to the state and economy is socially determined and can be also politically effective. Lucien Goldmann has shown, for instance, in *The Hidden God*, how the seventeenth-century mysticism of Pascal and Racine, with its world-denying ideology, is related to the incipient uselessness of the class of Noblesse de Robe, increasingly marginalized by the centralizing power of Louis XIV. This longing for a language beyond words, essentially a caress beyond identity, however, even when it consents to expression and manifestation by a mystical system, or when it simply refuses or denies interdiction, may still be far from being fulfilled. By definition, satisfaction of such "immortal longings" would be an aporia. *Having* what we want would imply a satisfaction, a freezing, a word that could be written and trusted to resummon the pleasure at will, "the death of endeavor and the birth of disgust," as Ambrose Bierce defined *achievement* in his *Devil's Dictionary*.

Heavenly Mathematics and the Case of Dee

Mathematics, even more purely than music, would be the ideal vocabulary for these mystical, all-too-human longings, satisfaction of which is a frank absurdity, and incessant displacement their only real motion—albeit a circular or hopefully (upward) spiralling one. Cabala has an affinity not only with mathematics, as well as with a mathematical-numerological literature, but also, among the arts, with that "frozen-mathematical music" which is architecture. The architectural metaphor is very prominent, for example, in Saint Teresa of Avila's masterpiece, *The Interior Castle* (1588), whose affinity with Cabala was studied by C. Swietlicki. On a more than merely symbolic level we have remarked on the influence of Giorgio's sephirotic schemes in the design, early in the sixteenth century, of San Francesco della Vigna, while another church Cabala shows up in is mentioned by Grözinger, who alludes to "Princess Antonia's kabbalistic altar painting in the modest church of Bad Teinach in the Black Forest."[62]

The numerical evaluation of the sacred letters, essential Cabala technique, among a few other equally abstract ones, owed its dissemination to this appeal to needs that are intrinsically incapable of satisfaction and therefore need to be transferred. Numbers, with less of the sentimental and emotional baggage that attaches to even the most neutral language, change into each other effortlessly, magically. The mystical "not here, not there"[63] finds in mathematics its ideal place where it can solve the contradictions of Rest and Motion, Being and Becoming, Duty and Desire—impossible, as Kant later established in the first two Critiques, to resolve on purely logical grounds. The mystical proclivities of such as Kepler and Newton very likely had much to do with their mathematical science, instead of being in competition with it; and certainly in the Renaissance, mathematicians were as likely, if not more so, to be cabalists as anyone else. An arithmetical work by William Ingpen, published in London in 1624, for example, is replete with references to Cabala, its title, *The Secret of Numbers*,[64] positively trumpeting its provenance in mystical mathematics. So it is no surprise that Ingpen starts off by citing Pico, who simply *incarnates* recognizably that permanent division and connection between the realms that is the paradox but fact of mystic life on earth: "Pico's art, which certifieth Christ's divinity is like a tree rooted invisibly in two different earths." Ingpen's arborial metaphor is ideal for a Christian Cabala drawing from two distinctly Platonic realms different types of nourishment. In other words the secret support of the written, of scripture, is in the nonwritten, the oral, and Ingpen is clear indeed as to the dual nature of this puzzling but insistent truth, according to a mathematics that does not hide from it: "There are two secrets among those Cabalists: one that is a simple Secret; the other a secret *cui non est simile* [an uncanny one], called the Secret of Secrets. The one is compounded of Art, Knowledge, wisdome, affection, power, habit of mind, and so forth; the other from extasie, voyce, inspiration, vision and whatsoever is given us from above."[65]

What indeed could be the secret of a number, behind the one, two, three, what awesome lesson or consolation lurks, waiting only for the right combination, formula or equation to be roused? Whole populations of Albigensians, the medieval avatar of the dualist Manicheans, died for the "two" (for instance, implied in the theory that good and evil are of separate provenance) in the bloody extirpations of the thirteenth century near where Cabala was being born or reborn. The two seems to command a good deal of attention also in Cabala, which, however, possibly benefiting from the experience of millennial persecution, was more discreet (for a few centuries a least, until the advent of Sabbatai) about it than the Medieval Manichees were willing to be. Qualifying the *two*, also, in traditional Cabala, would be the awe and deferral of the stubborn monotheism from which it arose, to a One above and behind all duality, a proto-Kantian categorical imperative that simply *must* be there.[66] That Cabala is not a passing moment in Ingpen's mathematical thought but something in which it is deeply imbued, is born out by a further perusal of his treatise, which turns up another awed allusion to Pico, a discussion of the "two Adams," and a detailed explanation of the cabalistic *sephiroth*, or emanations. In his development of the latter subject Ingpen demonstrates the depth of his studies by defining the grandiose and worldly eighth sephiroth as that of the "50 gates of intelligence, save one,"[67] referring, by the allusion to the missing gate, to the one that Moses did not enter, and very much in the spirit of a certain cabalistic modesty, which stresses rather the increased difficulty in the lives of even the most evolved people rather than any complacent ease and confidence in their redemption.

John Dee is certainly the central figure in the English Renaissance in the dissemination of the kind of mystical mathematics that surfaces in William Ingpen's book.[68] Catalytic for this current was Dee's preface to a translation of Euclid, published in 1570, which resumed and added to a Pythagorean-numerological tradition, passing it on eventually to the golden-age generation of Elizabethan literature of Spenser, Sidney, Chapman, and Shakespeare. Dee's most direct mentor in Cabala seems to have been Agrippa, and his reputation has fluctuated similarly. Although Agrippa's books were in Dee's famous library, this link has been established (by Yates) subjectively more on the matter of common ground than objective evidence. Josten thinks he has found Dee's handwriting in another cabalistic tome in Dee's library: *Iannis Cheradami Alphabetum Linguae Sanctae*, and also cites Dr. Meric Casaubon's introduction to his edition of 1659 of the conversations of Dee with Spirits: "John Dee was a Cabalistical man, up to his ears . . . as may appear to any man by his Monas Hieroglyphica, a book much valued by himself."[69] Clulee's recent remark that Dee "knew little of" Cabala[70] I think is based on an excessive literalism. Dee may not have been well versed in matters Hebrew and Rabbinical, but he certainly understood that Cabala was a way of getting people to think differently about things that they take the most for granted. Dee understood perfectly well indeed that what he called his *real* Cabala, as opposed to a *vulgar*, literal one, was a tool in his search, not a mere object, end, or goal. This is clearly in evidence in the letter of introduction he wrote to the Emperor Maximilian I, to whom he dedicated *Monas*, where he emphasizes specifically Cabala's extra-Semitic applications:

And now I come to the Hebrew cabalist who, when he will see that (the tree principal keys to his art, called) Gematria, Notariacon, and Tzyruph, are used outside the confines of the language called holy, and that, moreover, the signs and characters of that mystical tradition (which was received from God) . . . are brought together from whencesoever . . . from certain obvious and invisible things, then . . . he will call this art holy too; and he will own that, without regard to person, the same most benevolent God is not only [the God] of the Jews, but of all peoples, nations and languages; also that *no mortal may excuse himself for being ignorant of this our holy language*, which . . . I have called the real cabbala, or of that which is, as I call that other and vulgar one, which rests on well-known letters that can be written by man, cabbalistic grammar or the cabbala of that which is said. The real cabbala, which was born to us by the law of creation (as Paul intimates), is also [a] more divine [gift], since it invents new arts and explains the most abstruse arts very faithfully, as others, following our example, may try out in some other field.[71]

This holy language that "no mortal man may excuse himself from being ignorant of" is most certainly *not* Hebrew; and here Dee the magus intuitively anticipates modern findings that Hebrew was not the language the Jews brought to Canaan but the one they adopted there. Quite uncannily Dee slides here I think into a central mystery of Cabala, which was only hiding behind the garment of the notion that Hebrew is the language of God, which is that the divine language or creative principle is something else and other than language (as we know it), rather the *idea* of language than any particular one.

Whether or not the *Monas* is Dee's most important text, unquestionably there he is at his most cabalistic and I submit that though his Cabala may yield to Reuchlin's and others' in literal accuracy it yields to none in intensity and validity. Coincidentally, since we are on the subject of Cabala in the Age of Elizabeth, this *Monas* was equally a book that seems to have piqued Queen Elizabeth's interest particularly. Dee, who had published the book abroad, in Amsterdam in 1564, had sent her a copy, which had arrived ahead of his return that same year, and later recalls that they read the book together, at her request, in private audience: "Her Majestie very graciously vouchsafed to account herselfe my schollar in my booke . . . *Monas Hieroglyphica*; and said, whereas I had prefixed in the forefront of the book; *Qui non intelligit, aut taceat aut discat* [one who doesn't understand is either silent or speaks]: if I would disclose unto her the secretes of that booke she would *et discere et facere* [both speak and do]; whereupon her Majestie had a little perusin of the same with me, and then in most heroicall and princely wise did comfort me and encourage me in my studies philosophical and mathematical."[72]

Like Agrippa, Dee for centuries has been treated like a marginal, likely demonic figure and pretty much of a charlatan, and as with Agrippa, on the basis more of myth than any solid information, as if our culture needed to reject the "other" these figures stood for in order to define itself. Only recently has his (and Agrippa's) integrity and importance come to be more widely granted. In the context of Yates's *The Occult Philosophy in the Elizabethan Age*, he emerges, for instance as just about the most influential exponent of Christian Cabala of his time. As proved by a prolonged residence (1583–1589) in Bohemia as advisor at the magical court of Rudolph II of Bohemia, Dee's impact and influence were also European in scope. Yet his fortunes waxed and waned with the prestige of the Agrippan Cabala that he was promoting, which was in evident decline by the time of Dee's return to England. Paradoxically a magical, numerological-Pythagorean Cabala that Spenser had absorbed from Dee was structurally essential to *The Fairie Queene*, published at a time (early 1590s) when such magical systems of thought were passing out of fashion. By the time of the accession of James the decline of Dee had very nearly turned into positive disgrace, as anything to do with Agrippan magic was regarded as condign witchcraft, while even the relatively anodyne orthodox cabalistic magic of the pervasive Giorgio was coming under suspicion and worse. Dee was swept out by the same wave of political realism that was going to submerge Sir Walter Raleigh, himself evidently more than a dabbler in Cabala, numerology, alchemy, and the occult. Spenser and Sidney were saved from such fates by their early deaths, and as a matter of fact, because of this "antimagical" reaction, the former did not achieve the rewards or recognition from Elizabeth that his mighty epic about her should have entitled him to.

Although too late or weak to help the hapless Dee, who died in poverty in 1608, there were, however, revivals of the spirit of Elizabethan magic within the Jacobean age. John Dee is the key, according to Yates, to much of Shakespeare's later drama, which resists the new opposition to magic: While *Macbeth* would be a concession to the spirit of the times, in tune with its condemnation of all magic as witchcraft and equivocation, *King Lear* represents sympathetically the last days of the now useless John Dee. By the time of *The Tempest*, which was meant as a reply to Jonson's *Alchemist*, which, a sequel to Marlowe's influential earlier mockery of Agrippa, ridiculed Dee and magic, this sympathy had changed into a positive encomium. Prospero represents the ultimate triumph and redemption of John Dee, while the sublimely magical realism of *Winter's Tale*, *Pericles* and *Cymbeline* described his apotheosis, as well as that of the Christian Cabala he stood for, at least in the realm of art.

The Occult Sir Thomas Browne

The great German Christian cabalist, Knorr von Rosenroth, associate of F. M. Van Helmont, a.k.a. Peganius in the Conway circle, was also the German translator of Browne's fascinating encyclopedia of mistakes, *Vulgar Errors*,[73] where, as we shall notice, Cabala also occasionally peeks out at us. In fact, probably no major writer of the seventeenth century was better informed about Cabala (and everything else) than Sir Thomas Browne (1605–1682), author of some of the most compelling and thoughtful prose, and about some of the most bizarre subjects, of English literary history. Browne's knowledge of cabalism has been documented by Joseph Blau,[74] who indicates, by primary citations to the text, that Browne had read Paul Ricius *Heavenly Agriculture*, probably in Pistorius's *Artes Cabalisticae* of 1587. Blau also cites, in particular, Browne's acquaintance with the work of Athanasius Kircher, encylopedist of the occult, in particular the *Oedipus Aegyptiacus*, in which Kircher expounds the nature of the sephirotic system. These *sephiroth* then appear in the context of cabalistic letter analysis, or *gematria*, in the magisterial concluding chapter of Browne's Pythagorean-numerological-mystical prose fantasy, *The Garden of Cyrus*, on the '5' or fabulous quincunx, which

> same number in the Hebrew mysteries and Cabalistical accounts was the character of Generation, declared by the Letter He, the fifth of their Alphabet. According to that Cabalisticall *Dogma*, If Abram had not had this Letter added unto his name, he had remained fruitless, and without the

power of generation:[75] ... so in divine and intelligent productions, the mother of Life and Fountain of souls in Cabalisticall Technology is called *Binah*; whose Seal and Character was *He*. So that being sterill before, he received the power of generation from that mesure and mansion in the Archetype; and was made conformable unto *Binah*. And upon such involved considerations, the ten of *Sarai* was exchanged into five. If any shall look upon this as a stable number, and fitly appropriable unto Trees, as Bodies of Rest and Station, he hath herein a great Foundation in nature, who observing much variety in legges and motive Organs of Animals, as two, four, six eight, twelve, fourteen, and more, hath passed over five and ten, and assigned them unto none. And for the stability of this Number, he shall not want the sphericity of its nature, which multiplied in it self, will return into its own denomination, and bring up the rear of the account.[76] Which is also one of the Numbers that makes up the mysticall Name of God, which, consisting of Letters denoting all the sphaericall Numbers, ten, five, and six, Emphatically sets forth the Notion of *Trismegistus*, and that intelligible Sphere, which is the Nature of God.[77]

Browne's numerological system assigns odd numbers to plants, starting with the *one*, corresponding to the single trunk of the tree or stem, while even numbers are assigned to animals, whose appendages tend to come in twos. As mentioned in about the middle of the above passage, the tree, as is fitting for one of those vegetable "bodies of rest and station," as opposed to moving animal bodies, corresponds to the odd numbers in the cabalistic hermeneutics involved in the relation of five, and its multiple ten, both to the letters of Sarah's name and to the sephiroth of Binah, the fifth letter of which is the same as the fifth letter of Sarah. This sphere of Binah, a feminine element of mercy and love in Cabala, and very high up in the sephirotic system, Browne calls that of the "mother of Life and the Fountain of souls." It is characteristic also that in this *Garden of Cyrus* where Browne's allusions to Cabala seem to be more direct, forthright, and essential than anywhere else in his works, the tree is his essential metaphor and symbol. As well as being a living manifestation of the presence of the structure of the macrocosm in the microcosm, the tree suggests its cabalist quality as metaphor and symbol of the emanation of the *sephiroth*. Two paragraphs later, indeed, we find Browne mentioning the sephiroth explicitly, explaining what they are, and working out some very odd analogies between the configuration of the harp David uses in scripture to calm Saul and the generally tranquilizing qualities of these spheres of being that relate to five or its multiples, all in connection with "the Cabalisticall Doctors, who conceive the whole *Sephiroth* or divine emanations to have guided the ten-stringed Harp of *David*, whereby he pacified the evil spirit of *Saul*, in strict numeration doe begin with the Perihypate Meson, or si fa ut, and so place the Tiphereth answering C sol fa ut, upon the fifth string."[78]

Additionally for Browne, the figure of the tree functions on another mystical level to support a syncretic Christian humanism, as a symbol of the cross and the promise of resurrection, linking us also to higher levels, through the patterns of the bark and the form of the leaves, which Browne remarks are permeated by the Platonic-Timaen quincunx, or structure by fives. Browne, for whom even the dark sciences of the Occult in all their splendidly challenging heterodoxy must function in supreme harmony, here even works out an alchemically tinged Astrology, carefully grounded however in the "lower," but essential, realm of botany, a complex correspondence that is established by the fact that "the Leaves of the Olive and some other Trees solstitially turn, and precisely tell us, when the Sun is entred in Cancer."

Recognizably cabalistic concepts seem, in general, to be a part of Browne's philosophical vocabulary, working in concert with alchemical, gnostic, Pythagorean, and hermetic ones, which seem to be invoked especially when, as apparently was often the case for him, scrupulosity forces him outside of the strictly Christian, or even a purely empirical or historical, framework. As Browne remarks so coyly and I think charmingly in a little text on the surprisingly speculative subject of the *date* of the beginning of the world (he accepts the Biblical version but is trying to determine it exactly), which he tucked into *Vulgar Errors*, he would have *preferred* to rely on written history rather than to have resorted to conjecture, in the matter of creation: "Some indeed there are, who have kept Records of time, and of a considerable duration, yet do the exactes thereof afford no satisfaction concerning the beginning of the world, or any way point out the time of its creation. The most authentick Records and best approved antiquity are those of the Chaldeans; yet in the time of Alexander the Great, they attained not so high as the flood . . . The Arcadians I confess, were esteemed of great antiquity, and it was usually said they were before the Moon."[79] All explanation about some of the things that concern us most is for Browne one version or another of *hearsay*, which would make Cabala for him, whose very meaning is that of an oral tradition, paradigmatically useful as a style of thought, exegesis, and interpretation. This is because, as is typical of mystical discourse in general, it is a word about "last things" that does not claim, by definition, to be the last word. Perfectly in tune with the variety of Cabala, in particular, seems to me to be Browne's very frequent insistence on the necessity for alternative and alternate texts, one filling some of the gaps in the other. So we find Browne, in a philosophical summum with which he begins, very reluctantly it seems, and backwards, as it were, his strange literary career, *The Religio Medici* [1642], enjoying the equal appreciation the Pagans ostensibly had of the Books of Nature and God, whereas the Christians are faulted for being able to honor only the latter: "Thus are there two bookes from whence I collect my divinity; besides that written one of God, another of his servant Nature, that universall and public Manuscript, that lies expans'd unto the eyes of all: those that never saw him in the one, have discovered him in the other: . . . surely the Heathens knew better how to joyne and reade these mystical letters, than wee Christians, who cast a more carelesse eye on these common Hieroglyphicks, and disdain to suck Divinity from the flowers of Nature; which I define not with the Schooles, the principle of motion and rest, but that streight and regular line, that setled and constant course the wisedome of God hath ordained the actions of his creatures."[80]

The fact that Browne was a physician also probably played a part in his favoring here, at least for temporary tactical reasons, an earthy Paganism over an ethereal Christianity. In the Renaissance generally there was an especially strong relation between medicine and Cabala, based on the tendency of the latter to coalesce one's spiritual or astral body with one's physical body, its health, activities, and, of course, sexuality. Cabala, whether in its Jewish or

Christian avatar, may be thought of, in this way, as a "return of the repressed" of Paganism, an alternative whereby one could include the world and the body in one's calculations, without abandoning one's faith in an eventual heavenly destiny. Doctors, additionally, given the urgency of the situations they were professionally bound to deal with would perhaps be more open anyway to new options and styles of diagnosis and therapy. Accordingly, Cabala seems always to enter into Browne's text as an active and practical agent, never just as evidence in a purely theoretical matter. Although we can in no way define Browne's magic as Agrippan, in the sense of a ritual manipulation and transformation of reality, he does assign a theurgic power to the very ideas he invokes, which become effective symbolic actions in his system. The advance of Browne's cabalism over a more engaged one of Agrippa and Dee lies in this notion of his of the force of understanding, anticipating Hegel in the sense that by process of intellect we "overcome" and are equipped to pass on to higher problems.

An example of this might be the way he deploys the recognizably cabalistic notion of the "line" in his texts to resolve the problem of God's ostensible distance from human affairs and concerns. The concept of *tsimtsum* or withdrawal of a Deity behind the line of accessibility was so clearly cabalistic by the seventeenth century that so astute a reader as Leibniz unhesitatingly labeled Spinoza's God, indifferent to the plans and pleas of humanity, as the *ein soph* of Cabala.[81] It has, accordingly, seemed likely, for instance, to William Dunn, commenting in *Sir Thomas Browne, A Study in Religious Philosophy*, that the "streight and regular line" of God, mentioned in the last sentence cited, is an allusion to the familiar cabalistic concept of a line of withdrawal or retraction behind which an unknowable, unreachable *ein soph* retreats.[82] This retreat leaves the world to its own devices, or to follow, in Browne's language, its own pagan "law of Nature." Interestingly, the *metaphor of the line* is picked up again by Browne in the section immediately following the one we have just quoted from the *Religio Medici* (Sect. 16), where the *crooked* line of those who follow Fortune is disapproved of, compared to the straight line of those who follow God's Nature, or more precisely where God *left* us in Nature. The latter line is preferred for its clarity and simplicity; whereas the former, blurring separations, inducing false hopes and illusions is ultimately a "way full of Meanders and Labyrinths, whereof the Devill and Spirits have no exact Ephemerides . . . this we call Fortune, that serpentine and crooked line, whereby he drawes those actions his wisedome intends in a more unknowne and secret way."[83] While acknowledging it, grudgingly, Dunn is severe on the overall impact of Cabala on Browne, faulted for a science-impeding habit to see resemblences everywhere: "That phrase, 'delightful truths' tells the story. It is the story of the fatal malady of Greek and patristic and Cabbalist sciences . . . They could see resemblances but not differences . . . [and had] the inordinate habit of reading more unity into things than the facts justified."[84] Whereas Blau had pointed out that Browne was guided in studies of Cabala by the seventeenth-century encyclopedist of the occult, Athanasius Kircher, and by the Christianizing cabalists, Ricius and Pistorius, Dunn ties Browne's specifically Christian Platonist understanding of the subject rather with Henry More's *Conjectura Cabalisticae*, of 1654 (*The Garden of Cyrus* was published in 1658).

More was surely a *specialist* in Cabala, who, as a matter of fact, corresponded with Knorr Rosenroth, editor of the *Kaballah Denudata*, on such arcane but then urgent matters as whether or not the *sephiroth* were spherical in shape. More's 'letters to the editor', in fact, were printed by Rosenroth in the renowned anthology, which appeared in two volumes in 1677 and 1684. More's Cabala, though strictly even fanatically Christian, was eventually very much influenced by the gnostic drama of Luria's late sixteenth-century accretions. The Lurianic notion of the Breaking of the Vessels, at creation, insufficient to hold the creative light pouring through them, corresponds, in terms of devolution and desperation to the English Christian Platonists' concept of a separation of the upper and lower realms, the ideal and the real, heaven and earth, that are moving inexorably apart. This "worsening" situation, for the Luria-imbued heretic Sabbatai Zevi, would justify and necessitate prodigiously original and antinomian acts of *tikkun* or repair. For the Christian Platonists, redemptive schemes seem to focus more on an individual's exemplary rescue of himself through expanding intellectual and philosophical consciousness.

Specifically, for W. P. Dunn, Browne and More share in a certain idealizing Platonic-Timaen vision of the world, which comes across most vividly in Browne's mystical celebration of the quincunx,

The Garden of Cyrus. Within the text(s) of Browne the way the Cabala functions, according to Dunn, is to help resolve the questions of the separations of the realms of upper and lower, heaven and earth, spirit and matter, good and evil, which, already divided at first, are drifting ever further apart. It accomplishes this, Dunn concludes, by supplying a notion of correspondences and analogies,[85] so that one would be able to recognize and work on and towards the ideas of the higher realm even though one is trapped in a baser one of carnality.

What must strike even a casual reader of Browne is the nonexclusionary, noncondemnatory nature of his mentality, infrequent indeed in a polarized and polarizing century. However rare or incredible the event or phenomena, Browne will manage somehow to accept and understand it. Eager to grasp things on an empirical and sensory level, he will, nevertheless, shift to a hieroglyphic, symbolic, and allegorical one when the notion requires it, as even Witchcraft, Alchemy, and a certain Cabala of the Stars, Plants, and Letters enter into the domain of his calculations.[86] For a Cabala of Stars and Letters, allusions are strewn through the work. We may cite the following, almost at random, from an arcane disquisition in *Vulgar Errors* over whether or not there were rainbows before Noah: "Cabalistical heads, who from that expression in Esay [Isa. 34.4: 'And all the host of heaven shall be dissolved . . .'], do make a book of heaven, and read therein the great concernments of earth, do literally play on this, and from its [the rainbow] semicircular figure, resembling the Hebrew letter Caph, whereby is signified the uncomfortable number of twenty, at which years Joseph was sold, which Jacob lived under Laban, and at which men were to go to war: do note a propriety in its signification; as thereby declaring the dismal Time of the Deluge."[87]

For Leonard Nathanson, accordingly, the fundamental problem in *Religio Medici* is that of epistemology or the question of *how* we decide that we know something. Nathanson describes Browne as deploying, in order to elucidate this matter in a variety of ways, a triune Platonic hierarchy of, from lowest to highest: (1) *nomos*, or custom; (2) *physis*, or nature; (3) *idea*, or reason.[88] The purpose of this battery would be to establish some security in the realm of knowledge, as well as to reconcile apparent contradictions (for instance, between an empirical study of nature, discursive reason, and the practice of faith), at least to the extent that one can live with them. In Browne's ascending epistemology, therefore, a problem would be considered solved by referring it to the next highest plane. If the study of nature conflicts with the use of reason, it is reason that would determine the issue; and this accounts for Browne's "explaining away" only apparent singularities, his reason insisting, as in *Religio* that "there are no *Grotesques* in Nature."[89] To Nathanson's handy system we think it pertinent to add, nevertheless, a fourth, Platonic level, one that could be called hieroglyphic, allegorical, or simply intuitive. It is, in fact, the burden of Browne's powerful meditation on mortality, *Urn Burial*, according to Frank Huntley, to demonstrate the futility of relying *solely* on the use of either custom, nature, or reason in dealing with such crucial problems as death and immortality. It is the purpose of *Urn Burial*'s strange companion text (published, bound together, in 1658), *The Garden of Cyrus*, to answer the questions[90] left hanging on the three lower Platonic levels on a fourth, symbolic, and allegorical one, the latter book playing heaven to the former's earth. Here, Cabala, in itself a mystical, intuitive, prophetic, and syncretic allegory of scripture, is ideally suited to function as Browne's higher explanatory paradigm, which would be why it is so germane to the magisterial final section of the *Garden of Cyrus*.

At the very least, for even the most improbable notions, for instance that storks only live in free countries, or that Jewish people stink [sic],[91] Browne will be fascinated by the rationales and uses for the allegiance and support they have attracted in the past, rescuing some kind of meaning and validity for things that seem, on other levels, confessedly unreal and fantastic. Even if there are no grounds to believe something, the fallacy becomes something worthy in itself of study. Yet where there is a really substantial incentive to believe or at least respect something, however incredible or unlikely, Browne will find a way: so in his account of the pelican, short of food, who will feed its young with its own blood, ripping up its breast with its bill to do so, although Browne's comprehensive search turns up not the slightest shred of empirical or historical confirmation, that strangely sacrificial feeding becomes *compelling* on an whole different level when allusion is made to its thorough appropriateness, validity and power, taken in the hieroglyphic-allegorical sense as a representation of the crucifixion.[92]

Additionally, Browne teases us in conclusion, although no one has ever witnessed a pelican feeding its young this way, the beak *is* long and pointed enough to open up its own breast!

Browne's reader becomes very much aware of the precedence of interpretation and construction over mere data, evidence, or facts. The *fact* that, for instance, the archeological findings on which *Urn Burial* was based were erroneous, that the remains were not Roman, as Browne supposed, but Saxon, in no way detracts from the power and wisdom of this work, still as effective as ever. In one hilarious little piece, buried among the *Miscellany Tracts*, Browne is even not above inventing a Borgesian or Rabelaisian fable, according to which he supplies a correspondent with a list of odd titles of books that could not possibly exist, or which, more precisely, could possibly exist but which we know do not. Browne alerts his reader he is looking for such unlikely items, which he has seen in a catalogue, as:

1. A Poem of Ovidius Naso, written in the Getick Language, during his exile at Tomos, found wrapt up in Wax at Sabaria, on the Frontiers of Hungary, where there remains a tradition that he died, in his return towards Rome from Tomos, either after his pardon or the death of Augustus . . . 7. A particular Narration of that famous Expedition of the English into Barbary in the ninety fourth year of the Hegira, so shortly touched by Leo Africanus, whither called by the Goths they besieged, took and burnt the City of Arzilla possessed by the Mahametans, and lately the seat of Gayland . . . 14. King Mithradates his Oneirocritica . . . A Tragedy of Thyestes, and another of Media, writ by Diogenes the Cynick . . . Seneca's Epistles to S. Paul . . . 16. Josephus in Hebrew, written by himself . . . 19 . . . *Mazhapha Einok*, or the Prophecy of Enoch, which AEgidius Lochiensis, a learned Eastern Traveller, told Peireschius that he had found in an old Library at Alexandria containing eight thousand volumes. 20. A Collection of Hebrew Epistles, which passed between the two learned Women of our age, Maria Molinea of Sedan, and Maria Schuman of Utrecht."[93]

This wish list of books is followed by two others of equally dubious nature: one of desired pictures, paintings, and engravings; another of diverse objects that suggest a vaguely magical provenance, of the sort gathered by John Dee's erstwhile employer, the strange King Rudolph of Bohemia, the original occult collector, whose magical museum was scattered after the advent of the Hapsburgs in 1621. Browne, for instance, is curious to handle such delights as: "8. A large Ostridge's Egg, whereon is neatly and fully wrought that famous Battel of Alcazar, in which three Kings lost their lives . . . 9. The Skin of a Snake bred out of the Spinal Marrow of a Man . . . 20. A Ring found in a Fishes Belly taken about Gorro; conceived to be the same wherewith the Duke of Venice had wedded the Sea . . . 23. *Batrachomyomachia*, or the Homerican Battel between Frogs and Mice, neatly described upon the Chizel Bone of a large Pike's Jaw."[94]

Here, more nakedly than elsewhere where we know we are being led on, we cannot but recognize that improbabilities, inventions, and fictions are all meaningful to Browne for what they reveal about the forms, needs, and designs behind them. The "fact" for the Renaissance cabalist, like the dream, joke, or symptom today, is a sign which means that there is some urgent meaning, often an unsuspected one, calling to be read.[95] Mere empirical or historical reality on the other hand rather deludes by attracting more attention to itself than is warranted, while providing us with a shelter more dangerous and porous than ignorance, that is the illusion we know something and can stay somewhere or rest with something. Accordingly, Browne would favor a style like Cabala, for which the very highest word we can know, or Torah, can be by no stretch of the imagination taken as a real *word* of God. So for Browne all earthly manifestations, as well as all we can say or know we know about fall finally into the category of the insufficient.

In the pride of the virtuous, for Browne, therefore, would lurk the evils of complacency; while in the anger of the wicked there is an energy that is a good in itself. This is a complex and humanitarian ethics of ambiguity that Browne articulates eloquently in his most naked text, in the sense of least figurative, symbolic, and ornate, the *Christian Morals*, his last book, published posthumously (1715) and written in the rare second-person imperative, usually reserved for the Decalogue.

Most interesting for Browne, ultimately, is to see things differently, whichever side of the good/evil fence we see ourselves or are seen as being on, we need to discover a modesty that this rediscovery of our own limits reconstitutes. This, indeed, is the "inversion" that elicits a disapproval from Dunn, since he thinks that the cabalists read more unity into things than the facts warranted. Specifically, Dunn implies that Browne and his Cabala-imbued literary generation, obsessed with similarities, missed the differences and qualities of events and objects.[96] Dunn is not the first to point out the dangers, temptations, and excesses of Cabala. Here and in previous chapters, we have commented on a number of works and authors that attacked Cabala during its heyday, and often for very good reasons; but Browne's was not the kind of spirit and mind that liked to sacrifice one truth for the sake of another.

Cabala, prominent among the other heterdox recourses on what we have called the fourth and decisive hieroglyphic-allegorical epistemological level, helped him, therefore, plug the holes, at least temporarily, opened up in the fabric of belief by a "new philosophy," which, as lamented by John Donne, "calls all into doubt." Where for instance, written scripture comes into direct contradiction with historical and scientific research, a factor that begins to disturb things in an age when archeology is being invented, then the founding notion of Cabala, that of an oral law, which qualifies, complements, and guides the written one, is pertinent. The scripture, according to this *cabal* or tradition, would have just been a word of circumstance anyway, subject to the correction, therefore, of another conjuncture, and to emendation by the absolute voice, which is the original intention to speak, in comparison to which, *all* words are vain.

As an example of the way Cabala works to substantiate a conception for which sheer scripture is insufficient we may take a passage from that exploratory book of philosophical-religious conjectures, *The Religio Medici*. The problem Browne has set for himself here is to ground the notion of the microcosm, essential for the dignity of humanity, as he conceives it, in some kind of numinous authority or standard, when, essentially, all he has to go on is the very spare (but famous) statement from scripture that God made man in his own image. Significantly it is the notion of a secret and oral law, or Cabala, that provides the supporting framework the writer discovers, and lets his reader find with him, almost as if by surprise, but which has always already been there, obscure, hidden, unnoticed, but nourishing, all the more effectively so because we do not know that we know it. On the other hand whatever we knew we knew would be scripture, written, a form of ignorance and vanity, and, at the very least, incomplete: "That wee are the breath and similitude of God, it is indisputable, and upon record of holy Scripture, but to call ourselves a Microcosm, or little world, I thought it onlely a pleasant trope of Rhetorick, till my neare judgement and second thoughts told me there was a real truth theirin: for first wee are a rude masse, and in the ranke of creatures which only are, and have a dull kinde of being not yet privileged with life, or preferred to sense or reason; next we live the life of plants, the life of animals, the life of men, and at last the life of spirits, running on in one mysterious nature those five kinds of existences, which comprehend the creatures not onley of the world, but of the Universe; this is man the great and true *Amphibium*, whose nature is disposed to live not onely like other creatures in divers elements, but in divided and distinguished worlds; for though there be but one world to sense there are two to reason: the one visible, the other invisible."[97]

It should be remarked, also, that Cabala and other mystical styles to which Browne resorts are not just one of a battery of explanatory paradigms, the difference between which would be nugatory, but very much in the way of being a *privileged* and higher recourse, which tend to be invoked when all others have failed or have been revealed as insufficient. They are the kind of prayer we utter when we have done all we can do to help ourselves. References to Cabala, as to Alchemy, Magic, Astrology, and Hermeticism, tend to come in the concluding portions of sections or arguments, or even to comprise the ends in themselves. The allusion to the Cabala of Ricius, which, for Blau, shows Browne to be well versed in the subject, appears at the end of a cute little essay in *Vulgar Errors* whose subject is the significance of scutcheons or banners of the Tribes of Israel. In this text Browne proceeds, in the manner of Montaigne (to whom he has been frequently compared) and a certain Agrippa, by displaying a complex array of information, scholarship, and authority on the subject, soon reaching the point where the very possibility of coming to any conclusion at all seems vertiginously unlikely. However, the mystical is not simply just another option in a set of alternatives, among which history is soon to opt for the empirical, as is suggested by Jonathan Post in his recent book on Browne. Post is so impressed by the similarities of Browne to Montaigne in the matter of the incipiently open form of the essay,[98] created for the purpose of entertaining hypotheses, as, to my mind, risk conflating them, thereby missing an essential difference. Where for Montaigne the mystical would be merely another choice, level, or option, in Browne a concluding paragraph to this little essay on Tribes of Israel rather resolves the matter in favor of Cabala. What is here implied is that, although all the evidence, and the records and words to represent it, are insufficient, a mystical, here cabalist, paradigm would come closest to the truth. This is because, although there is no more to be said, empirically, logically, or philosophically (Nathanson's Platonic epistemology of *physis, nomos, ratio*) for this cabalistic-allegorical approach, Ricius being merely another source, it appeals by way of its elegance, range, simplicity, and dignity, a medicine, perhaps, whatever its mysterious composition, that *works*: "But more widely must we walk, if we follow the doctrine of the Cabalists, who in each of the four banners inscribe a letter of the Tetragrammaton, or the quadriliteral name of God: and mysterizing their ensigns, do make the particular ones of the twelve Tribes, accommodable unto the twelve signs in the Zodiack, and the twelve moneths of the year: But the Tetrarchical or general banners, of Judah, Reuben, Ephraim, and Dan, unto the signs of Aries, Cancer, Libra and Capricornus: that is, the four cardinal parts of the Zodiack, and season of the year."[99] Here we find Browne, floating on cabalist wings from heaven to earth, taking in at one glance and in the excitement of a single inspiration, Biblical history, astrology, the twelve months, and four seasons, concluding and resolving, aesthetically, if not logically, an issue that threatened to dissolve into sheer endlessness and undecidability. Similarly other cabalistic-mystic flights in Browne tend to take off at privileged points in his texts. This is so for his most direct borrowing of a zoharic motif, an hermeneutics that caught Pico's fancy too. This was the addition of the fifth letter to the name of Abraham, in Hebrew, the 'h' that made generation possible.[100] Browne takes up this numerological matter in the *fifth* and concluding section of *Garden of Cyrus*, an essay about the number five, where the author very likely sees the future of five, that is of posterity, being at stake.

We should not assume, on the other hand, that the mystical would constitute any kind of *final* word for Browne, whose texts are permeated by a profound sense of our ultimate ignorance, and the equality of all creatures, lettered or not, before the unfathomable mystery and challenge of our brief and puzzling existence. He delights in stressing the shadows and darkness created by the very light of knowledge, and, on the other side, the light emerging only by dint of the darkness of ignorance. One is wise, as Browne says so well in his works of direct statement that open and close his writing career, *Religio Medici* and *Christian Morals*, who knows how and when to turn his mind and his words off. Nevertheless, the mystical is as close as we can come to partaking in a fundamental mystery that we still cannot claim to control, as a way, if nothing else, of admitting our ignorance, while confessing to an appetite for eternity, for "something else," that can help make us human. So it is that Browne flies above the very earthly subject of ethics, which has been his subject, in the last paragraph of his last book, *Christian Morals*, for a sublime statement that, through his allusion to the mystery of "the kiss of the spouse," conveys a cabalistic motif of the coming of the Shekinah. This very same statement, he also makes a point of reminding us, he has made *verbatim* before (in the penultimate paragraph of *Urn Burial*), where Browne resolves mystically, although in a modest spirit of contingency and insufficiency, that perennial contradiction between flesh and spirit, time and eternity, here and the hereafter that it has been the particular mission of the Cabala of the Renaissance to relieve and relive: "And if, as we have elsewhere declared, any have been so happy as personally to understand Christian Annihiliation, Extasy, Exolution, Transformation, the Kiss of the Spouse, and Ingression into the Divine Shadow, according to Mystical Theology, they have already had an handsome Anticipation of Heaven."

Cabala in the Baroque Renaissance

Generally the major writers of the English Renaissance, who are influenced by Cabala, like Browne, Spenser, Milton, along with some other more specialized but very impressive and influential figures like Henry More and Thomas Vaughan, who made their profound studies of the subject a matter of personal commitment, seem to know exactly how they want to use it and how seriously they want to take it. For Spenser the *Shekinah* figure will lend substance to the idea of Sapience in the "Hymn to Heavenly Beauty," in the *Four Hymns*, as a way of imparting sensuality to an intellectualized and idealistic Platonism. Spenser, indeed, borrows, more or less directly, from The Zohar, in which spirits like to visit us in our sleep, specifically in the Red Cross Knight's dream of simulation and seduction in *The Fairie Queene*—an episode whose cabalistic quality is further stressed by the Agrippan name of the enchanter, Archimago. In a more general but probably more pervasive way, Giorgio's "orthodox Cabala," as transmitted to Spenser's generation by the authoritative John Dee, participates in the mystically benign hierarchical structure of *The Fairie Queene*, while also serving to dispel the specter of demonism from the extraordinary intermingling of the divine and earthly in the same epic.

In Milton, Cabala or an allied tradition, that of Hebrew-Gnostic "merkabah mysticism," supplies the imagery of the chariot at a strategic moment of the War in Heaven in *Paradise Lost*, where it is deployed by Christ both as a doomsday weapon against the legions of rebel angels he single-handedly confounds and also as a "getaway car." Relevant also to Milton is the attention focused by a certain cabalistic tradition on the problem, role and use of evil in a divinely created universe, reflections of which likely contributed to the complexity of the titanic figure of Satan in *Paradise Lost* and *Paradise Regained*, as well as to the credibility of the adjustment that Adam and Eve, and even Milton's Jesus, are able to make to an imperfect world.

For Browne, cabalistic notions, like that of an oral or written law, or of the line behind which the Deity has withdrawn, seem to fill a gap where more traditional explanations fail or where empirical sense tends to threaten faith. For the poets and thinkers of the "Platonic Renaissance" of the seventeenth century, Cudworth, Traherne, the Vaughan brothers (twins, Henry and Thomas, respectively, poet and alchemist) and Henry More, Cabala supplies sensual, literal (through letters) communication, relation, and correspondence between an ideal realm of ideas and a real one, colonized by science and power politics and therefore drifting ever farther away.

The minor writers, on the other hand, who are influenced by Cabala seem to be much more confused as to where exactly it fits in. It is, in fact, just this very confusion that makes their work revelatory about the effect of Cabala, as well as a denied need for it that the more masterly ones disguise and incorporate. This is indeed why I have sometimes lingered over writers like Henoch Clapham, otherwise probably unworthy of extended notice. Perhaps because they approach the subject without a clear sense of their own vision and purpose, beyond the limited horizons of just doing one's job, they often are ambivalent, confused, and ironic about a Cabala that they nevertheless seem to be fascinated by, a drug or experience, an inebriation, as one of them called it, that they can neither like or do without. In short, their popular Cabala seems to be an equivalent to the artificial paradises we enter through the portals of hallucinogenic substances, ecstatic sexuality, or speed and movement in our own by now thoroughly secular age, unsatisfactory recourses, of course, but as close to eternity as we can come. These are experiences that we come away from chastened and ashamed, but we have no substitute for, because they are themselves the substitutes.

The Vacant Hours of John Lightfoot

Meanderings in the STC collection turned up a few works of this minor sort, several of which I have already discussed, in which obsession with Cabala coexists also with disavowals of it, as well as with sheer misapprehension. One such ambiguous presentation is that of John Lightfoot's *Erubhim, or Miscellanies Christian and Judaicall*, published in London in 1629. Although here he seems anything but eager to claim special acquaintance with his "sacred" subjects, Lightfoot was, in fact, one of the major English Hebraists and Biblical scholars of his epoch. Lightfoot figures very prominently in H. F. Fletcher's account of Renaissance Hebraism: "The very best Christian scholars of the time made an attempt at an acquaintance with the rabbis, indeed, in the Buxtorfs, father and son, in Pococke, in Lightfoot, and in many others of the century, we have some the greatest Gentile rabbinical scholars who ever lived."[101] Fletcher, in another book, mentions also that, coincidentally, Milton's first tutor at Cambridge, William Chappell, was "tutor in 1617 to John Lightfoot, the greatest Semitic scholar of the seventeenth century,"[102] who is promoted, a little later, into someone "whom many scholars have styled the greatest Semitic scholar the English-speaking world has produced."[103] Showing this same ambivalence we have mentioned in connection with other authors that want to bring such hidden knowledge out into the open, but perhaps without a clear notion of what they want to do with it, Lightfoot claims at the beginning of his book that it was "penned for recreation at Vacant Houres," but nevertheless proceeds to grapple seriously with some of the profoundest mysteries of Cabala. First of all, he expounds the nature and function of the *Shekinah*, which, however, he also misrepresents. In turning her so directly into a Christian channel—"Shekinah they use for a title of God, but more expecially of the Holy Ghost"—Lightfoot seems to know nothing at all of a Neoplatonic quality of the Shekinah as emanation-from-the-absolute, nor her sensual presence and function as copulating female—as it is she who inhabits the cabalist's wife on Sabbath eve, when intercourse is enjoined. Conflating occult traditions, Lightfoot then alludes to the number mysticism of the "Alchemical cabalists who have extracted number out of the word 'Jehovah'." We find Lightfoot also, interestingly, referring to even more recondite cabalistic myths elsewhere: for instance, the legend that Adam was separated from Eve for 130 years after the Fall, and during this time fathered many children by the devil-women who visited him in his dreams.

Dreaming, from Adam to André Breton

Dreams are, indeed, a privileged area in occult traditions generally, as they are in more standard Biblical exegesis. Probably one reason for the Surrealists' deep grounding in occultism, especially in the 1920s, before their turn to political revolution, was this fascination they shared and at least partly derived from mystical traditions. Freud himself, important to the Surrealists, was, at the very time he was composing *Interpretation of Dreams,* greatly obsessed with the traditions and texts of Semitic and Christian demonism, which naturally would have included Cabala;[104] Michel

Leiris, that most word-possessed of the Surrealists, in the diaries he kept during the 1920s, is prone to alchemical or quasi-cabalistic glosses for his heavily dream-obsessed text. Whereas in Cabala the dream, as opposed to the waking vision, is always malefic, for the Surrealists, as for Freud, the dream was as likely to be an illumination as a warning, or in the Romantic-Symbolist tradition of Gerard de Nerval, even "a second life." Michel Leiris's lifelong search for an oneiric language that can "take off" at a certain point, to float as an entity of its own,[105] is harmonious with the dimension of the numinous Cabala finds in the very letters of scripture. Artaud also liked to mention Cabala explicitly, and Breton and Tzara seem to see their work, at least partly, as a continuation of other related traditions (Alchemy, in particular, but also Hermeticism, Tarot, and Magic), while rejecting the idea that any God went along with them; while the *Grand Jeu* group, including Daumal and Gilbert-Lecomte, eventually broke from Surrealism because it wasn't mystical enough (anymore). Roger Gilbert-Lecomte, leader of *The Grand Jeu* group, seems to have been deeply imbued with Cabala and a familiar of The Zohar, which combined with Vedanta helped create his visionary approach to modern art. Cabalistic notions of the withdrawal of the divine corresponded, for Gilbert-Lecomte, to a necessity for the artist to deploy an extraordinary strategy of Rimbaud-type dérèglement (disorganization of the senses).[106]

A Surrealist critique, based on Marx's indictment of the alienations and reifications of Capitalism combines with a Lurianic Cabala's idea of the retreat of the divine to form one of the formidable currents of resistance of modern art to the temper of our times. Occultism, with its strange sense of mission, after having helped inspire Surrealism, probably was not so much dropped as transcended and continued in other forms: revolution, art, the unconscious. Cabala, in its quality as a secret tradition, might also be an interesting metaphor for Surrealism, which can be seen as a hidden dimension of culture, just as Cabala was supposed to have been hidden in Torah. Having said that, it is necessary to mention that, although the reason-defying occult certainly had an impact and an influence, neither Surrealism, nor any other modernism or postmodernism, is a mysticism, even an atheist or failed one. Although the world might seem to be represented mystically by the Surrealists and others, their art, for instance, that of the "desiring machines" of Duchamp, Roussel, and Tanguy, would be rather an antimysticism, whereby there is no hint of a belief in the presence of anything beyond the screen or face of representation. The so-called mystical novel of today, such as it exists, is reactionary. For example, in Brooks Hansen's *The Chess Garden* (1995), the "other world" is presented just as if it is really there, without the (redeeming) irony of Borges, say, to whom Hansen has been mistakenly compared. Items in *this* world are transformed by authorial fiat by a spiritualizing, vitalizing influx from that other one, in a process of co-optation that a certain French current, from Sartre to Sollers, once would have called a "shameful idealism." Such demonic dreams as Lightfoot alludes to may be read, accordingly, abstracted from their theosophical context as messages from another world or dimension, as figures of repressed sexual desire, and of subliminal release of revelatory and revolutionary artistic energies.

Dreams are, of course, quite significant in Cabala, but always, at least in The Zohar, from a malefic point of view, as opposed to visions, which imply the reality-transforming energy of waking activity: one is vulnerable in somatic states generally, especially ones that one falls into, to the visits of nomadic unclean spirits who like nothing better than to "suck ones seed," as in the Knight's dream of a virtual Una in *The Fairie Queene*, as well as the Serpent's approach, in dream, to Eve in *Paradise Lost*. The names of the women, according to Lightfoot, who were the unhappy Adam's seducers were culled from pagan, pre-Christian, Hebrew, and gnostic sources, a provenance like that Milton drew on for his demons in *Paradise Lost*. The women, according to Lightfoot, who invaded and continue to threaten Adam's sleep are Lilith, Ogareth, Maleth, and Naamah.

Elsewhere he alludes to the cabalistic idea that "mistaking of a letter, in Hebrew, destroys the world," a notion derived from the other, oral and secret, of the "two laws" given to Moses. However, a little farther on, in a section entitled "Of the Cabalist," we find him manifesting that same ambivalence with which he started, as he says, about the cabalists, that "their trading is cheifly in numbers, strange trices and flights of invention." He suggests by this vulgar wording that cabalists are in the business of mystifying people for profit. As tends to be the case where one of these ambivalent authors feels out of their depth, or otherwise vulnerable in relation to the implications of Cabala, Lightfoot then refers us, for further information, to someone else, in this case to a German Rabbi whose name, Latinized, is Buxodorsius, and, in particular, to his book, *Abbreviatura*, for information about the techniques of *notorikon* and *geometrion*.[107]

Fludd's Wild Jig

An important and very influential thinker and writer, whose attitude toward Cabala and related occult styles was anything but hesitating was Robert Fludd (1574–1637), whose name is one of those that have endured as being synonymous with seventeenth-century "magical lore," with its intimations of universal integration into a Great Chain of Being that soon would not be enough to hold us all together. In one of his dreams, Michel Leiris finds himself, for instance, dancing a jig with "l'alchimiste Robert Fludd."[108]

With Fludd there surfaces, in particular, a relation between Rosicrucianism and Cabala, which may have been a sequel to Dee's enigmatic stay in Bohemia in the 1580s. In 1614, in T. M. Luhrmann's words, "A strange German text proclaimed the founding of a secret brotherhood dedicated to religious and intellectual reform . . . Thus emerged the Rosicrucian fraternity, whose existence has long been the subject of historical and occult debate." Luhrmann, who mentions he had been reluctant to accept Yates's mostly intuitive intimations as to links between Rosicrucianism and Cabala, through Dee, has to admit, after a comprehensive comparative perusal, that this founding text of the movement, the mysterious *Fama Fraternitas* was very likely modeled on Dee's *Monas*.[109] The *Fama Fraternitas Rosae Crucis* was followed in the next year (1615) by *Chymische Hochzeit Christiani Rosenkreuz*, fictitiously dated 1459, which purported to be an account of the life, ideas, and (al)chemical adventures of the legendary founder of the order, Christian Rosenkreuz. The editor and translator of Comenius's *Labyrinth of The World*, Matthew Spinka, asserts bluntly in a note to that book: "Their authorship is now traced with practical certainty to John Valentine Andreae, [who] . . . had written these Rosicrucian books in order to satirize the conditions of his day. But his subtle irony was misunderstood by some of his readers, and his story was taken quite seriously by some of them."[110] Comenius, whose philosophical framework we have described as cabalist, had indeed enough esteem for the Lutheran reformer Andreae (1586–1654) to all but plagiarize him in *Labyrinth of The World*. Chapter XIII of the *Labyrinth* is, dizzyingly, then, a satire of the ideal Rosicrucian community, already, according to Spinka, a satire.

Yates's basic theory is that the frustrated idealism of the sixteenth-century Cabala of Harmony, derived from Giorgio, was sublimated and channeled into the Rosicrucian movement, to which she has devoted a book, *The Rosicrucian Enlightenment*, where Fludd, indeed is a central figure. For Yates Rosicrucianism was one of the primary conduits or vehicles through which Cabala survives into modern times.[111] The first English translation from The Zohar was, indeed, accomplished by an eminent Rosicrucian, S. L. G. MacGregor Mathers; and the merest glance at Rosicrucian literature today is likely to turn up allusions to cabalist-sounding sephiroth and numerology.[112] Fludd was indeed steeped in Cabala as well as in the other heterodoxies of the Renaissance. Fludd, like Pico, Agrippa, Paracelsus, and Bruno gave to his presentations of these subjects a powerful sense of his own mercurial, demiurgic, creative personality, whose syncretic energy it was to fuse things into one. Evidence of how successful he was in disseminating his ideas is manifest both in the frequency and bitterness with which he was attacked and the prestige of those who were opposing him. Pierre Gassendi (1592–1655), his formidable antagonist, was both an illustrious correspondent of Descartes and the foremost representative of a current of seventeenth-century French libertine materialism. The libertine radicals were quite a powerful force, including among their number important and daring writers who scandalized their time, such as Cyrano de Bergerac and Charles Sorel, while even Molière, apparently, at least for a time, was connected to them. The libertine current represented a radical-empirical extension of the implications of Cartesian thinking to include the rejection of all moral and religious obstacles to pleasure, knowledge, and power, a turn that was very much resented and resisted by magical (Fludd, T. Vaughan) as well as religious-philosophical (H. More, the Cambridge Platonists, Pascal) thinkers of the seventeenth century.

In 1631 Gassendi published an *Examination of the Philosophy of R. Fludd*, in which he systematically ridicules Fludd, singling out for special disdain Fludd's idiosyncratic version of Cabala, supposed to be obsessed with a *Light* which, emanating by way of the Sephiroth and uniting with a World Spirit forms a kind of World Soul. Fludd here is regarded as a (wild) sort of Neoplatonic emanationist or even flat pantheist to whom the vocabulary of Cabala would be secondary to a mystical vision already waiting to be confirmed. More recently, Waite has objected that Fludd's Cabala was derived rather from some of the bizarre modifications of the tradition late in the Renaissance, as conveyed in the controversial *Gali Razia*,[113] a sixteenth-century unsigned Safed-circle text whose rationalizations of scriptural immorality foreshadowed the Sabbatian inversions of the next century, than from the more orthodox *Zohar*, which Waite supposes he did not even know.[114] Waite criticizes Fludd for following Paracelsus in making Cabala only an adjunct to his own personal mysticism, becoming, essentially, merely "his own cabalist." This is a judgment that might apply equally, beyond the immediate context of Waite's concern, which was to establish the relative degree of fidelity of the writer to his own esoteric-theosophical idea of "the secret doctrine of Kaballah," to the situations of mystical movements, especially in the late Renaissance.

In a general sense, then, Fludd's theosophical schemes, of which a radical and experimental Cabala was certainly an essential component, were part of a tendency widespread in Western society and sympathetically documented by de Certeau in *The Mystic Fable*, that placed social life and mystical truth on a collision course one with the other. From Zevi's "heretical Cabala" to Urban Grandier's subliminal-sensual appeal to the "possessed of Loudun," to the extravagant designs of such as Fludd, and also the English Platonists, a similar urgency and dismay is to be sensed at the coming final triumph of secular culture, to be consolidated by the eighteenth century. Essentially, according to de Certeau, what happens to mysticism in the seventeenth century is its abandonment to the will or whim of the individual, consequence of the evaporation of institutional support, which tends to expel those with such inclinations and visions out of social and religious contexts, or at least put them in a nomadic posture regarding the establishment.

However, in Hegelian terms, probably not so far from Scholem's, mystical nomadism is then relayed by eighteenth-century and later Enlightenment and Revolution, invented then on a terrain that has been cleared of traditional authority and hierarchy. This *aufhebung* or transcendence was sometimes the matter of a single lifetime, for instance, that of an eighteenth-century Sabbatian-Frankist cabalist notable who became Junius Frey, member of the Revolutionary Convention, and eventually earned the distinction of dying with Danton: "When the outbreak of the French Revolution again gave a political aspect to their [Sabbatians] ideas, no great change was needed for them to become the apostles of unbounded political apocalypse."[115] A metamorphosis from cabalist to *philosophe* is accomplished in the short and stormy life of Solomon Maimon, who passed from deep absorption in The Zohar to being an important figure in the German Enlightenment. Before Maimon drank himself to death in a nobleman's castle, he wrote a sensational autobiography, very much in the iconoclastic spirit of Rousseau's *Confessions*, as well as having turned himself into a recognized authority on Kantian ontology and metaphysics.

Fludd's most systematically cabalistic work was the appropriately titled *Mosaical Philosophy* (London, 1638, 1659), whose full title expresses this over-reaching response of the embattled mysticism of the time: *Mosaicall Philosophy, grounded upon the essential truth or Eternal Sapience.*[116] It is interesting also that attacks on Fludd came from such diverse provenance. If Gassendi's bias is libertine epicurism and secularism, which Fludd's platonic extravagance offends, Mersenne, whom we have met before[117] as a prestigious Catholic opponent of the classical Christian Cabala of the early Renaissance author Franciscus Georgius, entered the lists as an opponent of Fludd's pandemic and dramatic obsession with his own strange brew of cabalistical alchemy. In a public *Letter*, published in 1631 (responding to the earlier publication in Latin of Fludd's book on Cabala) he castigates Fludd, in Thorndike's paraphrase, "for thinking all scripture has alchemical significance, and for saying that Moses was an alchemist in describing creation, as were David, Solomon, Jacob, Job . . . Similarly true cabalists are nothing but alchemists."[118]

The Christian Cabala of the later Renaissance was largely a Protestant phenomenon, promulgated by Lutheran enthusiasts like

Pistorius and Rosenroth, whereas its opponents tended more and more to be Catholics. The "nasty" job of attacking Cabala and other eclectic threats appears to have devolved mostly on Jesuits, while, as a matter of fact, the Catholics had frequently supported (and added to) it, especially on the Franciscan side, early in the Renaissance. However Fludd's Cabala was surely dangerous and threatening in a whole new way, which throws light both on Mersenne's Catholic attacks on it and on the need of the libertine, Gassendi, to demarcate himself and his current from it: for Fludd's Cabala, whose standard was the alchemical search for the "philosopher's stone," whose style was theosophical extravagance and provocation, was profoundly a pagan, or at least a Gnostic, therefore pre- or para-Christian one; and its urgency, drama, and apocalyptic mood is, indeed, very much in harmony with what Scholem has suggested were the eventually cataclysmic implications of the rediscovery of the Cabala of the late Renaissance of its Gnostic roots. For with this reawakened Gnosticism rose the specter of the incessant conflict between Manichean antipodes, as well as a justification of the maximization of the principle of evil as a prelude and passage to a new creation.

Scholem, who has described himself as a Jewish anarchist, regarded the long-range effects of the Sabbatian movement, however disturbing at the time, as quite salutary, in the sense of being a mystical precondition for more secular and practical struggles of our own century. Through cabalist heresy the Jews gained a sense of entitlement, which, even after the eschatological messianism had largely fallen away or dissolved into a more innocuous Hasidism, remained to inspire Zionist dreams and realizations. Scholem has, of course, been challenged on this interpretation, running counter as it does to the Jewish anathema that has attached to "apostate" Sabbatai and his even more "shameful" Frankist acolytes; for, just as in Freudian terms, many don't like owing civilization to patricide, there are those who won't be indebted to cabalist heresy for the State of Israel!

This same historical urgency that turned Fludd's Cabala into an abstruse pagan and alchemical myth may be seen operating in the grandiose schemes of the figures connected with the Platonic Renaissance of seventeenth-century England, whose most prominent theoretical statement was Ralph Cudworth's *True Intellectual*

System of the Universe, of 1668. Here the function of Cabala, rather than that of a *revival* of pagan or gnostic paradigms, was that of a redefinition of these elements to fit into the Christian forms that were being so widely questioned. Cabala's great malleability and flexibility leant itself readily and credibly to such complications, which were meant to strengthen Christianity with all the resources, ironically, of the "undesirables" that the Church had defined itself against by excluding in the first place. Waite, always suspicious of Christian versions of Cabala, which he tends to see as distortions or even betrayals, is severe and ironic on the contradictions of Cudworth and the Christian Platonism he stands for, although respectful of the intellectual scrupulosity of the individual: "The chief thesis of the INTELLECTUAL SYSTEM is that behind the tapestries and embroideries of pagan mythology there is the doctrine of monotheism, and that civilized man in reality has never worshipped but one God, whose threefold nature was a 'Divine Cabbala' or revelation, successively depraved and adulterated till it almost disappears for Cudworth among the 'particular unities' of Proclus and the later Platonists."[119] However, to make of Cabala an adjunct of the classical myth of The Golden Age, as Cudworth does, is, for Waite, to alter history by fiat and to enlist entropy in the service of a mystical nostalgia.

Unquestionably the dramatic, gesture-provoking escalation of Cabala of the school of Isaac Luria helped the Christian Platonists of the seventeenth century define their age as a degenerate one, especially when the *withdrawal* of the numinous from the world is seen, in a concession to the new scientific spirit, as happening progressively and *within* history. Coincidentally Henry More, Christian Platonist, and probably the most notable English Christian Cabalist of the century, student of the eminent seventeenth-century scholar of the Apocalypse, Joseph Meade, also tended to advocate the anteriority of Cabala, an archeology whose discovery was human devolution from an initial position close to divinity. One of More's other ambitious suggestions, meant to exploit the accumulated prestige of mystical numerology and printed in correspondence that was published as an appendix to Knorr Von Rosenroth's *Kabbalah Denudata* of 1677, which, as a matter of fact, *featured* Lurianic texts, was that the Cabala was Pythagorean in origin. Since what More has very much in mind when he talks of Cabala are premonitions and anticipations of Christianity, essentially he is attempting to extend the borders of the latter, historically, philosophically, and mystically (into a realm of a divine mathematics) at a time when its territorial limits, that is, its relevance, are very much in question. Luria's Cabala, which was an adaptation to a Jewish position of "permanent exile," imparted to these Christian schemes a sense of drama and crisis, of timeliness, that would have been missing from the more static and patient zoharic, or prezoharic models. From Luria's ideas of voluntary "divine absence," prelude to a "breaking of the vessels" could be developed the revolutionary notion of a world in urgent need of repair, awaiting its messiah that could and should be, ultimately, anyone and everyone. A world from which the divine is missing is tantamount, symbolically, especially when a messianic component is introduced, to a confession of faith in a pantheistic ideal of one where the *restored* divine would be, or should be everywhere. This "stretching" of Cabala in the late Renaissance, whether in the Jewish direction of the astounding Sabbatai Zevi and his prophet Nathan or in the hermeneutic extravagance of its Christianizing, Platonizing, or Paganizing acolytes, was obviously both symptom and result of a climate of uncertainty and doubt, one in which the unthinkable needs to be thought and whatever secret answers humanity has been harboring tend to surface and be disseminated. The reminder may be useful that we are dealing here with the Age of the Baroque, commonly thought of in cultural history as a time when *style* claims an attention all of its own, while being defined in terms that emphasize effects of planned discontinuity, interruption, and discordance—of shock, in short, both to the nervous system and to all settled systems of belief and expectations. These are reasons the Baroque is often thought of as a protomodernism, indeed having to wait for modernity to discover it, the way the Gothic waited for the Romantics.

Thomas Vaughan and the Return of Agrippa

"Baroque" might be an apt appellation, in any case, for the kind of cabalist Thomas Vaughan [1621–1665] was, that very strange and questionably Christian poet, mystic, magician, philosopher, *and* practicing alchemist, and a disciple of the omnivorous Agrippa, as

well as his seeming avatar in the Platonic Renaissance (and Resistance, in Cassirer's sense) in England of the seventeenth century.
Vaughan's relation to Agrippa is a curious one, to say the least, one
that surely conveyed some kind of defiant statement, analogous,
possibly to one's claiming currently Timothy Leary, or better yet,
Aleister Crowley, or Eliphas Levi as one's mentor or saint. Long
before Vaughan fell under his spell Agrippa was widely considered,
even in unorthodox places, bad company. Jean Bodin, himself an
eccentric Hebraizing Christian who wound up as his own kind of
archaic Jew, had singled out Agrippa for special scorn in his
Démonomanie (1580) for what he considered, in contradistinction
to pagan magicians, his *intentional* malevolence and subversion:
"[The pagans] resorted to it [sorcery] through ignorance and error,
in good faith and assuming they were doing good: but Agrippa
practiced it through detestable impiety: for he was the greatest
sorcerer of his time."[120] Bodin's attitude was to impact soon on no
less an authority than the King of Scotland, soon to be James I of
England, who in 1587 published a *Daemonologie*, where he, according to Yates, "has much more to say about 'the Divel's school wich
thinks to climb to knowledge of things to come mounting from
degree to degree on the slippery scale of curiosity,' believing that
circles and conjurations tied to the words of God will raise spirits.
This is clearly 'practical Cabala' interpreted as a black art, a fruit
of that tree of forbidden knowledge of which Adam was commanded
not to eat. James's work, if read in Manchester [Dee's home], would
not have helped Dee's reputation."[121] As a matter of fact, in 1589
Dee returned home from his mysterious Bohemian mission to find
his home burned and library sacked. This latter had included a
"fabulous" collection of occult lore and was a kind of miniacademy,
Yates opines, where the generation of Sidney and Spenser imbibed
their blends of "divine mathematics," Neoplatonism, Hermeticism,
and Giorgian Cabala.

There seemed to have been pretty much of a consensus that
Agrippa and his acolytes had crossed a line that a tradition of
astrological and cabalistic ritual, from Ficino to Campanella, hov-
ered uncomfortably near. This was a vague but very important
border that divided a heavenly or at least acceptable magic from a
clearly demonic one. With Agrippan magic we clearly cross this
line, as here, even for tolerant spirits, it was generally granted that

"the demons have come out into the open and dominate the scene."[122] With this in mind we may suppose that Vaughan's paraded attachment to Agrippa must have constituted a dramatically iconoclastic provocation and sensation. Indeed, it would be difficult to exaggerate the extent of Vaughan's defiant identification with Agrippa and his bold reality-transforming legacy except by invoking, perhaps, a presumed belief in metempsychosis (or psychosis), whereby the former would be the latter reborn.

Vaughan's special delight is in throwing the insults, easy enough to find, to Agrippa's memory, in the teeth of the detractors, resuming and reiterating the shameful demonic appellations as so many badges of merit, while proclaiming his absolute devotion to a figure he treats like a combination of a god and father, extolling: "Cornelius Agrippa, that Grand Archimagus, as the antichristian *jesuits* call him. He is indeed my Author and next to God I owe all that I have unto him."[123] Vaughan's strange hero worship extended to his editing of the spurious fourth, notoriously demonic book, of Agrippa's *Occult Philosophy* for publication in 1665. Agrippa's revenge has been that later ages often gave Vaughan the credit for being its author.

Although Thomas Vaughan has been regarded as having sacrificed a poetic talent that was comparable to that of his twin brother, Henry, on the altar of his mystical career and mission,[124] a notable exception was his extravagant ode to Agrippa, just about as near to an *apotheosis* as one writer can fashion for another, and one, I think, that yields nothing in hyperbole to Milton's *Lycidas*, or Shelley's *Adonais*. This adoring text was printed with Vaughan's 1651 edition of Agrippa's *Occult Philosophy*. Vaughan's determination to disseminate news of his worship of Agrippa is evident also from his having printed the same piece, together with a full-page engraving of a portrait of the Magus, in a book he published[125] the year before:

An Encomium on the Three Books of Cornelius Agrippa, Knight

Great, glorious penman! whom I should not name	1
Lest I might seem to measure thee by fame:	
Nature's apostle and her choice high-priest,	
Her mystical and bright evangelist	
How am I rapt when I contemplate thee	5

And wind myself above all that I see!
The spirits of thy lines infuse a fire
Like the world's soul, which make me thus aspire.
I am unbodied by thy books, and thee,
And in thy papers find my ecstasy;   10
Or if I please but to descend a strain,
Thy Elements do screen my soul again.
I can undress myself by thy bright glass,
And then resume th'enclosure, as I was.
Now I am earth, and now a star, and then   15
A spirit: now a star and earth again
Or if I will ramasle [sic] all that be,
In the least moment I engross all three
I span the Heaven and Earth, and things above,
And, which is more, join natures with their Jove.   20
He crowns my soul with fire, and there doth shine
But like the rainbow in a cloud of mine.
Yet there's a law by which I discompose
The ashes, and the fire itself disclose,
But in his emerald still he doth apear;   25
They are but grave-clothes which he scatters here.
Who sees the fire without his mask, his eye
Must needs be swallowed by the light, and die
These are the mysteries for which I wept,
Glorious Agrippa, where thy language slept,   30
Where thy dark texture made me wander far
Whiles through that pathless Hight I traced the star;
But I have found those mysteries, for which
Thy book was more than thrice-piled o'er with pitch.
Now a new East beyond the stars I see,   35
Where breaks the day of thy divinity:
Heaven states a commerce here with man, had he
But grateful hands to take, and eyes to see.
Hence you fond school-men, that high truths deride
And with no arguments but noise, and pride;   40
You that damn-all but what yourselves invent
And yet find nothing by experiment;
Your fate is written by an unseen hand,
But his three books with the three worlds shall stand.[126]

Whether (entirely) consciously meant or not there are elements
above that correspond particularly well to cabalistic styles of
thought. Cabalistic, first of all the astral mobility of the subject (l.

13–16), flying back and forth from earth to the stars, while passing at will between body and spirit, all on the wings of a *technique*. Also, there is a clear allusion to the veil that Moses was said to both have been born with and worn on his return from Sinai (1.27), or symbolically, to a mystery of secrecy, disguise, and protection, which especially fascinated the cabalists. This would make of Agrippa, after Christ, the "new Moses." Then, there is the declaration of the congress between human and divine (1. 37–38) brought on by Agrippan alchemy, suggesting those moments of descent of God and his Shekinah into, respectively, the midnight Eden and conjugal bed of the worshiper. Finally the division of the cosmos into three worlds (1. 44), one for each of the books of Agrippa, corresponds to typically triune cabalistic image of elemental, celestial, and spiritual spheres, for each one of which we are supposed to possess a separate soul. A god-like exemption from contingency is claimed, additionally, in the last three lines of the poem, for Agrippa's books, and by implication for the cabalist-mage-alchemist, Vaughan himself, who follows in their starry wake.

Vaughan's Cabala, however, would be a mélange of the conventional with the eccentric and even heretic. His promotion of Agrippa, for instance, to the status of a Moses or Simon ben Yohai, with himself, it is hinted certainly, as the latest mystic avatar, suggests what was soon to become, on the Jewish side, the Sabbatian deviation in Cabala. In Vaughan Cabala passes beyond being a *personal* style or faith, which it already is somewhat for Browne, Fludd, and also the Christian Platonists, to being a matter of personality, or what we might call today a "cult of personality," as also for his Jewish heretical contemporary, Zevi. With Vaughan, however, the sense of messianic energy and mission is obviously an internal and solitary one, whereby one can work only toward a transformation in one's own being, rather than being a matter of "bringing up" a whole people, as was the Sabbatian project.

The Messiah of the Baroque.   Vaughan's master in Cabala was, indeed, as he made no secret, the mercurial, by then widely regarded as demonic genius, Agrippa, whom he claims as his spiritual forefather. According to Waite, who himself perhaps would be a modern-esoteric version, at least in spirit, of the pyrotechnic cabalist of the Vaughan-Agrippa variety: "Vaughan, in his early works, confesses himself a disciple of Agrippa, and THE THREE BOOKS OF OCCULT PHILOSOPHY represent the general measure of his knowledge concerning the Esoteric Tradition of the Jews."[127] Now although nothing is easier in the history of Christian Cabala than to underestimate the seriousness of Agrippa's contribution, unquestionably Vaughan was being provocative when he foregrounded Agrippan magic in a century when ritual magic itself was on the defensive, or at least beginning to yield to that more effective magic "empiricks" was offering, and when, in fact, there must have been other approaches even to Cabala open to him. However, magic, especially with the aura of special forces and faculties Agrippa was able to convey with it, was the perfect embodiment of Vaughan's very personal and eccentric orientation, where the individual is accorded the discretionary power of so much possibility. Ultimately, even this Faustian Vaughan appears not so much interested in formulas, letters, and rituals as he is in the posture and potential of an individual in relation to energies of transformation, coded and disguised in a Cabala or name of the divine. One senses, in his version of Agrippa, more the provocation, hubris, and demonism in his daring to claim such a mentor than a literal belief in rites. Even in Vaughan as alchemist, we feel his pride in his achievement, which, he advertises,[128] takes precedence over the success of the actual operation or experiment. In this sense he extends as much the mystically syncretic spirit of Pico as that of the more practically oriented Agrippa into an age that was turning away from such a theater of individuality toward other, more impersonal scenes in which ego-assaulting notions like *human nature*, anchored in Cartesian mechanism (as relayed in the eighteenth century by La Mettrie's "man as machine," or in our own by varieties of conditioning psychologies), were to assume the only part.

We may, accordingly, think of Vaughan's style as Baroque because his emphasis is rather on shocking the reader into a kind of recognition than communicating any specific doctrine, at least through recipe or formula. In a passage, for example, which Waite cites, from a text called *The Antiquity of Magic*, he even distances himself, indeed, from the kind of manipulative Cabala that Agrippa had developed a reputation for promoting. Vaughan here projects rather a sense of the possibility of garnering higher powers, which involves a vision of allowing the unobstructed influx of the divine into the individual, whose fundamental role is simply to *be* there, rather than to act, through rites or formulas, to enhance the process. Waite's reading-paraphrase-citation of this text isolates not letters and numbers and their manipulation as catalytic cabalistic recourses, but instead Vaughan's use of the motif of *Jacob's Ladder* as a sign of the feasibility (and urgency) of the absorption into the personality of the individual of the aura and energy of the divine. For this act and style, which we are calling Baroque, because of the readiness with which Vaughan shifts perspectives, the (Agrippan) contortions were only, ostensibly, meant as mask and preliminary: "He recognizes also a metaphysical tradition [Kaballah] in which the greatest mystery is the symbolism of Jacob's Ladder. 'Here we find the two extremes—Jacob is one, at the foot of the ladder, and God is the other, Who stands above it, *emittens formas et influxus in Jacob, sive subjectum hominum* [emitting form and influx to Jacob, or the human subject]. The rounds or steps in the ladder signify the middle nature, by which Jacob is united to God.' With this symbolism he contrasts the 'false grammatical Kabbala' which 'consists only in rotations of the alphabet and a metathesis of letters in the text, by which means the scripture hath sufered many racks and excoriations.' The true Kabbalah only uses letters for artifice, that is, with a view to concealment."[129]

Much more so than for the earlier Renaissance, the Cabala of the seventeenth century needs to be understood in terms of the individuals who promote and utilize its imagery and symbolism, each one lending the force, eccentricity, and particular energy and imagination of his own personality and priorities. Whereas in its earlier development the identity of its sages, even its authors, is often dubious and obscure, if not mythical or pseudepigraphical, as the Cabala of the Renaissance becomes more urgently ideological person and personality start to assert themselves. Perhaps we may point to the Christian Cabalists of the fifteenth and early sixteenth centuries as beginning this evolution toward identity. By 1550 we are more familiar with the personalities of Pico, Reuchlin, Postel, and Agrippa than with that of Moses de Leon, who nevertheless wrote The Zohar, without which there never would have been a Cabala, or at least not one of anywhere near its prestige, scope, and influence, Christian or otherwise! Whatever the distinctions we may make between Jewish community and anonymity and Christian individuality (God must know *who* I am if I am to be saved, a factor which would be nugatory if it is a matter of rescuing a people), by the end of the sixteenth century Jewish names, like those of Luria and Cordovero, have attached themselves irremediably to Cabala, which really cannot be understood apart from them. In the next century, from names like Zevi's and Nathan's there emanates, at least for a while, a positively Biblical aura and authority. *They* have become, titanically, miraculously, marvelously, the Simon ben Yohais, no longer distant and comforting, nonthreatening and reassuring entities, summoned only in moments of confusion or ecstasy, but actual beings, and, as such, exigent, demanding, and critical, like a Moses suddenly appearing on your doorstep or in your living room. So in Vaughan's abrupt shift from the image of letters to that of the ladder, as presented in Waite's reading above, what may stand out might be the *"sive subjectum hominem* [virtual human subject]." That Jacob face to face with the terror, promise, and occasion of the divine, for the later Cabala, turns out to be oneself.

Sexual Mysticism and Philosopher's Stone.   The texts of Thomas Vaughan yield manifold evidence, as Waite has been cunning enough to suspect, that his perspectives have been very largely shaped by Cabala, which, along with Alchemy, provides essential metaphors, as well as adding the guarantee of scriptural authority, for the challenge of passage through the mysteries of personal transformation. For Vaughan, as for Cabala, "every secret is truth, and *every substantial truth is secret,"*[130] while the fact that Moses was born with a veil over his face symbolizes the ineluctable disguise every revelation must at first wear as well as assigning our highest and most urgent earthly role to the duty or burden of its lifting, called, indeed, by Vaughan, "the greatest mystery." Vaughan's self-ascribed mission was to succeed at a cabalist alchemy that was at once practical (he died sensationally and prematurely at the age of forty-four, in 1665, through inhaling the fumes of mercury from an operation gone awry) and symbolical, in the sense that the Philosopher's Stone for him was a metaphor, as Jung was going to describe it, of psychic healing and wholeness, for a mystic transformation. In the extended title of a book published in 1645, *Secrets*

Revealed, he even claimed to have "by Inspiration and Reading/ attained to the Philosopher's Stone/at his age of Twenty-Three Years," actually rushing into print with his recipe, since he was twenty-three that same year.

By way of answering the question as to where a young man goes after discovering The Philosopher's Stone at the age of twenty-three, we may cite a later, more general and philosophical work, *Anthroposophia Theomagica*. Here we find Vaughan explaining the creation very much in the spirit of Lurianic withdrawal, flavoring his Cabala also with the salt of a little Hermetic imagery: "God before his work of *Creation* was wrapped up and contracted in himself. In this state the Egyptians stile him *Monas solitario*, and the Cabalists *Aleph tenebrorum*."[131] Vaughan then describes the very instant of creation in terms of this all-powerful, wonder-working, opening first letter, but whose quality has changed suddenly from shadow to light, which he calls the *Aleph Lucidum*. Hebraic and cabalistic also is Vaughan's account of a primordial division of souls between those that belong to "Ruach" or to "Nephesh," representing separate female and male principles respectively, but which are joined eventually by what he calls the "hieroglyph" of marriage. In another essay, bound with the *Anthroposophia*, *Anima Magica Abscondita*, he extols what he calls the "conjugal mystery of ejaculation,"[132] whereby the two souls, representing also upper and lower Platonic cosmic categories, are joined.

The ideal sexual act, like the "Kiss of the Spouse" Browne liked to think awaited us, may be thought of as the perfect alchemical operation, melting the divided cosmic levels into a universal unity and harmony. The fall, for Vaughan, would not be a sexual one but rather a fall into matter, from which "mystic sex" as well as the alchemical projection that is its metaphor would provide an ascent. The doctrines of Vaughan, which open up the realm of existence to the constant incursions of the divine, as was true generally with Cabala, eliminate the guilt generated by any "original sin,"[133] but also enhance and invent the individual, who has been provided with the means, and implicitly assigned the duty, of inviting the numinous *here and now*. Vaughan, is specific even about the particular sephiroth from which such "rays" descend, alluding boldly to those *"living Eternall Influences* which daily and hourly proceed from him. Hence he is called of the Cabalists Cether."[134]

Here he even calls, very much in the spirit Pico's "dignity," "Man, God's playfellow," and he culls out of zoharic texts or accounts the familiar image of a periodic recreation of Eden that ineluctably attracts the divine, where "we might *Enter the Terrestriall Paradise, that Hortus Conclusus* of Solomon, where God descends to walk."[135] This intimacy and congress of the levels is called by Vaughan, in an image that fuses mystic sex, alchemy, and Edenic intermingling, "that mysterious Kisse of God and Nature."[136] In this Age of the Baroque when people start creating their own systems, anticipating Blake's maxim that "I must create my own or be enslaved by another man's," the Cabala of Sir Thomas Browne, though I think of comparable authenticity, profundity, and sincerity, and certainly more livable (and literary), seems tame and cautious by contrast with Thomas Vaughan's. Henry More was closer to Vaughan, by way of his unrelenting and consistent idealism, but probably found him, for that reason, more of a threat. In fact, More found it imperative to enter the lists against him in a vigorous "pamphlet war."[137] Vaughan wanted to push that Cabala he had absorbed from the Cambridge Platonists into a more radical, ecstatic, and alchemical place than More, the philosophical mystic, could consent to. If we may call More's Cabala a patient and scrupulously intellectual one, where the Lurianic urgency and world repair or *tikkun* it enjoins, is very much a matter of the mind, we might qualify Browne's Cabala as modest, in the sense of allowing, as also The Zohar likes to do, for the possibility of wisdom coming through unsuspected, only apparently ignorant sources. Vaughan's ambitions are Faustian by contrast, elitist and demanding products of a soul that seeks only its own. Whereas More could only *exclude*, Browne could *include* a life style like Vaughan's, with its projections, passions, and dangers, in the range of behavior that could be understood and even admired, as his respectful correspondence with the alchemist, Elias Ashmole, shows. Browne was a sympathetic friend of John Dee's son, ostensibly believing his claims to have witnessed his father's halcyon "projections" that drew gold out of dross matter. That Vaughan's extravagant ambitions would have posed no problem for Browne may be supposed from a letter the latter wrote in 1658 to Elias Ashmole, offering to send to the famous alchemist texts that the late younger Dee had left with him: "whereof I receaved from Dr Arthur Dee, my familiar freind, sonne unto old Dr Dee the mathematician; hee lived many yeares and dyed in Norwich, from whom I have heard many accounts . . . concerning his father and Kelley; hee was a persevering student in Hermeticall philosophy and had noe small encouragement, *having seen projections made*; And with the highest asseverations hee confirmed . . . that hee had ocularly, undeceavably, and frequently beheld it in Bohemia, and to my knowledge, had not an accident prevented [death], hee had retired beyond sea and fallen upon the solemne processe of the great worke."[138]

Nevertheless Browne ultimately would likely feel more at home with More's theoretical-idealist Cabala than Vaughan's ecstatic-alchemical one. For Browne, Platonist to the core, the Kiss of the Spouse is nothing we should count on in any immediate sense. It is consolation, figure, hope, and aspiration, rather than a matter of an earthly intercourse and fruition, or actually *making* the gold out of our very dross matter of bones and flesh. As much as he was intrigued by it, Browne left alchemy to others. For Vaughan's exigent and maybe desperate spirit, on the other hand, inventing its own heretic Cabala, much like Sabbatai Zevi's but requiring no following, such defferal and modesty would have been merest temporizing. His attitude toward the mystical traditions, unlike Browne's, were not so much that they were meant to reform and improve life's quality, while enabling us to hope for better things eventually, but instead that they call, existentially, for an instant and irrevocable decision of transformation. In Vaughan's imagination and example the most prophetic passages of the Bible were never meant merely as promise of things likely to be or as rewards for certain behavior and compromises, but options that are challenges and choices, like Kierkegaard's paradoxes of faith were to be, which allow for only one decision: "This is the *pitch* and *place*, to which if any man *ascends*, he enters into *Chariots of Fire* with *Horses of fire*, and is *translated* from the *earth*, *soul* and *body*. Such was *Enoch*, such was Elijah."[139]

Cabala and the Game of the King's Bishop

Within England we may note affinities between the Puritan Revolution of the seventeenth century and the apocalyptic-millenarian quality of Cabala of the Age of the Baroque. Significantly Jews come very close to being readmitted into the country during the commonwealth, when an important cabalist leader of Amsterdam, Manasseh ben Israel, was even Oliver Cromwell's guest in London. Later on, even after their own revolution had failed or had been *aufgehoben,* the Sabbatian episode was followed with intense interest in England. In Sabbatai's announced year of the "new creation,"with the compellingly demonic number of 1666, Michael McKeon counts no less than eight English tracts dealing with the matter.[140] That particular quality, according to McKeon, of Jewish thought, especially in its apocalyptic aspects, that attracted the English religious revolutionaries was its promise of a transcendent redemption that could be experienced in an immanent and imminent way: "Christian millenarianism has from the beginning been greatly indebted to the messianic idea in Jewish thought, for an essential premise of this idea is the expectation of a fully historical and terrestrial coming which is of course simultaneously infused with profound spiritual meaning."[141] Ironically, while Jewish materialism has often been decried from the Platonic-spiritual heights of Christian orthodoxy, that fugitive and paradoxical joining of Heaven and Earth could appear to Christian radicals and utopians to be something they could and should borrow from Jewish mystics. One more step and Jewish messianism, hiding behind its Christian garment may be seen as one of the sources for our heavenly orgies of Woodstock and Height-Ashbury. Norman Cohn, indeed, has regarded our own hallucenogenically generated utopias as being another "up-to-date version of that alternative route to the Millennium, the cult of the Free Spirit.[142] For the ideal of a total emancipation of the individual from society, even from external reality itself—the ideal, if one will, of self-divinization—which some nowadays try to realize with the help of psychedelic drugs, can be recognized already in that deviant form of medieval mysticism."[143]

Whether or not it may have been exactly credible, also, that Sabbatai's apocalyptic career as savior was inspired by millenarian and antinomian English Puritan merchants he listened to at his father's house in Smyrna, the wide dissemination of the anecdote in Rycaut's very popular account of the messiah's career in *Three Famous Impostors* grants it the kind of virtual reality of something that might as well have been true. John Evelyn's *History of the*

Three Late Famous Imposters (1669) included the unsigned account of the historian, Sir Paul Rycaut, who, as English consul in Smyrna, birthplace of Sabbatai, was present during the entire episode of the messianic career and apostasy. This narrative was later republished under his own name in Rycaut's *History of the Turkish Empire* (1680). As an indication of with what interest Rycaut's accounts were followed by someone who knew a bit about Cabala, I've come across three references to this book in letters by Sir Thomas Browne to his son, Edward, the former absolutely insisting the latter read it. Rycaut was fourth, also, on a list Browne made of "Books Read . . . The books which my daughter Elizabeth hath read unto me at nights till she read them all out."[144]

According to Fixler's *Milton and the Kingdoms of God*, it is likely Rycaut may have invented the story of the connection between the "false messiah" and the English merchants in order to discredit millenarianism in an age of incipient restoration;[145] however, I think it may be argued that the very feasibility of such a claim establishes in itself a homology between English and Jewish apocalyptic movements, both grounded in a similarly exilic and chiliastic mentality, one with unquestionably political implications.

Much the same might be mentioned about other points of relation and contact, for instance, a very close correlation that has been noted between the kind of temptations that Christ is offered and eschews in Milton's *Paradise Regained* and those to which the Sabbatai was lost. Henry Oldenburg, the important Secretary of the English Royal Society, who had written a letter to Spinoza asking his opinion as to the affair of Sabbatai, was also a friend and correspondant of Milton's and, in fact, had visited with him a number of times in London about the time that the poet was writing *Paradise Regained*. According to Michael Fixler the temptations that Christ is offered and eschews in that strange epic of renunciation and exile—that of earthly power and status, women (actually, Satan in the epic just considers tempting Jesus with sex, but drops the idea), and messianic fame—are strangely identical with the "negative examples" set by Sabbatai. Fixler's notion is that Milton of this time, who had given up on the sublime hope for the coming, in any number sufficient to make a real difference, of a new man that would have gone along with the coming new kingdom, had taken a solitary path to salvation, that of unorthodoxy, introspection, and solitude, from which he was not to be lured by messianic-redemptive illusions, essentially demonic in provenance.[146] Also, the sexual "revolution within the revolution" as carried out by some passionate Diggers, Ranters, and Levelers among the English reformers, coincides equally with the practices of Sabbatai, who married a woman known for her license, and some of whose eighteenth-century and later Frankist followers lived together in varieties of group marriage, "holy" adultery, and incest. One may also find in the tracts of the English seventeenth-century antinomians, along with declamations of revelations of their own divinity, many autobiographical allusions to casual or adulterous sex, and general fooling around by radicals like Laurence Clarkson and Abiezer Coppe. These seemed to have often taken themselves for Greek gods on the loose, but were never short of female worshipers to indulge, humor, or otherwise participate in their divine exemption from supposedly no longer pertinent, or even existent, moral codes.[147]

Cabala, however, was larger that any particular faith or ideology, whether a conservative, radical, or syncretic (liberal) one. We may expect to find it on the insurrectionary side of the revolutionary barricades, but it was also useful at one time in the camp of the English King. Lancelot Andrewes,[148] for instance, who chaired the committee that translated the King James Bible and was one of the most important and most popular preachers of his time, was deeply imbued with the methods of cabalistic exegesis as well as much of the spirit of Cabala. Andrewes was multilingual to a degree that seems positively amazing, an attribute that applied, to some degree at least, as well to his listeners. Principally he carries his sermons on in four languages; in order of frequency, after English, Latin is spoken quite matter of factly, while *Hebrew* was next, more important even than the Greek, which he sometimes invokes. Andrewes's is a word-centered style of discourse, often whole sermons centering on arcane and erudite dissections and explications of all that hinges on a single syllable or letter, or on the merest shift of tense or voice that explains and confirms everything.

In the following passage, for example, Andrewes extrapolates vertiginously on the basis of a line from Psalms a prophecy of Christ's coming, "Filius Meus Tu, hoide genui est [Thou art My son, this day have I begotten thee]." This approach is, of course, quite orthodox as typology, that is the science of elucidating New Testament intimations from antecedent scripture. Yet his style of exposition seems also fully in continuity with Pico's awesome and controversial beginning statement that launched a theological movement, "There is no better proof of Christ's divinity than Cabala." Certainly the magical flights Andrewes is able to manage are thoroughly consistent with a letter and word-oriented approach as disseminated by the great Christian cabalists of the sixteenth century: the Ricius brothers, Reuchlin, and Agrippa. Here the pretext of Andrewes's far-ranging imaginations is the merest contrast in tense of a few words—between the "now" of "hodie" and the "past" of "genui est":

> There be that, because *hodie*, the present, is yet in *fieri*, and so not come to be perfect, understand by it His temporal generation as Man which is the less perfect, as subject to the manifold imperfections of our human nature and condition. And then by *genui*, which is in *factum esse*, and so done and perfect, understand His eternal generation as the Son of God, in Whom are absolutely all the perfections of the Deity.
>
> There be other, and they fly a higher pitch and are of a contrary mind, for whatsoever is past is in time say they, and so *genui* is temporal; and that *hodie*. Why? For there all is *hodie*; there is neither *heri* nor *cras*, no "yesterday" nor "tomorrow." All is "today," there. Nothing past, nothing to come—all present. Present as it were in one instant or centre, so in the *hodie* of eternity. "Past and to come" argue some, but if it be eternal, it is neither; all there is present. "To-day" then sets forth eternity best, say they, which is still present, and in being. But *genui*, that being past, cannot be His eternal at any hand, but must needs stand for His temporal.
>
> But whether of these it be: *genui*, His eternal as perfect, and *hodie*, as not yet perfect, His temporal; or *vica-versa*, *hodie* represents eternity best, and *genui* time, as being spent and gone; between them both, one way or another, they will show his begettings. You may weave *hodie* with *genui*, or *genui* with *hodie*, and between them both they will make up the two natures of Him That was the *hoide genitus* of this day. Concerning whom we believe; as first, that He is one entire person

and subsists by Himself, so second, that He consists of two distinct natures, eternal and temporal. The one as perfect God, the other as perfect Man.[149]

If the now of eternity and the past of time are separate and distinct words and concepts at the beginning of the analysis, as it develops they become closer, finally to be joined in a single phrase, echoing the psalmist, with which it concludes. Hereby Andrewes conciliates, according to a linguistic-cabalistic logic, a familiar eschatological paradox that much later Kierkegaard, more suspicious surely of "the word," had to leap—namely the fitting of the timelessness of Christ's appearance into a time that logically "has no place for Him."

Andrewes's manner of lengthy pyrotechnical exposition of the minutest alphabetical details, whether he learned it directly or indirectly from The Zohar or other cabalistic writings is zoharic to the limit, almost to the point of parody. Certainly reminiscent, for example, of the dazzling and vertiginous complexity of suggestion Cabala will find[150] in the merest stroke of a letter, point, or accent, is the microscopic intensity, for instance, of his gaze into the world of the meaning that separates the "insufflavit [breathed into]," in a text from John from a prior "sufflavit [breathed]": "It is first *sufflavit*, 'breathed,' and that was to keep correspondance with His Father, at the first. By breathing into Adam, the Father gave the soul, the Author of the life natural. *Ad idem exemplum*, the Son here by breathing gives the Holy Ghost, the Author of the life spiritual; the same passage, and the same ceremony held by both. But *insufflavit* is more, 'breathed it in,' 'into them.' This shows it pertains within, to the inward parts, to the very conscience, this act. His breath goeth, saith Solomon, *ad interiora ventris*, and His word with it, saith the Apostle, 'Through to the division of the soul and the spirit.' "[151] Words for Andrewes as for Cabala are living and procreative entities, whose speakers, as if taken in a divine blast of wind, are transformed and transforming beings. This sense of the holiness and energy of the spoken, voiced, and vocalized infuse his prose with a quality of imminent anticipation and uncanny event that recalls also a certain dialogical imagination of The Zohar.

Since The Zohar is many things but it is not too funny, a difference between the spirit of Cabala and Andrewes might be the latter's often very ingenious turn of phrase or thought, whereby the notion or aspect is so original as to draw attention to itself, and even, if grotesquely, amuse. This is his metaphysical wit, rediscovered for our own time by T. S. Eliot, whereby Andrewes can never resist a good pun. Thus breaking *Immanuel* down to its component meanings in Hebrew: Imm = with; anu = us; El = God, Andrewes proceeds to demonstrate the significance of these syllables with his hilarious pun offering the grim alternative between a choice for God or Satan: "If it be not Immanu-*El*, it will be Immanu-*Hell*."[152] Possibly none of Andrewes's games with words would captivate us less today than the one that the one he likes to play in his Sermons on Lent, as having been "lent" to us by God.

Hebrew itself invades Andrewes' is text very frequently, and I think ineluctably with the cabalistic intimations of secret, magical knowledge and power the study of that "sacred language" conveyed in the Renaissance. Andrewes likes to deploy his Hebrew to support his word and letter-focused arguments especially at places where it might not be so apparent that English is saying the same thing. What will happen next is that the meaning of the word in Hebrew is grafted live onto the English word, which is returned to us more meaningfully, and even politically [since sermons were often the "broadcast news" of the time]. If, for example, the Hebrew equivalent for the "compassion" also denotes "bowels" in the original, this meaning, for Andrewes would take precedence over the one we have assigned it in English:

> The word, which here is turned "compassions," in very deed (in Hebrew) properly signifieth "bowels" . . . These are the choice: for, of all parts, the bowels melt, relent, yield, yearn soonest. Consequently, the mercies from them, of all the other, the most tender, and, as I may say, the mercies most merciful. The best, 1. both because they are not dry, but full of affection, and come cheerfull (an easy matter to discern between a dry mercy, and a mercy from the bowels). 2. And because to mercy one may be inclined by somewhat from without; when that fails, where are we then? But the bowels are within Him, and when we have brought the cause within Him we are safe. *Quando causam sumit de Se et visceribus Suis*, that Mercy is best and yieldeth the best comfort.

But in this word of the Prophet's there is yet more than "bowels." *Mayim* were enough for them: *rachmayim* are more; are the bowels or the vessels near the womb, near the loin: in a word, not *viscera* only, but *parentum* viscera, the bowels of a father and mother, those are *rachmayim* , which adds more force a great deal.

And mention of this word is not unfit, whether we regard them (our enemies) *per quo itum est in viscera terrae* (in which place, God's bowels turned against them and toward us [Gunpowder Plot]), or whether we think, that His bowels had pity on our so many bowels, as should have flown about, all the air over, and light, some in the streets, some in the river, some beyond it, some I know not where.[153]

Andrewes's approach is cabalistic not only on the level of the (here scatalogical) extravagance of what he makes words do and the loads he makes letters carry, shifting them from profane to sacred shoulders and guts and back again at will. This fact alone, given the eminence of the preacher, would say much also about the penetration of cabalistic mentality in the period. For this is not just a foreign congregation, as was that of Henoch Clapham, cabalist *(malgré lui)* leader of an English congregation in the tolerant city of heretics, Amsterdam, but certainly one of the highest churchmen of the time and speaking from a most revered place, and in London, to an audience that would, presumably have regarding such reasoning as convincing.

Andrewes's general framework of ideas, even apart from his zoharic exegetical style, seems equally to be tinged with Cabala, or at least to depend on it in some meaningful ways. For instance, in explicating a moving little portion from the Gospel of John, Andrewes relies totally on a tradition, very reminiscent of the cabalistic one, whereby *hearing*, before vision, is the sense of faith.[154] That "tradition," which Cabala first of all signifies, in fact implies that not everything may be *inscribed*. The auditory organ, hierographical in its very shape (the "c," like the "kaph" in Hebrew, looks like an ear) is easily identifiable with Cabala, whose etymological provenance is *cabal* in Hebrew, one of whose meanings is "ear," while another is whatever is whispered there, questionable or even impossible to express out loud and publicly or to write: in short, the secret and oral tradition and mystery as *said* to Moses at the time of the Original Sinai Interview.

Cabal today, even in its profane and pejorative sense of "conspiracy" still retains this sense of audition, as of something whispered, *breathed* (from Latin *spiro*) with another. Andrewes begins his analysis by citing the text, which opens with Mary Magdalene, who has been weeping by the empty sepulchre because she thinks that the body of Christ has been stolen, significantly being *addressed* by two visiting Angels:

> *Woman, wy weepest thou? She said to them, They have taken*
> *away my Lord, and I know not where they have laid Him.*
> *When she had thus said, she turned herself about, and saw Jesus*
> *standing, and knew not that it was Jesus.*
> *Jesus saith to her, Woman why weepest thou? Whom seeketh thou?*
> *She supposing He had been the gardener, said to Him, Sir, if*
> *thou have borne Him hence, tell me where thou hast laid Him,*
> *and I will take Him thence.*
> *Jesus saith to her, Mary. She turned herself, and said to Him*
> *Rabboni, that is to say, Master.*

While it is evident that in the above what is spoken is more powerful than what is seen, it would appear to be, in itself, a slight basis for establishing that the ear as opposed to the eye is the organ of faith, unless the explicator is already rooted in a tradition according to which this is very much the case. Another paradigm, for instance a Kierkegaardian or Pascalian one, would regard as nugatory if not trivial, *how* Jesus appeared, focusing instead on the existential miracle of his being manifested at all, and on the leap believing it would require or presuppose. For Andrewes what the episode teaches, on the other hand, is a cabalistic lesson about the phenomenology and mystery of faith:

> All all this by a word of His mouth. Such power is there in every word of His; so easily are they called, whom Christ will but speak to.
> But by this we see, when He would be made known to her after His rising, He did choose to be made known by the ear rather than by the eye. By hearing rather than by appearing. Opens her ears first, and her eyes after. Her "eyes were holden"

till her ears were opened; comes aures autem aperuisti mihi [you opened, moreover, my ears], and that opens them.

With the philosophers, hearing is the sense of wisdom. With us, in divinity, it is the sense of faith. So, most meet. Christ is the Word; hearing then, that sense, is Christ's sense; *voce quam visu* [hearing rather than seeing], more proper to the word. So, *sicut audivimus* [so we hear] goes before, and then *sic vidimus* [so we saw] comes after. In matters of faith the ear goes first ever, and is of more use, and to be trusted before the eye.[155]

The breathless quality of the prose is not merely specific to the above but is eminently characteristic of Andrewes's style of composition and address, whereby he speaks to his auditory as if in a moment of passionate and emotional revelation and insight, voicing such truths as must have been conveyed to privileged prophets anciently. At such times one is in such throes one eschews grammar and sentence, gasping out fragments only, as in a "metaphysical" passage on the geography of Christ's body, reminiscent also of prezoharic and zoharic "heavenly anatomies": "This Temple of His body, the spirit from the flesh, the flesh from the blood was loosed quite. The roof of it, His Head, loosed with thorns, the foundation, His feet, with nails. The side aisles, as it were, His hands both, likewise. And His body as the body of the Temple, and with the spear loosed all."[156]

In another passage, where Andrewes is speaking in something like rapture of the difference between Christ's task and that of others who were accomplishing a divine mission, the quality of the style is such as to communicate rather the gaps between words, the silence of wonder that they summon, break, and to which they return: "For others, by Moses' example upon Jethro's advice and God's own allowance, may and do lay off and translate their burden, if it be too heavy, upon others, and so ease their part. Not so He. It could not be so in His. He, and He alone; He, and none but He; upon his own shoulders, and none but His own, bare He all. He 'trod the wine-press'; and bare the burden, *solus*, 'alone', et *vir de gentibus*, 'and all the nations, there was not a man with Him.': Upon His only shoulders did the burden only rest."[157]

Curiously for a figure who was so identified with royalist authority, Andrewes locates the organs of perceptions whereby we become aware of such mysteries as being *within* us. His prejudice against vision, even, involves merely a distancing from things as they reveal themselves externally, while thematic in his arguments are allusions to an *inner man* who knows better. If our own notions of interiority date from the Renaissance then Andrewes's text is a place where they appear explicitly and nakedly, as for instance in the following praise of inwardness, fortified and validated by Platonic and Hebrew precedent. Here, after discrediting the outward eyes, Andrewes finds himself wondering:

> Then, if not with his eyes, how? Yes; with his eyes too, though not of the body. Which to conceive, we are to take notice that there is in every man of us two men: (Plato had seen so much and set it down, and it is thought the Apostle took it from him;) 1. an outward, and 2. an inward man, we must allow him senses as a man; he must have eyes. So he hath; "having the eyes of your understanding lightened." Here are eyes; by them did Abraham, and even by them and by no other do we see Him.
>
> Those eyes many have besides, but see Him not for want of light. By what light saw he? He was a Prophet, and as a Prophet he might be in the Spirit and have the vision clearly represented before him, *in luce Prophetiae*. But without all question a "faithful" man he was, and so certain it is he saw it *in limine fidei*, "the light of faith," which "faith is the clearness or evidence of things not seen"; (ye know the place;) not seen—nay even of things invisible.[158]

This divided self of Andrewes's corresponds also to cabalistic separations whereby one's outer practice is merely a shield for an inner sincerity and conviction, quintessentially the style of the exile and Marrano. It is the particular quality of the Lurianic epoch in Cabala, as interpreted by Scholem, to see in this particular alienation of the Jews an image, figure, and symbol of the universal exile of humanity or of the human condition, as well as being a reflection of the predicament of the divine: "The Galut [exile] the Ari's Kabbalah saw as a terrible and pitiless state permeating and embittering all of Jewish life, but Galut was also the condition of the universe as a whole, even of the deity."[159] Andrewes's structural reliance on these categories of inner-outer, internal-external may represent, on the Christian cabalistic side, this Lurianic moment of a Marranization of the mainstream, as of some strange and estranged Society of Pariahs. This kind of mobile and mobilizing siege mentality would be appropriate for a time when all power and fixity is being challenged and threatened, prelude and overture to our own epoch of universal insecurity, when our place in society is based on factors (connected with the market, for instance) very largely beyond anyone's control. The escalation from a Lurianic to a Sabbatian consciousness would be in a shift from a descriptive to an imperative or hortatory mode, from the concept that all things are covered and disguised to an insistence that all that is true and real *must* show a lying face to the world: the "real" Jew must convert externally to another religion, and commit all the other sins, especially the sexual ones, that the Decalogue specifically warns against. Neither, of course, should real Christians, Jews, and cabalists in this way, be judged (only or mainly) by their actions or by the faces they are forced to show the world.

In any event, Andrewes's appeal to a hidden and secret dimension where only the truth is accessible is thoroughly cabalistic, and not the less so for the explicit allusions, firstly, to an "ancient theology" that connects Christianity to a prophetic pagan wisdom and, secondly, to the intuitive apprehensions of Abraham whose rejection of "idols that have eyes and see not" was one of the founding notions of Judaism. A *critical difference*, however, is Andrewes's locating the whereabouts of this hidden wisdom and exigent Cabala not in any sefirotic externalization, ecclesiastical, theosophical, or political system, or even any actual *cross*, but rather in the mind, instincts and especially intuitions of the individual. Such a mystical approach, in Andrewes's case, supports his conservative and loyalist agenda: We are to obey King James, in spite of what we see or what he's really saying, because we hear, *within* us, his voice, divinely a categorical imperative because of what is speaking through him. This Cabala, or hidden rule beyond all appearance, worked, however, as or more effectively, eventually in the Revolutionary Puritan opposition, as well as on its antinomian margins, with a slight but crucial modification whereby *the voice within us* would enjoin and compel rather insurrection than submission to hierarchy. If the inner man is higher than the outer one, whatever he says is more to be trusted than anything and anyone. Should he, as was bound to be the case, someday change his mind, all Hell would break loose. It might even appear self-evident that women have voices in them that need to be listened to. Eventually scripture itself, along with royalty, educational and cultural privilege and status, states, property, sexual and marital relations were to be put into question by people who began rather to believe in the Idea that lived and spoke within them than in the deceiving screens they merely saw in Its way.

Notes

Preface

1. Thorndike, *History of Magic and Experimental Science* (henceforward, *HM*), VI, 457, paraphrasing *Monas Hieroglyphica*, where Dee's exact text was: "Raising toward heaven our cabbalistic eyes (that have been illuminated by speculation in the mysteries), we shall behold an anatomy precisely corresponding to our monad" (Dee, 175). Noun, adjective, and adverbial permutations of the word Cabala occur throughout Dee's text, with approximately the validating force we might accord to the word *logical*.

2. The mysterious, nomadic ("female Rimbaud"), Russian-French Arabophile and convert to Islam, Isabelle Eberhardt (1877–1904) would relate, strictly speaking, rather to Sufism than Cabala. These have been, however, as Moshe Idel has brought out in his analyses of the Eastern inspiration of Abraham Abulafia's thirteenth-century meditative Cabala, often contiguous, sometimes even interchangeable discourses.

3. Cf. Yates, *The Occult Philosophy*; also French, Calder, in Bibliography.

4. *HM*,VI, 26.

Chapter One. *In the Beginning*

1. Scholem, *Major Trends*, 156–243.

2. That the question of who wrote the book continues to annoy is shown by Isaiah Tishby's irritated comment, in *The Wisdom of The Zohar: An Anthology of Texts*, on what seems like an otherwise valuable recent translation of The Zohar into Hebrew, the *Nizozei Zohar*, whose editor and commen-

tator, Reuben Margaliot, after having been praised for the parallels he "draws with the writings of medieval scholars," nevertheless "spoils everything by trying to show that these parallels point to an early date for the composition of The Zohar" (*The Wisdom of The Zohar*, I, 105). J. Abelson, editor of the standard English translation of The Zohar, which was published in 1933, had no doubts as to the work's antiquity ("Introduction," vol.1, xiii). An adroit middle position is occupied recently by Yehuda Liebes, who, in his *Studies in The Zohar*, affirms that de Leon, who identified with the messianism of his narrator, R. Simeon, was merely foremost among a mystical (discourse) community that "generated" The Zohar. As implied also by Liebes in "How The Zohar Was Written" (*Studies*, 85–138), what is still in question is no longer whether the work is of ancient or medieval provenance but whether in fact it should be mainly or mostly attributed to Moses de Leon.

3. Scholem, *Sabbatai Sevi: the Mystical Messiah*; but also passim in Scholem's work.

4. The provenance of The Zohar, and a fortiori, earlier cabalist texts, strictly speaking, is the late Middle Ages, but the wider dissemination and impact of Cabala, after the exile from Spain, definitive by 1492, was in the Renaissance.

5. *Les Grands textes de la Cabale: les rites qui font dieu.*

6. *Kabbalah*, 10–16, which I have been paraphrasing and citing.

7. An account, together with a bibliography of the challenges to Scholem's gnostic interpretation of Cabala, as well as the way he understands Gnosticism, is to be found in Michael Lieb's *The Visionary Mode*, 46, 104, 173ff., with bibliographical note.

8. In *The Strong Light of the Canonical*, Harold Bloom finds Freud and Scholem share a common project of reinvention of their traditions. David Bakan, in *Freud and the Jewish Mystical Tradition*, explores a possibility that Freud was influenced by cabalistic ideas (specifically from The Zohar), having been exposed to them in much the same way as Grözinger and Ripellino (see Bibliography) later were to opine Kafka was, through the proximity of Eastern European Jewry.

9. *Major Trends*, 190.

10. Tishby, I, 49–50.

11. In Ramon Martin's *Pugio fidei* (Sword of Faith) of the middle of the thirteenth century, a text that was articulate enough to stay in circulation for four centuries, Christian Cabala is very much a weapon in the wars of conversion. Duns Scotus and Raymund Lull, however, both flourishing in the early fourteenth century, may have been exceptions to this rule.

12. *Walter Benjamin*, 38.

13. Dan, *Gershom Scholem*, 313–26. According to Dan, for Scholem, (modern) Hasidism represents a (kind of) continuation, or popularization of Cabala, through a neutralization and suppression of its most radical and provocative elements; while, for Buber, Hasidism, with its antitheoretical bias, represents an outright rejection of the heritage of Cabala, thought to stand for eclectic and esoteric intellectualism and individualism.

14. Biale, *Gershom Scholem*, 81.

15. De Pauly considered himself an Angel Pope, following in the footsteps of the medieval inventor of this office, by self-appointment only, Joachim de Fiore, as well as those of an illustrious predecessor in zoharic translation, William Postel. De Pauly is commonly supposed to have translated interestingly but very unreliably and even to have made up a few stories. Nevertheless his Zohar was the one that impacted very heavily on the French Surrealist generation of the twenties and thirties, who would not have minded, doubtless, or would even have appreciated, his extravagance or duplicity.

16. Mopsik's translation is now up to four massive volumes, in addition to, in a separate volume, the intriguing zoharic commentary on the Book of Ruth, the very important *Midrash Ha-Neelam*, distinguished in Scholem's inventory by the name "mystical midrash" and not included in Sperling-Simon translation.

17. Excerpts from and references to The Zohar, unless otherwise noted, are to the five-volume edition (Soncino), translated by Maurice Simon and Harry Sperling, of 1933. Those who want to consult The Zohar in the Hebrew-Aramaic text as first published in the Mantua-Cremona edition of 1558 will find the folio references on the pages of this translation.

18. The Bahir, cited by Scholem, *The Origins of the Kabbalah*, 149.

19. Scholem, paraphrasing Isaac the Blind, *The Origins of the Kabbalah*, 198.

20. Ibid, 327.

21. A level of meaning that is still current, as in the context of Rudolf Otto's *The Idea of the Holy*: "The *Shekinah* is properly the *haunting presence* of Yahweh in The Temple of Jerusalem" (127n.).

22. *The Hebrew Goddess*, 79.

23. *The Essence of Judaism*, 89.

24. *Zohar I*, 324–25.

25. For a brilliant comparative analysis of Ramanuja and Sankara, see George Thibaut's comprehensive introduction to his translation of the *Vedanta Sutras of Badarayana, with Sankara's Commentary*. For a compelling existential-phenomenological analysis of transcendence as *secret*, immanence as *revelation*, cf. Lévinas, "Un Dieu homme," *Entre nous*, 69–76.

26. *The Hebrew Goddess*, 150–51; and especially "Kabbala and Hinduism," *The Jewish Mind*, 134–51.

27. *The Hebrew Goddess*, 90.

28. *Zohar I*, 329.

29. Nohrnberg, 30.

30. *Zohar, the Book of Splendour*, 10–11. My emphasis.

31. The translator mentions in a note that text is repeating a passage from earlier in The Zohar, so something is being omitted: eliminating and interpolating are of course in the great tradition of zoharic editing.

32. "Deux Modèles d'écriture: Essai sur le rapport entre ordre et liberté," *Revue Philosophique* 16 (1982): 483–86.

33. *Island*, 347–356.

34. Marie-Christine Leclerc, "Fouilles dans les ruines circulaires," *Critique* 555–56 (1993): 530.

35. Karl Erich Grözinger, *Kafka and Kaballah*: Angelo Maria Ripellino, *Magic Prague*.

36. See especially "Tailor's Dummies," in *The Street of Crocodiles*, 51–71.

37. *Sabbath's Theater*, 357, 402.

38. *Kabbalah*, 236.

39. Cf. "The Fragmentary Word of Maurice Blanchot," in my *I Am a Process with No Subject*, 94–122; and passim.

40. *L'Entretien infini*, 630, translation mine.

41. *Kabbalah*, 227.

42. Cf. Cynthia Ozick, "The Consensus That Plagues Israel."

43. *Kabbalah*, 26.

44. My personal experience, based on an abruptly ended conversation after browsing through some editions of The Zohar, all of which listed ben Yohai as the author, at a "Cabala Booth" at a bookfair.

45. Dan, *Jewish Mysticism and Jewish Ethics*, 94.

46. Scholem, *Zohar*, 32. Emmanuel Lévinas, characteristically, interprets this face to face sexual posture phenomenologically rather than mystically, that is, as an example of the essential humanity of the Jewish tradition, according to which, even in the throes of congress, the partners do not lose sight of the person and personality, "visage" (place, also, par excellence, of the miracle some have found in Christ, of *transcendent immanence*), of the other (*Difficile Liberté*, 55–56; cf. also *Entre Nous*, 102).

47. Cf. Mopsik's translation and commentary on the prezoharic *Lettre sur la sainteté: Le secret de la relation entre l'homme et la femme dans la Cabbale*, published together with Idel's essay, "Métaphores et pratiques sexuelles dans la Cabballe."

48. *The Mystic Fable*, 299—last words of the book.

49. Werblowsky, *Joseph Karo*, 263.

50. Scholem's "Hasidism, the Latest Phase," *Major Trends*, 325–50; "The Neutralization of the Messianic Element in Early Hasidism," *The Messianic Idea*, 176–201.

51. *Les Deux sources*, 1192; my trans.

52. Rosenzweig, 171.

53. *Zohar III*, 285.

54. *The Mystic Fable*, 303.

55. Idel, *Kaballah*, 5–6.

56. Agrippa's feminist numerology is commented by Blau, *The Christian Cabala* (henceforward, *CC*), 82. *Female Preeminence* has been reprinted recently in the anthology Diane Bornstein edited, *The Feminist Controversies of the Renaissance*. Agrippa's ingenious zoharic gender mathematics, long ago, become somewhat of a commonplace. For instance, it was cited prominently by Judge William, one of Kierkegaard's invented authors in *Stages on Life's Way*, 126–27, pleading for more respect for women than Kierkegaard's "seducer" authors accorded.

57. From "Sancta Maria Dolorum," in *Crashaw*: 180–81.

58. Tishby, I, *Wisdom of The Zohar*, 395–96; also Werblowsky, *Joseph Karo*, 216, who comments on the proximity, even identity, of the sphere of the Shekina to that of the demonic.

59. "Samael, Lilith," 22; Lilith's sway is in this world, so only preapocalypse.

60. I have been paraphrasing *The Wisdom of the Kaballah* reprint of selected portions of Mather's translation of Von Rosenroth's 1677 Latin anthology, which includes the important *Greater Assembly* "anatomy of God" chapter of The Zohar, entirely omitted from the Soncino edition.

61. *Zohar IV*, 334.

62. *Ethics*, Part II, Prop. II, end of note.

63. *Joseph Karo*, 130–34.

64. *The Holy Kaballah*, 377–405.

65. *Literature and the Occult Tradition*, 94–122.

66. *Fire*, 116. She mentions Saurat explicitly (127), so when she talks in these exalted pages, penned in Paris in the thirties, about "reading her Cabala" (283, 289), she's surely referring to the version he used, de Pauly's Zohar, the one consulted by the Surrealist generation (Gilbert LeComte, Artaud).

67. *Major Trends*, 228.

68. Tishby, I, 434.

69. *Joseph Karo*, 225–26.

70. Ibid, 134–38, for citations since last note.

71. *On the Mystical Shape of the Godhead*, 184 and 298n.

72. *Standing Again at Sinai*, 138–39. For a less polemical, but similarly "progressive" Cabala, see also David S. Ariel, "The Shekinah: The Feminine Aspect of God," *The Mystic Quest*: 89–109.

73. Peter Steinfels, "Presbyterians Try to Resolve Long Dispute," *New York Times* 17 June 1994, A24; and "MacNeil-Lehrer Report," *PBS* 16 June 1994.

74. *The Shorter Poems of Edmund Spenser*, 746n. (editor's note to poem).

75. *Literature and the Occult Tradition*, 222–37.

76. Mopsik and others (certainly Idel), whom I think of as "ecstatics," would view this as a misconception, fostered by philosophically oriented (Cartesian-Hegelian) scholars such as Scholem, who, true to their Platonic tradition, would privilege too much the mind over the body.

77. *Joseph Karo*, 47, 82, 118, 264.

78. Cf. Bradbrook, *The School of Night*; Yates, *The Occult Philosophy in the Elizabethan Age*.

79. For the Sufi link, very important in the "meditative" Cabala of de Leon's nomadic contemporary, Abraham Abulafia, which was also to play its part in the Safed "Renaissance," cf. Moshe Idel, *Studies in Ecstatic Cabala.*

80. This unusual line seems tied up with Cabala. It descends in the late Middle Ages, from Joachim de Flores, whose concept of World Cycles has been related to cabalistic notions of the succession of created worlds (*shemittoth*); then in the Renaissance it devolves upon the important Christian cabalist Galantino, to pass to the translator of The Zohar and *Sefer Yetzirah*, Postel; after which it touches on modern times in the person of Jean de Pauly, the first to render The Zohar comprehensively into any vernacular. Cf. n.15, above.

81. Idel, "Was Abraham Abulafia Influenced by the Cathars?" *Studies in Ecstatic Kaballah*, 33–44; Scholem, *The Origins of the Kaballah*, 197–98, 234–38, 463–65.

82. Reeves, *The Influence of Prophecy in the Later Middle Ages*, 271, 442.

83. Scholem, *Zohar*, 30; my emphasis.

84. *The Medieval Manichee.*

85. *New Light on the Renaissance*, 99.

86. *The Medieval Manichee*, 179.

87. *Stages* 554—comment from Kierkegaard's *Papiren*, in appendix to "In Vino Veritas."

88. This may be confirmed to be typical in Kierkegaard's Hegelian (in this respect) thought by consulting the topic "Jews" in the *Journals*, in the thematic Princeton edition.

89. De Certeau, *La Faiblesse de croire*, 120–21; trans. mine.

90. Thanks to Michael Stern, for pointing this out to me.

91. *L'Extase et l'errance*, 140; trans. mine.

92. *Musiques, Variations sur la pensée juive*, 58, 60–61. Coincidentally, de Certeau, in *Mystic Fable* interprets Abraham's leaving home similarly as a prototype for characteristically mystic nomadism (129—"leave your country"—the mystic's first commandment). Cf. also *Zohar I*, 271–333, for an extended commentary, "Lech Lecha" (God's words, enjoining the departure), on the symbolism of Abraham's voyage, as it develops in Genesis XII–XVII.

93. *L'Idole et la distance*, where the recrimination is thematic.

94. *Kabbalah*, 247.

95. *Mille Plateaux*, 9–37.

96. Ibid, 51, and passim.

97. The notion of a circle or community-generated Zohar is very much the gist of Liebes's *Studies in The Zohar*. See n.2 above.

98. Dan, *Gershom Scholem*, 155–56.

99. *On the Kaballah and Its Symbolism*, 30–31.

100. Citations from last paragraph from Scholem, *Zohar*, 89, 83, 121.

101. *Studies in Ecstatic Kabbalah*, 140. The Cabala of Abulafia, with connections to Sufism, as opposed to that of de Leon's, with which it is contemporary, is comparatively less text and discourse-oriented and correspondingly more a matter of meditative practice.

102. *Theodicy*, 348.

Chapter Two. *The Secret of Agrippa*

1. Blau, *CC*, 1–17.

2. *CC*, 25; Thorndike, *HM*, IV, 497 ff.

3. *The Holy Kabbalah* (henceforward *HK*).

4. *The Garden of Cyrus*, in *The Prose of Sir Thomas Browne*, 339–40.

5. Cf. also Vigée, *L'extase et l'errance*, 85–100, for a more cabalistic presentation of these "two aspects of God," as opposed to Lévinas's talmudic-existential one (*Entre Nous*, 261). That the two are one is a basic tenet of Cabala, a point that Vigée makes much of in his defense of *voice* in literary creativity against deconstructive textuality.

6. "Kabbala and Hinduism," *The Jewish Mind*, 134–51.

7. Blau, *CC*: 41–64. Reuchlin was eight years older, nevertheless it was the precocious Pico who initiated him into the mysteries of Cabala, when the former was on a visit to Florence.

8. Blau, *CC*: 7–8.

9. Meres, *God's Arithmetic* (1597), *passim*.

10. Fowler, *Spenser and the Numbers of Time*, 6–7.

11. Each of the projected twelve books of the epic (six were completed) was to correspond to a different virtue from Aristotle's *Ethics* (104, where you find a list of twelve, including Temperance, yet look in vain for Holiness), but Spenser adds a Pythagorean-numerological-cabalistic dimension to them.

12. "The Orders of Simulacra," *Simulations*; cf. especially 135–36, on the reality-assaulting effects of the *twin* towers of the World Trade Center in New York City, each making the other virtual.

13. Fowler, passim in *Spenser*.

14. Cited to by Fowler, *Spenser*, 247.

15. De Certeau, *Mystic Fable*, 168–69.

16. *Remains* (1614), 169; second emphasis mine.

17. *HK*, 458.

18. *Psychology and Alchemy*.

19. *CC*, 51. Blau is paraphrasing Reuchlin, and echoing the Abbot Tritheim.

20. *CC*, 121–44; 89.

21. *CC*, 78–88; Waite, *HK*, 452–55.

22. *Occult Philosophy*, 218.

23. *Agrippa and the Crisis of Renaissance Thought*.

24. De Certeau, *La Possession de Loudun*: 242; *l'Écriture de l'histoire*: 269; these incidents are the subject of two motion pictures, as well as of Aldous Huxley's book, *The Devils of Loudun*.

25. *Vanity*, 4.

26. *Vanity*, 5, for previous quote; 4–5, for this one. Emphasis Agrippa's or translator's.

27. *Le Masque et la lumière*, 180; 178. Trans. mine.

28. Ibid, 264–65. Second square brackets mine.

29. *Vanity*: 125.

30. Ibid, 342.

31. "We found the abundant scholar Cornelius Agrippa. At that time he bare the fame to be the greatest conjurer in Christendom" (Nashe, 297).

32. Nashe, 277–86.

33. Ibid, 286.

34. *Vanity*: 355, 360. Emphasis and square brackets mine. For Agrippa's anabaptist scorn of authority, see Zambelli, "Magic and Radical Reformation in Agrippa"; coincidentally, Paracelsus was also somewhat of a fellow traveler too, supporting the German Peasant Revolt (Williams, 81).

35. Scholem, *Major Trends*: 161.

36. Birnbaum, *The Life and Sayings of the Baal Shem.*

37. *Sanitarium*, 64.

38. *Vanity*, 360.

39. Nauert, 326n.

40. "Panurge Consults Herr Trippa," *Gargantua and Pantagruel*: 356–60.

41. *Doctor Faustus*: I.1, ll.109–16. Emphasis mine.

42. Shelley, 39.

43. Nauert, 195.

44. The amount of attention this "miracle" attracts seems disproportionate, indeed. Cf. *Doctor Faustus*: IV, 7, ll. 13–40.

45. *Errour on the Left Hand through Preposterous Zeale*, 48. Emphasis his, brackets mine. Errors on the left or right hand meant, from the point of view of Anglican centrism, anabaptist-atheist-anarchist-communist dissidence (left), or Catholic-conservative-Papist reaction (right). What was to be eschewed was extremism, either of reason or faith (which then becomes superstition). Interestingly it is reason that was leftist (sinister, as in Latin), and maybe still is. Cf. H. Schultz, 105.

46. Nauert, 118.

47. Ibid, 59n.

48. On Thenaud's unpublished cabalistic poem, see above, p. 79–80.

49. *Le Masque et la lumière*: 196, 265. Trans. and square brackets mine.

50. Cited by Nauert, 46.

51. *HK*, 452.

52. Ibid, 473–76.

53. Ernst Cassirer, *The Platonic Renaissance in England.*

54. Cf. Diane Bornstein's introduction to *Female Pre-Eminence.*

55. *CC*, 16.

56. *CC*, 96n.

57. Secret, *Le Zohar chez les kabbalistes chrétiens de la Renaissance* (henceforward, *ZK*), 14.

58. *Origins of the Kabbalah*, 49n.

59. Jean Bodin (1530–1596) was an anomalous, but immensely important and influential figure in European intellectual history of the sixteenth and seventeenth centuries. Though overtly Catholic, he manifested a deep affinity for Hebrew studies, and may even have considered himself a Jew.

60. *Major Trends*, 234.

61. Patai, "Philosophy: Faith and Arrogance," *Jewish Mind*, 126–34.

62. Spinoza was excommunicated by the *Jews* of Amsterdam, one of whom stabbed him to emphasize the point. The *Theological-Political* Treatise (1670), one of the few works Spinoza dared to publish in his lifetime, was put on the index by the *Catholics*.

63. *Concluding Unscientific Postscript*.

64. Cf. especially *Seduction* and *Fatal Strategies*.

65. *The Ethics*: Part I, Proposition XX; Part II, Proposition X.

66. *Major Trends*, 311; and for next quotation.

Chapter Three. *Bibliographica Kabbalistica*

1. *Agrippa*, 126.

2. Ibid, 48, where Scholem's *Major Trends*, 99–100, 144–45, is cited in support of concluding sentence.

3. *CC*, 18.

4. *Agrippa*, 122.

5. Ibid, 126.

6. *ZK*, 21.

7. *A History of Philosophy* (henceforward *HP*), I, 319.

8. *The Influence of Prophecy*, 442.

9. Secret, *ZK*, 27.

10. Ibid, 26n.; my translation from Secret, who cites in Latin.

11. Ibid, 29n.; my translations of titles, all from Latin, except Tasso's Italian.

12. *Origins*, 39ff.

13. *Major Trends*, 74.

14. *The Medieval Manichee.*

15. *Major Trends*, 214.

16. *HK*, 462.

17. Blau, *CC*: 19.

18. *HK*, 134.

19. *Major Trends*, 145.

20. *Artes cabalisticae.*

21. Frances Yates, *Giordano Bruno and the Hermetic Tradition.*

22. *Literature and the Occult Tradition*, 222–37.

23. Scholem, *Bibliographica Kabbalistica* (henceforward, *BK*), 118.

24. Marin Mersenne. *Questions on Genesis.* Cf. extended title in Bibliography, where Mersenne announces his opposition to the (by then) classical early sixteenth-century Christian (Franciscan) Cabala of Georgius, eventual source, according to Yates, of Cabala in the Elizabethan generation of Dee, Sidney and Spenser.

25. *Major Trends*, 283.

26. *Sabbatai Sevi*, 61–65.

27. There is of course no central authority of Cabala, as also there is no pope of Judaism. Zevi may have betrayed Judaism but not Cabala; in this sense he may be regarded as true a cabalist as anyone else (Luria, Cordovero, Baal Shem Tov, Nahman of Bratslav). It has been Scholem's genius, nerve, and effrontery to attach a nonpejorative "heretic," which others may regard as redundant, to Sabbatian Cabala.

28. *BK*, 68.

29. *History of the Jews* (henceforward *HJ*), IV, 423–76.

30. *CC*, 61.

31. *ZK*, 17–19.

32. Thorndike, *HM*, VI, 411.

33. Blau, *CC*, 87.

34. *The Mystic Fable*, 206–99.

35. *ZK*, 18.

36. Thorndike, *HM*, VII, 282.

37. Secret, *ZK*, 11, 26–27n.

38. "Structure as Prophecy," 55.

39. "The Diffusion of the Christian Interpretation of the Cabala in English Literature."

40. *Major Trends*, 252–53.

41. *ZK*, 23.

42. *HK*, 462n.

43. *CC*, 97n.

44. Ibid, 97.

45. Ibid, 89.

46. *ZK*, 10.

47. The whole of Riccio's handy digest is translated into English by Blau, *CC,* 65–72.

48. *HK*, 428–32.

49. *HJ*, IV, 481.

50. *CC*, 39; as cited by Blau, Montecuccolus leaves out the adjective *Hebrew* (which you find in Garzia's version), maybe not wanting to rub it in!

51. *BK*, 51.

52. *HM*,VII, 304.

53. *CC*, 28.

54. *HK*, xxviii (preface); square brackets mine.

55. Ibid, 428–32; Graetz, *HJ*, IV, 480–82.

56. *HK*, 430.

57. Ibid, 430–31.

58. *Milton and the Christian Tradition*, 62–63; Thorndike,*HM*, VII, 410–14.

59. *BK*, 156.

60. *ZK*, 11–13.

61. *HJ*, III, 621–22.

62. *HM*, VI, 463.

63. *The Mystic Fable*, 264.

64. *HM*, V, 660–61.

65. *HP*, II, 357, 403; Nicolson, *The Conway Letters*, 310–11.

66. *HM*,VII, 229. His son, Franciscus Mercurius, was later to invent a sign language for the deaf, based on the letters of the Hebrew alphabet.

67. Spector, 310–11; previous quote, Nicolson, *The Conway Letters*, 454; ibid 40–51, 318n., 309–22, 324, and passim for whole entry. Cf. also Cassirer, *Individual and Cosmos in Renaissance Philosophy*.

68. *HM*, VI, 430.

69. *The Mystic Fable*, 80.

70. *La Société de consommation*.

71. Scholem, *Kaballah*: 274ff.; Williams, 351ff. and passim for roots of libertinism in sixteenth-century Reformation (marginal) sects, which took Presdestination to mean "I can do no wrong."

72. *BK*, 53.

73. *The Spanish Christian Cabala*, 43–80.

74. According to Canetti's brilliant study, "Kafka's Other Trial," this same "impossible" symbolic role was one that Kafka "wrote" for women in his life, whom he rather played against each other in a tormenting, if creatively catalytic, dialectic of intimacy and distance.

75. Kermode, 47, 123, 144–45.

76. *Amerika*, xi.

77. *Magic Prague*.

78. *Kafka and Kaballah*.

79. Kahn, 86.

80. "Scholem: Unhistorical or Jewish Gnosticism," in *The Strong Light*, p. 56.

81. "Gershom Scholem's Ten Unhistorical Aphorisms on Kaballah," *Modern Critical Views*: 99–123.

82. Ibid, 101.

83. *Kabballah*, 236; Hercenberg; "Deux Modèles d'écriture"; and Rattray's "Les secousses transatlantiques du Grand Jeu," on the surrealist, R. G. Lecompte's obsession with The Zohar.

84. "Ten Unhistorical Aphorisms," 122–23.

85. See Fowler, in Bibliography, and for numerological school of critics generally, *Silent Poetry*, which he edited.

86. "Structure as Prophecy," 41.

87. *CC*, 36.

88. *Triumphal Forms*, 21.

89. Charles Bouillé (1470–1553), follower of the Neoplatonic natural philosophy, derived from Nicholas of Cusa, of the identification of the world with the essence of God.

90. Geralamo Cardano (1501–1576), Italian mathemetician, philosopher, and physician.

91. *HP*, II, 372; emphasis mine.

92. "The Greatness of Gershom Scholem," 147.

93. *Joyful Wisdom*, 233–34.

94. *CC*, 65–67.

95. *Triumphal Forms*, 155.

96, Swietlicki, 19–20.

97. *CC*, 32.

98. *ZK*, 11; see also extended title of Mersenne's work in Bibliography.

99. Thorndike, *HM*,VI, 499.

100. *CC*, 103–105.

101. *HM*, VI, 219.

102. *CC*, 87.

103. *HM*, VI, 430.

104. *CC*, 98.

105. *BK*, 152.

106. *HM*, VII, 84–85.

107. Ibid, 324.

108. *HP*, II, 373. This "interference in the course of Nature" would also be what could determine the doctor as (the acceptable) demonic.

109. *HM*,VI, 550–51.

110. *HP*, II, 373.

111. Walker, 72.

112. *HM*, VII, 274; emphasis mine.

113. Ibid,V, 649–50.

114. *BK*, 92.

115. Ibid, 40.

116. *ZK*, 14 and 14n., where Secret cites his own unpublished thesis on Duret (see Bibliography); exclamation point Secret's.

117. Union Catalogue, The Library Company, Philadelphia.

118. *HK*, 376.

119. For this fascinating mystical lineage, cf. Bibliography: Ansari, James, Miller, and Parkinson—all helpfully annotated in Spector.

120. *HM*,VII, 183–84.

121. Tishby, I, 402–406.

122. *BK*, 41; where Scholem wonders, however, how well Fludd, who thought *Zohar* was a rabbi, knew his Cabala.

123. Spector, 354, annotation of Joscelyn Godwin's *Athanasius Kircher*.

124. *HM*,VII, 567–68.

125. *HK*, 72–72n.

126. Ibid, 218.

127. *HM*,VI, 388–89.

128. Scholem, *Zohar*, 119–20.

129. *BK*, 96, for comments on both books of Lobkowitz.

130. *HP*, II, 355, 371, 406; also *BK*, 96.

131. *HM*, VII, 605.

132. *BK*, 152.

133. Recipes for this "medicine" descend from at least as far back as manuscripts attributed to Lull, which had "the property of curing infirmity of a month's duration in a day" (*HM*, IV, 58, VIII, 388; ibid, for next quote).

134. *HM*,VI, 525.

135. *BK*, 7.

136. Thorndike, *HM*, V, 124 (from chapter 7, entirely on Champier).

137. Ibid, 213 (from an inventory of publications connected with the Conjunction of 1524).

138. Ibid, 219; next quote, 218.

139. Ibid, 316; 315, for previous quote, both Thorndike's paraphrases.

140. Ibid, 635–39.

141. *BK*, 44.

142. *HM*,V, 262.

143. Ibid, VI, 537; end of citation is direct quote from Godelmann, emphasis mine.

144. Ibid, VII, 275.

145. Ibid, 323.

146. Ibid, VIII, 483; VII, 330, for next quote.

147. *BK*, 138.

148. *HM*, VIII, 414–15. Romain Gary's novel, *The Gasp* (1973) is weirdly about an attempt to garner the immense energy occult tradition has long attributed to our last breath of life.

149. Ibid, 272.

150. Ibid, VII, 330.

151. *BK*, 21; *HM*, VII, 17, 45.

152. *HM*, VII, 64.

153. VII, 477.

154. Ibid, VIII, 321.

155. Ibid, 561.

156. *BK*, 85.

157. Ibid, 64.

158. *HM*, VIII, 492.

159. *The Conway Letters*, 82 (for last quote), 400–401, 406, 408, 429, 431, and passim.

160. Ibid, 352; square brackets mine.

161. Ibid, 192n.

162. Ibid, 208n.

163. Ibid, 173, 323.

164. George Keith, from around 1670, frequented the Conway cabalists, attributing his earlier Quaker conversion to More's *Immortality of the Soul*, published in 1659 (More who mistrusted Quakers, who he thought were descended from the antinomian Family of Love of the sixteenth century, protested that he had been misread). Eventually Keith left the Quakers, seduced, Nicolson says, "when he came under the influence of More and Van Helmont—and of their cabbalism—at Ragley" (*Conway*, 341n.). Later, however, he wanted to make it very clear that he was *not* the author of *Two Hundred Queries*, going so far as to publish a pamphlet (see Bibliography), in Philadelphia, in 1692, which contains "Mr. Keith's denial of the accusation made 'by a certain person . . . for being the Author of a certain Book, called, *The Two Hundred Queries*' " (*Dict. Cat. of N.Y. Pub. Lib.*, p. 83).

165. *Kaballah*, 201ff.

166. *Two Hundred Questions*, 54.

167. Ibid, 66.

168. Ibid: 129, 153, 39—in topic order since last note.

169. Ibid, 153.

170. In zoharic Cabala, reincarnation would have been looked upon rather grudgingly, as a last recourse and punishment for the sin of dying childless (Liebes, 71), whereas for the later Lurianic Cabala it would be rather the reward of another chance to redeem creation.

Chapter Four. *Kiss of the Spouse*

1. Blau, *CC*, 34.

2. Ibid, 35.

3. Ibid, 63 (for previous paragraph also).

4. *Spiritual and Demonic Magic*, 219.

5. See also, "Cabala as Anathema," in previous chapter.

6. *The Occult Philosophy*, n.7, 205; generally on "cabalistic" Shakespeare: 29–36; 127–59, and her *Shakespeare's Last Plays*.

7. *Spiritual and Demonic Magic*, 112–19.

8. *The Occult Philosophy*, 129–30.

9. Ibid, 129.

10. See "Agrippa and His Shadow," in chapter 2, above.

11. STC 13858 and 13859 (revised edition of 1620), pp. Ccj, Cciij.

12. *CC*, 64.

13. Denis Saurat, *Literature and the Occult Tradition*, 163–237.

14. Yates, *The Occult Philosophy*, 104–105.

15. STC 3935.

16. *Giordano Bruno and the Hermetic Tradition*.

17. *Spiritual and Demonic Magic*, 69–70.

18. Ibid, 69, Walker citing Paul Kristeller on Lazzarelli and de Corigio.

19. For Thomas Vaughan as very much the *Agrippan* alchemist, see William Newman's "Thomas Vaughan as Interpreter of Agrippa von Nettesheim," who deals with the connection objectively (scientifically), neglecting, however, the dimension of the *scandal* of such an association. I'll return to Vaughan's "Agrippa complex" later in this chapter.

20. *HM*, VI, 529.

21. *The Occult Philosophy*, 64–72, 91–92. Yates relies for her interpretation of the Bodin-Agrippa-James-Dee-syndrome on Walker, *Spiritual and Demonic Magic*, 71–78.

22. *God's Arithmetic*, first few pages.

23. *Kafka and Kaballah*, 182, my emphasis. See also above, chapter 1, "The One and the Two Many."

24. On Clapham, see above, 92.

25. *Spiritual and Demonic Magic*, 42–50.

26. *The Revelation of St. John Revealed*, fol. 129.

27. Ibid, fol.166.

28. The merkabah, through John Milton's acquaintance probably with Henry More's *Cabalistic Conjectures* (1654), shows up as Christ's doomsday weapon chariot, deployed in Book VI, 1. 710ff., in *Paradise Lost* (1667), with which the legions of Satan are decimated; see J. F. Adamson's "Milton's Version of the War in Heaven."

29. See above, 139ff.

30. See "The Paradox of Secrecy," chapter 2, above.

31. *A New Document Concerning the Early Kaballah* (in Hebrew).

32. *Jewish Mysticism and Jewish Ethics*, 33.

33. This indeterminacy is compounded vertiginously and exponentially in the Hasidic notion, according to Schechter, of an " 'expanded' Torah . . . (which) comprised not only the Law, but also the contributions of later times expressing either the thoughts or the emotions of sincere men" (160–61).

34. See above, 27ff.

35. *Mountain Gloom and Mountain Glory*, 79.

36. See above, 61ff.

37. My *I Am a Process with No Subject*, 95ff.

38. 4th section of *Elohim-Triune*, 7th stanza.

39. HM, *VII*, 229.

40. *A Brief of the Bible*, 3, 14.

41. *An Abstract of Faith*, 12.

42. Ibid.

43. *Chronological Discourse*, 62.

44. Ibid, N3.

45. *Error on the Right Hand*, 48.

46. Graetz, V, 18–50.

47. Nashe, 276–86.

48. The phrase is Ernst Bloch's, cited by Scholem, who, by way of example, alludes to David Joris (d. 1556), a Dutch mystical-political revolutionary who had a mass following and an enormous impact. For an impeccably scholarly, comprehensive survey of the whole movement, together with its theological concomitants and cultural consequences, cf. Williams, *The Radical Reformation*.

49. Cohn, 157, 257ff., 268–70; Williams, 362ff.; deconstruction of Halloween my own.

50. *The Occult Philosophy*, 66; and n.14, 199, where she refers to Wallace Kirsopp, *The Family of Love in France*. Münzer, Joris and The Family of Love tend to become conflated, in a broad range of English Renaissance texts, from Thomas Nashe to Sir Thomas Browne and Henry More, as the paradigmatic bugaboo and warning of the consequences of extremism in religion.

51. *Cambridge Guide to English Literature.*

52. Jonas, 92–96.

53. *Microcosmos*, 231.

54. *Spiritual and Demonic Magic*, 201, where Walker cites an elaborate praise of magic Bacon published both in Latin and English.

55. Malcolm W Browne, "How Brain Waves Can Fly a Plane."

56. Edgar Wind, *Pagan Mysteries in the Renaissance*; Jean Seznec, *La Survivance des dieux antiques*, which, curiously, had appeared in English and Japanese translations long before its publication in French (1993).

57. For this moralization, especially of Ovid (a challenge for any ethical system, one that Marlowe and Shakespeare were eventually to defy in the naked Ovidian erotics of *Hero and Leander* and *Venus and Adonis*, respectively) in action a particularly good place to go is to John Gower's (Chaucer's contemporary) incessant invocations of them in his consummate, if somewhat strained epic summa of the allegorical style, *Confessio Amantis*. The modern *locus classicus* for this whole subject is still C. S. Lewis, *The Allegory of Love*.

58. *Twilight of the Idols*, 71–72.

59. Thomson, 10.

60. "Psychoanalysis and Its History," *Heterologies*, 14; n.34, 238.

61. See n.8, chapter 1.

62. *Kafka and Kabbalah*, 5.

63. A leitmotif of de Certeau's, *The Mystic Fable*, where see especially his essay on the seventeenth-century itinerant mystic, Jean Labadie, who passed ecstatically, memorably, and radically through religions and places, "Labadie the Nomad," 271–94. Cabalists, from Moses de Leon, Abraham Abulafia through to Agrippa, Nathan, and Zevi, were always great travelers, for whom there may have been a Holy Land but not one to stay in; while urgently restless and mercurial characters like the alchemist-cabalists John Dee and Thomas Vaughan may have been what Blake later was to call "mental travelers."

64. See above, 165.

65. Ingpen, 15.

66. See above, 218ff.

67. Ingpen, 16, 64–66.

68. The next three paragraphs follow closely Yates, *The Occult Philosophy* (and *Shakespeare's Last Plays*), and also Swietlicki, 32–34. I mean this less as a reading of Shakespeare than of John Dee and the Christian Cabala for which he (among many other things, of course) stands. There is a consensus, even among sceptics (of Yates), that Dee's "alchemy" is to be taken in the sense of a search for the gold within: "man, not metal is the subject of (Dee's) alchemical transmutations" (Josten, intro. to Dee's *Monas Hieroglyphica* 101).

69. Dee, 106, 84.

70. Clulee, 118.

71. Dee, 133–35; brackets Josten's, emphasis mine.

72. Cited, French, 38–39; trans. in brackets mine.

73. *Pseudodoxia Epidemica: or, Enquiries into Very Many Received Tenents and Commonly Presumed Truths.*

74. "Browne's Interest in Cabalism."

75. Zoharically, it was a willingness to "go down" (leave home) that awarded Abraham the medal or potion of paternity, the "h" that transformed him from a mere Abram.

76. 5x5=25. The 5 at the end represents the return to the 5 at the beginning, a circle or sphere that is a figure of eternity. As Browne mentions in the next sentence, 5 shares this kind of perfection with 6 ("hexameral" creation in 6 days) and 10 (Decalogue), comprising with the H occurring twice the four letters of the Hebrew Tetragrammaton, or *name* of God.

77. The allusion to Trismegistus is, of course, to Hermeticism. This passage in *not* coincidentally from chapter 5 of *The Garden of Cyrus* (*Prose*, 339–40). Cyrus suggests a mystical resonance also, for he was the King of Persia (550–529) who was supposed to have allowed the Jews to return home from their Babylonian exile and rebuild their temple. Cyrus's adventures, lessons, and ideas are the subject of the *bildungsroman* that is the baroque (seasoned with a heavy dose of reincarnation theory, à la F. M. Van Helmont), belated and probably final product of High Renaissance Cabala, *The Travels of Cyrus*, by Chevallier Ramsay (Andrew Mitchell), of 1705 (but symptomatically popular, since reprinted as late as 1795). Ramsay's odd (for an increasingly rational age) theories attracted some bemused attention later from David Hume, who enjoyed their originality but nevertheless placed them in the purgatory of "Impious Conceptions of the Divine" (chap. 13), in the niche of a note to the (discreetly posthumous) *Natural History of Religion* (1757).

78. *The Prose of Sir Thomas Browne*, 328.

79. *The Works of Sir Thomas Browne*, II, 401. Browne goes on to allow, hilariously, that, according to a Censorinus this may mean *not* that the Arcadians were here before there was a moon (as Ovid and Seneca thought) but before it entered into calculations of the calendar.

80. *The Prose of Sir Thomas Browne*, 21–22 (Part I, Sect. 16).

81. "God's indifference" is not *only* an elitist notion: "Praised . . . and hallowed be His holy Name . . . *though He transcends all our blessings, hymns, praises and exaltations that we may ever offer in this world*" ("Mourner's Kaddish," in current use, emphasis mine).

82. Dunn, 99.

83. *The Prose of Sir Thomas Browne*, 23 (Part I, Sect. 17).

84. Dunn,131.

85. Dunn, 86–88; 131–32.

86. On Browne and Witchcraft: Post, 16–19, who alludes to a case where Browne's "toleration" ironically led to an execution, because he testified that he thought that there might well be such a thing as sorcery; for Alchemy, the correspondence with Ashmole and Lilly, *Works*, IV, 291–98; for a Cabala of Plants, the whole design generally of *The Garden of Cyrus*.

87. *Works*, II, 495.

88. *The Strategy of Truth*, 60.

89. *The Prose of Sir Thomas Browne*, 20 (sect. 15).

90. *Sir Thomas Browne*, 204–23.

91. *Works*, II, 256; 297–303.

92. Ibid, 338–40

93. From "*Musaeum Clausum*, or *Bibliotheca Abscondita*: containing some remarkable books, antiquities, pictures, and rarities of several kinds, scarce or never seen by any man now living" (*Works*, III, 109–12).

94. Ibid,117–19.

95. Bakan intimates the compatability of Freudian interpretation with cabalistic hermeneutics in *Freud and the Jewish Mystical Tradition*.

96. Dunn's Cabala is pretty much conflated and deflated with other Renaissance heterodoxies, while missing, I think, also the sexual, political-apocalyptic, and transgressive qualities that made it such a catalytic force, especially in the later Renaissance.

97. *The Prose of Sir Thomas Browne*, 41–42 (Part I, Sect. 34).

98. Post, 64–66.

99. *Works*, II, 361.

100. See n.75, above.

101. *Milton's Rabbinical Readings*, 307.

102. *Milton's Semitic Studies*, 51n.

103. Ibid, 89. Lightfoot was an important collaborator in Brian Walton's monumental *Polygot Bible* (1657), published in ten languages and dialects—eight Semitic and two classical.

104. Bakan, 221–31.

105. "The Rules of Michel Leiris' Game," in my *I Am a Process*, 70–93.

106. Michel Random, "Méditations Sur le Grand Jeu."

107. For Lightfoot citations and allusions from p. 261: *Erubhim*, 20–23; 28.

108. *Journal*, 78. Some of the other names associated with Renaissance Cabala that recur in Leiris's journals are Paracelsus and Sir Thomas Browne. Of the latter he translated and published passages from *Religio Medici* and *Urn Burial* in the 1920s, which activity seemed to occupy in Leiris's notebooks a talismanic place, if not function. Leiris also reviewed very favorably, after citing Nerval, a French translation of Dee's Cabala-imbued *Hieroglyphical Monade* in *La Révolution Surréaliste* in 1927.

109. Luhrmann, "An Interpretation of the *Fama Fraternitas* with Respect to Dee's *Monas Hieroglyphica*," 1, 8.

110. Comenius, 164. This "practical certainty" is not shared by Luhrmann, who, in the article mentioned above, published in 1986, forty-four years later, does not mention Andreae.

111. *The Occult Philosophy*, 167.

112. e.g., passim: Regardie's *My Rosicrucian Adventure*; see "cabbala" and in index of *The Confessions of Aleister Crowley*, by the Rosicrucian rebel and everyone's astral bad boy.

113. *HK*, 469.

114. Scholem would agree; see n.122, chapter 3.

115. Scholem, *Major Trends*, 320.

116. Scholem, *BK*, 46.

117. See above, n.24, chapter 3.

118. *HM*, VII, 441–42.

119. *HK*, 481–82.

120. "usoient par ignorance, & par erreur, & y alloient à la bonne foy pensant bien faire: mais Agrippa en a usé, par impieté detestable: car il a esté toute sa vie le plus grand sorcier qui fut de son temps" (*Démonomanie*, cited in Walker, nn.174–75).

121. *The Occult Philosophy*, 91–92.

122. Walker, 86.

123 *Anthroposophia Theomagica*, 50.

124. I've come across this intimation twice, admittedly in obscure places: (1) J. R. Tuttin, writing in introduction to a little book that appeared in 1896, *Secular Poems by Henry Vaughan, Silurist: Including a Few Pieces by His Twin Brother Thomas, "Eugenius Phialethes"*; (2) Eva Martin, "Thomas Vaughan, Magician," *Fortnightly Review* (1924).

125. *Anthroposophia*, 52 (portrait of Agrippa); 54–56 (poem), which Tuttin reprinted, 60–62. Newman (n.19 above), in "Thomas Vaughan as Interpreter of Agrippa," mentions the poem, but takes no account of the scandal of Vaughan's proclaimed descent from the demonic Agrippa.

126. Numbering of the lines mine; "ramasle" in l.17, whatever it means, is spelled the same in both versions I consulted.

127. *HK*, 473–74. Waite was editor of Thomas Vaughan's *Complete Works* (1919).

128. See extended title of Vaughan's *Secrets Revealed* in Bibliography.

129. *HK*, 474–75.

130. *Anima Magica Abscondita*, 31.

131. *Anthroposophia*, 7.

132. *Anima Magica*, 28. Language as blunt as this would argue against Newman, who, in "Thomas Vaughan as Interpreter of Agrippa von Nettesheim," dismisses the notion of sexual mysticism in Vaughan as a theosophical fantasy of Waite's.

133. Vaughan parts here from Agrippa, who was apparently a partisan of the orthodox doctrine, very foreign to zoharic Cabala, that the "original sin" was *sexual*. See above, 93ff., where I opine, however, that Agrippa, in this respect, might have been being merely provocative.

134. *Anima Magica*, 13.

135. Ibid, 19.

136. Ibid, 27.

137. The trail of this episode can be followed through entries under "Vaughan" in Conway, *The Conway Letters*.

138. *Works*, IV, 293; emphasis mine: projection=making gold.

139. *Anima Magica*, 41.

140. "Sabbatai Sevi in England."

141. Ibid, 167.

142. The Cult of the Free Spirit is a tradition of religious antinomianism and heterodoxy, which Cohn traces back to twelfth-century Joachimite prophecies up through a seventeenth-century English avatar of Levellers, Ranters, and Fifth Monarchists.

143. Cohn, 286.

144. *Works*, IV, 140, 145, 148; III, 331.

145. Fixler, 244–45.

146. Ibid, 221–71.

147. Cohn, 309ff. for a Ranter-Leveller anthology; Scholem, "The Crypto-Jewish Sect of the Dönmeh (Sabbatians) in Turkey," *Messianic Idea*, 142–66; Hill, 247–60.

148. I've consulted for Andrewes: Mitchell, *English Pulpit Oratory*; Reidy, *Bishop Lancelot Andrewes*; Welsby, *Lancelot Andrewes*; Andrewes: *The Private Devotions*; *Ninety-Six Sermons*, 5 vols. (chronological, within topics: Ash Wednesday, Nativity, Gunpowder Plot, etc.).

149. "Seventeenth Nativity Sermon," I, 295–96.

150. Cabala's focus on language was remarked on by Reuchlin: "He (Raziel) gave Adam divine words, to be interpreted allegorically, in the way of Kabbalah. No word, no letter, however trifling, not even the punctuation, was without significance" (*On the Art of the Kabbalah*, 69).

151. "Ninth Holy Ghost Sermon," III, 271.

152. "Ninth Nativity Sermon," I, 145.

153. "Fourth Gunpowder Sermon," IV, 274–75; square brackets and italics mine; in Andrewes's text words printed in Hebrew accompany their English transcription.

154. Elliot Wolfson's recent *Through a Speculum That Shines* reverses this "received wisdom" by arguing very well for the cogency of sight; however, that the *vision* in *visionary* needs to be taken more seriously may attest also to the strength of this tradition of "faith in sound."

155. "Fourteenth Resurrection Sermon," III, 4 (Andrewes's italics for scriptural citation, which he also quotes in the Latin Vulgate: his audience clearly needing to hear both), 21–22.

156. "Tenth Resurrection Sermon," II, 355.

157. "Second Nativity Sermon," I, 26.

158. "Eighth Nativity Sermon," I, 128.

159. *The Messianic Idea*, 43; Ari (The Lion) = Luria.

Bibliography

Adamson, J. F. "Milton's Version of the War in Heaven." *JEGP* LVII (October, 1958): 690–703.

Agrippa, Heinrich Cornelius. *De Origine Peccato* (On original sin), 1518.

———. *De Triplici ratione cognoscendi Deum* (The Threefold way of understanding God). 1515.

———. *Female Pre-eminence.* Trans. of 1670, unattributed. In *The Feminist Controversies of the Renaissance.* Ed. Diane Bornstein. New York: Scholastic Facsimiles and Reprints, 1980. First published in 1542 as *De Nobilitate et praecellentia foeminei sexus.*

———. *On the Vanity of the Arts and Sciences.* London, 1694. Earliest English edition: *Of the vanitie and uncertainty of artes and sciences.* Trans. James Sandford. London: Henry Wykes, 1569. Pub. in Latin: *De incertitudine et vanitate omnium scientarum declamatio inuectiva.* Cologne, 1531. French trans. Paris, 1582.

———. *Three Books of Occult Philosophy or Magic.* Trans. I. F. London, 1651. Rpt.: *Three Books of Occult Philosophy or Magic: Book One— Natural Magic.* Chicago: Hahn & Whitehead, 1898. Rpt. New York: Weiser, 1975. Pub. in Latin: *De occulta philosophia libri tres.* Cologne, 1533. Rpt.: Ed. V. Perrone Campagni. Leiden and New York: E. J. Brill, 1992.

Alazraki, Jaime. "Borges and the Kabbalah." *Tri-Quarterly* 25 (1972): 240–67.

Andrewes, Lancelot. *Ninety-Six Sermons.* Ed. J. P. Wilson and James Bliss. Oxford: Library of Anglo-Catholic Theology, 1861–65. 5 vols. Rpt. 1865–72. First published, 1629, ed. William Laud and John Buckeridge; rpt., 1631, 1635.

———. *The Private Devotions.* Trans., and ed. F. E. Brightman, with an essay by T.S. Eliot. New York: Living Age, 1961.

Anonymous. *Adumbratio Kabbala Christianae Application Doctrina Hebraenum Cabbalisticum ad Dogmata Herr Foederis ad conversionem Judaeum* (Cabala as adumbration of Christianity, application of the Hebrew cabalistic doctrine to Foederis's dogmatics for the purpose of converting the Jews). Francfurt ad Moenum, 1614.

———. *Bericht eines Cabalisten Über die 4 figuren des grossen Ampitheatri Khunradi* (A cabalist view of the four figures of Khunrath's *Great Ampitheatre*). An appendix to Heinrich Khunrath's *De Igne magorum philosophorumque secreto* (The secret light of magicians and philosophers). Strassburg, 1608.

———. *Opusculum de Auditu Kabbalistica sive ad omnes scientias introductorum* (A short essay on cabalistic phonics as an introduction to all sciences). Venice, 1518. Paris, 1578.

Ansari, Asloob Ahmad. "Blake and the Kabbalah." *William Blake: Essays for S. Foster Damon*. Providence: Brown University Press, 1969: 199–220.

Ariel, David S. *The Mystic Quest*. New York: Schocken, 1988.

Aristotle. *Ethics*. Trans. J. A. K. Thomson. London: Penguin Classics, 1976.

Baeck, Leo, *The Essence of Judaism*. Intr. Irving Howe. Trans. Victor Leonard Pearl and Victor Grabenwieser. New York: Schocken, 1964. 1st English ed., 1948.

Bakan, David. *Freud and the Jewish Mystical Tradition*. 2nd ed. New York: Schoken, 1958.

The Bahir (Book of Brightness). In *The Early Kaballah*. Ed. and intr. Joseph Dan; pref. Moshe Idel. Trans. Ronald C. Kiener. New York: Paulist Press, 1986: 55–69.

Banes, Daniel. *The Provocative Merchant of Venice*. Silver Springs, Md.: Malcolm House, 1975

Baudrillard, Jean. *Fatal Strategies*. Trans. Philip Beitchman and W. G. J. Niesluchowski. New York: Semiotext(e)-Autonomedia, 1990.

———. *Seduction*. Trans. Brian Singer. New York: Saint Martin's Press, 1979.

———. *Simulations*. Trans. Philip Beitchman, Paul Foss and Paul Patton. New York: Semiotext(e)-Autonomedia, 1983.

———. *La Société de consommation*. Paris: Gallimard, 1970.

Bayley, Harold. *A New Light on the Renaissance Displayed in Contemporary Emblems*. London: J. M. Dent, 1909. Rpt. New York: Blom, 1967.

Beeckman, Isaac. *Journal tenu de 1604 à 1634*. Ed. C. de Ward. The Hague, 1939–53. 4 vols.

Beitchman, Philip. *I Am a Process with No Subject*. Gainesville: University of Florida Press, 1988.

Bergson, Henri. *Les Deux sources de la réligion et de la morale. Oeuvres Complètes*. Paris: Presses Universitaires Françaises, 1959.

Bernegger, Mathias. *Orationes Duae de Cabbala*. Strassburg, 1640.

Beyerlinck, Laurens. *Magnum Theatrum*. 1631.

Biale, David. *Gershom Scholem, Kaballah and Counter-History*. Cambridge: Harvard University Press, 1979.

———. "Gershom Scholem's Ten Unhistorical Aphorisms on Kaballah," *Modern Critical Views: Gershom Scholem*. Ed. Harold Bloom. New York: Chelsea House, 1987: 99–123.

Birnbaum, Salomo, and Maximilian Hurwitz, eds. *The Life and Sayings of The Baal Shem*. Trans. Irene Birnbaum. New York: Hebrew Publishing Co., 1933.

Bitaudus, Johannes, Antonius de Villon, and Stephanus de Claues. *14 Theses in Opposition to Paracelcists, Cabalists, and Dogmatic Peripatetic Physicians*. Paris, 1624.

Blanchot, Maurice. *L'Entretien infini*. Paris: Gallimard, 1969.

———. *Le Livre à venir*. Paris: Gallimard, 1959.

Blau, Joseph Leon. "Browne's Interest in Cabalism." *PMLA* XLIX (1934): 963–64.

———. *The Christian Interpretation of the Cabala in the Renaissance*. New York: Columbia University Press, 1944.

———. "The Diffusion of the Christian Interpretation of the Cabala in English Literature," *Review of Religion* VI (1941–42): 146–68.

Bloch, Ernst. *The Principle of Hope*. Vol. 2. Trans. Neville Plaice, Stephen Plaice, and Paul Knight. Cambridge: MIT Press, 1986. 3 vols.

Bloom, Harold. *Kaballah and Criticism*. New York: Seabury Press, 1975.

———. *The Strong Light of the Canonical: Kafka, Freud and Scholem as Revisionists of Jewish Culture and Thought*. New York: City College Papers (#20), 1987.

Bodin, Jean. *De la démonomanie des sorciers*. Paris, 1580.

Boehme, Jacob. *De Signatura Rerum* (The Signature of Things). 1621; *The Signatures of All Things*. London: Everyman's Library, 1912.

Bongus, Peter. *The Mysterious Meaning of Numbers*. London, 1585.

Bradbrook, Muriel. *The School of Night*. New York: Russell and Russell, 1965. Originally published, London, 1936.

Brocard, James. *The Revelation of St. John Revealed*. Trans. (from Latin) and pref. by J. Sanford. London, 1582. STC 3810.

Brognolo, Candido. *Alexicacon, hoc est, opus maleficius ac morbis maleficis* (Alexicacon, on evil and evil spells). Venice 1668. 2 vols., in folio.

Browne, Malcolm W. "How Brain Waves Can Fly a Plane." *New York Times* 3 July 1995.

Browne, Sir Thomas. *Christian Morals*. Cambridge: The University Press, 1715.

———. *The Prose of Sir Thomas Browne*. Ed. Norman J. Endicott, N.Y.: Doubleday-Anchor, 1967.

————. *The Works of Sir Thomas Browne.* Ed. Geoffrey Keynes. Chicago: University of Chicago Press, 1964. 4 vols.

Bruno, Giordano. *Cabala del cavallo pegaseo. Con l'aggiunta dell Asino cillenico* (Cabala of the horse Pegasus, to which is joined the Silenian Ass). Parigi (Paris), 1585. London: J. Charlewood, 1585. STC 3935.

Burggrav, Johann Ernst. *Introductio in vitalem philosophiam. In speciali explicatione morborum agitur de curationum mysteriis, indicationum impendiis remediorum arcanis* (Introduction to vital philosophy, with special explanation on the cure of disease through mysteries and the arcane remedies indicated). Frankfurt, 1623.

Burgo Novo, Archangelus. *Apologia fratris Archangeli de Burgonovo pro defensione doctrinae Cabalae contra rev. D. Petrum Garziam Mirandulam impugnantem et conclusiones cabalisticae LXXI secundam opinionem propriam ejusdem Mirandulae ex ipsis Hebraeorum sapentum fundamenti Christianum religionem.* (The apology of brother Archangelus of Burgonovo in defense of cabalistic doctrines against Rev. Peter Garzia's attack on Mirandula and the seventy-one cabalistic conclusions drawn by Pico de Mirandula from Hebrew wisdom, source of the Christian religion). Basel, 1560. Bologna, 1564. In Pistorius's *Artis cabalisticae scriptores.* Basel, 1587.

Calder, I. F. "John Dee Studied as an English Neo-Platonist." Diss. Univ. London, 1952.

Camden, William. *Remains.* London, 1614. STC 4522.

Canetti, Elias. "Kafka's Other Trial." *The Conscience of Words.* Trans. Joachim Neugroschel. New York: Farrar Straus Giroux, 1984: 60–139.

Casaubon, Meric. *A True and Faithful Relation of What Passed for Many Years Between Dr. John Dee . . . and Some Spirits.* London, 1659.

Cassirer, Ernst. *Individual and Cosmos in Renaissance Philosophy.* Oxford: Blackwell, 1963).

————. *The Platonic Renaissance in England.* Trans. Pettegrove. Knoxville: University of Tennessee Press, 1953.

Castiglione, Pietro Maria. *Admiranda naturalis ad renum calculos curandos* (Natural wonders especially adapted for kidney ailments). Milan, 1622.

Certeau, Michel de. *L'Écriture de l'histoire.* Paris: Gallimard, 1975.

————. *La Faiblesse de croire.* Paris: Seuil, 1987.

————. *Heterologies: Discourse of the Other.* Trans. Brian Massumi. Minneapolis: University of Minnesota Press, 1986.

————. *The Mystic Fable.* Trans. Michael B. Smith. Vol. 1. Chicago: University of Chicago Press, 1992.

————. *La Possession de Loudun.* Paris: Juillard, 1970.

Chamisso, Ioao Bravo. *De medendis corporis malis per manualem operationem* (On healing the body of ills through manual manipulation). Coimbra, 1605.

Champier, Symphorien. *Prognosticon Libri* (Prognosicating Books). Lyon, 1521.

Cheradam, Jan. *Iannis Cheradami Alphabetum Linguae Sanctae, mystico intellectu refertum* (Jan Cheradam's holy sacred language, intellectually and mystically expounded). Paris, 1532.

Cicogna, Strozzi. *Palagio de gl'incanti & delle gran maraaviglie de gli spiriti & di tutta la natura . . . in iii prospettive, Spirituale, celeste & elementare* (Palace of the enchantments and of great marvels of spirits and of all nature according to three perspectives, spritiual, celestial, and elementary). Venice, 1605. Cologne, 1606 (in Latin). 8 vols.

Clapham, Henoch. *An Abstract of Faith Ground on Moses and Applyed to the Common Creede.* London, 1606. STC 5328.

―――. *Briefe of the Bible Drawne into English Poetry.* London, 1596. STC 5332.

―――. *A Chronological Discourse.* London, 1609. STC 5336.

―――. *Elohim Triune, displayed by his workes Physicall and Metaphysicall, in a poem of diverse form.* London, 1601. STC 5329.

―――. *Errour on the Left Hand through Preposterous Zeale.* London, 1608. STC 5342.

―――. *Error on the Right Hand through Frozen Securitie.* London, 1608.

Clulee, Nicholas H. *John Dee's Natural Philosophy: Between Science and Religion.* London and New York: Routledge, 1988.

Cohn, Norman. *The Pursuit of the Millenium.* New York: Oxford University Press, 1970. 2nd ed., revised and expanded. First published, 1957.

Comenius, Amos. *The Labyrinth of the World.* Trans. Matthew Spinka. Chicago: The National Union of Czechosovak Protestants in America, 1942. First published, Lezno (Poland), 1631.

Conway, Anne. *The Conway Letters.* Ed. Marjorie Hope Nicolson. New Haven: Yale University Press; London: Oxford University Press, 1930. Revised edition, ed. Sarah Hutton. Oxford University Press, 1992.

―――. *The Principles of the Most Ancient and Modern Philosophy.* Ed. Peter Lopson. The Hague/Boston/London: Martinus Nijhoff. Publishers, 1982. Originally published in Latin, Amsterdam, 1690; English trans. J. C. London, 1692.

Crashaw, Richard. *The Verse in English of Richard Crashaw.* New York: Grove Press, 1949.

Croll, Oswald. *Basilica Chymica* (Chemical temple). Francfurt, 1609.

Crowley, Aleister. *The Confessions of Aleister Crowley.* Ed. John Symonds and Kenneth Grant. New York: Bantam, 1971.

Cudworth, Ralph. *True Intellectual System of the Universe.* London, 1668.

D'Allones, Olivier Revault. *Musiques, Variations sur la pensée juive.* Paris: Christian Bourgois, 1979.

Dan, Joseph. *Gershom Scholem and the Mystical Dimension of Jewish History.* New York: New York University Press, 1987.

————. *Jewish Mysticism and Jewish Ethics.* Seattle: University of Washington Press, 1986.

————. "Samael, Lilith and the Concept of Evil in Early Kabbalah." *AJS Review* 5 (1980): 17–40.

D'Aquin, Philippe. *Interprétation de l'arbre de la Cabale enrichy de sa figure tirée des plus anciens auteurs hébreux.* Paris, 1625.

Davies, John. *Microcosmos.* London, 1603. STC 6333.

Dee, John. *Monas Hieroglyphica mathematice cabalistice anagogiceque explicata* (The hieroglyphic monad, mathematically, cabalistically and anagogically expounded). Antwerp, 1564. Trans. C. H. Josten. *Ambix* 12 (1964): 84–221.

Deleuze, Gilles, and Guattari, Félix. *L'Anti-Oedipe: Capitalisme et Schizophrénie.* Paris: Éditions de Minuit, 1975.

————. *Mille Plateaux: Capitalisme et Schizophrénie.* Paris: Éditions de Minuit, 1980.

Donne, John. "The Second Anniversary of the Progress of the Soul." *The Complete Poetry.* Ed. John T. Shawcross. New York: Doubleday Anchor, 1967: 289–306.

Dunn, William. *Sir Thomas Browne, A Study in Religious Philosophy.* Minneapolis: University of Minnesota Press, 1950.

Duret, Claude. *Thresor de l'histoire des langues de cest univers* (Compendium of a universal history of languages). Cologne, 1613.

Eberhardt, Isabelle. *The Oblivion Seekers.* Trans. Paul Bowles. San Francisco: City Lights Books, 1972.

Eco, Umberto. *The Island of the Day Before.* Trans. William Weaver. New York: Harcourt-Brace, 1994.

Elysius, Joannes. *Satis metuendi diluvii verissima liberatio* (Most true liberation from the fearful enough flood). Bologna, 1522. Naples, 1523.

Erastus, Thomas Liebler. *Disputationum de medicina nova P. Paracelsi* (Disputation on the new medicine of Paracelsus). 1572.

Eusebio, Father Juan Nuremberg. *Occulta Filosofia.* Madrid, 1633.

Evelyn, John. *History of the Three Late Famous Imposters.* London, 1669.

Evoli, Cesare de. *De divinis attributis quae Sephirot ab Hebraeus nuncupata* (Divine attributes called in Hebrew sephiroth). Prague, 1571. Venice, 1573, 1580, 1589.

Fixler, Michael. *Milton and the Kingdoms of God.* Evanston, Ill.: Northwestern University Press, 1964.

Fletcher, Harris F. *Milton's Rabbinical Readings.* New York: Gordian, 1967. Orig. published, 1930.

————. *Milton's Semitic Studies.* New York: Gordian, 1966. Orig. published, 1926.

Fludd, Robert. *Mosaicall Philosophy, grounded upon the essential truth or Eternal Sapience.* London, 1638, 1659.

Fowler, Alastair. *Silent Poetry, Essays in Numerological Analysis.* Ed. Alastair Fowler. New York: Barnes & Noble, 1970.

———. *Spenser and the Numbers of Time.* London: Routledge & Kegan Paul, 1964.

———. *Triumphal Forms: Structural Patterns in Elizabethan Poetry.* Cambridge: Cambridge University Press, 1970

Franck, Adolphe. *Kabbale ou philosophie religieuse des Hebreux.* Paris, 1843.

French, Peter. *John Dee, The World of an Elizabethan Magus.* London: Routledge and Kegan Paul, 1972.

Garcia, Pedro. *Petri Garsie Episcopi Usselen. ad santissimum patrem et dominum Innocentium papam VIII in determinationes magisteriales contra conclusiones apologiales Iannis Pici Mirandulani* (Pedro Garcia, Bishop of Ussellus, to the most holy father and lord, Pope Innocent VIII, in magisterial judgement against the apologies of Pico della Mirandula). Rome, 1499.

Gaffarel, Jacques. *Abdita Divinae Cabalae Mysteria, contra Sophisticorum logomachiam defensa* (The hidden mystery of the divine Cabala, a defense against the logic-mongering of sophisticates). Paris 1625.

———. *Codicum cabbalisticorum manuscriptorum quibus est usus Iannes Picus, comes Mirandulanus index* (Index of manuscripts used by Pico in his study of Cabala). Paris, 1651.

Galantino. Peitro. di. Galantini. *De arcanis Catholicae veritatis contra obstinatissimum Judaeorum nostra tempestatis perfidium; ex Talmude, aliusque Hebraicis libris nuper excerptum* (Of arcane Catholic truth against the perfidious obstinacy of the Jews of our time, with excerpts from Talmud and other more recent Hebrew books). Ortona Di Mare, 1518. Basel, 1550, 1561, 1591. Frankfurt, 1603, 1612, 1672.

Garzoni, Tommaso. *La Piazza Universale* (The universal fortress). Venice, 1585.

Georgius, Franciscus. *De Harmonia mundi totius cantica tria* (Three cantos on the harmony of the whole world). Venice, 1525. French trans. Paris: La Boderie (brothers), 1578.

Gikatila, R. Joseph. *Sha'are orah* (The gates of light). Abbreviated Latin trans. Paulus Riccius, as one of the tracts comprising *De Coelesti agricultura* (Heavenly agriculture), published 1510–20. Latin trans. *Portae lucis* Paulus Riccius. Augsburg, 1516. In Pistorius's *Artis cabalisticae scriptores.* Basel, 1587. Written in Hebrew-Aramaic, c. 1280.

Godelmann, Johann Georg. *De magis veneficis et lamiis recte cognoscendis et puniendis* (On discovering and punishing magicians, sorcerers, and witches). Franckfurt, 1591.

Godwin, Joscelyn. *Athanasius Kircher: A Renaissance Man and the Quest for Lost Knowledge*. London: Thames and Hudson, 1979.

Goethe, Johann Wolfgang von. *Faust*. Trans. Charles E. Passage. New York: Library of Liberal Arts, 1965.

Goldmann, Lucien. *Le Dieu caché*. Paris: Gallimard, 1955.

Gower, John. *Confessio Amantis*. Ed. Russell A. Peck. New York: Rinehart, 1968.

Graetz, Heinrich. *History of the Jews*. Trans. Bella Löwu and "various hands." Philadelphia: Jewish Publication Society of America, 1891–95. 5 vols.

Grimmelshausen, H. J. C. von. *Courage the Adventuress and The False Messiah*. Trans.Hans Speier. Princeton, N.J.: Princeton University Press, 1964.

———. *Simplicissimus*. Trans. A. T. S. Goodrick. Lincoln: University of Nebraska Press. 1962.

Grözinger, Karl Erich. *Kafka and Kaballah*. Trans. Susan Hecker Ray. New York: Continuum, 1994.

Guinther of Andernach. *De medicina veteri et nova* (On medicine old and new). 1571.

Hackspan, Theodor. *Miscellanearum sacrorum libri duo, quibus accesit ejusdem exercitatis de Cabbala Judaica* (Two books of miscellanies, in which is explained the practice of Jewish Cabala). Altdorf, 1660.

Hadrianus, Finus. *In Judeos flagellum ex sacris scriptis excerptum* (The Jews scourged by their own Bible). Venice, 1538.

Halevi, Judah. *The Kuzari*. Trans. Hartwig Hirschfeld. New York: Schocken, 1964.

Hansen, Brooks. *The Chess Garden: The Twilight Letters of Gustav Uyterboeven*. New York: Farrar, Straus, and Giroux, 1995.

Haydn, Hiram. *The Counter Renaissance*. New York: Grove Press, 1950.

Heer, Henry van. *Spadocrene, hoc est fons Spadanus* (The Eunuch's fountain of sterility). Liege, 1614.

Heilbronner, Jacob. *Daemonomania Pistoriana. Magica et cabalistica morborum curandorum ratio a Ioanne Pistorio* (Pistorius's demon-mania, his magical and cabalistic method of curing every disease). Palantine, 1601.

Helmont, Franciscus Mercurius. *Two Hundred Queries Concerning the Doctrine of the Revolution of Humane Souls, and Its Conformity to the Truths of Christianity*. Trans. "A Lover and Searcher after Hidden Truth." London, 1684.

Henning, Johan. *Cabbalalogia sive brevis institutio de Cabbala cum veterum Rabbinorum Judaica tum Poëtarum Paragrammatica* ("Cabalogy"? or brief introduction to Cabala through ancient Jewish rabbis and poetic examples). Leipzig, 1683.

Hercenberg, Dov. "Deux Modèles d'écriture: essai sur le rapport entre ordre et liberté." *Revue Philosophique* 16 (1982): 483–86.

Hill, Christopher. *The World Turned Upside Down, Radical Ideas During the English Revolution*. New York: Viking, 1972.

Hochstraten, Jacob. *Destructio Cabbalae* (Destruction of Cabala). Cologne, 1518.

———. *De Cabala an toleranda* (Must Cabala be allowed?). Cologne, 1519.

Howard (Henry), Earl of Northampton. *Defensative Against the Poyson of Certain Prophecies*. London, 1583. STC 13858.

Huntley, Frank Livingstone. *Sir Thomas Browne, A Biographical and Critical Study*. Ann Arbor: University of Michigan Press, 1962.

Iadertinus, Federicus Chrisogonus. *Federico Chrisogoni Nobilis Iadertini Artium et Medicine doctoris subtilissimi et Astrologi excellentissimi de mode Collegiandi Pronosticandi et Curandi Febres: Necnon de humana felicitate ac denique de fluxu et refluxu maris* (Federico Iadertinus, noble, most skilled doctor of arts and medicine, member of the excellent college of astrology and prognostication, also expert at curing fevers, inducing human felicity, and determining the effects of the tides). Venice, 1528.

Idel, Moshe. *Kabbalah: New Perspectives*. New Haven: Yale Univerity Press, 1988.

———. "Métaphores et pratiques sexuelles dans la Cabballe." *Lettre sur la sainteté: le secret de la relation entre l'homme et la femme dans la Cabbale*. Paris: Verdier, 1986: 329–58.

———. *Studies in Ecstatic Kaballah*. Albany: State University of New York Press, 1988.

Ingpen, William. *The Secret of Numbers*. London, 1624. STC 14089.

James VI, King of Scotland; I, King of England. *Daemonologie*. London, 1597.

James, Lara De Witt. *William Blake: The Finger on the Furnace*. New York: Vantage Press, 1979.

Javary, Geneviève. *Recherches sur l'utilisation du thème de la Sekina dans l'apologétique chrétienne du XV au XVIII siècle*. Lille: H. Champion, 1978.

Jonas, Hans. *The Gnostic Religion*. Boston: Beacon Press, 1958. 2nd ed., revised.

Jung, C. J. *Psychology and Alchemy*. Trans. R. F. Hull. 2nd ed. Princeton, N.J.: Princeton University Press, 1968.

Kafka, Franz. *Amerika*. Intr. Klaus Mann. Trans. Edwin Muir. New York: New Directions, 1946.

———. *The Castle*. Trans. Willa and Edwin Muir. New York: Schocken, 1992.

———. *The Trial*. Trans. Willa and Edwin Muir. New York: Schocken, 1992.

Kahn, Robert. "Prier pour le petit bossu, politique et désespoir dans la correspondance Benjamin-Scholem, 1933–40." *Les Temps Modernes* 584 (1995).

Keith, George. *Truth and Innocency Defended Against Calumny and Defamation, in a Late Report Spread Abroad Concerning the Revolution of Souls*. Philadelphia, 1692. 20 p.

Kermode, Frank. *The Genesis of Secrecy: On the Interpretation of Narrative*. Cambridge: Harvard University Press, 1979.

Khunrath, Henry. *Ampitheater of the Only True Eternal Wisdom, of Christian, Cabalistic, Divine Magic*. London, 1609. Hanover, 1609 (in Latin).

Kierkegaard, Søren. *Concluding Unscientific Postscript*. Trans. David F. Swenson and Walter Lowrie. Princeton, N.J.: Princeton University Press, 1968.

———. *Journals and Papers*. Ed. and trans. Howard V. Hong and Edna H. Hong. 4 vols. Princeton, N.J.: Princeton University Press, 1967–75.

———. *Stages On Life's Way*. Ed. and trans. Howard V. Hong and Edna H. Hong. Princeton, N.J.: Princeton University Press, 1988.

Kircher, Athanasius. *Arithmology Concerning the Hidden Mysteries of Numbers*. Rome, 1665.

———. *Mundus Subterraneus* (Underground world). 12 vol. Amsterdam, 1663–65.

———. *Oedipus Aegyptiacus* (Egyptian Oedipus). Rome, 1623.

Knittel, Caspar. *Via Regia ad Omnes Scientias et Artes* (The royal road to all sciences and arts). Prague, 1682. Nürnberg, 1687.

Kosinski, Jerzy. *The Hermit of 69th Street*. New York: Henry Holt, 1988.

Langer, Mordecai George (Jiri). *Nine Gates to the Chassidic Mysteries*. Trans. Stephen Jolly. New York: McKay, 1961.

Lapide, Cornelius. *Commentaria Bibliorum Chuonradi Pellicani* (Biblical commentaries of Conrad Pellican). Zurich, 1532.

———. *In Pentateuchum In hebreo innuitur mysterium Trinitatis et incarnationis. Sic enim Habet Audi . . . idem innuitur ab Isaia VI, 3 . . . quod veteres Rabbini, ut R. Simeon filius Joai sic exponunt . . . teste Galantino Lib. 2, cap. I* (On the Hebrew Pentateuch's mysteries of the trinity and incarnation; the same were heard in Isaiah VI, 3 . . . which the ancient Rabbis and also Rabbi Simeon ben Yohai expounded . . . from the Galantini text, Bk. 2, chapter 1). Antwerp, 1618.

Lauret, Christophorus. *Hazoar temporis Messiae* (The Zohar in the Messiah's time). Paris, 1610.

Lazzarelli, Lodovico. *Crater Hermetis* (The crater of Hermes). Paris, 1505.

Leary, Timothy. *The Politics of Ecstasy*. New York: Putnam's, 1969.

Le Loyer, Pierre. *Discours, et histoires des spectres*. Angers, 1586. Paris, 1605.

Lebenwald, Adam A. *Von des Teufels List und Betrug in der Hebraer Cabbala* (Hebrew Cabala as the devil's cunning and fraud). Salzburg, 1680.

Leclerc, Marie-Christine. "Fouilles dans les ruines circulaires." *Critique* 555–56 (1993): 520–36.

Leibniz, G. W. *Theodicy*. Trans. E. M. Huggard. New Haven, Conn.: Yale University Press, 1952.

Leiris, Michel. *Journal, 1922–89*. Jean Jamain, ed. Paris: Gallimard, 1992.

———. *"Le Monade Hieroglyphique*, de John Dee." *Révolution Surréaliste* 9–10 (1927): 61–63.

Leo the Hebrew (psuedonym, R.Juda, son of Isaac Abravanel, also known as Leon Abrabenel-Medigo). *De Amore*. In Pistorius's *Artis cabalisticae scriptores*. Basel, 1587. Orig. published in Italian as *Dialoghi d'amore*. Rome, 1535. Rpt. Venice, 1541. Latin trans. Sarrazin. Vienna, 1564. Spanish trans. Juan Costa, 1584. French trans. Pontus de Thiard, 1580.

Lévinas, Emmanuel. *Difficile Liberté*. Paris: Albin Michel, 1976.

———. *Entre nous: essais sur le penser-à-l'autre*. Paris: Grasset, 1991.

Lewis, C. S. *The Allegory of Love*. London: Oxford University Press, 1936

Lieb, Michael. *The Visionary Mode: Biblical Prophecy, Hermeneutics and Cultural Change*. Ithaca, N.Y.: Cornell University Press, 1991.

Liebes, Yehuda. *Studies in The Zohar*. Trans. Arnold Schwartz, Stephanie Nakache, and Penina Peli. Albany: State University of New York Press, 1993.

Lightfoot, John. *Erubhim, or Miscellanies Christian and Judaicall*. London, 1629. STC 15593.

Lobkowitz, Johann Caramnel. *Cabalae Totius brevissimum Specimen* (Brief explanation of the whole Cabala). Brussels, 1643.

———. *Cabbalae Theologicae Excidium* (Overthrow of Cabala theology). Rome, 1657.

Lovejoy. Arthur O. *The Great Chain of Being*. New York: Harper Torchbooks, 1956.

Luhrmann, T. M. "An Interpretation of the *Fama Fraternitatis* with Respect to Dee's *Monas Hieroglyphica*." *Ambix* 33, Part 1 (1986): 1–10.

Maccaby, Hyam. "The Greatness of Gershom Scholem." *Modern Critical Views: Gershom Scholem*. Ed. H. Bloom. New York: Chelsea House, 1987: 137–54.

Maimon, Solomon. *Solomon Maimon: An Autobiography*. Trans. (abridged) J. Clark Murray. Ed. Moses Hadas. New York: Schocken, 1967.

Marin, Jean Baptiste. *Astrologia Gallica* (Gallic astrology). Paris.1661.

Marion, Jean Luc. *L'Idole et la distance*. Paris: Grasset, 1989.

Marlowe, Christopher. *The Complete Plays*. Ed. J. B. Steane. New York: Penguin Classics, 1969.

Martin, Eva. "Thomas Vaughan, Magician." *Fortnightly Review* 687 (1924): 405–16.

Mathers, S. L. G, trans. *The Wisdom of the Kaballah*. Ed. Dagobert Runes. New York: Citadel Press, 1967. Trans. K. Rosenroth's *Kaballa Denudata*, 1677–84. First pub. as *The Kabbalah Unveiled*. London, 1887.

McKeon, Michael. "Sabbatai Sevi in England." *AJS Review* 2 (1977): 131–79.

Meres, Francis. *God's Arithmetic*. London, 1597. STC 17833.

Mersenne, Marin. *Observationes et emendationes ad Francisci Georgii Veneti problemata: in hoc opere, cabala evertitur, editio vulgata et inquistores sanctae fidei catholicae ab haereticorum atque politicorum calumniis accurate vindicantur* (Observations and emendations of the problematics of the Venetian Franciscus Georgius; hereby Cabala is refuted and the holy Bible as well as the sacred Inquisition of faithful Catholics are vindicated from the calumnies of heretics and politicos). Paris, 1623.

———. *Quaestiones celeberrimae in Genesim* (Frequently asked questions on Genesis). Paris, 1623.

Mirandola, Pico della. "Cabalistic Conclusions." Trans. A. E. Waite, *The Holy Kabbalah*: 445–53.

———. "Oration on the Dignity of Man." Trans. Elizabeth Livermore Forbes. *The Renaissance Philosophy of Man*. Eds. Ernst Cassirer, Paul Oskar Kristeller, and John Herman Randall, Jr. Chicago: University of Chicago Press, 1945: 213–54.

Mitchell, W. Fraser. *English Pulpit Oratory from Andrewes to Tillotson, a Study of Its Literary Aspects*. London: Russell and Russell, 1962; orig. pub., 1932.

Monceaux, François de. *Disquisitio de magia divinatrice et operatrice* (Disquisition on divining and operative magic). Paris, 1683.

Montaigne, Michel de. *Essais*. Ed. A. Thibaudet. Paris: Gallimard (Pléiade), 1950.

Montecuccolus, Carolus. *In cabalam introductio* (Introduction to Cabala). Modena, 1612.

Mopsik, Charles. *Les Grandes textes de la cabale: les rites qui font dieu*. Paris: Verdier, 1993.

———. Ed., trans.: *Lettre sur la sainteté: le secret de la relation entre l'homme et la femme dans la Cabbale*. Paris: Verdier 1986.

———. Ed., trans.: *Le Livre de Ruth* (Midrach ha-Neélam). Paris: Verdier, 1987.

———. Ed., trans.: *Le Zohar.* Paris: Verdier, 1981–96. 4 vols. (5 planned).

More, Henry. *Conjectura Cabbalistica, or a Conjectural Essay of Interpreting the Mind of Moses, According to a Threefold Cabbala, viz., Literal, Philosophical, Mystical or Divinely Moral*. London, 1654.

Mornay, Philip de. *Trewness of Christian Religion*. Trans. Sir Philip Sidney and Arthur Golding. London, 1587. STC 18149.

Nashe, Thomas. *The Unfortunate Traveller and Other Works*. Ed. J.B. Steane. London: Penguin Classics, 1985.

Nathanson, Leonard. *The Strategy of Truth, A Study of Sir Thomas Browne*. Chicago: University of Chicago Press, 1967.

Nauert, Charles. G., Jr. *Agrippa and the Crisis in Renaissance Thought*. Urbana: University of Illinois Press, 1965.

Newman, Beth S. "John Donne and the Cabala." *Jewish Quarterly* 23 (1975): 312–36.

Newman, William, "Thomas Vaughan as Interpreter of Agrippa von Nettesheim." *Ambix* 29 (1982): 125–40.

Nicolson, Marjorie Hope. *Mountain Gloom and Mountain Glory*. Ithaca, N.Y.: Cornell University Press, 1959.

Nietzsche, Friedrich. *Joyful Wisdom*. Trans. Thomas Common. New York: Frederick Ungar, 1960.

———. *Twilight of the Idols*. Trans. R. J. Hollingdale. New York: Penguin, 1975.

Nin, Anaïs. *Fire: Diaries, 1934–37*. New York: Harcourt-Brace, 1995.

———. *Incest: Diaries, 1932–34*. New York: Harcourt-Brace, 1992.

Nohrnberg, James. *The Analogy of the Faerie Queene*. Princeton, N.J.: Princeton University Press, 1976.

Obicius, Hyppolitus. *De nobilitate medici contra illius obtretatores* (Of the dignity of medicine, against its detractors). Venice, 1619.

Otto, Julius Conrad. *Gali Razia id est Occultorum detectio* (Uncovering the mysteries of the Gali Razia, or the revealed mysteries). Korberi, 1605. Stettin, 1613.

Otto, Rudolf. *The Idea of the Holy*. Trans. John W. Harvey. London and New York: Oxford University Press, 1958.

———. *Mysticism, East and West*. Trans. Bertha L. Bracey and Richenda C. Payne. New York: Meridian, 1957.

Ozick, Cynthia. "The Consensus that Plagues Israel." *New York Times* 2 Dec. 1995: A21.

———. *The Shawl*. New York: Alfred A. Knopf, 1989

Parkinson, Thomas. "The Sun and Moon in Yeats's Early Poetry." *Modern Philology* 50 (1952): 50–58.

Patai, Raphael. *The Hebrew Goddess*. 3rd ed. Detroit, Mich.: Wayne State University Press, 1990.

———. *The Jewish Mind*. New York: Scribners, 1977.

Patrides, Constantinos. *Milton and the Christian Tradition*. New York and London.: Oxford University Press, 1969.

Pauly, Jean de, trans. *Zohar, le livre de la splendour*. Paris: E. Leroux, 1906–11. 6 vols.

Peranzanus, Nicolaus de Monte Sante Marie in Cassiano. *Vaticinium de vera futuri diluvii declaratione . . . cum determinatione ultimorum dierum huius mundi cum laudibus astrologie aliisque rebus occultis ex intimarum mathematicarum cabalisticarum que scientia depromptis* (Prediction and true declaration of a future flood . . . with determination of the last days of the world with praises on astrology and other matters taken from the innermost science of mathematicians and cabalists). Ancona, 1523.

Pererius, Benedictus, S.J. *Adversus fallaces et superstitiosas artes; id est, De Magia, de observatione somniorum, et de divinatione astrologica*

(Against fallacious and superstitious arts; of magic, dreams, and astrological divination). Venice, 1592.

Peucer, Caspar. *Commentarius de praecipuis divinationum generibus, in quo a prophetiis, authoritate divina traditis, et a physicis coniecturis, discernuntur artes et imposturae diabolicae* (Commentary on the best divinatory methods; and to what extent divine authority as well as physical principles are represented theirin, as well as a discovery of diabolical arts and imposture). Wittenburg, 1553. French trans., 1584. Frankfort, 1593.

Piccioli, Antonio. *Rapiti Renovati* (Raptures renewed). Bergamo, 1587.

Pistorius, Johannes. *Artis cabalisticae hoc est reconditae theologiae et philosophiae scriptorum* (Of the cabalistic arts, their philosophical and theological writings). Basel, 1587.

———. *De vera curandae pestis ratione* (A method for a real cure of disease). Frankfurt, 1568.

Plaskow, Judith. *Standing Again at Sinai: Judaism from a Feminist Perspective.* San Francisco: Harper, 1991.

Pollard, A.W., and G. R. Redgrave. *A Short-Title Catalogue of Books Printed in England, Scotland and Ireland, and of English Books Printed Abroad, 1475–1640.* London, 1926. Listed here as STC, with identifying number.

Post, Jonathan S. *Sir Thomas Browne.* Boston: Twayne, 1987.

Postel, Guillaume. *Abrahami patriarchae liber Jezirah; sive, Formationis mundi, patribus quidem Abrahami tempore revelatus, sed ab ipso etiam Abrahamo expositus Isaaco, et per profetarum manus posteritati conservatus . . . Vertebat ex Hebraeis et comentariis illustrabat . . . Gulieumus Postellus Restitutus* (The Sefer Yetzirah of the Patriarch Abraham; or of the creation of the world, revealed by the ancients in the time of Abraham, that this same Abraham expounded to Isaac, and which was conserved in the caring hands of posterity . . . Translated from the Hebrew and accompanied by commentaries . . . William Postel Restored (born again?)). Paris, 1552.

Rabelais, François. *Gargantua and Pantagruel.* Trans. J. M. Cohen. London: Penguin Classics, 1983.

Ramsay, Chevalier (Andrew Michael). *The travels of Cyrus, to which is annexed a discourse on the the theology and mythology of the pagans.* London, 1795. Orig. published, 1715.

Rattray, David. "Les secousses transatlantiques du Grand Jeu." *Europe* 782–83 (1994): 30–35.

Reeves, Marjorie. *The Influence of Prophecy in the Later Middle Ages—A Study of Joachism.* New York and London: Oxford University Press, 1969.

Regardie, Israel. *My Rosicrucian Adventure.* St. Paul: Llewellyn Publications, 1971.

Reidy, Maurice F., S.J. *Bishop Lancelot Andrewes, Jacobean Court Preacher*. Chicago: Loyola University Press, 1955.

Reuchlin, Johannes. *On the Art of the Kabbalah*. Trans. Martin and Sarah Goodman. Intr. (1983, Abaris Books) Lloyd Jones. Intr. Moshe Idel. Lincoln and London: University of Nebraska Press, 1993. Originally published as *De Arte cabalistica*, 1517.

——. *De Verbo Mirifico* (The wonder-working word). Basel, 1494.

Ricius, Paulus. *De coelesti agricultura* (Heavenly agriculture). In Pistorius's *Artes cabalisticae*. Basel, 1587. Originally published as a series of tracts, 1510–20.

——. *Portae, Lucis (sic). Hec est porta Tetragrammaton* (Gates, Light: This is the gate to the Tetragrammaton). Augsburg, 1516. Trans. of R. Joseph Gikatila's. *Sha'are orah*, composed c. 1280.

——. *In cabalistarum, seu allegorizantium eruditionem isagoge* (On Cabala, or digest of erudite allegory). Augsburg, 1514.

Ripellino, Angelo Maria. *Magic Prague*. Trans. Daven Marinelli. Berkeley: University of California Press, 1994. First published in Italian, 1973.

Rittangel, Iohannes Stefanus. *Liber Jezirah qui Abrahamo patriarchae adscribitur, una cum commentario Rabi Abraham F.D. super thirty-two semitis sapientiae, a quibus liber Jezirah incipit; translatus et nois illustratus* (The Sefer Yetzirah ascribed to the Patriarch Abraham, with a commentary of Rabbi Abraham, expounding the thirty-two paths of knowledge, which the Sefer Yetzirah invented; translated and accompanied with notes). Amsterdam, 1652.

——. *De veritate religionis Christianae . . . pars secunda de Judaeorum cabbala, qua S. Scriptorum interpretantur* (True Christian religion . . . second part of the Jewish Cabala, as interpreted by Holy Scripture). Frankfurt, 1699.

Riviera, Cesare. *Il magico mondo de gli heroi*. Mantua, 1603. Rpt. Milan, 1605.

Rosenroth, Christian Knorr von., ed. and trans. *Kabbala denudata*. (Cabala revealed). Sulzbach (vol. 1), 1677; Frankfurt (vol. 2), 1684.

Rosenzweig, Franz. *The Star of Redemption*. 2nd ed. New York: Hill and Wang, 1930.

Rostvig, Maren-Sofie. "Structure as Prophecy." *Silent Poetry*. Ed. Fowler. New York: Barnes and Noble, 1970: 32–72.

Roth, Philip. *Sabbath's Theater.* New York: Houghton-Mifflin, 1995.

Runciman, Steven. *The Medieval Manichee, A Study of the Christian Dualist Heresy*. New York: Viking, 1961.

Saurat, Denis. *Literature and the Occult Tradition*. Trans. Dorothy Bolton. Fort Washington, New York: Kennicut Press, 1966. Originally published, 1930.

Schechter, Solomon. *Studies in Judaism*. Philadelphia: Jewish Publication Society, 1958.

Schickardt, Wilhelm. *Bechinath Happeruschim* (Inquiry into exegesis) Tubingen, 1624.

Scholem, Gershom G. *Bibliographica Kabbalistica.* Leipzig: W. Drugalin, 1927.

———. *Kabballah.* New York: Meridian, 1978

———. *Major Trends in Jewish Mysticism.* New York: Schocken, 1971; first pub., 1941.

———. *The Messianic Idea in Judaism.* New York: Schocken, 1971.

———. *On the Kaballah and Its Symbolism.* Trans. Ralph Manheim. New York: Schocken, 1965.

———. *On the Mystical Shape of the Godhead: Basic Concepts in the Kaballah.* Trans. Joachim Neugroschel. New York: Schocken, 1991.

———. *The Origins of the Kabbalah.* Ed. R. J. Zwi Werblowsky. Trans. Allan Arkush. Princeton, N.J.: Princeton University Press and Jewish Publication Society, 1987.

———. *Sabbatai Sevi: the Mystical Messiah.* Trans. R. J. Zwi Werblowsky. Princeton, N.J.: Princeton University Press, 1973.

———. *Walter Benjamin, the Story of a Friendship.* Trans. Harry Zohn. Philadelphia: Jewish Publication Society of America, 1981.

———. *Zohar, the Book of Splendour.* New York: Schocken, 1949.

Schoock, Martin. *Physica caelestis* (Celestial physics). Amsterdam, 1663.

Schott, Caspar. *Magia universalis naturae et artis* (Universal magic of nature and art). Wurtzburg, 1657–59. 4 vols.

———. *Physica Curiosa* (Strange physics). Hebipoli, 1667.

Schultz, Bruno. *The Street of Crocodiles.* Trans. Celina Wieniewska. New York: Penguin, 1977.

Schultz, Howard. *Milton and Forbidden Knowledge.* New York: Publications of the Modern Language Society, 1955.

Secret, François. *Le kabbalisme chrétien à la Renaissance . . . d'après le Thresor de l'histoire des langue de Claude Duret.* Diplôme des Hautes Études, 1954. Unpublished.

———. *Le Zohar chez les kabbalistes chrétiens de la Renaissance.* Paris: Mouton, 1964.

Sefer Yetzirah. Ed. and trans. Aryeh Kaplan. York Beach, Maine: Samuel Weiser:, 1990

Sennert, Andreas. *Dissertatio Peculiaris de Cabbala* (Special discourse on Cabala). Wittenburg, 1655.

Seznec, Jean. *La Survivance des dieux antiques.* Paris: Champs Flammarion: 1993.

Shelley, Mary. *Frankenstein.* New York: New American Library, 1965.

Sherman, William. *John Dee and the Politics of Reading and Writing in Elizabethan England.* Amherst: University of Massachusetts Press, 1995.

Spector, Sheila A. *Jewish Mysticism: An Annotated Bibliography on the Kabbalah in English*. New York & London: Garland Publishing, 1984.

Spenser, Edmund. *The Faerie Queene*. Ed. Thomas P. Roche, Jr. London: Penguin, 1978.

———. *The Shorter Poems*. Ed. William A. Oram et al. New Haven, Conn.: Yale University Press, 1989.

Sperber, Julius. *Kabbalisticae precationes* (Cabalistic prayers). Magdeburg, 1600. Amsterdam, 1675.

Spinoza, Benedict. *Chief Works*. Trans. R. H. M. Elwes. New York: Dover, 1951. 2 vols.

Steeb, Johann Christoph. *Dulcedo de forti sive Elixir solis et vitae, vera per dulcem liquorem auri solutio radicalis atque auri potabilis genuina praeparation noviter reperta mathematice hieroglyphice anagogice caballistice introducta* (Sweet potion or the only true elixir of the brave, the newly discovered potable gold interpreted hieroglyphically, mathematically, anagogically and cabalistically). Amsterdam, 1673, 1675.

———. *Coelum sephiroticum Hebraeorum per portas intelligentiae Moysi revelatas, interiores naturalium rerum characteres ex vetustissima Hebraica veritate explicans* (The heavens of the Hebrew sephiroth, revealed through the Mosaic gates of wisdom, explained from the most ancient Hebrew truths). Mainz, 1679.

Steidner, Johann. *Jüdische ABC Schul im Buch Yezirah von dem Geheimniss des dreyeinigen wahren Gottes und Schöpfers Jehova* (The Jewish alphabet school of The Sefer Yezirah on the mysteries of the trinity of the true God and Jehovah's holy spirit). Augsburg, 1665.

Suavius, Leo (Jacques Gohory). *Theophrasti Paracelsi philosophiae et medicinae universae compendium* (Compendium of the philosophy and universal medicine of Paracelsus). Paris and Frankfurt, 1568.

———. *Discours fait en la défense de la philosophie et médecine antiques contre la nouvelle paracelsique*. Paris, 1575. Signed "Jacques Gohory."

Swietlicki, Catherine. *The Spanish Christian Cabala: The Works of Luis de Leon, Santa Teresa de Jesus and San Juan de la Cruz*. Columbia: University of Missouri Press, 1986.

Tentzel, Andreas. *Medicina Diastatica ad distans et beneficio mumialis transplantationis operationem et eficaciam habens multa abstrusioris philosophiae et medicinae arcana continet* (Diastatic medicine, at a distance, together with benefits and efficacy of mummia (human remains) transplantation, containing many rather abstruse medical and philosophical arcana). Jena, 1629. Rpt. Erfurt, 1666.

Teresa , Saint of Avila. *The Interior Castle*. Trans. Benedictines of Stanbrook Abbey. London, 1912.

Thenaud, Jean. *La Saincte et tréscrestienne cabale*. Paris, 1519. Unpublished manuscript.

Thomson, Thomas. *A Diet for Drunkards*. London, 1612. STC 24027.

Thorndike, Lynn. *History of Magic and Experimental Science*. New York: Columbia University Press and Macmillan, 1923–1958. 8 vols.

Tilyard, E. M. *The Elizabethan World Picture*. London: Chatto and Windus, 1956.

Tishby, Isaiah. *The Wisdom of The Zohar: An Anthology of Texts*. Trans. (from Modern Hebrew of Fischel Lachower and Isaiah Tishby) David Goldstein. New York: Oxford University Press, 1989. 3 vols.

Torreblanca, Francisco. *Daemonologia sive de magia naturali* (Demonology or on natural magic). Mainz, 1623.

Vaughan, Henry. *Secular Poems by the Silurist, Including a Few Pieces by His Twin Brother Thomas , "Eugenius Philalethes."* Intr. and ed. J. R. Tuttin. London: Hull Press, 1893.

Vaughan, Thomas. *Anima Magica Abscondita or A Dissertation of the Universal Spirit of Nature, with His Strange, Abstruse, Miraculous Ascent and Descent*. London, 1650.

———. *Anthroposophia Theomagica, or A Discourse of the Nature of Man and His Seate after Death, by Eugenius Philalethes*. London, 1650.

———. *Secrets Revealed or An Open Entrance to the Shut-Palace of the King Containing the Greatest Treasure in CHYMISTRY ever yet so plainly Discovered composed by a most famous English-man styling himself Anonymous, Eyraneus Philaletha Cosmopolita who by Inspiration & Reading attained to the Philosopher's Stone at his age of Twenty Three Years* (spaces = line separations). London: William Cooper, 1645.

Vedanta Sutras of Badarayana, with Ramanuja's Commentary and *Vedanta Sutras of Badarayana, with Sankara's Commentary*. Ed., and trans. George Thibaut. Delhi: Motilal Banarsidas, 1962; New York: Dover, 1962. First pub. 1890, 1904. 2 vols.

Vickers, Brian, ed. *Occult and Scientific Mentalities in the Renaissance*. Cambridge: Cambridge University Press, 1984.

Vigée, Claude. *L'Extase et l'errance*. Paris: Grasset, 1982.

Vincenti, G. M. *Il Messia venuto, historia spiegata e provata agli Hebrei in cento discorsi* (The Messiah is come, explained and proved by stories from the Hebrew in 100 lessons). Venice, 1659.

Voysin, Joseph de. *Disputatio Cabalisticae R. Israel filii R. Mosis de Anima adjectis commentariis ex Zohar aliisque rabbinorum libris, cum iis quae ex doctrina Platonis convenere* (Cabalistic disputation on the soul, of Rabbi Israel, son of Rabbi Moses, with additional commentaries on The Zohar from the books of several Rabbis, all in harmony with Platonic doctrines). Paris, 1635.

————. *Observationes in proemium Pugionis fidei* (Observations in praise of *The Sword of Faith*). Preface to Raymond Martin's *Pugio fidei*. Leipzig, 1687.

Waite, A. E. *The Holy Kabbalah*. New York: Citadel, 1992. First published, 1929.

Walker, D. P. *Spiritual and Demonic Magic, from Ficino to Campanella*. London: Warburg Institute and University of London, 1958.

Welsby, Paul A. *Lancelot Andrewes, 1555–1626*. London: S.P.C.K., 1956.

Werblowsky, R. J. Zwi. *Joseph Karo, Lawyer and Mystic*. Philadelphia: Jewish Publication Society, 1980.

————. "Milton and the *Conjectura Cabbalistica*." *Journal of the Warburg Institute* XVIII (1955): 90–113.

Wier, Johann. *De praestigiis daemonum et incantationibus et veneficiis* (On demonic wonders, both incantations and spells). Basel, 1564. Rrpt. as *De lamiis* (She-devils), Basel, 1584.

Williams, George. *The Radical Reformation*. London, 1962.

Wind, Edgar. *Pagan Mysteries in the Renaissance*. New York: Norton, 1969. 2nd ed. revised.

Windelband, Wilhelm. *A History of Philosophy*. Trans. (originally published, 1901) James H. Tufts. New York: Harper and Brothers, 1958. 2 vols.

Wolfson, Elliot R. *Through a Speculum That Shines: Vision and Imagination in Medieval Jewish Mysticism*. Princeton, N.J.: Princeton University Press, 1994

Yates, Frances. *Giordano Bruno and the Hermetic Tradition*. London: Routledge and Kegan Paul, 1979.

————. *The Occult Philosophy in the Elizabethan Age*. London: Routledge, 1979.

————. *The Rosicrucian Enlightenment*. London: Routledge and Kegan Paul, 1972.

————. *Shakespeare's Last Plays: A New Approach*. London: Routledge, 1975.

Yurick, Sol. *Metatron*. New York: Semiotext(e)-Autonomedia, 1985.

Zambelli, Paola. "Magic and Radical Reformation in Agrippa of Nettesheim." *Journal of the Warburg Institute* 29 (1970): 69–103.

Zara, Antonio. *Anatomia ingeniorum et scientarum* (Anatomy of skills and sciences). Venice, 1615.

The Zohar. Ed. J. Abelson. Trans. Maurice Simon and Harry Sperling (with Dr. Paul Levertoff., vols. 3 & 4). London and New York: Soncino Press, 1933. 5 vols. Rpt. 1984.

Zumthor, Paul. *Le Masque et la lumière: la poétique des grands rhétoriquers*. Paris: Seuil, 1978.

Index

Abelson, J., the antiquity of The
Zohar, 31, 294n.2
*Abdita Divinae Caballae
Mysteria* (Gaffarel), 143–44
Abraham, 40, 73, 291
Abulafia, Abraham, 29, 57, 54,
71, 72, 81, 124–25, 162, 173,
223, 293, 299n.79
Acquinas, Saint Thomas, 62,
135, 182
Adam, 37, 40, 42, 189, 197, 228,
261
Adamson, J. F., The War in
Heaven in Milton's *Paradise
Lost*, 311n.28
Admiranda naturalis (P.
Castiglione), 195
*Adversus fallaces et superstitiosis
artes* (Pererius), 130
Agrippa, Henry Cornelius von
Nettesheim, xiii, xiv, 4, **65–
113**, 115–19, 124, 130, 155,
157 170, 174–76, 183, 186–87,
192–93, 195–96, 198, 200,
210–11 214–18, 220, 225, 232,
238, 242, 244, 249, 256, 265,
270–72, 274–76, 284., 301n.31,
311n.19, 317nn.120, 125, 133;
Anabaptist-populist leanings,

301n.34; "anxious style," 94–
95; hidden influence of the
neopagan Lazzarelli, 117–20
*Agrippa and the Crisis in
Renaissance Thought* (Nauert),
118
ain soph, 20, 48, 60, 63, 79, 147,
211, 249. *See* Sephiroth
Albigensians, 50–51, 241
Albion's England (Warner), 211
The Alchemist (Jonson), 245
alchemy, xiv, 78, 90, 247, 256,
280, 314n.68, 315n.86
alectromancy, 200
aleph, 61, 105
Alexicacon (Brognolo), 199
The Allegory of Love (Lewis),
313n.57
Alphabetum Linguae Sanctae
(Iannis), 242
alumbrados, 151
Amsterdam, 173, 230, 287
Anabaptism, 86, 230–32, 301n.34
The Analogy of the Fairie Queene
(Nohrnberg), 22
*Anatomia ingeniorum et
scientarum* (Zara), 131–32, 211
Ancient Theology, 291. *See also*
Hermes

Andreae, John Valentine,
assumed author of Rosicrucian
pamphlet, 264–65. *See also*
Spinka, ed., *The Labyrinth of
the World* (Comenius)
Andrewes, Lancelot, xii, **283–92**,
318n.148, 319n.155
"angel popes," 49, 120, 295n.15,
299n.80
angels, 21, 107
Anthroposophia Theomagica
(Vaughan), 278–79
Anima Magica Abscondita
(Vaughan), 317n.130, 132
Anonymous, 176–77, 187
L'Anti-Oedipe (Deleuze-Guattari),
59–60
The Antiquity of Magic
(Vaughan), 275–76
Apocalypse, 269, 280
apocatastasis, 14
Apologia (for Pico by Burgo
Novo), 139
"The Apology of Raymond
Sebond" (Montaigne), 81
Of Arcane Catholic Truth
(Galantino), 120–21, 133–34
Arendt, Hannah, 128
Ariel, David S., 298n.72
Aristotle, 60–62, 64, 300n.11;
Christianization of, 64
ars notoria, 189, 196
ars Paulina, 196
Artes cabalisticae (Pistorius),
134
Ashmole, Elias, 315n.86
Astrologia Gallica (Morin), 199f
Astrology, 90, 174–75, 188–89,
191, 193, 247, 256
Atheneum, 226
aufhebung, 267
Augustine, Saint, 132, 165, 226
Austin, J. L., 27
authority, 20
automatic writing, 47–48. *See
also* Breton, Karo, Surrealism

Baal Shem Tov, 87
Bacon, Francis (Lord Verulam),
97; on magic, 235, 313n.54
Bacon, Roger, 235
Baeck, Leo, 19
Bakan, David, Freud and Cabala,
161, 239, 294n.8, 315n.95. *See
also* Certeau, Dreams, Freud,
Grözinger, Jung, Kafka, Langer,
Ripellino, Surrealism
Bakhtin, Mikel, 20, 84
Banes, Daniel, Shakespeare and
Cabala, 212. *See also* Yates
baroque, 39; Age of the Baroque,
270, 276, 279, 281
Barthes, Roland, 26
Basilica Chymica (Croll), 176
Bathsheeba, 234
Baudelaire, Charles, 99; art as
inebriation, 237
Baudrillard, Jean, 156–57;
indirect communication, 108;
seduction and simulation, 73.
See also Debord, Kierkegaard,
simulation
Bayley, Harold, 51
Bechinath Happeruschim
(Schickardt), 197
Beckett, Samuel, 60
Beeckman, Isaac, 173
beginning, 104–108, 226
Beitchman, Philip, 296n.39,
312n.37
Ben Yohai, Simon, 1, 20, 24, 30,
32, 44, 55, 133, 177, 274,
294n.2. *See also* de Leon
Benjamin, Walter, 125, 161, 163;
and Gershom Scholem, 7–9
Bergson, Henri, 36
Bernegger, Matthias, 178
Berukhim, Abraham ha-Levi, 127
beth, 73
Beyerlinck, Laurens, 197
Biale, David, 8; on Scholem's
"Unhistorical Aphorisms" and
Kafka as cabalist, 162–64

Bible, the, 6, 9, 71, 163
Bibliographica Kabbalistica
(Scholem), xi, 177; Duret as
having compiled the first one
(1613), 277
Bierce, Ambrose, 239
Binah, 246
Blake, William, 178, 313n.63
Bitaudus, Johannes, Antonius de
Villon, and Stephanus de
Claues, Stephanus, 181
Blanchot, Maurice, 27, 29, 56,
224, 226
Blau, Joseph, xi, 80, 101, 118,
125, 129–30, 134, 136–38,
143–44, 165, 169–72, 172, 177,
180, 210, 214, 245, 250,
300n.7. *See also* Secret
Bloch, Ernst, 312n.48
Blood Libel, 19
Bloom, Harold, 28–29, 133, 135,
161–62, 164
Bockelson, Jan (John of Leyden),
231
Bodin, Jean, 81, 103, 186, 194,
217, 271, 303n.59, 317n.120
Body, the, 155; and cabalistic
physicality, 157
Boehme, Jacob, 178, 183
Bohemia, and John Dee's
"mission" there, 215
Bongus, Peter, 124, 164–65
Borges, Jorge Luis, 28, 162, 253
Bornstein, Diane, 297n.56
Bouillé, Charles, 167, 307n.89
Bourdieu, Pierre, xiii
Bradbrook, Muriel, 211
Breaking of the Vessels, 136, 203
Breath, 288
*Briefe of the Bible Drawne into
English Poetry* (Clapham),
228–29
Breton, André, 29, 162, 262
Brocard, James, 210, 220–21,
225
Brognolo, Candido, 199

Browne, Sir Thomas, xii, 67,
154, 172, 183, 187, 193, 211,
215, 216, 217, 225, 237,
245–58, 259, 274, 279, 280,
282, 315nn.86, 93, 316n.108
Bruno, Giordano, xi, 48, 97, 170
Buber, Martin, 7–8, 61, 295n.13
Burggrav, Johann Ernst, 178,
181
Burgo Novo, Archangelus de, 79,
139–40, 169, 179, 221. *See also*
Garzia

Cabala, x–xii, 2, 4, 16–18, 21–27,
28–29, 32–36, 41–42, 45, 51,
57, 62, 64, 115, 117, 127, 132–
33, 142, 154, 158–59, 162,
171–72, 175, 178, 186, 190,
193, 195–98, 207, 211, 213,
222–23, 226, 229, 238, 245,
248–50, 255–57, 274, 277, 280,
284; and astrology, 174;
attraction for Christians, 20;
devolution of its image, 76;
and Dualism, 50: early Cabala,
14; and the East, 70; as "fad,"
100; heretical, 111, 162, 234,
266, 304n.27; as inebriation,
238; Jewish Cabala, x, 127;
and literary modernity. 28–29;
as literature, xii–xiii; meaning
of word, 16; Neopagan, x–xi,
90, 120, 192; Neoplatonic, 78;
orthodox (Giorgio), 259; and
Pico's "conclusions," 67–71; of
plants, 315n.86; and
Spinoza,146–47; three worlds
of, 49. *See also* Christian
Cabala, Judaism
Cabala del cavallo pegaseo
(Bruno), 126
De Cabala an toleranda
(Hochstraten), 128
Cabala of the Renaissance, ix–xii,
2, 237, 276, 294n.4; of the late
Renaissance, 268

Cabalae Totius brevissimum
  (Lobkowitz), 182
In Cabalam introductio
  (Montecuccolus), 142
Cabalistic Art (Reuchlin), 76,
  139, 209–10, 318n.150
Cabalistic bibliography (in
  Giorgio), 170
"Cabalistic Conclusions" (Pico),
  67–71
In cabalistarum, seu
  allegorizantium (Riccio), 169,
  305n.47
Caballeria, Pedro de la, 102
Cabbalalogia (Henning), 200
Cain, Sons of, 83, 234
Calder, I. F., xiv
Cambridge Platonists, xii, 97,
  148, 201, 266, 279
Camden, William, 75, 182
Campanella, Tommaso, 183, 271
Canetti, Elias, 306n.74
Capital (Marx), 11
capitalist economy, 64, 90–91
Cardano, Geralamo, 307n.90
Casaubon, Meric, 242
Cassiodorus, Flavius Magnus
  Aurelius, 165
Cassirer, Ernst, 165, 171
Castellamare, Bishop of, 190
Castiglione, Baldassaro, 213
Castiglione, Pietro, 195
The Castle (Kafka), 116
Catholicism, 112; Trinitarianism
  and cabalistic *sephiroth*, 142
Certeau, Michel de, 35–36, 38,
  54, 59, 74–75, 130–31, 151,
  155, 166, 180, 238–39,
  299nn.89, 92, 301n.24,
  313n.63. *See also* Jesuits,
  Lacan, Mystics
Chamisso, Ioao Bravo, 155, 173
Champier, Symphorien, 117, 188
Chapman, George, 215
Chappell, William, 261
chariot (*merkabah*), 73, 311n.28

Charles V, 133
chemistry, 190
The Chess Garden (Hansen), 263
Christ, x, 53, 149, 248, 284;
  Agrippa's cabalistic (humble)
  Christ, 86–87; body of, 289; in
  Paradise Lost as driver of
  chariot, or *merkabah*, 74, 259;
  reincarnation(s), 205; resists
  Sabbatian temptations in
  Paradise Regained, 282; in
  time, 285; as transcendent-
  immanence, 297.n.46
Christian, 186, 206, 236, 249,
  270
Christian Cabala, x–xii, 5–6, 33,
  49–50, 75, 96, 125, 134, 143
  144, 169, 170, 187, 201, 222,
  227, 244, 267, 314n.68; in
  Christian apologetics of
  Renaissance, 38
The Christian Cabala (Blau), 101
Christian Morals (Browne), 254,
  258
On Christian religion (Ficino),
  121
A Chronological Discourse
  (Clapham), 229
Church fathers, early, 176
Chymische Hochzeit Christiani
  Rosenkreuz (Andreae), 264
Cicogna, Strozzi, 174
circumcision, 68
City of God (Augustine), 226
Clapham, Henoch, 92, 219–21,
  228–29, 232, 260, 287
Clarkson, Laurence, 232, 283
Clulee, Nicholas, xiii, 242
Codicum cabbalisticorum quibus
  est uses Iannes Picus
  (Gaffarel), 143–44
De Coelesti Agricultura (Riccio),
  139, 145
Coelum sephiroticum
  Hebraeorum (Steeb), 184–85
Cohn, Norman, 281, 318n.142

Colet, John, 209
Comenius, Amos, 145–46, 264–65, 316n.110
Commentaria Bibliorum Chuonradi Pellicani (Lapide), 133
Commentary on Divinatory Methods (Peucer), 171
communism, 186
community, 37, 277
conditioning, 275
Confessio Amantis (Gower), 313n.57
The Confessions of Aleister Crowley, 316n.112
Conjectura Cabbalistica (More), 201
Conjunction, of February 1524, 188, 309n.137
conspiracy, 288
conversion, 4, 102, 141
Conway, Anne, Countess of, 153–54, 201–204; "Aspasia-Mary" of Christian cabalist circle at Ragley, 155
The Conway Letters (Conway-More, Nicolson ed.), 153–54, 201–04, 310n.164
Coppe, Abiezer, 232, 283
Cordovero, Moses, 47, 63, 134–35, 277
Corigio, Joannes Mercurius de, 216–17
correspondences, 41, 251
The Counter Renaissance (Haydn), 161
The Courtier (Castiglione, Hoby trans.), 213
Crashaw, Richard, 39
Crater Hermetis (Lazzarelli), 48, 117–19, 216
creator continuans, Acquinas' Christian adjustment of Aristotle, 62
Crispus, J. P., Franciscan and defender of Pico, 79, 169

Croll, Oswald, 176
Cromwell, Oliver, and readmission of Jews to England, 129, 281
Crowley, Aleister, 271, 316n.112
Cudworth, Ralph, 157, 202, 259, 268, 269
cultural capital, xiii
curiosity, 76
Cusa, Nicholas de, 76
Cymbeline (Shakespeare), 245
Cyrano, 265
Cyrus, the Great, 314n.77

Daemonologia sive de magia naturali (Torreblanca), 195–96
Daemonologie (James VI, King of Scotland, later James I, of England), 217
D'Allones, Olivier Revault, 56
Dan, Joseph, 40, 223, 295n.13
Daniel & Sons, 121
Dante, 204
D'Aquin, Philippe, 182
Daumal, René, 262
David, King, 234
Davies, John, **232–36**, 238
Davies, John (Sir), 233
De Leon, Moses, 1–2, 4–6, 20, 30–32, 59–60, 65, 80, 173, 223, 276, 294n.2, 300n.101
De Man, Paul, 26
De Pauly, Jean, 10, 43, 144, 295n.15, 299n.80
De la démonomanie des sorciers (Bodin), 186, 194
Debord, Guy, 108. *See also* Society of the Spectacle
Decalogue, 18, 108, 291
deconstruction, 55, 84, 300n.5
Dee, Arthur, 279–80
Dee, John, xii–xiv, 157, 161, 170, 185–87, 193, 211, 215, 217–18, 243–45, 249, 259, 293n.1, 316n.108; Queen Elizabeth as reader of Dee's *Monas*, 243–44. *See also* Yates

John Dee and the Politics of Reading and Writing (Sherman), xiv

John Dee's Natural Philosophy (Clulee), 242

"John Dee Studied as an English Neo-Platonist" (Calder), 294n.3

John Dee, The World of an Elizabethan Magus (French), xiv

Defensative Against the Poison of Certain Prophecies (Howard), 210, 214

Deleuze, Gilles, **55–60**. *See also* Guattari, Rhizome

demonic, the, 196, 297n.58, 307n.108

DeQuincey, Thomas, 237

dérèglement, 262. *See also* Daumal, Gilbert-Lecomte, Rimbaud, Surrealism

Derrida, Jacques, 27, 56

Descartes, René, 47, 97, 152–54, 275, 298n.76

desire, female, 38; Mystical Heresy and the Impasse of Desire, 238–40

desiring machines, 262–63

Destructio Cabbalae (Hochstraten), 128

d'Étaples, Lefevre, 95, 188

"Deux Modèles d'écriture" (Hercenberg), 306n.83

Les Deux sources de la réligion et de la morale (Bergson), 36

devil, in medicine, 171–72; Renaissance semiotics of, 186

The Devils of Loudun (Huxley), 301n.24

Dialoghi d'amore (Medigo), 141, 145

dialogic style, 19, 27. *See also* Bakhtin

Dialogues on Two Systems of the World (Galileo), 198

Diaspora, 31, 63

A Diet for Drunkards (Thomson), 238

difference, 56

Digby, Everard, 210

Discours fait contre la nouvelle paracelsique (Gohory/Suavius), 192–93

Discours et histoires des spectres (Le Loyer), 172

Discoverie of Witchcraft (Scot), 217

Disputatio Cabalisticae (Voysin), 147

Disputatio de medicina nova P. Paracelsi (Erastus), 151

Disquisitio de magia divinatrice et operatrice (Monceaux), 200

Dissertatio Peculiaris de Cabbala (Sennert), 183

De divinis attributis quae Sephirot ab Hebraeus nuncupata (Evoli), 193

Doctor Faustus (Mann), 89

Doctor Faustus (Marlowe), 88, 214

Dominicans, the, 52, 66, 76, 80, 128–29, 130

Don Quixote, 31

Dönmeh (Islamic Sabbatians), 159, 318n.147

Donne, John, 126, 165, 255

Dostoevsky, 20

Dreams, 237; from Adam to André Breton, **261–64**; epistemological status in Zohar, 22–23

Dresnitz, Solomon, 48

Dualism, 42, 61, 70; Albigensian-Cathar compared to cabalistic, 14, 50–52; and Gnostic Cabala of *Bahir*, 122; in Kafka and Spenser, 218–19. *See also* Gnosticism

duality, 73, 301n.12. *See also* Agrippa, Baudrillard, Kierkegaard, Daumal

Duchamp, Marcel, 263
Dulcedo de forti sive Elixir (Steeb), 184–85
Dunn, William, 249–51, 255, 315n.96
Duret, Claude, 177, 308n.116

Eastern European Jewry, and endurance of Cabala, 294n.8
Eberhardt, Isabelle, xii, 293n.2
Eckhart, Meister, compared to Sankara and Ramanuja, 20; on *gelassenheit*, 74
Eco, Umberto, 28; open work, 162
L'Écriture de l'histoire (Certeau), 301n.24
ecstatics (French), 2, 135, 298n.76. *See also* Vigée, Mopsik
Eden, 47; Paradise Now, 52
Egypt, 132
Eleazer, of Worms, 72
eleventh commandment, 158
Elias, as avatar of Christ, 205
Eliot, T. S., 286
Elizabeth, (deposed) Princess of Bohemia, correspondent of Descartes, 154
Elizabeth, Queen of England, Age of Elizabeth, 213; Cabalas of the Age of, 187, **215–19**; talk with Dee about *Monas Hieroglyphica mathematice cabalistice*, 243–44; in *Fairie Queene*, 126–27
The Elizabethan World Picture (Tilyard), 233
Elohim, 70
Elohim Triune (Clapham), 219, 221
Elysius, Joannes, 188–89
"An Encomium on the Three Books of Agrippa," (Vaughan), 272–74

English Civil War, xii; interest in Sabbatian episode and débacle in England, 281; Puritan Merchants and Sabbatai (at Smyrna), 281; Ranter-Leveler promiscuity and Sabbatian sexuality, 283; and Sabbatian heresy, 86, 230, 280–83. *See also* Cohn, Fixler, Hill
English Romanticism, 28
Enlightenment, 132–33, 267
L'Entretien infini (Blanchot), 29–30
Entre Nous (Lévinas), 300n.5
Erasmus, 209
Erastus, Thomas Liebler, 151
Errour on the Left Hand through Preposterous Zeale (Clapham), 229, 302n.45
Errour on the Right Hand through Frozen Securitie (Clapham), 229–30, 302n.45
Erubhim, or Miscellanies Christian and Judaicall (Lightfoot), 260
Esau, 234
eschatology, 50
The Essence of Judaism (Baeck), 19
The Eternal Gospel (Joachim of Fiore), 120
Ethics (Aristotle), 300n.11
Ethics (Spinoza), 146–47
Euclid, Dee's Preface to, 242
The Eunuch's Fountain of Sterility (Heer), 152
Eusebio, Father, 198–99
Eve (Biblical), 98
Evelyn, John, 281–82. *See also* English Civil War, Rycaut
evil, 14–15, 111–12, 234; cabalistically intertwined with good, 67–69
Evoli, Cesare de, 193
Examination of the Philosophy of R. Fludd (Gassendi), 266

exile, 65; Cabala as ideology of, 32–33; definitive after expulsion from Spain, 127; as the human condition, 290; in Lurianic Cabala, 179; rhetoric of in Agrippa, 84, 94–95. *See also*, Certeau, Labadie, *galuth*

Expositio Virgiliana (Fulgentius), 236

L'Extase et l'errance (Vigée), 55–56, 300n.5

La Faiblesse de croire (Certeau), 54, 299n.89

The Fairy Queen (Spenser), 22, 38, 73, 126, 215, 259

faith, 148

The False Messiah (Grimmelshausen), 159

Fama Fraternitas Rosae Crucis (Andreae), 264

Family of Love, 232, 310n.164, 312n.50

Fatal Strategies (Baudrillard), 303n.64

Faustian, 275

Febres, de humana felicitate ac de fluxu maris (Iadertinus), 191

Female Pre-eminence (Agrippa), 38

feminine, the, 38; female principle, 44; feminism, 98; feminist numerology, 297n.56. *See also* Patai, Shekinah

Ficino, Marsilio, xii, 65, 121, 195, 211, 271; controversial astrology, 176, 193

fifty gates of understanding, 77

Finnegan's Wake, 6, 60, 163

Fire: Diaries, 1934–37 (Nin), 298n.66

Fish, Stanley, 133

Fisher, John, Bishop of Rochester, 299

Fixler, Michael, 282–83

Fletcher, H. F., 260–61

floods, anticipating through Astrology and Cabala, 189

Fludd, Robert, 180,199, **264–68**; does jig in Leiris' dream, 264; Rosicrucian-cabalist, 265

flux, in The Zohar and modernism, 60

fortress, as mystical metaphor, 109

"Fouilles dans les ruines circulaires" (Leclerc), 296n.34

Fourteen Theses in Opposition to Paracelcists, cabalists (Bitaudus, Villon, and Claues), 181

Fowler, Alastair, 73, 124, 165, 170

fragmentation, 150, 153; the fragmentary, 164

Franciscans, the, 66, 79 129, 130

Franck, Adolphe, 100–101, 137

Frank, Joseph (Sabbatian), 19, 48, 11–12, 128, 144; Frankists, 158, 283

Free Spirit, Cult of, 318n.142

French, Peter, xiv

French cabalists, 56. *See* ecstatics

French Symbolists, 8

Freud, Sigmund, 39, 268, 294n.8, 315n.95; Cabala between Freud and Jung, 78–79; interpreting the dreams of Cabala and Surrealism, 261–62; and Sabbatianism, 238–39; Scholem's Cabala and Freud's unconscious, 3. *See also* Bloom, Bakan

Freud and the Jewish Mystical Tradition (Bakan), 315n.95

Frey, Junius, 267

Fulgentius, 236

Gaez, Gilles, 210

Gaffarel, Jacques, 143–44, 180

Galantino, Pietro, 49, 117, 119, 120–21, 133–34, 170, 299n.80. See also "angel pope," Viterbo

Gali Razaya, 128, 266. *See* Berukhim, J. Otto

Galileo, 198. *See* Bernegger

galuth, 32. *See* exile

Garden of Cyrus (Browne), 245–46, 67, 251–52, 257, 314n.77, 315n.86

Gargantua and Pantagruel (Rabelais), 88

garment, 69, 107, 281

Gary, Romain (Émile Ajar), 162, 309n.148. *See* mumia

Garzia, Pedro, Bishop of Ussel, 65, 179; on Pico's most controversial "Cabalistic conjecture," 139; defender of (orthodox) Astrology, 193. *See also* Burgo Novo

Garzoni, Tomasso, 116, 159

The Gasp (Gary), 320n.108

Gassendi, Pierre, 265–67

gematria, 66, 73, 93, 221, 229

Genesis, 178, 226

The Genesis of Secrecy (Kermode),160

George of Ragusa, 143

Georgius, Franciscus, 79, 117, 142, 165, **169–71**, 187, 216, 232, 244, 267, 271; influence on architecture, 170; and Shakespeare, 211–14; and Spenser, 215

German Romantics, 8

Gershom Scholem, Kaballah and Counter-History (Biale), 8

Gershom Scholem and the Mystical Dimension of Jewish History (Dan), 60, 295n.13

Gikatalia, Joseph, 72, 103, 140–41, 223; importance of Ricci's Latin translation of *Sha'are Orah*, 169

Gilbert-Lecomte, Roger, 262; obsession with Zohar, 306n.83. *See also* Daumal, Grand Jeu, Rattray, Rimbaud, Surrealism

gilgul, 20, 122, 127. *See* reincarnation

Glanvill, Joseph, 203. *See* reincarnation

Gnosticism, 43, 46, **47–52**, 70, 78, 121, 132, 247, 294n.7; in *Bahir*, 122; Cabala as Gnostic revival, 2–3; and Cartesian cogito, 46–47; challenges to (Scholem's) Gnostic Cabala, 294n.7; in Milton, 127; in Nietzsche, 167–68; sects of Antiquity, 234. *See also* Albigensians, Dualism, Jonas, Kafka, Scholem, Runciman

Godelmann, Johann Georg, **194–95**, 196

God's Arithmetic (Meres), 218

Goethe, xi, 89

Gohory, Jacques, 192–93. *See* Suavius

Golding, Arthur, 172. *See* Mornay

Gower, John, 313n.57. *See also* allegory

Graetz, Heinrich, xi, 2, 4, 131, 144, 149, 167; on Leo the Hebrew, 141; on Raymond Martin, 148

Grand Jeu, 262. *See* Daumal, Gilbert-Lecomte

Les Grandes textes de la Kaballe: les rites qui font dieu (Mopsik), 2

Grandier, Urban, 82, 266. *See* Loudun

The Great Chain of Being (Lovejoy), 233

Greater Assembly, the (Idra-Rabba), 41, 298n.60

"The Greatness of Gershom Scholem" (Maccaby), 167

Grimmelshausen, H. C., first published novel about Sabbatai, 159

Grözinger, Karl Erich, 161, 218–19, 240, 294n.8
Guinther of Andernach, 171

Hackspan, Theodor, 198
Hadrianus, Finus, 121
Halevi, Judah, 53
Halloween, 231
hallucinogens, 260, 281
Hansen, Brooks, 263
De Harmonia mundi totius cantica tria (Georgius), 79, 169–71
On the Harmony of the Earthly Sphere (Postel), 121
Hasidism, x, 295n.13, 312n.33; as anti-Cabala, 7–8; as neutralization of Cabala, 36
Haydn, Hiram, 166, 168
Hazoar temporis Messiae (Lauret), 177
hearing, 287; sense of faith, 289
heavenly anatomies, 20, 41. See also Greater Assembly
Hebrew, 101, 182, 185–86, 260, 283, 290; Renaissance Hebraism, 260
Hebrew and talmudic hours (Schoettgen), 121
Hebrew Cabala as Devil's Cunning (Lebenwald), 186
The Hebrew Goddess (Patai), 18, 21
Heer, Henry van, 152
Hegel, 53, 106, 176, 249, 267, 298n.76
Heidegger, 27
Height-Ashbury, 181
Heilbronner, Jacob, 149
Henning, Johan, 200
Henry IV, King of France, 172
Henry VII, King of England, 210
Henry VIII, King of England, 210
Hercenberg, Dov 28
Heredia, Paulus, 102, 120

Hermes, 195, 216, 247; hermeticism, 216, 229, 271; Thrice-Great, xiv, 78; Trismegistus, 246, 314n.77
The Hermit of 69th Street (Kosinski), 28
Hero and Leander (Marlowe), 313n.57
Heterologies: Discourse of the Other (Certeau), 238–39
Hezekiah, King 109
Hieroglyphica (Valeriano), 165
Hill, Christopher, 230
History of Magic and Experimental Science (Thorndike), xi, 166, 293n.1. See Thorndike
History of Philosophy (Windelband), xi, 120, 152, 165–66, 168, 174–75, 183
History of the Jews (Graetz), xi
History of the Three Late Famous Imposters (Evelyn), 281–82
History of the Turkish Empire (Rycaut), 281–82
Hobbes, Thomas, 152
Hochstraten, Jacob, 128
The Holy Kabbalah (Waite), 43–45, 67–71, 77–78, 137, 141–42, 144–45, 178, 181, 266, 269, 277
The House of Incest (Nin), 43
Howard, Earl of Northampton, 210, 214
Hume, David, 314n.77
Huntley, Frank Livingstone, 252
Huxley, Aldous, 301n.24
"Hymn to Heavenlie Beauty" (Spenser), 126, 215

I Am a Process with No Subject (Beitchman), 296n.39, 312n.37
Iadertinus, Federicus, 191
Iamblichus, 115, 229
Iannis, Cheradami, 242
The Idea of the Holy (Otto), 295n.21

Idel, Moshe, 2, 29–30, 32, 56, 63–64, 162, 293n.2, 294n.6, 297n.42, 298n.76, 299n.79, 300n.101

L'Idole et la distance (Marion), 299n.93

Immortality of the Soul (More), 310n.164

Incest: Diaries, 1932–34 (Nin), 43

Individual and Cosmos in Renaissance Philosophy (Cassirer), 306n.67

The Influence of Prophecy in the Later Middle Ages (Reeves), 121

Ingpen, William, 165, 240–42

The Interior Castle (Saint Teresa), 159, 240

Interprétation de l'arbre de la Cabale (D'Acquin), 182

Introductio in vitalem philosophiam (Burggrav), 178

Iraneus, 132, 206

Isaac ben Samuel of Acre, 4

Isaac the Blind, 16, 72; apocatastasis, 14; Blanchot on a famous fragment, 29–30; letter warning cabalists not to write, 223–24

Isaac de Lattes, 10

Islam, 54, 112, 128, 234

The Island of the Day Before (Eco), 28

Israel, 40, 132

Jacob, 15, 234; ladder, 276

James, VI of Scotland, I of England, 217, 271, 291

James, William, 150

Javary, Geneviève, 38

Jellinek, Aaron, 4

Jesuits, 130–31, 150, 268. *See also* Certeau

The Jewish Mind (Patai), 21

Jewish Mysticism: An Annotated Bibliography on the Kabbalah (Spector), 201, 308n.119

Jewish Mysticism and Jewish Ethics (Dan), 297n.45

Joachim of Fiore, Joachimism, 49, 120, 318n.142; angel pope, 295n.15, 299n.80; world cycles, 50

Job, 15

Jonson, Ben, 245

Joris, David, 245

Josten, C. H., 242; Dee's alchemy as inner search, 314n.68. *See also Monas*

Joseph Karo, Lawyer and Mystic (Werblowsky), 43, 47–48, 297n.58

Joubert, Joseph, 227

Journals (Kierkegaard), 299n.88

Journals (Leiris), 261–62, 316n.108

The Joyful Wisdom (Nietzsche), 168

Juan de la Cruz (Saint John of the Cross), 159

In Judeos flagellum (Hadrianus), 121

Judaism, 8, 37, 53–54, 132, 205, 236; fragmented authority, 14, 304n.27; Jewish millenarianism, 230; Jewish sects, 2; and Trinitarianism, 143; segregation of sexes, 21; sexism, 18

Judische ABC Schul im Buch Yezirah (Steidner), 184

Jung, Carl Gustav, 78, 277

Kaballah (Scholem), 132

Kabballah and Criticism (Bloom), 29

Kabbalah Denudata (Rosenroth), 117, 134, 136, 250, 269

Kabbalah: New Perspectives (Idel), 213

On the Kaballah and Its Symbolism (Scholem), 61–62

The Kaballah Unveiled (Mathers trans.), 10

Kabbale ou la philosophie religieuse des Hebreux (Franck), 100–101

Kabbalisticae precationes (Sperber), 172

Kafka, Franz, xii, 116, 133, 146, **159–64**, 193, 218, 294n.8, 306n.74; dualism, 218–19; paradox of (divine) mercy and justice, 70; and women, 159–60, 306n.74. *See also* Benjamin, Biale, Bloom, Canetti, Grözinger, Kermode, Ripellino, Scholem

Kafka and Kaballah (Grözinger), 161

Kafka's Other Trial (Canetti), 306n.74

Kant, Immanuel, 133, 236, 240–41

Karo, R. Joseph, Safed Kaballahist, 47. *See* Werblowsky

Keats, John, 149

Keith, George, Quaker notable, 310n.164

Kelley, Edward, 193

Kermode, Frank, 160

Khunrath, Heinrich, 176, 195

Kierkegaard, Soren, 98, 106, 108, 280, 285, 288, 297n.56; critique of aesthetics, xiii; hidden Christ, 164, Jews, 53, 176

Kircher, Athanasius, **180–81**, 245

The Kiss of the Spouse, 280

Knittel, Caspar, 200

Kosinski, Jerzy, 28, 162

The Kuzari (Halevi), 53

La Boderie, brothers, 211

La Mettrie, Julien de, 275

Labadie, Jean, 313n.63

The Labyrinth of the World (Comenius), 145–46, 264–65

Lacan, Jacques, 27, 166

Laing, R. D., 58

Langer, Jiri, 161

Lapide, Cornelius à, 131, **133–34**

Lauret, Christophorus, 177

Lazzarelli, Ludovico, 48, **117–19**, 124, 188, 192, Agrippa's borrowings from, 117–18; demonic magic, 216–17; Neopagan Cabala, x. *See also* Bruno, de Corigio, Hermes, Pimander, T. Vaughan, Walker

Le Loyer, Pierre, 172

League of the Elect, 231

Leah, 108

King Lear (Shakespeare), 244–45

Leary, Timothy, 271

Lebenwald, Adam, 186

Lech Lecha, 299n.92, 314n.75

Leclerc, Marie-Christine, 296n.34

Leibniz, G. W., 102, 152; and Anne Conway, 155; on Spinoza as cabalist, 41, 147, 249

Leiris, Michel, 261–62, 316n.108

Leon, Fra Luis de, 159

Lessing, Gotthold Ephraim, 133

Levelers, 86, 318nn.142, 147. *See also* Cohn, Hill, Ranters

Levi, Eliphas, Abbé Louis Constant, 271

Lévinas, Emmanuel, 27; transcendent immanence, 296n.25, 297n.46; the two sides (mercy and justice) of God, 70, 300n.5

Lévy-Bruhl, Lucien, 166

Lewis, C. S., 313n.57

Liber Jezirah (Rittangel), 183

Libertinism, 158, 265, 306n.71

Lieb, Michael, 294n.7

Liebes, Yehuda, 294n.2, 300n.97, 310n.170

Light from the East (Glanvill), 203

Lightfoot, John, **260–64**, 316n.103

Lilith, 297n.59; and Nin, 43; in
Paradise Lost, 127, 263; and
the Shekinah, **38–47**, 159
Literature and the Occult
Tradition (Saurat), 311n.13
Le Livre à venir (Blanchot), 224
Lobkowitz, Johann Caramnel, 182
Loudun, the Possessed of, 82,
266, 301n.24. See Certeau,
Grandier, Huxley
Love's Labor's Lost
(Shakespeare), 211–14
Lovejoy, Arthur, 233
Lowry, Malcolm, 28
Lull, Raymond, 173, 294n.11;
potable gold, 308n.133
Luria, Rabbi David, 4
Luria, Isaac, 47, 117, 134–35,
196, 250, 277, 279, 310n.170,
319n.154; in England, 154,
202–204, 269–70. See also
Breaking of the Vessels,
Gilgul, More, Safed, Tikkun,
Tsimtsum, F. M. Van Helmont,
Vital
Luther, Martin, 129, 267

Macbeth (Shakespeare), 244
Maccaby, Hyam, 167
Macrobius, 165
maggid, 35, 47, 55
Maggid Mesharim (Karo), 47
Magia universalis (Schott), 184
magic, xiii, 99–100, 103, 118,
150, 158, 172, 181, 183, 194,
218, 256, 271, 275; divinatory
175; natural, 181; objective
(heretical), 175–76; subjective,
175. See also Agrippa,
Lazzarelli, Walker
Magic Prague (Ripellino), 161
"Magic and Radical Reformation
in Agrippa" (Zambelli), 301n.34
A Magical and Cabalistic
Method of Curing Every
Disease (Heilbronner), 149–51

Il magico mondo de gli heroi
(Riviera), 195
De magis veneficis et lamiis
(Godelmann), 194–96
Magnum Theatrum (Beyerlinck),
197
magus, 118
Maimon, Solomon, 115, 132, 267
Maimonides, 105, 149, 155, 226,
303n.61
Major Trends in Jewish Mysti-
cism (Scholem), 1, 43, 122, 127
malkuth, 39, 160
Mallarmé, Stéphane, 17, 62
Manasseh ben Israel, 230
Mann, Klaus, 160
Mann, Thomas, 89
Margaliot, Reuben, 293–94n.2
Marion, Jean-Luc, 56, 299n.93
Marlowe, Christopher, 48, 90,
170, 172, 232, 234, 302n.44,
313n.57; Agrippa as Marlowe's
Faustus, 88–89, 214, 217. See
also School of Night
marranos, 33, 291
Martin, Eva, 317n.24
Martin, Raymond, 148, 294n.11
Marx, Karl, 92, 231
Marxism, 8, 152
Mary, 19
Mary, Princess, 210
Le Masque et la lumière: la
poétique des grands rhétoriquers
(Zumthor), 84–85, 94
mathematics: Heavenly Math-
ematics and the Case of Dee,
240–45; mystical, 190, See also
Bongus, Dee, duality, Fowler,
Ingpen, Meres, Milton, numer-
ology, Peranzonus, Pythagoras,
Quarnström, Spenser,
Windelband
Mathers, S. L. G., 10, 265. See
also Rosicrucians
Matthys, Jan, 231
McKeon, Michael, 281

Meade, Joseph, 269
De medendis corporis malis per
    manualem operationem
    (Chamisso), 173
Medicina Diatastica (Tentzel),
    197
De medicina veteri et nova
    (Guinther of Andernach), 171
medicine, 174, 248–49; Cabala as
    medicine, 149–59; the devil as
    doctor, 171–72, 307n.108
The Medieval Manichee
    (Runciman), 51–52, 122
Medigo, Leon Abrabanel (Leo the
    Hebrew), 141, 145
Mendelssohn, Moses, 132, 149
The Merchant of Venice
    (Shakespeare), 212
Meres, Frances, 218
Mersenne, Père Marin, 127, 132,
    142–43, 170, **179–80**, 268,
    304n.24
messiah, 66, 111; messianic
    movements, 158
The Messiah is Come, Proved by
    Stories from the Hebrew
    (Vincenti), 121
The Metamorphosis (Kafka), 146
"Métaphores et pratiques
    sexuelles dans la Cabballe"
    (Idel), 297n.47
Metatron (Yurick), 81, 168
Microcosmos (Davies), 233–35
midnight, 32
Midrash Ha-Neelam, 295n.15
Midsummer Night's Dream
    (Shakespeare), 212
Mille Plateaux (Deleuze-
    Guattari), 59–60
Milton, John, 12, 74, 127, 146,
    202, 237, 259, 263, 282,
    311n.28. See also Adamson,
    Fixler
Milton and the Christian Tradi-
    tion (Patrides), 145
"Milton and the Conjectura

Cabbalistica" (Werblowsky),
    202–203
Milton and Forbidden Knowledge
    (H. Schultz), 302n.45
Milton and the Kingdoms of God
    (Fixler), 282–83
Milton's Rabbinical Readings
    (Fletcher), 260
Milton's Semitic Studies
    (Fletcher), 261
"Milton's Version of the War in
    Heaven" (Adamson), 311n.28
Miscellanearum sacrorum . . . de
    Cabbala Judaica (Hackspan),
    198
Miscellany Tracts (Browne), 252
Mithridates, Flavius, 102
modernism, 59, 226
Mohammed, 54
Molière, 265
Molitor, Franz Josef, 7–8
Monas Hieroglyphica
    mathematice cabalistice (Dee),
    242–44, 293n.1
Monceaux, François de, 200
Montaigne, Michel de, 81, 88,
    157–58, 256–57
Montecuccolus, Carolus, 142,
    305n.50
moon, 178–79, 182, 315n.79
Mopsik, Charles, 2, 10, 294n.5,
    295n.16, 297n.47, 298n.76
morality, 12–13, 41
More, Henry, 138, 153–55, 201,
    203–204, 250, 269, 279–80,
    310n.164, 318n.137; arrival of
    Lurianic Cabala in England,
    202; source of merkabah in
    Paradise Lost, 311n.28. See also
    Adamson, Browne, Cambridge
    Platonists, Cassirer, Conway,
    Keith, Glanvill, Leibniz, Milton,
    Nicolson, Peganius (Von
    Rosenroth), reincarnation, Rust,
    Spector, Van Helmont, T.
    Vaughan, Werblowsky

Morin, Jean Baptiste, 199
Mornay, Philip de, 172
Mosaicall Philosophy (Fludd), 267
Moses, 18, 123, 223, 263, 274, 277
Mount Sinai, 15
*Mountain Gloom and Mountain
    Glory* (Nicolson), 226
mumia, 197
Mundus Subterraneus (Kircher),
    180–81
Münster Rebellion, 86, 230.
    See also Anabaptist, Bloch,
    Bockelson, Cohn, Halloween,
    Matthys, Münzer, Nashe,
    Williams
*Musiques, Variations sur la
    pensée juive* (d'Allones), 56
My Rosicrucian Adventure
    (Regardie), 316n.112
*The Mysterious Meaning of
    Numbers* (Bongus), 165
The Mystic Fable (Certeau),
    35–36, 38, 130–31, 151,
    299n.92, 313n.63
The Mystic Quest (Ariel), 278n.72
*On the Mystical Shape of the
    Godhead* (Scholem), 45, 26
Mysticism East and West (Otto),
    20
Mystics, x, 238; discourse of, 36,
    59, 248; mystical experience.
    86; mystical nomadism, 266,
    299n.92, 313n.63; mystical
    text, 8. See also Certeau,
    Labadie, *Lech Lecha*

Naked Lunch, 120
Nathan of Gaza, 111, 149, 173,
    270
Nathanson, Leonard, 251–52
The Natural History of Religion
    (Hume), 314n.77
Natural Religion, 183, 204
Nauert, Charles, 82, 93; Agrippa
    and Lazzarelli, 117–18
Neander, M., 161

Neoplatonism, x, xii, 2, 48, 66,
    80, 96, 126, 213, 229, 271;
    Jewish, 122. *See also* Pico
Nephesh, 278
Nerval, Gérard de, 262
*A New Document Concerning the
    Early Kaballah* (Scholem), 223
A New Light on the Renaissance
    (Bayley), 299n.85
Newman, William, 311n.19,
    317nn.125, 132
Newton, Isaac, 198
Nicolson, Marjorie Hope, 153–54,
    201, 203, 226, 310n.164. *See
    also* Conway, More, Van
    Helmonts
Nietzsche, Friedrich, 27, 41–42,
    69, 116, 162, 164, 166–68,
    236–37
Nin, Anaïs, xii, 43, 298n.66
Ninety-Six Sermons (Andrewes),
    283–92, 318n.148
De nobilitate medici (Obicius), 155
Nohrnberg, James, 22
notorikon, 66, 73–74
Nouveau Essais (Leibniz), 155
Novalis, 226
numerology, 90, 164–65, 190,
    307n.85; in Browne, 245–46;
    Renaissance literature, 73–74.
    See also Bongus, Dee, Fowler,
    Iamblichus, mathematics,
    Pythagoras
numinous, the, xi–xiii, 160. *See*
    Otto

Obicius, Hyppolitus, 155
*The Occult Philosophy in the
    Elizabethan Age* (Yates), 212–13,
    242–44, 312n.50, 314n.68, 271
occult traditions, 91; and Surre-
    alism, 262
Occulta Filosofia (Eusebio),
    198–99
Oedipus Egyptiacus (Kircher),
    181, 245

one, the, 218, 241; The One and
the Two Many, 60–64. *See* two
Ophites, 83, 234
Oporin, J., 137
oral and the written, the, 11,
16–17, 19; oral law, 100; *voice*
as supplement, 57
Oration on the Dignity of Man
(Pico), 68
Orationes Duae de Cabbala
(Bernegger), 178
original sin, 278, 317n.133
Origins of the Kabbalah
(Scholem), 102, 122
Orpheus, 195
other side, the, 13, 39, 103, 107
Otto, Julius Conrad, 127
Otto, Rudolph, xii, 20, 57,
295n.21. *See* numinous
OuLiPo, 140. *See* Perec
*The Overthrow of Cabalist
Theology* (Lobkowitz), 182
Ovid, 236, 313n.57
Ozick, Cynthia, 296n.42

*Pagan Mysteries in the Renais-
sance* (Wind), 236, 313n.56
Paganism, 248–49
Palagio de gl'incanti (Strozzi), 174
Paracelsus, Theophrastus
Bombastus, 90, 155, 157, 174,
178, 181, 192, 230, 265–66,
316n.108; Paracelsan Alchemy,
xii; Peasant Revolt sympa-
thizer, 301n.34; potable gold,
185; and Vitalism 152–53, 178
Paradise Lost (Milton), 74, 127
Paradise Regained (Milton), 259,
282
Pardes, 98
Pardes rimmonim (Cordovero),
134–34
Pascal, Blaise, 102, 148, 288
Patai, Raphael, 296n.26; Cabala
and Indian religion, 70–71; the
feminine-divine in Judaism,

18–19; sexually suggestive
statuary in the Second
Temple, 21
Patrides, Constatinos, 145
Peganius, 202, 243. *See*
Rosenroth
Pellican, Conrad, 133. *See*
Lapide
In Pentateuchum (Lapide), 133–34
Peranzanus, Nicolaus, 189–90
Perec, George, 190
Pererius, Benedictus, 130
Pericles (Shakespeare), 245
Peucer, Caspar, 171
Pfefferkorn Controversy, 129
Philo, 18, 48, 181
*Philosophie der Geschichte oder
Über die tradition* (Molitor), 7
Physica caelestis (Schoock), 199
Piccioli, Antonio, 194
Pico della Mirandola, xiii–xiv,
4–5, 36, 49, **65–72**, 77, 79, 96,
115, 117, 142–47, 170, 172–73,
186–87, 209, 211, 237, 240,
265, 275–76, 279, 284; Cabalis-
tic Conclusions, 67–71; Chris-
tian Cabala, x, 34, 102. *See
also* Burgo Novo, Garzia,
Neoplatonism
Pimander (Hermes Trismegistus),
95, 117, 188, 192
Pirke Abot, 160
Pistorius, Johannes, 49, 117, **134–
41**, 145, 149–50, 169, 196, 245
Plaskow, Judith, 45, 298n.72
Plato, 60
Platonic Discourse on Love
(Pico), 145
*The Platonic Renaissance in
England* (Cassirer), 302n.53,
174
Platonism, 48–49, 61, 64–66, 72,
105, 108, 153, 181, 202, 241,
250–51, 259, 268, 290. *See*
Cambridge Platonists,
Neoplatonism

Plotinus, 48
Pollard and Redgrave, xi
Polygot Bible (Walton), 316n.103
Polytheism, 48
Porphyry, 48, 229
La Possession de Loudun
(Certeau), 301n.24
Post, Jonathan, 257, 315n.86
Postel, William, 121, 187, 199,
237, 276, 295n.15, 299n.80;
translator of Sefer Yetzirah,
101, 123–26, 140–41; transla-
tor of Zohar (unpublished),
101–02, 136–38, 144
potable gold, 185, 308n.133
The Principle of Hope (Bloch),
312n.48
*The Principles of the Most
Ancient and Modern Philoso-
phy* (Conway), 154–55
Problemata (Mersenne), 170
Prognosticon Libri (Champier),
188
In Prooemium Pugionis fidei
(Voysin pref. to Martin),
147–48
Protestantism, 138, 267
*The Provocative Merchant of
Venice* (Banes), 212
pseudepigraphy, 3, 123
psychoanalysis, 78
Pugio fidei (Martin), 148
The Pursuit of the Millennium
(Cohn), 281, 318n.142
Pynchon, Thomas, 28, 162
Pythagoras, 190, 200, 205
Pythagorean, 73, 90, 98, 165,
216, 247, 269, 300n.11. *See
also* numerology

*Quaestiones celeberrimae in
Genesim* (Mersenne), 142,
179–80
Quakers, 310n.164. *See* Keith
quincunx, 245, 247, 250. *See*
Browne, *The Garden of Cyrus*

Rabelais, François, 20, 88, 253
Rachel, 108
The Radical Reformation (G. H.
Williams), 306n.71, 312n.48
Raleigh, Sir Walter, 48, 211, 213,
215, 244. *See* The School of
Night
Ramanuja, 20, 296n.25
Ramsay, Chevallier, 314n.77
Rapiti Renovati (Piccioli), 194
Rattray, David, 306n.83
Raya Mehemna, 6, 31
Recenati, Menaheim, 72, 80, 143
*Recherches sur l'utilisation du
thème de la Sekina* (Javary),
38
redemption, 206–207
Reeves, Marjorie, 121. *See*
Joachimism
Regardie, Israel, 316n.112. *See*
Rosicrucians
reincarnation, 153, 310n.170,
314n.77; Cabala as Reincarna-
tion, **201–207**. *See also gilgul*,
Glanvill, Luria, More, Rust, F.
Van Helmont,
Religio Medici (Browne), 255,
258, 316n.108
religion, ix, xii; religious and
sexual liberation, 232; subversive in Renaissance, 230
Remains (Camden), 182
Renaissance, 3, 5–6, 12, 39,
42, 50, 73, 91, 99, 115,
294n.4; later Renaissance,
61, 315n.96
Reuchlin, John, 4, 49, 71–73,
76, 79–80, 102, 115, 117,
139, 142, 152, 183, 186, 193,
200, 209–11, 214–15, 276,
318n.150; Dominicans, 66,
128–29. *See also* Pfefferkorn
Controversy
Revelation, 205
*The Revelation of St. John
Revealed* (Brocard), 220

Revolution, 261–62, 267. *See also* English Civil War, Münster Rebellion, F. M. Van Helmont (Reincarnation-Revolution)

Rhizome: Cabala as Rhizome, **55–60**. *See* Deleuze and Guattari

Riccio, Paul, 49, 117, 139, 140–41, **169**, 202, 229, 245, 256–57, 284, 305n.47; translated Gikatilia's *Gates of Light*, 102–103, 140–41, 169

Richard II (Shakespeare), 197

Richard III (Shakespeare), 234

Ricoeur, Paul, 56–57

Rimbaud, 262

Ripellino, Angelo Maria, 161, 294n.8

Rittangel, Iohannes Stefanus, 183

Riviera, Cesare, 195

Romantic (and Symbolist) poetics, 237, 262

Rosenkreuz, Christian, 264. *See also* Andreae, J. Dee, Rosicrucians

Rosenroth, Knorr Von, 29, 117, 134, 136, 138, 140, 169, 183; connections with Conway circle, 153–54, 201–202; correspondence with More, 138, 250, 269. *See* Conway, I. Luria, More, Peganius, F. M. Van Helmont

Rosenzweig, Franz, 36–38, 61, 226

The Rosicrucian Enlightenment (Yates), 264–65

Rosicrucians, xi, 10, 151, 264–65, 316n.112. *See also* Andreae, Comenius, Crowley, J. Dee, Fludd, Mathers, Regardie, Spinka, Yates

Rostvig, Maren-Sofie, 133, 165

Roth, Philip, 28

Rousseau, Jean Jacques, 133

Roussel, Raymond, 263

ruach, 278

Rudolph II, King of Bohemia, 185, 193, 215, 244. *See also* J. Dee, Kelley

Runciman, Steven, 51–52, 122

Runes, Dagobert, 10

Russo, Baruchiah (Osman Baba), 158. *See* eleventh commandment, Sabbatian

Rust, George, 203

Rycaut, Sir Paul, 281–82. *See* Evelyn

"Sabbatai Sevi in England" (McKeon), 281

Sabbatai Sevi: The Mystical Messiah (Scholem), 127–28

Sabbath's Theatre (Roth), 28

Sabbatians, ix, 3, 21, 50, 132–33, 143, 173, 196, 239; and Cambridge Platonists, 203; and English millenarianism, 230; heretical Cabala, 185, 304n.27; and libertinism, 158; and modernist literature, 162; news followed in England, 281; and F. M. Van Helmont, 201. *See* Frank, McKeon, Nathan, Scholem, Zevi

Safed, x, xii, 47, 85, 128, 134, 142, 155, 299n.79. *See also* Berukhim, Cordovero, *Gali Razaya*, Karo, Luria

La Saincte et tréscrestienne Kaballahe (Thenaud), 79–80

Salomon, Johannes, 121

"Samael, Lilith and the Concept of Evil in Early Kabbalah" (Dan), 40, 297n.59

San Francesco della Vigna, Church of (Venice), 170, 240

Sanatorium Under the Sign of the Hourglass (Schultz), 87

"Sancta Maria Dolorum" (Crashaw), 39

Sanctae linguae erotemata
(Neander), 121
Sankara, 20, 296n.25
Sapience, 215, 259
Sarah, 246
Sartre, 263
Satan, 14. *See* apocatastasis
Satis metuendi diluvii verissima
liberatio (Conjunction of 1524
and expected deluge, Elysius),
188–89
Saurat, Denis: read by Nin,
298n.66; sexual Cabala, 43, 45;
on the *Shekinah* in Spenser's
"Hymn to Heavenlie Beauty,"
126, 215. *See* Sapience
Savanarola, 191, 193
Schechter, Solomon, 312n.33
Schickardt, Wilhelm, 197
schizoanalysis, 58
Schlegels, Friedrich, and August
Wilhelm, 226
Schoettgen, Christian, 121
Scholem, Gershom, xi,, 16–17, 23,
30, 43–45, 102, 105, 111, 121–
24, 132–33, 135, 159, 177, 197,
204, 223, 226, 233, 267–68,
293n.1, 294nn.2, 8, 312n.48; on
the Bahir, 122; and Benjamin,
7–9; challenges to Scholem's
Gnostic Cabala, 2–3, 294n.7;
establishing Moses de Leon as
the author of The Zohar, 1–7;
exile (*galut*) of humanity and
God, 290; on *Gali Razaya*, 127–
28; on Hasidism, 268; Hegelian-
ism of, 54, 267, 298n.76; Kafka's
heretical Cabala, 161–64; on
Rosenzweig, 61–62; Sabbatai's
apostasy, 231–32
Schoock, Martin, 199
School of Night, 211, 213
The School of Night (Bradbrook),
211
Schott, Caspar, 184
Schultz, Bruno, xii, 28, 87, 162

Schultz, Howard, 302n.45
Science, 100, 140, 158
Scot, Reginald, 217
Scotus, Duns, 294n.11
"The Second Anniversary"
(Donne), 126
"Les secousses transatlantiques
du Grand Jeu" (Rattray),
306n.83
secrecy, 106; Manifestly the
Hidden, **223–25**; The Paradox
of Secrecy, **108–13**
Secret, François, xi, 100, 120,
131, 148, 177, 308n.116;
opposes Blau's underestimation
of Renaissance Cabala, 125,
129–30, 136–38, 144, 170
The Secret Light of Magicians and
Philosophers (Khunrath), 176
The Secret of Numbers (Ingpen),
240
Le secret de la relation entre
l'homme et la femme dans la
Cabbale (Mopsik trans.),
297n.47
Secrets Revealed (Vaughan), 277–
78
Secular Poems by Vaughan
brothers (Tuttin, ed.), 317n.124
seduction, 108
Seduction (Baudrillard), 306n.64
Sefer Bahir, 11, 13, 102, 121–22,
196, 295n.18
Sefer Yetzirah, 11, 184; Postel
trans., 101, 123–26, 140–42;
influence on Lazzarelli, 216.
See Rittangel, *Liber Jezirah*
Sennert, Andreas, 183
Sephiroth (or Sefiroth), 46, 48,
76, 88, 121; and Christian
Trinity, 142–43; in *Merchant of*
Venice, 212; Platonic, as
opposed to Aristotelian *ain*
soph, 60–63; would correspond
to Ramanuja's rather than
Sankara's Vedanta, 20

Serres, Michel, xiv

Sex,, 71, 106; arousing sculpture in Jewish Temple, 21; demonic visits in The Zohar and *Fairie Queene*, 22; and Leo the Hebrew, 145; Sabbath eve sex with the Shekinah, 33–34, 37–38; Sabbatian and English antinomian promiscuity, 232; sexual Cabala, 43–47; Sexual Mysticism and the Philosopher's Stone, 277–80; in Vaughan, 317n.132

Seznec, Jean, 236, 313n.56. *See* allegory

Sha'are Orah (Gikatalia), 103, 140

Shakespeare, xii, 170, 206, 234, 242, 244–45, 313n.57; The School of Night and *Love's Labor's Lost*, 211–14. *See also* Banes, Bradbrook, School of Night, Yates

Shakespeare's Last Plays (Yates), 314n.68

She-devils (Wier), 194

Shekinah, 36–37, 99, 111, 122, 177, 213, 215, 219, 258–59, 295n.21, 298n. 72; in English literature (Spenser, Donne, Milton), 126–27; as Goddess in Judaism, 18–19; Lilith and the Shekinah, **38–47**, 159, 297n.58; as Sabbath eve sexual consort, 22, 33–34, 52

Sherman, William, xiv

Short Title Catalogue (Pollard and Redgrave), xi

Sidney, Sir Philip, 170, 213, 215, 242, 244. *See* Mornay

De Signatura Rerum (Boehme), 178

Silent Poetry (Fowler, ed.), 307n.85

Simon, Maurice, and Sperling, Harry, translators of The Zohar, 10, 226

Simplicissimus (Grimmelshausen), 159

Simulations (Baudrillard), 301n.12

Singer, I. B., 162

1666 (year), 184, 281

Sixtus IV, Pope, 65, 209

Sixtus V, Pope, 210

Smith,Reverend Henry, 214–15

La Société de consommation (Baudrillard), 306n.70

Society of Pariahs, 291

Society of the Spectacle, 206

Sollers, Philippe, 26, 263

Solomon Maimon: An Autobiography, 267

In Somnium Scipionis (Macrobius), 165

Sorel, Charles, 265

The Spanish Christian Cabala (Swietlicki), 159, 240

Spector, Sheila, 201, 308n.119

Spenser and the Numbers of Time (Fowler), 300n.10

Spenser, Edmund, xii, 48, 126, 172, 190, 211, 213, 219, 237, 242, 244, 263; Archimago, Agrippan enchanter in *Fairy Queen*, 22, 38, 259; numerological-symbolic meaning of Una and Duessa in *Fairy Queen*, 73; Queen Elizabeth as Spenser's Shekinah for the Israel of Britain, 215; the Red Cross Knight's zoharic sex dream in *Fairy Queen*, 22, 259; Sapience as Shekinah in "Hymn to Beauty," 45–46. *See also* Nohrnberg, Saurat

Sperber, Julius, 172

Spinka, Matthew, 265

Spinoza, Baruch Benedict, 62, 107, 160, 204, 249; amor intellectus dei, 110; banned by Catholics, excommunicated by Jews, 303n.62; epistemology

compared to three worlds of
Cabala, **146–47**; removal of
God from human affairs, 41–
42. *See also* Leibniz, Natural
Religion, Nietzsche
Spiritual and Demonic Magic
(Walker), 48, 175–76, 210, 216,
235, 313n.54
Stages on Life's Way
(Kierkegaard), 297n.56
Standing Again at Sinai
(Plaskow), 45
Stapleton, Michael, 233
The Star of Redemption
(Rosenzweig), 36–37
Steeb, Johann, 184–85
Steidner, Johann, 184
Stern, Michael, 296n.90
Stoeffler, Johann, 188
The Strategy of Truth
(Nathanson), 251–52
Street of Crocodiles (Schultz), 28,
296n.36
*The Strong Light of the Canoni-
cal* (Bloom), 294n.8
Structuralism, 28
"Structure as Prophecy"
(Rostvig), 133, 165
Studies in Ecstatic Cabala (Idel),
229n.79, 301n.101
Studies in Judaism (Schechter),
312n.33
Studies in the Zohar (Liebes),
294n.2
Suavius, Leo, xiii, 192–93. *See*
Gohory
Sufism, 49, 293n.2, 299n.79,
300n.101. *See also* Abulafia,
Eberhardt, Idel
Summa Contra Gentiles (Acqui-
nas, in Hebrew trans.), 182
Surrealism, 29, 47, 57, 162, 237,
295n.15; Dreaming from Adam
to André Breton, **261–64**
La Survivance des dieux antiques
(Seznec), 313n.56

Swedenborg, Emmanuel, 178
Swietlicki, Catherine, 159, 240
syncretism, 207

tabernacle, 24
Talmud, 9, 49, 75
Tamburlaine, 234
Tanguy, Ives, 263
Tantra, 21, 71
Tao Te Ching, 224
Tasso, F., 121
technology, 125–26
The Tempest (Shakespeare), 212
"Ten Unhistorical Aphorisms on
Kabbalah" (Scholem), 161–64
Tentzel, Andreas, 197
Teresa, Saint, 116, 159, 194, 240
Tetragrammaton, 67, 70, 150,
233
Theatre of Human Life
(Zwinger), 197
themurah, 66, 73–75
Thenaud, Jean, 79–80, 95, 188
Theodicy, 13, 234
Theodicy (Leibniz), 234
Theologian of Revolution, 231,
312n.48
Theological-Political Treatise
(Spinoza), 107, 303n.62
Theology (Asclepius), 188
*Theophrasti Paracelsi
philosophiae et medicinae
universae* (Suavius), 192–93
Theoria Analytica (Digby), 210
theosophy, 47, 178
theurgy, 47, 72, 81, 173, 249
Thibaut, George, 296n.25
32 (cabalistic number), 74
37 Demonstrationes (Saloman),
121
Sir Thomas Browne (Huntley),
252, 315n.90
Sir Thomas Browne (Post), 257,
315n.86
"Thomas Vaughan, Magician"
(Martin), 317n.124

"Thomas Vaughan as Interpreter of Agrippa von Nettesheim" (Newman), 311n.19
Thomson, Thomas, 238
Thorndike, Lynn, xi, xiv, 151–52, 166, 172, 176, 180–81, 184–86, 194–196, 198–99, 228, 293n.1
Three Books of Occult Philosophy or Magic (Agrippa), 272
three worlds (of Cabala), 49, 80, 146–47, 174
Thresor de l'histoire des langues (Duret), 177
Through a Speculum that Shines (Wolfson), 319n.154
Thus Spake Zarathustra (Nietzsche), 168
tikkun, 136, 203, 279
Tikkune Zohar, 6, 31
Tilyard, E. M., 233
Tishby, Isaiah, 10, 44, 293–94n.2, 297n.58
Torah, Pentateuch, 9, 11, 16, 18, 37, 40, 63, 95, 135, 223, 227, 234, 312n.33
Torreblanca, Francisco, 195–96, 199
The Travels of Cyrus (Ramsay), 314n.77
tree (of the sefiroth), 39, 182
Trewness of Christian Religion (Mornay), 172
The Trial (Kafka), 70
Tritheim, Abbot Johannes, 80, 195, 301n.19
Triumphal Forms (Fowler), 307n.88
A True and Faithful Relation of what passed between Spirits and Dee (M. Casaubon), 242
True Intellectual System of the Universe (Cudworth), 268–69
tsimtsum, withdrawn divine, 35, 50, 63, 135
Turner, Cyril, 234
Tuttin, J. P., 317nn.124, 125

typology, 125, 183, 284
Twenty Familiar Arguments on the Coming of the Messiah (F. Tasso), 121
Twilight of the Idols (Nietzsche), 236–37
two, the, 219, 241. See the one
Two Hundred Queries about the Revolution of Souls (F. Van Helmont), 201–207
two laws, the, 95–96
Two Treatises on the Hierarchies of Dionysius (Colet), 209
Tzara, Tristan, 262

Universal Castle (Garzoni), 116, 159
Unvollziehbarkeit, unrealizability, 163
Urn Burial (Browne), 252, 259, 316n.108
Utopianism, 2, 8

Valeriano, 165
Valois, House (French Royal) of, 170, 232
Van Helmont, Franciscus Mercurius, 152–55, **201–207**, 228, 245, 306n.66, 313n.77; impact, with More and Conway, on Keith, 310n.164; revival of pre-Christian cyclical time, 206–207. See also Conway, Luria, More, Rosenroth
Van Helmont, Johannes, 152–53, 228
Vanini, Lucilio, xi
On the Vanity of the Arts and Sciences (Agrippa), 157
Vaticinium diluvii ex intimarum cabilistcarum (Peranzanus), 189
Vaughan, Henry, 259, 317n.124
Vaughan, Thomas, 97, 157, 238, 259, 265, 311n.19, 317n.123–36;

Messiah of the Baroque, 274–77; polemic with More, 279, 318n.137; Sexual Mysticism and the Philosopher's Stone, 277–80; and the Return of Agrippa, 270–74, *See also* alchemy, Dee, Browne, More, Newman, Waite

Vedanta Sutras of Badarayana with Sankara's Commentary (Thibaut trans.), 296n.25

Venus and Adonis (Shakespeare), 313n.57

De vera curandae pestis (Pistorius), 149–50

De Veritate religionis Christianae (Rittangel), 183

Via Regia ad Omnes Scientias et Artes (Knittel), 200

Vigée, Claude, 55–56, 300n.5

Vincenti, G. M., 121

Virgil, 236

Virgin Wisdom, 178

Vision, 22, 319n.154

The Visionary Mode (Lieb), 294n.7

Vital, Hayim, 47, 135

Vitalism, 152–53, 178

Viterbo, Egidio, 49–50, 119–21, 170; projected Zohar translation, 136–37. *See also* Agrippa, Galantino, Joachimism, Reeves

Vivaldus, M., 121

Voysin, Joseph de, 147–48. See also R. Martin, Pascal

Vulgar Errors (Browne), 256

Waite, A. E., xi, 77, 123–24, 136–37, 141–42, 144–45, 178, 181, 266, 269, 317n.27; "The Mystery of Sex," 43–45; translation and commentary, Pico's "Cabalistic Conclusions," 67–71; on Vaughan, 275–77

Walker, D. P., 48, 216, 235, 313n.54; heretical vs. accept-able magic, 175–76, 210. *See also* Agrippa, de Corigio, Ficino, Lazzarelli, Yates

Walton, Brian, 316n.103

Walter Benjamin, the Story of a Friendship (Scholem), 7

Warner, William, 211. *See* Bradbrook, School of Night

Webster, John, 234

Werblowsky, R. Zvi, 43, 47–48, 202–203, 297n.58

Widmanstadius, J. A., 138

Wier, Johann, 194, 196

Williams, G. H., 306n.71, 312n.48

Williams, Raymond, 230

Wind, Edgar, 236, 313n.56. *See also* allegory

Windelband, Wilhelm, xi, 120, 152, 165–66, 168, 174–75, 183

The Winter's Tale (Shakespeare), 245

The Wisdom of the Zohar (Mathers trans., Runes ed.), 10

The Wisdom of the Zohar (Tishby), 10, 44, 293–94n.2, 297n.58

Witchcraft, 315n.86

Wittgenstein, Ludwig, 106

Wolfson, Eliot, 319n.154

On the Wonder-Working Word (Reuchlin), 49, 76, 139, 214–15

world cycles (*shemittoth*), 50, 299n.80. *See* Joachimism

The World Turned Upside Down (Hill), 318n.147

worship, power of, 36–37

Yates, Frances, xi, xiv, 170, 214–15, 232, 242–44, 293n.3; Family of Love, 312n.50; Rosicrucianism and Cabala, 264–65; Shakespearean Cabala, 210–13, 314n.68. *See also* Banes, Bruno, Fludd, Dee

Yeast, as zoharic impurity, 34
Yeats, William Butler, 178
Yurick, Sol, 81, 168

Zambelli, Paola, 301n.34
Zara, Antonio, 131–32, 211
Zarathustra, 168
Zeal of Christ (Vivaldus trans. of Caballeria), 121
Zelus Christi (Caballeria), 121
Zen Buddhism, 71
Zevi, Sabbatai, 2, 9, 19, 86, 128, 135, 144, 148–49, 173, 184, 250, 266, 270, 304n.27; apostasy, 111–12, 231; English Puritans and antinomians, 232, 280–83. See also McKeon, Nathan, Sabbatians, Scholem
Le Zohar (Mopsik, trans.), 295n.16

Le Zohar chez les kabbalistes chrétiens de la Renaissance (Secret), 100–102
The Zohar (Sperling and Simon trans.), ix, xi, **1–65**, 71, 84, 87, 94, 99, 105, 205, 216, 226, 234, 293–94n.2, 294n.4, 295n.17, 300n.17; on circumcision, 68–69; dimensions, 10; literary extravagance, 23–30; on secrecy, 107–10; sexual Cabala, 33–34, 37–38, 46–47. *See also* Abelson, Ben Yohai, Bloom, Cabala, De Leon, Idel, Liebes, pseudepigraphy, Scholem
Zohar, the Book of Splendour (Scholem), 23, 62–63, 182
Zumthor, Paul, 84–85, 94, 190
Zwinger, Theodor, 197

IATZ5470   6-3-98   help